P9-CEZ-076

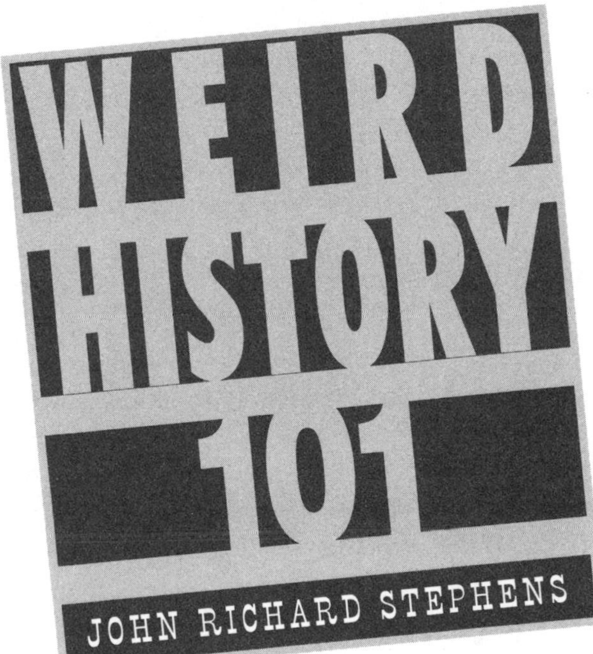
WEIRD
HISTORY
101
JOHN RICHARD STEPHENS

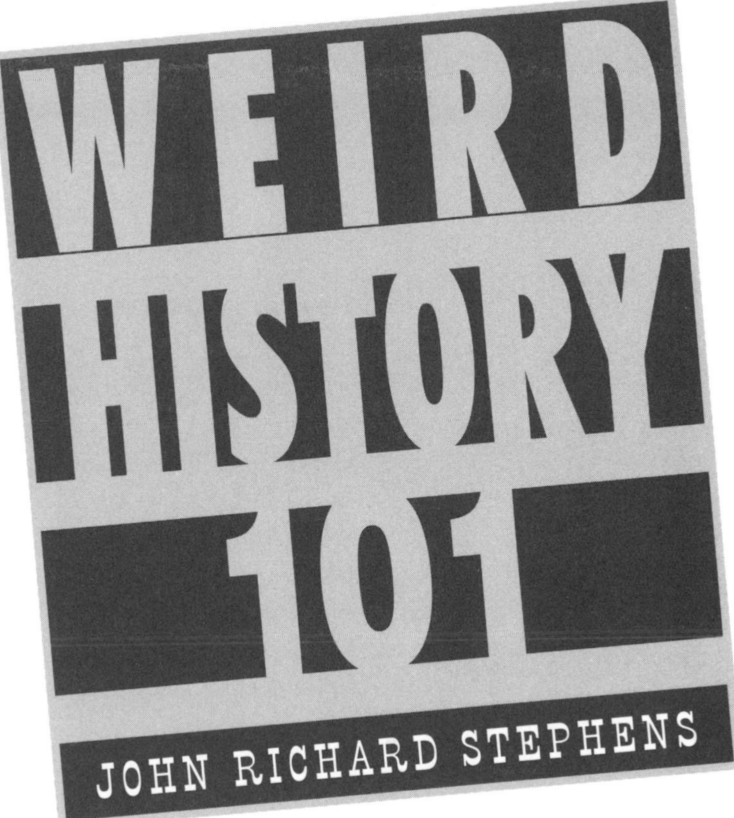
WEIRD
HISTORY
101
JOHN RICHARD STEPHENS

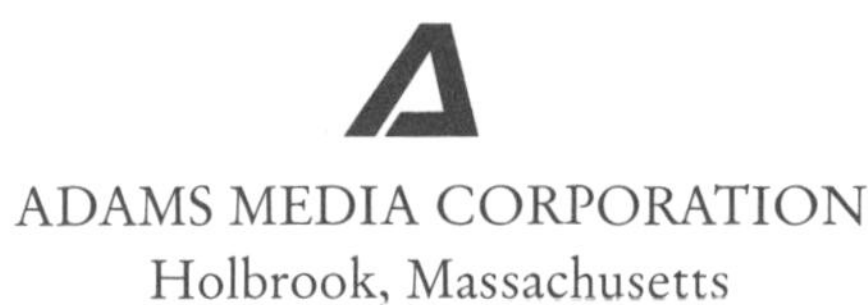
ADAMS MEDIA CORPORATION
Holbrook, Massachusetts

Published by
Adams Media Corporation
260 Center Street, Holbrook, MA 02343

ISBN: 1-55850-715-9

Printed in the United States of America

J I H G F E

Library of Congress Cataloging-in-Publication Data
Stephens, John Richard.
Weird history 101 / by John Richard Stephens.—1st ed.
p. cm.
ISBN 1-55850-715-9
1. United States—History—Sources. 2. Curiosities and wonders—United States—History—Sources. I. Title.
E173.S826 1997
973—dc21 97-7531
CIP

This book is available at quantity discounts for bulk purchases.
For information, call 1-800-872-5627.

Visit our home page at http://www.adamsmedia.com

Aknowledgments

John Richard Stephens wishes to express his appreciation to Martha and Jim Goodwin; Scott Stephens; Marty Goeller; Joyce Whiteaker and Gary Wood; Terity, Natasha, and Debbie Burbach; Branden, Alisha, and Kathy Hill; Jeff and Carol Whiteaker; Doug, Michelle and Christopher Whiteaker; Bill and Norene Hilden; Doug and Shirley Strong; Frank and Marybeth DiVito; Stan and Barbara Main; Carl Chafin; and to his agent, Charlotte Cecil Raymond.

Answers from Back Cover

1. George Bush
2. Warren G. Harding
3. Gerald Ford

Other Presidential comments may be found in the American Presidents section.

Contents

This book is dedicated to
Dr. Hunter S. Thompson

"I think we are in rats' alley
Where the dead men lost their bones."

—T. S. Eliot, *The Waste Land* (1922).

Eyewitness REPORTS

Eyewitness to Custer's Last Stand

On June 25, 1876, Lieutenant Colonel George Custer and 225 of his men died in the Battle of Little Bighorn. Custer's final battle made him a legend and stirred up considerable controversy.

Custer's first battle was at Bull Run in 1861. At that time, he was a second lieutenant and had just graduated from the U.S. Military Academy. Two years later, at the age of twenty-three, he was a brigadier general. His brigade fought at Gettysburg and in Shenandoah Valley. He was promoted to major general before the end of the Civil War. Like many others, he reverted to his regular rank of captain when the war was over. He was a lieutenant colonel at the time of his death. After the war, he spent many years fighting Native Americans.

In his book, *My Life on the Plains*, which was originally published serially from 1872 to 1874, Custer wrote:

> It is to be regretted that the character of the Indian as described in [James Fenimore] Cooper's interesting novels [such as *The Last of the Mohicans*] is not the true one. . . . Stripped of the beautiful romance with which we have been so long willing to envelop him, transferred from the inviting pages of the novelist to the localities where we are compelled to meet with him, in his native village, on the war path, and when raiding upon our frontier settlements and lines of travel, the Indian forfeits his claim to the appellation of the *noble* red man. We see him as he is, and, so far as all knowledge goes, as he ever has been, a *savage* in every sense of the word; not worse, perhaps, than his white brother would be, similarly born and bred, but one whose cruel and ferocious nature far exceeds that of any wild beast of the desert.

This was Custer's view of Native Americans. It wasn't long after writing this that Custer found himself marching through the Black Hills country of the Sioux in Montana. The Treaty of 1868 designated the Black Hills and the Powder River area as Native American land, saying, "No white person or persons shall be permitted to settle upon or occupy any portion of the territory, or without consent of the Indians to pass through the same." The Black Hills were sacred to the Native Americans, who believe they were the home of the gods. Warriors went there to talk to the Great Spirit and to receive visions. Shortly after signing the treaty, gold was discovered there—billions of dollars worth. The government offered to lease mineral rights for $400,000 a year or to buy the mountains for $6 million. The Native Americans refused.

Tremendous pressure was put on Washington D.C. to open the land to mining. Without seeking permission to enter Native American land, the government sent in the Army on a reconnaissance mission. Custer's regiment was sent out ahead of the main forces to scout out the situation. Coming upon an encampment, Custer underestimated the camp's size and decided to attack while he still had the element of surprise. He divided his 650 men into 3 columns and went up against the camp of between 2,500 and 5,000 Native Americans, including about 1,500 warriors led by Chiefs Sitting Bull and Crazy Horse. The column under Major Reno was the first to attack the camp, but they were forced to retreat. The remnants of his column joined up with the force under Major Benteen. They held off the Native Americans for almost two days before they were rescued. Shortly after Reno's original attack, Custer's column attacked the camp. Hopelessly outnumbered, Custer and five troops of the 7th Cavalry were completely wiped out. The only surviving eyewitnesses to Custer's Last Stand were the Native Americans.

Kate Bighead was there. Although there are many accounts of the Battle of Little Bighorn by Native Americans who were there, this one is probably the most descriptive.

> I was with the Southern Cheyennes during most of my childhood and young womanhood. I was in the camp beside the Washita River, in the country the white people call Oklahoma, when Custer and his soldiers came there and fought the Indians [November 1868]. Our Chief Black Kettle and other Cheyennes, many of them women and children, were killed that day. It was early in the morning when the soldiers began the shooting. There had been a big storm and there was snow on the ground. All of us jumped from our beds, and all of us started running to get away. I was barefooted, as were almost all of the others. Our tepees and all of our property we had to leave behind were burned by the white men.
>
> The next spring Custer and his soldiers found us again [March 1869]. We then were far westward, on a branch of what the white people call Red River, I think. That time there was no fighting. Custer smoked the peace pipe with our chiefs. He promised never again to fight the Cheyennes, so all of us followed him to a soldier fort [Fort Sill]. Our people gave him the name Hi-es-tzie, meaning Long Hair.
>
> I saw Long Hair many times during those days. One time I was close to where he was mounting his horse to go somewhere, and I took a good look at him. He had a large nose, deep-set blue eyes, and light-red hair that was long and wavy. He was wearing a buckskin suit and a big white hat. I was then a young woman, 22 years old, and I admired him. All of the Indian women talked of him as being a fine-looking man.

"Brothers, I have listened to a great many talks from our great father [President Jackson]. But they always began and ended in this: 'Get a little further; you are too near me.'"

—Speckled Snake, Creek, 1829, after President Jackson recommended that the Cherokees, Chickasaws, Choctaws, Creeks, and Seminoles move west beyond the Mississippi. He was more than 100 years old when he said this.

My cousin, a young woman named Me-o-tzi, went often with him to help in finding the trails of Indians. She said he told her his soldier horses were given plenty of corn and oats to eat, so they could outrun and catch the Indians riding ponies that had only grass to eat. All of the Cheyennes liked her, and all were glad she had so important a place in life. After Long Hair went away, different ones of the Cheyenne young men wanted to marry her. But she would not have any of them. She said that Long Hair was her husband, that he had promised to come back to her, and that she would wait for him. She waited seven years. Then he was killed.

Me-o-tzi mourned when she learned of his death. I was not then with those people, but I heard that she cut off her hair and gashed her arms and legs, for mourning. Her heart was much the more sad on account of his having been killed in a battle where the Northern Cheyennes fought against him. About a year later she married a white man named Isaac. They had several children. . . .

I came to the Northern Cheyennes when their reservation was in the Black Hills country [1868-1874]. White people found gold there, so the Indians had to move out. The Cheyennes were told they must go to another reservation, but not many of them made the change. They said it was no use, as the white people might want that reservation too. Many Cheyennes, and many Sioux also, went to live in the hunting ground between the Powder and Bighorn Rivers. White Bull and White Moon, my two brothers, left to go to the hunting ground, and I went with them. Word was sent to the hunting Indians that all Cheyennes and Sioux must stay on their reservations in Dakota. But all who stayed on the reservations had their guns and ponies taken from them, so the hunters quit going there.

The band of Cheyennes where I dwelt had forty family lodges. In the last part of the winter we camped on the west side of Powder River, not far above the mouth of Little Powder River. Soldiers came early in the morning [March 17, 1876]. They got between our camp and our horse herd, so all of us had to run away afoot. Not many of our people were killed, but our tepees and everything that was in them were burned. Three days later, all of us walking, we arrived at Crazy Horse's camp of Ogallala Sioux.

The Ogallalas gave us food and shelter. After a few days the two bands together went northward and found the Uncpapa Sioux, where Sitting Bull was the chief. The chiefs of the three bands decided that all of us would travel together for the spring and summer hunting, as it was said that many soldiers would be coming to try to make us go back to the reservations.

The three tribal bands grew larger and larger, by Indians coming from the Dakota reservations, as we traveled from place to place and as the grass came up. Other tribal bands—Minneconjou Sioux, Blackfeet Sioux, Arrows All Gone Sioux—came to us. There were then six separate tribal camp circles, each having, its own chiefs, wherever we stopped. In some of the six camp circles were small bands of other Sioux—Burned Thigh, Assiniboines, and Waist and Skirt people.

All of us traveled together to the west side of lower Powder River, on west across Tongue River, and to the Rosebud Valley. The grass grew high and our ponies became strong. Our men killed many buffalo, and we women tanned many skins and stored up much meat, as we camped from place to place up the Rosebud Valley . . . .

The chiefs from all the camps, in council, decided we should move down the Little Bighorn

River to its mouth, so our hunters could go across to the west side of the Bighorn and kill antelope in the great herds they had seen there. All of the Indians crossed to the west side of the Little Bighorn and moved the first part of the expected journey to the mouth of this stream. The plan was to stay at this camp but one night, and to go on down the valley the next day.

The next morning [June 25, 1876] I went with an Ogallala woman to visit some friends among the Minneconjoux Sioux, up the valley toward where was the Uncpapa camp circle, at the upper or south end of the camps. We found our women friends bathing in the river, and we joined them.

"We have been running up and down this country, but they follow us from one place to another."

—Chief Sitting Bull

Other groups, men, women and children, were playing in the water at many places along the stream. Some boys were fishing. All of us were having a good time. It was somewhere past the middle of the forenoon. Nobody was thinking of any battle coming. A few women were taking down their lodges, getting ready for the move on down the valley that day. After a while two Sioux boys came running toward us. They were shouting:

"Soldiers are coming!"

We heard shooting. We hid in the brush. The sounds of the shooting multiplied—pop—pop—pop—pop—pop—pop! We heard women and children screaming. Old men were calling the young warriors to battle. Young men were singing their war songs as they responded to the call. We peeped out. Throngs of Sioux men on horses were racing toward the skirt of timber just south of the Uncpapa camp circle, where the guns were clattering. The horsemen warriors were dodging through a mass of women, children and old people hurrying afoot to the benchland hills west of the camps.

From our hiding place in the brush we heard the sounds of battle change from place to place. It seemed the white men [Major Reno's column] were going away, with the Indians following them. Soon afterward we got glimpses of the soldiers crossing the river above us. Many of them were afoot. Then we saw that the Indians were after all of them, shooting and beating them.

I came out and set off at running toward our Cheyenne camp circle, the last one, at the north end down the river, more than a mile from where I had been hiding. In all of the camps, as I went through them, there was great excitement. Old men were helping the young warriors in dressing and painting themselves for battle. Some women were bringing war horses from the herds. Other women were working fast at taking down their tepees. A few were loading pack horses with tepee belongings, while others were carrying heavy burdens on their backs. Many were taking away nothing, leaving the tepees and everything in them, running away with only their children or with small packs in hands. I saw one Sioux woman just staying at one spot, jumping up and down and screaming, because she could not find her little son.

Clouds of dust were kicked up by the horse herds rushed into the camp circles, as well as by the horses that had been picketed near at hand by the Indian camp policemen and had been mounted and ridden to the fight when came the first alarm. The mounted Indians were still going to the place where had been the fighting, south of the Uncpapa camp. But before I got to my home lodge all of them were riding wildly back down through the camps. It appeared they had been beaten and were running away. But I soon learned what had happened. I heard a Cheyenne old man calling out:

"Other soldiers are coming! Warriors, go and fight them!". . .

I crossed the river and followed up the broad coulee where the warriors had gone and were still going. The soldiers [Custer's column] had lined themselves out on a long ridge nearer to the river and a little lower than the ridge far out where we first had seen them. By the time I got close enough to see well, the Indians were all around the soldiers, I think. Most of the warriors, when they got where they wanted to go, left their ponies back in gulches and hid themselves for crawling forward along little gullies or behind small ridges or knolls. The soldiers also got off their horses. . . .

The Indians were using bows and arrows more than they were using guns. Many of them had no guns, and not many who did have them had also plenty of bullets. But even if they had been well supplied with both guns and bullets, in that fight the bow was better. As the soldier ridge sloped on all sides, and as there were no trees on it nor around it, the smoke from each gun fired showed right where the shooter was hidden. The arrows made no smoke, so it could not be seen where they came from. Also, since a bullet has to go straight out from the end of a gun, any Indian who fired his gun had to put his head up so his eyes could see where to aim it. By doing this his head might be seen by a soldier and hit by a soldier bullet. The Indian could keep himself at all times out of sight when sending arrows. Each arrow was shot far upward and forward, not at any soldier in particular, but to curve down and fall where they were. Bullets would not do any harm if shot in that way. But a rain of arrows from thousands of Indian bows, and kept up for a long time, would hit many soldiers and their horses by falling and sticking into their heads or their backs.

The Indians all around were gradually creeping closer to the soldiers, by following the gullies or dodging from knoll to knoll. On the southern side, where I stopped to watch the fight, almost all of the Cheyennes and Ogallala Sioux had crawled across a deep gulch at the bottom of a broad coulee south of the ridge where the soldiers were, and about half way between them and the river. There was a long time—the old men now say they think it must have been about an hour and a half—of this fighting slowly, with not much harm to either side. Then a band of the soldiers on the ridge mounted their horses and came riding in a gallop down the broad coulee toward the river, toward where were the Cheyennes and the Ogallalas. The Indians hidden there got back quickly into the deepest parts of the gulch or kept on going away from it until they got over the ridge just south of it, the ridge where I was watching. The soldiers who had come galloping stopped and got off their horses along another ridge, a low one just north of the deep gulch.

Lame White Man, the bravest Cheyenne warrior chief, stayed in hiding close to where the small band of soldiers got off their horses. From there he called to the young men, and they began creeping and dodging back to him. The Ogallala

Sioux chiefs also called to their young men, and these also returned to the fight. Within a few minutes there were many hundreds of warriors wriggling along the gullies all around those soldiers.

I saw one of the white men there kill himself, with his own gun, just after they got off their horses. Soon afterward I saw another one do the same act. From where I was I had a clear view of the soldiers, and their saddled horses standing near them showed all of the warriors where the white men were. I think that only a few soldiers, maybe not any of them, were killed by the Indians during the few minutes of fighting there. I could not see the creeping Indians well enough to know when any one or another of them might have been killed or wounded. After a little while I heard Lame White Man call out:

"Young men, come now with me and show yourselves to be brave!"

On all sides of this band of soldiers the Indians jumped up. There were hundreds of warriors, many more than one might have thought could hide themselves in those small gullies. I think there were about twenty Indians to every soldier there. The soldier horses got scared, and all of them broke loose and ran away toward the river. Just then I saw a soldier shoot himself by holding his revolver at his head. Then another one did the same, and another. Right away, all of them began shooting themselves or shooting each other. I saw several different pairs of them fire their guns at the same time and shoot one another in the breast. For a short time the Indians just stayed where they were and looked. Then they rushed forward. But not many of them got to strike coup blows on living enemies. Before they could get to them, all of the white men were dead. . . .

I started to go around the east end of the soldier ridge. Just then I saw lots of Indians running toward that end of the ridge, and the soldier horses there were running away. Pretty soon I saw that all of the white men there were dead and the warriors were among them getting their guns. I did not see how they were killed, but I think they must have killed themselves. The Indians crowded on westward along the ridge and along its two sides. I followed, but keeping myself back so I would not be hit by a bullet. I stopped to look over a little hill and watch a band of soldiers [Custer and the remnants of his column] on the ground at the north slope of the ridge. Warriors were all around those men, creeping closer and closer. The white men's horses were all gone from there. After I had been looking but a few minutes at those men I saw them go at shooting each other and shooting themselves, the same as I had seen it done by the soldiers down toward the river.

The remaining white fighters collected in a group at the west end of the ridge, where our men say there now is a big stone having an iron fence around it. At that time there must have been hundreds of warriors for every white soldier left alive. The warriors around them were shifting from shelter to shelter, each one of them trying to get close enough to strike a blow of some kind upon a living enemy, as all warriors try to do when in a fight. Many hundreds of Indian heads were being popped up for a quick look and then jerked down again for a movement forward a little farther. The soldiers must have seen many of those heads, but they must have been puzzled as to which ones to shoot at. The remaining soldiers were keeping themselves behind their dead horses. The Indians could get only some glimpses of the white men, but it was easy enough to see where they were. . . .

The shots quit coming from the place where the soldiers were lying behind their dead horses. All of the Indians jumped up and ran toward them, supposing all of them were dead. But there were seven of the white men who sprang to their feet and went running toward the river. All of the hundreds of boys came tearing in on their horses, to strike blows upon the dead white men, as that was considered a brave deed for a boy. There was such a rush and mixup that it seemed the whole world had gone wild. There was such a crowd, and there was so much dust and smoke in the air, that I did not see what happened to the seven men who ran down the hillside. Hundreds of Sioux and Cheyenne warriors were after them. The talk I heard afterward was that all of them, and all of the others who had been hidden behind the horses, killed themselves. The Indians believe that the Everywhere Spirit made all of them go crazy and do this, in punishment for having attacked a peaceful Indian camp.

While I was looking at the last fighting, I saw back along the ridge a living soldier sitting on the ground, in plain view. He was just sitting there and rubbing his head, as if he did not know where he was nor what was going on in the world. While I was watching him, three Sioux men ran to him and seized him. They stretched him out upon his back. They went at this slowly, and I wondered what they were going to do. Pretty soon I found out. Two of them held his arms while the third man cut off his head with a sheath-knife.

I went riding among the Indians at different places on the battlefield. . . . I saw several different ones of the soldiers not yet quite dead. The Indians cut off arms or legs or feet of these, the same as was done for those entirely dead. . . .

Women from many families brought lodgepole travois, dragged by ponies, to take away the dead or wounded Indians. Some of the women, mourning, for their own dead, beat and cut the dead bodies of the white men. . . .

The Indians got guns, cartridges, horses, saddles, clothing, boots, everything the soldiers had with them. During the battle, all of the women and children and old people had been watching from the western hills across the valley. They kept themselves ready to run away if their warriors should be beaten, or to return to the camps if their side should win.

"Tell your people that since the Great Father promised that we should never be removed we have been moved five times. I think you had better put the Indians on wheels so you can run them about wherever you wish."

—Anonymous chief, 1876

After a long time of this watching, all the time in doubt, they saw a band of horsemen coming across the river and toward them. As the horsemen got into good view it was seen that all of them had on blue clothing and were mounted on soldier horses. It appeared the Indian warriors all had been killed, and these men were soldiers coming to kill the families. Women shrieked, some of them fainted. Mothers and children ran away into hiding. One woman grabbed her two little boys and set out running up a gulch. She was so excited that in picking them up she seized their feet and slung them upside down over her shoulders. It soon became known, though, that these men were our own warriors bringing the horses and the clothing of the dead soldiers.

Noisy Walking died that night. Six of our Cheyenne young men now were dead. Twenty-four Sioux warriors had been killed. Many more Indians would have been killed if the Everywhere Spirit had not caused the white men to go crazy and turn their guns upon themselves. Even as it was, in all of the camps there was much mourning and sadness of heart. The night before, there had been dancing and the usual gayety of Indian young people. But on this night there were so many sorrowing people that all feelings of joy were forgotten.

We Cheyennes buried our dead that afternoon. We placed them in hillside caves out from the camps. Some of the Sioux left their dead warriors in burial tepees set up as they had been when in use by the living people. Other Sioux put their dead on scaffolds, near the camps. One of our lost warriors was Chief Lame White Man, the most important war leader among the Cheyennes. He was killed soon after I last had seen him, when he called the young men for fighting the soldiers who rode down toward the gulch near the river. Although I had seen him just before his death I did not learn of it until after I got back to our home camp. He was 37 years old, and he left a widow and two daughters. Each of the other five dead Cheyennes was a young and unmarried man. . . .

I may have seen Custer at the time of the battle or after he was killed. I do not know, as I did not then know of his being there. All of our old warriors say the same—none of them knew of him being there until they learned of it afterward at the soldier forts or the agencies or from Indians coming from the agencies.

But I learned later something more about him from our people in Oklahoma. Two of those Southern Cheyenne women who had been in our camp at the Little Bighorn told of having been on the battlefield soon after the fighting ended. They saw Custer lying dead there. They had known him in the South. While they were looking at him some Sioux men came and were about to cut up his body. The Cheyenne women, thinking of Me-o-tzi made signs. He is a relative of ours, but telling nothing more about him. So the Sioux men cut off only one joint of a finger. The women then pushed the point of a sewing awl into each of his ears, into his head. This was done to improve his hearing, as it seemed he had not heard what our chiefs in the South said when he smoked the pipe with them. They told him then that if ever afterward he should break that peace promise and should fight the Cheyennes the Everywhere Spirit surely would cause him to be killed.

Through almost sixty years, many a time I have thought of Hi-es-tzie as the handsome man I saw in the South. And I often have wondered if, when I was riding among the dead where he was lying, my pony may have kicked dirt upon his body.

Chief Red Horse said that toward the end of the fighting, the "soldiers became foolish, many throwing away their guns and raising their hands, saying, 'Sioux, pity us; take us prisoners.' The Sioux did not take a single soldier prisoner, but killed all of them; none were alive for even a few minutes."

In 1887, a newspaper reporter interviewed Chief Sitting Bull. While Sitting Bull didn't see Custer himself, he did describe what his people told him they saw. Sitting Bull pointed at a map and said:

> "Any way it was said that up there is where the last fight took place, where the last stand was made, the Long Hair stood like a sheaf of corn with all the ears fallen around him."
>
> "Not wounded?"
>
> "No."
>
> "How many stood around him?"
>
> "A few."
>
> "When did he fall?"
>
> "He killed a man when he fell. He laughed."
>
> "You mean he cried out."
>
> "No, he laughed; he had fired his last shot."
>
> "From a carbine?"
>
> "No, a pistol."
>
> "Did he stand up after he first fell?"
>
> "He rose up on his hands and tried another shot, but his pistol would not go off?"
>
> "Was any one else standing up when he fell down?"
>
> "One man was kneeling; that was all. But he died before the Long Hair. . . . I did not see it. It was told to me. But it is true."

An Arapahoe warrior who was riding with the Cheyenne reported:

> When I reached the top of the hill I saw Custer. He was dressed in buckskin, coat and pants, and was on his hands and knees. He had been shot through the side and there was blood coming from his mouth. He seemed to be watching the Indians moving around him. Four soldiers were sitting up around him, but they were all badly wounded. All the other soldiers were down. Then the Indians closed in around him, and I did not see anymore. Most of the dead soldiers had been killed by arrows, as they had arrows sticking in them. The next time I saw Custer he was dead, and some Indians were taking his buckskin clothes. The Indians were quarreling, each trying to take the clothes away from the other.

"If you white men had a country which was very valuable, which had always belonged to your people, and which the Great Father had promised should be yours for ever, and men of another race came to take it away by force, what would your people do? Would they fight?"

—Anonymous chief, 1876

Sioux Chief White Bull was one of several warriors who claimed to be the one that killed Custer. In his account of what happened he said:

> I charged in. A tall, well-built soldier with yellow hair and mustache saw me coming and tried to bluff me, aiming his rifle at me. But when I rushed him, he threw his rifle at me without shooting. I dodged it. We grabbed each other and wrestled there in the dust and smoke. . . . He tried to wrench my rifle from me, and nearly did it. I lashed him a cross the face with my quirt,[1] striking the *coup*. He let go, then grabbed my gun with both hands until I struck him again. . . . He hit me with his fists on jaw and shoulders, then grabbed my long braids with both hands, pulled my face close and tried to bite my nose off. I

1 A riding whip with a short stalk and a lash of braided leather.

> yelled for help: "Hey, hey, come over and help me!" I thought that soldier would kill me. . . . He drew his pistol. I wrenched it out of his hand and struck him with it three or four times on the head, knocked him over, shot him in the head and fired at his heart. . . . *Ho hechetu*! That *was* a fight, a *hard* fight. But it was a glorious battle, I enjoyed it.

Chief White Bull said he didn't know who it was he had fought until a warrior who knew Custer came up and said, "Long Hair thought he was the greatest man in the world. Now he lies there."

General Edward Godfrey arrived on the scene three days after the battle and described Custer's burial:

> All the bodies, except a few, were stripped of their clothing, according to my recollection nearly all were scalped or mutilated, and there was one notable exception, that of General Custer, whose face and expression were natural: he had been shot in the temple and in the left side. Many faces had a pained, almost terrified expression. . . . I had just identified and was supervising the burial of Boston Custer, when Major Reno sent for me to help identify the dead at Custer Hill. When I arrived there General Custer's body had been laid out. He had been shot in the left temple and the left breast. There were no powder marks or signs of mutilation. Mr. F. F. Girard, the interpreter, informed me that he preceded the troops there. He found the naked bodies of two soldiers, one across the other and Custer's naked body in a sitting posture between and leaning against them, his upper right forearm and hand supporting his head in an inclining posture like one resting or asleep.

Custer's resounding defeat was dubbed a "massacre" though it was actually a battle. A massacre is what Custer had intended to do to the Native Americans. His attack violated the orders of his superiors; still, the government used it as an excuse to rescind the Treaty of 1868. The military assumed control of the reservations in Sioux country, and the Native Americans became prisoners of war—even those who had not left the reservation or been involved in the battle. Their horses and guns were confiscated. After the government passed a law transferring the Black Hills and the Powder River country to the United States, the reservations were moved onto land that had already been deforested in Missouri. Seeking revenge, the U.S. Army set out to kill any Native American they could find who had not moved to Missouri. Custer died, but his legend haunted the Native Americans.

Dinner with Attila the Hun

I sometimes wonder what it would be like to meet some famous historical leader, like Attila the Hun, face to face. Of course, that's impossible short of someone inventing a time machine or unless we continue to exist as individuals in the afterworld. But we can get an idea of what an encounter with Attila might have been like because there survives an account written by someone who did meet him.

Attila (c. A.D. 406-453) became the king of the Huns, also known as Scythians,[2] in A.D. 434 and

[2] This is under the broader use of the name *Scythian*, which refers to a number of barbarian tribes. Not all Scythians were Huns.

ruled them for nineteen years. His territory included what is now the Netherlands, Germany, Eastern Europe, and Russia. He also launched invasions into Turkey and Greece, which were then part of the Eastern Roman Empire (the Byzantine Empire), and into France and Italy, which were then part of the Western Roman Empire. It was fugitives fleeing from Attila into lagoons on the Adriatic who laid the foundations of the city of Venice. For a while, the Eastern Empire paid him seven hundred pounds of gold every year to keep him from invading them again. All this earned him the appellation "the Scourge of God." He was quite a guy, but it was best to stay on his good side since he had a tendency to crucify or impale on stakes anyone who displeased him.

The brutality of the Huns followed the tradition of the earlier Scythians. Several centuries earlier, the Greek historian Herodotus[3] (c. 485-430 B.C.) wrote that the Scythians sometimes beheaded their enemies and made the skulls into drinking cups by binding the outside with leather and gilding the interior with gold. They also made coats, capes, and cushions out of their victim's skins, he said, explaining, "The Scythian soldier scrapes the scalp clean of flesh and, softening it by rubbing it between the hands uses it thenceforth as a napkin. The Scyth is proud of these scalps and hangs them from his bridle rein; the greater the number of such napkins that a man can show, the more highly is he esteemed among them. Many make themselves cloaks by sewing a number of these scalps together."

Herodotus went on to say that they drank the blood of the first enemy they killed and mixed it with wine when making toasts to their agreements and alliances. In addition, they'd use the bloody wine to dip their arrows, swords, and javelins in. They considered it a terrible disgrace if, when the tribes gathered each year, they hadn't killed someone since their last meeting. They also went in for human sacrifices.

Toward the end of Attila's reign in A.D. 448, Priscus of Panium, who was a Goth, was sent along with two ambassadors of the Eastern Roman Empire to see Attila. He recorded his journey and, while his original book has been lost, some of it was included in Jordanes's *History of the Goths* (sixth century A.D.). Here is his description of Attila:

> His army is said to have numbered 500,000 men. He was a man born into the world to shake the nations, the scourge of all lands, who in some way terrified all mankind by the dreadful rumors noised abroad concerning him. He was haughty in his walk, rolling his eyes hither and thither, so that the power of his proud spirit appeared in the movement of his body. He was indeed a lover of war, yet restrained in action, mighty in counsel, gracious to suppliants and lenient to those who were once received into his protection. He was short of stature, with a broad chest and a large head: his eyes were small, his beard thin and sprinkled with gray: and he had a flat nose and a swarthy complexion showing the evidences of his origin.

The embassy reached Attila's camp eight miles east of the Danube River. Their first encounter with him did not go very smoothly.

> While we were thus engaged Attila summoned us through Scottas [one of Attila's men], and so we came to his tent, which was guarded by a band of

[3] It should be noted that Herodotus was biased against the Scythians.

barbarians around it. When we made our entrance we found Attila sitting on a wooden seat. As we stood a little apart from the throne, Maximinus [one of the ambassadors] went forward, greeted the barbarian, and gave him the letters from the emperor, saying that the emperor prayed that he and his followers were safe and sound.

He answered that for himself the Romans would have whatever they wished. Straightway, he turned his words against Bigilas, calling him a shameless beast and asked why he desired to come to him when he knew the terms made by him and Anatolius for peace, adding that he had said that no ambassadors ought to come to him before all the fugitives had been surrendered to the barbarians.

Bigilas [the other ambassador] said that there was not a single refugee of the Scythian race among the Romans, for all of them had been surrendered. Attila became even angrier and, railing at him violently, said with a shout that he would have impaled him and given him to the birds for food if he had not thought it an outrage to the law of embassies to exact this punishment from him for his effrontery and recklessness of speech. He said there were among the Romans many refugees of his race whose names, written down on a piece of paper, he ordered his secretaries to read out. When they had gone through all of them, he ordered Bigilas to depart without more ado. He sent Eslas with him to tell the Romans to send back to him all the barbarians who had fled to them from the time of Carpileon, who as the son of Aëtius, the general of the Romans of the West, had been a hostage at his court. . . .

Bigilas expressed surprise that though Attila had seemed mild and gentle to him when he had made the former embassy now he railed at him harshly.

After capturing a town, Genghis Khan would order the inhabitants to gather outside the town's walls, and then his men would proceed to slaughter them. Each man was ordered to kill at least fifty people, and they had to bring a sack full of ears to their officers to prove it.[4] *At Nichapur in 1221, they killed 1,748,000 people in just one hour—which is more than all the people murdered in Auschwitz. But then, the Mongols weren't worried about keeping their crimes hidden as the Nazi's were.*

The emissaries then proceed on to Attila's capital, where they met him again. His capital was farther east from the Danube, near what is now the Hungarian–Slovakian border in the area known as Transylvania.

> We crossed certain rivers and came to a very large village in which the dwelling of Attila was said to be more notable than those elsewhere. It had been fitted together with highly polished timbers and boards and encircled with a wooden palisade, conceived not for safety but for beauty. Next to the king's dwelling that of Onegesius was outstanding, and it also had a circuit of timbers but was not embellished with towers in the same way as Attila's. Not far from the enclosure there was a large bath which Onegesius, who had power second only to Attila among the Scythians, had built, fetching the stones from the land of

[4] During the Vietnam War, some American officers also had their men collect the ears of dead Vietnamese to confirm their body counts. Some of these were then nailed up on display, and some soldiers kept them as trophies. The American colonists did much the same thing with Native American scalps.

Pannonia. There is neither stone nor tree among the barbarians living in those parts, but they use imported wood. . . .

Maidens came to meet Attila as he entered this village, advancing before him in rows under fine white linen cloths stretched out to such a length that under each cloth, which was held up by the hands of women along either side, seven or even more girls walked. There were many such formations of women under the linen cloths, and they sang Scythian songs. When he came near the house of Onegesius (for the road to the palace led past it), the wife of Onegesius came out with a host of servants, some bearing dainties and others wine, and (this is the greatest honor among the Scythians) greeted him and asked him to partake of the food which she brought for him with friendly hospitality. To gratify the wife of his intimate friend, he ate sitting on his horse, the barbarians accompanying him having raised the silver platter up to him. Having also tasted the wine proffered to him he went on to the palace, which was higher than the other houses and situated on a high place.

Attila invited both parties of us to dine with him about three o'clock that afternoon. We waited for the time of the invitation, and then all of us, the envoys from the Western Romans as well, presented ourselves in the doorway facing Attila. In accordance with the national custom the cupbearers gave us a cup for us to make our libations before we took our seats. When that had been done and we had sipped the wine, we went to the chairs where we would sit to have dinner. All the seats were ranged down either side of the room, up against the walls. In the middle Attila was sitting on a couch with a second couch behind him. Behind that a few steps led up to his bed, which for decorative purposes was covered in ornate drapes made of fine linen, like those which Greeks and Romans prepare for marriage ceremonies. I think that the more distinguished guests were on Attila's right, and the second rank on his left, where we were with Berichos, a man of some renown among the Scythians, who was sitting in front of us. Onegesius was to the right of Attila's couch, and opposite him were two of the king's sons on chairs. The eldest son was sitting on Attila's own couch, right on the very edge, with his eyes fixed on the ground in fear of his father.

When all were sitting properly in order, a cupbearer came to offer Attila an ivy-wood bowl of wine, which he took and drank a toast to the man first in order of precedence. The man thus honored rose to his feet and it was not right for him to sit down again until Attila had drunk some or all of the wine and had handed the goblet back to the attendant. The guests, taking their own cups, then honored him in the same way, sipping the wine after making the toast. One attendant went round to each man in strict order after Attila's personal cupbearer had gone out. When the second guest and then all the others in their turn had been honored, Attila greeted us in like fashion in our order of seating.

After everyone had been toasted, the cupbearers left, and a table was put in front of Attila and other tables for groups of three or four men each. This enabled each guest to help himself to the things put on the table without leaving his proper seat. Attila's servant entered first with plates full of meat, and those waiting on all the others put bread and cooked food on the tables. A lavish meal, served on silver trenchers, was prepared for us and the other barbarians, but Attila just had some meat on a wooden platter, for this was one aspect of his self-discipline. For instance, gold or silver cups were presented to the other diners, but his own goblet was made of wood. His clothes, too, were simple, and no trouble was taken except to have them clean. The sword that hung by his side, the clasps of his barbarian shoes and the bridle of his horse were all free from gold, precious stones or other valuable decorations affected by the other Scythians. When the food in the first plates was finished we all got up, and no one, once on his feet, returned to his seat until he had, in the same order as before, drunk the full cup of wine that he was handed, with a toast for Attila's health. After this honor had been paid him, we sat down again and second plates were put on each table with other food on them. This also finished, everyone rose once more, drank another toast and resumed his seat.

As twilight came on torches were lit, and two barbarians entered before Attila to sing some songs they had composed, telling of his victories and his valor in war. The guests paid close attention to them, and some were delighted with the songs, others excited at being reminded of the wars, but others broke down and wept if their bodies were weakened by age and their warrior spirits forced to remain inactive. After the songs a Scythian entered, a crazy fellow who told a lot of strange and completely false stories, not a word of truth in them, which made everyone laugh. Following him came the Moor, Zerkon, totally disorganized in appearance, clothes, voice and words. By mixing up the languages of the Italians with those of the Huns and Goths, he fascinated everyone and made them break out into uncontrollable laughter, all that is except Attila. He was presented to Aspar, son of Ardaburius, during the time he spent in Libya and was captured when the barbarians invaded Thrace and was brought to the Scythian kings. Attila could not endure the sight of him, but Bleda [Attila's brother[5]] was exceedingly pleased with him, not only when he uttered comical words but also when he walked about in silence and moved his body clumsily. . . .

He [Attila] remained impassive, without any change of expression, and neither by word or gesture did he seem to share in the merriment except that when his youngest son, Ernas, came in and stood by him, he drew the boy towards him and looked at him with gentle eyes. I was surprised that he paid no attention to his other sons, and only had time for this one. But the barbarian at my side, who understood Latin and what I had said about the boy, warned me not to speak up, and said that the seers had told Attila that his family would be banished but would be restored by this son. After spending most of the night at the party, we left, having no wish to pursue the drinking any further.

Alcohol wasn't the barbarians only vice—they also had an affinity for marijuana. Most scholars believe Herodotus was referring to it when he wrote,

> They . . . have a tree, which bears the strangest produce. When they meet together in companies they throw some of it upon the fire round which

5 Priscus is speaking of when Bleda was still alive. Earlier in his narrative, he wrote, "When Attila's brother Bleda who ruled over a great part of the Huns was slain by Attila's treachery, the latter united all the people under his own rule." Bleda was killed in 445.

they are sitting, and presently, by the mere smell of the fumes which it gives out in burning, they grow drunk, as the Greeks do with wine. More of the fruit is then thrown on the fire, and, their drunkenness increasing, they often jump up and begin to dance and sing. Such is the account which I have heard of these people.

In Siberia, in 1994, a container full of marijuana was discovered in the 2,000-year-old grave of a twenty-year-old Scythian princess and priestess, among the many other articles buried with her.

Scythian funerals were decidedly unpleasant affairs. According to Herodotus:

> When a king dies, they dig a great square pit, and, when it is ready, they take up the corpse, which has been previously slit open, cleaned out, and filled with various aromatic substances, crushed galingale [an aromatic plant], parsley seed, and anise; it is then sewn up again and the whole body coated over with wax . . . .
>
> [The king's body is then carried in a wagon from tribe to tribe until the funeral cortege reaches the land of the Gerrhi, the most isolated of the Scythian tribes.]
>
> Here the corpse is laid in the tomb on a mattress, with spears fixed in the ground on either side to support a roof of brush laid on wooden poles, while in other parts of the great square pit various members of the king's household are buried beside him: one of his concubines, his butler, his cook, his groom, his steward, and his chamberlain—all of them strangled. Horses are buried too, and gold cups (the Scythians do not use silver or bronze), and a selection of his other treasures. . . . This ceremony over, everybody with great enthusiasm sets about raising a mound of earth, each competing to make it as big as possible. . . .
>
> When a year is gone by, further ceremonies take place. Fifty of the late king's attendants are taken . . . and are strangled, with fifty of the most beautiful horses.
>
> When they are dead, their bowels are taken out and the cavity cleaned, filled full of chaff, and straightway sewn up again. This done, a number of posts are set into the ground, in sets of two pairs each; atop every pair of stakes half the rim of a wheel is placed to form an arch. Then strong stakes are run lengthwise through the bodies of the horses from tail to neck, and they are set on top of the rims so that the arch supports the shoulders of the horse, while the one behind holds up the belly and quarters, the legs dangling in mid-air. Each horse is given a bridle, which is stretched out in front of the horses and fastened to a peg.
>
> The fifty strangled youths are then mounted on the fifty horses. To effect this, a stake is passed through their bodies along the course of the spine to the neck, the lower end of which projects from the body and is fixed into a socket made in the stake that runs lengthwise down the horse. The fifty riders are thus ranged in a circle round the tomb and so left.

It's said Attila died of a hemorrhage on his wedding night. Priscus explained that the Huns, "as it is the custom of that race, cut off a part of their hair and disfigured their faces horribly with deep wounds, so that the gallant warrior should be mourned not with the lamentations and tears of women, but with the blood of men." He also said:

Centuries later, another famous dictator also had problems on his wedding night, but of a completely different sort. Napoleon and Josephine were in the middle of passionate sex when Napoleon suddenly cried out. She thought he was crying in ecstasy, but actually her dog had bitten his leg. As M. de Ravine put it, "All night the disappointed Josephine had to put compresses on her invalid's wound. He huddled in the bed and loudly moaned that he was dying of rabies."

His body was placed in the midst of a plain and laid in state in a silken tent as a sight for men's admiration. The best horsemen of the entire tribe of the Huns rode around in circles, after the manner of circus games, in the place to which he had been brought and told of his deeds in a funeral dirge in the following manner:

Attila, the great king of the Huns,
the son of Mundzucus,
the ruler of the most courageous tribes;
enjoying such power as had been unheard of
 before him,
he possessed the Scythian and Germanic
 kingdoms alone
and also terrorized both empires of the
 Roman world
after conquering their cities, and
placated by their entreaties
that the rest might not be laid open to plunder
he accepted an annual tribute.
After he had achieved all this with
 great success
he died, not of an enemy's wound, not
 betrayed by friends,
in the midst of his unscathed people,
happy and gay,
without any feeling of pain.
Who therefore would think that this
 was death
which nobody considers to demand revenge?

When they had mourned him with such lamentations, a *strava*, as they call it, was celebrated over his tomb with great reveling. They connected opposites and showed them, mixing grief over the dead with joy. Then in the secrecy of night they buried the body in the earth. They bound his coffins, the first with gold, the second with silver, and the third with the strength of iron, showing by such means that these three things suited the mightiest of kings: iron because he subdued the nations, gold and silver because he received the honors of both empires. They also added the arms of foemen won in the fight, trappings of rare worth, sparkling with various gems, and ornaments of all sorts whereby princely state is maintained. And that so great riches might be kept from human curiosity, they slew those appointed to the work—a dreadful pay for their labor; and thus sudden death was the lot of those who buried him as well as of him who was buried.

Attila's kingdom crumbled soon after his death. Historians now question his historical significance. Although he seriously threatened the Roman empires, he didn't win any decisive victories against them. Perhaps his greatest achievement was that he united the Huns for a short while. He appears in Scandinavian legends under the name Atli, and in German legends, such as the *Nibelungenlied*, under the name Etzel.

Watching Gettysburg and Other Civil War Battles

In 1863, General Robert E. Lee launched an offensive invasion into the North. As Northern and Southern forces came together for the Battle of Gettysburg in Pennsylvania, Lee thought this would be a decisive victory for the South and hoped it would lead to European mediation of the war. He also wanted to move the battle zone away from Virginia. After three days of intense fighting, Lee was forced to withdraw.

Gettysburg was the biggest and bloodiest battle ever fought on American soil. In all, 5,662 men were killed there, while both sides reported an additional 10,584 missing and 27,203 wounded. The battle *was* a turning point in the war, but against the South. The war continued for two more years, but Lee was never again able to invade the North and was forced to fight the remainder of the war from a defensive position.

One eyewitness to this important battle was newspaper reporter Samuel Wilkeson. His description of the Confederate bombardment just prior to Major General George E. Pickett's suicidal charge on July 3, 1863—the final day of the three-day battle—appeared in The *New York Times* a few days later. Lying next to him as he wrote was the body of his own son, Lieutenant Bayard Wilkeson, who had been killed in the first day of battle.

> Who can write the history of a battle whose eyes are immovably fastened upon a central figure of transcendingly absorbing interest—the dead body of an oldest born, crushed by a shell in a position where a battery should never have been sent, and abandoned to death in a building where surgeons dared not to stay?. . .
>
> For such details as I have the heart for. The battle commenced at daylight, on the side of the horseshoe position, exactly opposite to that which [Confederate Lt. Gen. Richard S.] Ewell had sworn to crush through. Musketry preceded the rising of the sun. A thick wood veiled this fight, but out of the leafy darkness arose the smoke and the surging and swelling of the fire. . . .
>
> Suddenly, and about ten in the forenoon, the firing on the east side and everywhere about our lines ceased. A silence of deep sleep fell upon the field of battle. Our army cooked, ate and slumbered. The rebel army moved 120 guns to the west, and massed there [Lt. Gen. James] Longstreet's corps and [Lt. Gen. A. P.] Hill's corps to hurl them upon the really weakest point of our entire position.
>
> Eleven o'clock—twelve o'clock—one o'clock. In the shadow cast by the tiny farmhouse, sixteen by twenty, where [Union Major] General [George G.] Meade had made his headquarters, lay wearied staff officers and tired reporters. There was not wanting to the peacefulness of the scene the singing of a bird, which had a nest in a peach tree within the tiny yard of the whitewashed cottage. In the midst of its warbling a shell screamed over the house, instantly followed by another and another and in a moment the air was full of the most complete artillery prelude to an infantry battle that was ever exhibited. Every size and form of shell known to British and to American gunnery shrieked, moaned, whirled, whistled, and wrathfully fluttered over our ground. . . .Through the midst of the storm of screaming and exploding shells an ambulance, driven by its frenzied conductor at full speed, presented to all of us the marvelous spectacle of a horse going rapidly on three legs. A hinder one had been shot off at

the hock. . . . During this fire the houses at twenty and thirty feet distant were receiving their death, and soldiers in Federal blue were torn to pieces in the road and died with the peculiar yells that blend the extorted cry of pain with horror and despair. Not an orderly, not an ambulance, not a straggler was to be seen upon the plain swept by this tempest of orchestral death thirty minutes after it commenced.

General Richard Ewell fought bravely at Gettysburg, but he sometimes thought he was a bird and would eat only a few grains of wheat or sunflower seeds at a meal. He also sat in his tent for hours quietly chirping to himself.

An even more graphic account of how devastating artillery could be was related by Captain Thomas Livermore of the New Hampshire Infantry in his book, *Days and Events, 1860-1866* (1920). Here he describes the Battle of White Oak Swamp, which took place on the Virginia peninsula on June 30, 1862.

> The enemy's fire was unremitting, and from noon until dark we endured the slow torture of seeing our comrades killed, mangled, and torn around us, while we could not fire a shot, as our business was to lie and wait to repel attacks and protect our batteries. With every discharge of the enemy's guns, the shells would scream over our heads and bury themselves in the woods beyond, burst over us and deal death in the ranks, or ricochet over the plain killing whenever they struck a line. . . .
>
> The shot hit some of our men and scattered their vitals and brains upon the ground, and we hugged the earth to escape this horrible fate, but nothing could save a few who fell victims there. I saw a shot strike in the 2d Delaware, a new regiment with us, which threw a man's head perhaps twenty feet into the air, and the bleeding trunk fell over toward us. The men seemed paralyzed for a moment, but presently gathered up the poor fellow's body in a blanket and carried it away. I do not know that I have ever feared artillery as I did then, and I can recollect very well how close I lay to the ground while the messengers of death, each one seemingly coming right into us, whistled over us. . . .
>
> I had just reached my place when the order was given to rise up and face about. A cannon shot came quicker than the wind through my company, and close by me. Tibbetts fell and Nichols fell. We reached the line designated with a few hasty steps, and resumed our line with faces to the front. Nichols got up, and came back to the captain and said, "Captain, I am wounded and want to go to the rear." The poor fellow held up one arm with the other hand, for it dangled only by a strip of flesh. Some men went forward and hastily gathered up Tibbetts in a blanket and bore him away; the shot had gone through his body. We felt a little safer now. Hazzard's battery withdrew, cut to pieces, and with Captain Hazzard mortally wounded; and for a short time it seemed as if the rebels would fire unmolested, but Pettit galloped up with his battery of 10-pounder Parrotts and went into action, and then iron did fly, and the rebels had their hands full. Captain Keller sat up on a knapsack in front of us and gave warning when the shells were coming, and perhaps saved lives by it; anyhow it was a brave thing to do.

What it was like to be in a battle with bullets whizzing all around comes across even more strongly in this next account by Private Oliver W. Norton of the Pennsylvania Volunteers. Amazingly, he survived the fierce all-day battle at Gaines's Mill on June 27, 1862, which was also during the Virginia peninsula campaign. This account is from Norton's book, *Army Letters, 1861-1865* (1903).

Union General John Sedgwick was killed during the Battle of Spotsylvania on May 9, 1864, while watching Confederate troops. His last words were, "They couldn't hit an elephant at this dist. . . ."

The order was given to face about. We did so and tried to form in line, but while the line was forming, a bullet laid low the head, the stay, the trust of our regiment—our brave colonel, and before we knew what had happened the major shared his fate. We were then without a field officer, but the boys bore up bravely. They rallied 'round the flag and we advanced up the hill to find ourselves alone. It appears that the enemy broke through our lines off on our right, and word was sent to us on the left to fall back. Those in the rear of us received the order but the aide sent to us was shot before he reached us and so we got no orders. . . .

I returned to the fight, and our boys were dropping on all sides of me. I was blazing away at the rascals not ten rods off when a ball struck my gun just above the lower band as I was capping it, and cut it in two. The ball flew in pieces and part went by my head to the right and three pieces struck just below my left collarbone. The deepest one was not over half an inch, and stopping to open my coat I pulled them out and snatched a gun from Ames in Company H as he fell dead. Before I had fired this at all a ball clipped off a piece of the stock, and an instant after another struck the seam of my canteen and entered my left groin. I pulled it out, and, more maddened than ever, I rushed in again. A few minutes after, another ball took six inches off the muzzle of this gun. I snatched another from a wounded man under a tree, and, as I was loading, kneeling by the side of the road, a ball cut my rammer in two as I was turning it over my head. Another gun was easier got than a rammer so I threw that away and picked up a fourth one. Here in the road a buckshot struck me in the left eyebrow, making the third slight scratch I received in the action. It exceeded all I ever dreamed of, it was almost a miracle.

Then came the retreat across the river; rebels on three sides of us left no choice but to run or be killed or be taken prisoners. We left our all in the hollow by the creek and crossed the river to Smith's division. The bridge was torn up, and when I came to the river I threw my cartridge box on my shoulder and waded through. . . .

Before the May 1863 battle near Chancellorsville, Virginia, Confederate General Thomas "Stonewall" Jackson gave orders for his men to shoot any unknown soldiers who approached their lines and ask questions later. During the battle, Jackson and some of his troops swung around attacking Union General Joseph Hooker's men from the side, routing them. Returning from the successful battle, Jackson was approaching his own lines when he was gunned down by his own men. Though his three wounds didn't kill him, they did weaken him, and he died of pneumonia a few days later.

Sunday night we lay in a cornfield in the rain, without tent or blanket. Monday we went down on the James River, lying behind batteries to support them. Tuesday the same—six days exposed to a constant fire of shot and shell, till almost night, when we went to the front and engaged in another fierce conflict with the enemy. Going on to the field, I picked up a tent and slung it across my shoulder. The folds of that stopped a ball that would have passed through me. I picked it out, put it in my pocket, and, after firing sixty rounds of my own and a number of a wounded comrade's cartridges, I came off the field unhurt, and ready, but not anxious, for another fight.

The Heavy Costs of the Civil War

The total number of Americans killed in the Civil War is greater than the combined total of Americans killed in all other wars. About 618,000 soldiers died, plus an unknown number of civilians. Some estimates of the dead range as high as a million—or about 8 percent of the population. It was also an extremely expensive war that completely devastated the South. The total direct and indirect costs of the war are estimated at more than $15 billion.

If war had somehow been avoided, it's very likely slavery would have soon disappeared in the South, as it did throughout the rest of the world.[6] And it probably would have done so without the rise of the Ku-Klux-Klan-style hate groups, the tremendous number of lynchings,[7] and the resentment that still exists today.

Although there were well over 3 million slaves in America when the Civil War began, less than 20 percent of the Southerners had slaves, and most of them had just one or two. Only 8,000 landowners—or less than one tenth of 1 percent of the slave-state populations—had 50 or more slaves in 1850. There was also a large antislavery movement in the South before the war, and at times, more antislavery groups were in the South than in the North. In fact, the Virginia legislature debated abolishing slavery for two weeks in 1832 before taking a vote, with seventy-three voting for keeping it and fifty-seven for abolishing it. What's more, a motion to condemn slavery as an evil failed by only seven votes.

Many poor Southern whites didn't support the war since they felt they'd only be fighting for the slaveowners, and when General Sherman made his famous march through Georgia, his army got larger because thousands of white Southerners volunteered to join his forces. At the same time, two thirds of the Confederate army in front of Sherman disappeared through desertion.

Slavery was much harsher in the Caribbean, West Indies, and South America than in the South. Only 4.5 percent of all the slaves brought into the New World ended up in the United States, the other 95.5 percent went to Latin American plantations. Brazil alone received ten times as many slaves as the United States. But by the Civil War, the United States had the world's largest slave population. The reason for this was that in Latin America, slaves died faster than they were born, primarily because of disease. Still, slavery disappeared in Latin America without armed conflict. Brazil was the last country in the Western

6 A small amount of slavery still exists today in a few out-of-the-way places.

7 Between 1882 and 1903, 2,060 African-Americans were lynched. It wasn't until 1949 that an entire year went by without one African-American lynching.

Hemisphere to abolish slavery, and it did so in 1888. When the Civil War began, slavery had already essentially vanished in western Europe and most of Latin America. England had abolished it almost thirty years earlier.

Toward the end of the Civil War, many in the South were talking about abolishing slavery in order to hold onto their independence. A month before the war ended, Jefferson Davis authorized a diplomat to tell Britain and France that the Confederacy would emancipate the slaves if they would officially recognize the South's independence. At about the same time, General Robert E. Lee told the Confederate Congress that African-Americans were essential in order to win the war, so they authorized him to recruit up to 300,000 slaves into the army. Even the Jackson *Mississippian* ran an editorial that said, "Let not slavery prove a barrier to our independence. If it is found in the way—if it proves an insurmountable object of the achievement of our liberty and separate nationality, away with it! Let it perish!" Of course, by then it was too late.

One of the results of the Civil War was that states' rights decreased while there was an increase in the powers of the federal government. Before the war, you could say the country considered itself the United *States* of America, whereas afterwards, it became the United States of *America*. If the war hadn't occurred, it's likely the two world wars would have drawn the country together and increased the authority of the federal government to some degree, but the states would be much more independent than they are today, and there would be a much smaller central government. The states would probably handle most internal matters, and the federal government would probably focus primarily on foreign policy.

Battle of the *Monitor* and the *Merrimac*

Actually, the *Monitor* never fought the *Merrimac*. The U.S.S. *Merrimack*[8] was a Union ship that was set on fire and sunk when Northern forces abandoned the Norfolk Navy Yard in 1861. She was later raised by the Confederates, covered with armor plating, and rechristened the C.S.S. *Virginia*. So the famous sea battle was actually the battle of *Monitor* and the *Virginia*. It's possible the name of the battle was changed because some in the Union didn't believe the Confederacy had the right to change the name of a Northern ship, or it might have been changed because "the Battle of the *Monitor* and the *Merrimac*" just sounds better.

It's not known when the first armored ships were built. The ancient Greeks said they had one in the third century B.C. named the *Syracusa*, that had eight armored catapult turrets, a gymnasium, a pool, gardens, and a temple. It was sort of a combination luxury liner and superfreighter that could carry 1,800 tons of wheat. The huge lead-plated ship, built under Archimedes' supervision, was so big it could enter only one harbor though they didn't realize this until after it was built. It made only one voyage—from Sicily to Egypt—where it was given to Ptolemy of Alexandria as an oddity. The Koreans also said they built an armored ship in 1592, but this has yet to be confirmed. The French did build the ironclad *Gloire* in 1859, and the British had the *Warrior* in 1860.

[8] Although the name of the ship was spelled both with and without the "k," official Navy records spell it with the "k." The *Merrimac* spelling is more common today.

The Confederates quickly began experimenting with ironclads. The C.S.S. *Manassas* was a renamed and converted tug that successfully attacked Northern ships in the Mississippi on October 12, 1861. The Union also had armored gunboats, which they used to capture Fort Henry, Tennessee, on February 6, 1862.

The *Monitor–Virginia* battle was the first battle between two ironclads and was also one of the first between two ships solely powered by steam. The battle came about because the Union established a blockade against the South to prevent foreign shipping from providing aid to the Confederacy. Although most countries respected the blockade, it was still a difficult task to close off more than 3,500 miles of coastline with a dozen major ports and about two hundred smaller ones—especially since the North had only twenty vessels.

The C.S.S. *Virginia* was the first of the two ships to be built, and usually it easily destroyed the wooden ships it went up against, so the North built the U.S.S. *Monitor* specifically to take on the *Virginia*. This was a small, more maneuverable vessel. The flat deck of this ship rose just inches out of the water. Sitting on deck was the revolving gun turret, which was roughly shaped like a large tin can. Some called it a "cheesebox on a raft." It had two guns and was entirely made of iron. The *Virginia* carried ten guns inside its sloping armored shielding and has been described as resembling "a floating barn roof." The *Virginia* often attacked ships by ramming them.

The famous battle between the ironclads was fought on March 9, 1862, and lasted five hours. The evening before the battle, the *Monitor* had reached the grounded steam-frigate *Minnesota*, which had run aground attempting to attack the *Virginia*. Here is a description of what it was like to be inside the *Monitor* from Lieutenant William F. Keeler, the *Monitor*'s acting paymaster.

> As a light fog lifted from the water it revealed the *Merrimac* with her consorts lying under Sewall's Point. The announcement of breakfast brought also the news that the *Merrimac* was coming, and our coffee was forgotten. . . .

Like most Americans, Civil War soldiers loved to drink liquor. If they couldn't buy it, they made it. The ingredients in one Union recipe for home brew were "bark juice, tar-water, turpentine, brown sugar, lamp-oil and alcohol." Sometimes the Confederates would drop some raw meat in theirs and let it ferment for a month or so to give it "an old and mellow taste." The soldiers gave their rot-gut names like "Oh! Be Joyful," "Bust-Head," "Pop Skull," "Tanglefoot," and "Nockum Stiff."

> Everyone on board of us was at his post, except the doctor and myself, who having no place assigned us in the immediate working of the ship were making the most of our time in taking a good look at our still distant but approaching foe. A puff of smoke arose from her side and a shell howled over our heads. Capt. Worden, who was on deck, came up and said more sternly than I ever heard him speak before, "Gentlemen, that is the *Merrimac*, you had better go below."
>
> We did not wait [for] a second invitation but ascended the tower and down the hatchway, Capt. W. following. The iron hatch was closed over the opening and all access to us cut off. As we passed down through the turret the gunners were lifting

a 175 lb. shot into the mouth of one of our immense guns. "Send them that with our compliments, my lads," says Capt. W.

A few straggling rays of light found their way from the top of the tower to the depths below which was dimly lighted by lanterns. Everyone was at his post, fixed like a statue; the most profound silence reigned—if there had been a coward heart there its throb would have been audible, so intense was the stillness.

I experienced a peculiar sensation; I do not think it was fear, but it was different from anything I ever knew before. We were enclosed in what we supposed to be an impenetrable armor—we knew that a powerful foe was about to meet us—ours was an untried experiment and our enemy's first fire might make it a coffin for us all.

Then we knew not how soon the attack would commence, or from what direction it would come, for with the exception of those in the pilothouse and one or two in the turret, no one of us could see her. The suspense was awful as we waited in the dim light expecting every moment to hear the crash of our enemy's shot.

Soon came the report of a gun, then another and another at short intervals, then a rapid discharge. Then a thundering broadside and the infernal howl (I can't give it a more appropriate name) of the shells as they flew over our vessel was all that broke the silence and made it seem still more terrible.

Mr. Green says, "Paymaster, ask the Capt. if I shall fire." The reply was, "Tell Mr. Green not to fire till I give the word, to be cool and deliberate, to take sure aim and not waste a shot."

O, what a relief it was, when at the word, the gun over my head thundered out its challenge with a report which jarred our vessel, but it was music to us all. . . . Until we fired, the *Merrimac* had taken no notice of us, confining her attentions to the *Minnesota*. Our second shot struck her and made the iron scales rattle on her side. She seemed for the first time to be aware of our presence and replied to our solid shot with grape and canister[9] which rattled on our iron decks like hailstones.

One of the gunners in the turret could not resist the temptation when the port was open for an instant to run out his head; he drew it in with a broad grin. "Well," says he, "the damned fools are firing canister at us."

The same silence was [again] enforced below that no order might be lost or misunderstood.

The vessels were now sufficiently near to make our fire effective, and our two heavy pieces were worked as rapidly as possible, every shot telling—the intervals being filled by the howling of the shells around and over us, which was now incessant.

The men at the guns had stripped themselves to their waists and were covered with powder and smoke, the perspiration falling from them like rain.

Below, we had no idea of the position of our unseen antagonist, her mode of attack, or her distance from us, except what was made known through the orders of the Capt. . . .

The sounds of the conflict at this time were terrible. The rapid firing of our own guns amid the clouds of smoke. . . mingled with the crash of solid shot against our sides and the bursting of shells all

9 Grapeshot was a cluster of connected iron balls which was shot from a cannon, whereas canister shot was a metal can filled with small shot and scrap metal that scattered when fired.

around us. Two men had been sent down from the turret, who were knocked senseless by balls striking the outside of the turret while they happened to be in contact with the inside. . . .

At this time a heavy shell struck the pilot-house—I was standing near, waiting an order, heard the report which was unusually heavy, a flash of light and a cloud of smoke filled the house. I noticed the Capt. stagger and put his hands to his eyes—I ran up to him and asked if he was hurt.

"My eyes," says he. "I am blind."

With the assistance of the surgeon I got him down and called Lieut. Green from the turret. A number of us collected around him; the blood was running from his face, which was blackened with the powder smoke. [A direct hit had dislocated the top of house and driven splinters of iron into his eyes.] He said, "Gentlemen, I leave it with you, do what you think best. I cannot see, but do not mind me."

The quartermaster at the wheel, as soon as Capt. W. was hurt, had turned from our antagonist and we were now some distance from her. We held a hurried consultation and "fight" was the unanimous voice of all.

Lieut. Green took Capt. W's position and our bow was again pointed for the *Merrimac*. As we neared her she seemed inclined to haul off and after a few more guns on each side, Mr. Green gave the order to stop firing as she was out of range and hauling off. We did not pursue as we were anxious to relieve Capt. W. and have more done for him than could be done aboard.

Our iron hatches were slid back and we sprang out on deck, which was strewn with fragments of the fight. Our foe gave us a shell as a parting fire which shrieked just over our heads and exploded about 100 feet beyond us.

The battle ended in a draw. At one point, the *Virginia* rammed the *Monitor* and probably would have caused considerable damage if the iron ram on her prow hadn't been knocked off in battle the previous day.

The *Monitor* sank in a storm nine months later, whereas the *Virginia* was scuttled a year after that when the Confederates fled Norfolk. In 1862 and 1863, the Union ordered the construction of fifty-nine more monitors—fourteen of which would have had two gun turrets—but only just over half these were actually built. They fought successfully in many other battles. The South also continued building ironclads.

Even the British and Italian navies built monitors of varying sizes. Britain's *Roberts* class of monitors was so large it displaced 7,800 tons. Monitors were used in both World War I and World War II.

Love Letter from a Dead Man

During the Civil War, Major Sullivan Ballou of the 2nd Rhode Island seemed to sense that he was about to die when he wrote to his wife in Smithfield a week before he was killed in the battle known in the North as the First Battle of Bull Run and in the South as the First Battle of Manassas. This battle, which took place on July 21, 1861, was the first major land engagement of the war. It's very likely his wife didn't receive this letter until after he was dead.

July 14, 1861
Camp Clark, Washington
My very dear Sarah:

The Indications are very strong that we shall move in a few days tomorrow. Lest I should not be able to write again, I feel impelled to write a few lines that may fall under your eye when I shall be no more. . . .

I have no misgivings about, or lack of confidence in the cause in which I am engaged, and my courage does not halt or falter. I know how strongly American Civilization now leans on the triumph of the Government, and how great a debt we owe to those who went before us through the blood and sufferings of the Revolution. And I am willing—perfectly willing—to lay down all my joys in this life, to help maintain this Government, and to pay that debt. . . .

Sarah my love for you is deathless, it seems to bind me with mighty cables that nothing but Omnipotence could break; and yet my love of Country comes over me like a strong wind and bears me unresistibly on with all these chains to the battle field.

The memories of the blissful moments I have spent with you come creeping over me, and I feel most gratified to God and to you that I have enjoyed them so long. And hard it is for me to give them up and burn to ashes the hopes of future years, when, God willing we might still have lived and loved together, and seen our sons grown up to honorable manhood, around us. I have, I know, but few and small claims upon Divine Providence, but something whispers to me—perhaps it is the wafted prayer of my little Edgar, that I shall return to my loved ones unharmed. If I do not my dear Sarah, never forget how much I love you, and when my last breath escapes me on the battle field, it will whisper your name. Forgive my many faults, and the many pains I have caused you. How thoughtless and foolish I have often times been! How gladly would I wash out with my tears every little spot upon your happiness. . . .

But, O Sarah! if the dead can come back to this earth and flit unseen around those they loved, I shall always be near you; In the gladdest days and in the darkest nights . . . *always*, *always*, and if there be a soft breeze upon your cheek, it shall be my breath, as the cool air fans your throbbing temple, it shall be my spirit passing by. Sarah do not mourn me dead; think I am gone and wait for thee, for we shall meet again. . . .

Human Sacrifice at a Viking Funeral

For several centuries, the Vikings were the scourge of Europe. Every spring they would set forth in their ships for foreign shores where they would plunder, pillage, and conquer with a savage devotion. Their courage was bolstered by their war gods, Odin and Thor. Although at first they were little more than pirates, by the ninth century they were launching full-fledged invasions. They devastated cities and villages, demonstrating an enthusiasm for burning monasteries and cathedrals, along with a particular passion for slaughtering priests and nuns. At that time a large portion of Europe's treasure was in its churches, and the pagan Vikings seemed to delight in raiding them. On the positive side, they did help spark the economic revival that led Europe out of the Dark Ages by putting much of Europe's wealth back into circulation.

These reckless marauders, with names like Harald Bluetooth, Halfdan the Black, Eric

Bloodax, and Ivar the Boneless, sacked most of Europe's cities at one time or another. Simeon of Durham, who witnessed the Viking raid on Lindisfarne in A.D. 793, said, "The pagans arrived like stinging hornets and spreading on all sides like fearful wolves, robbed, tore, and slaughtered not only beasts of burden, but even priests and monks and nuns. They came to the church at Lindisfarne and destroyed everything. Some of them polluted the holy places. Their mouths frothed, their eyes stared, they howled like wild beasts." One Viking had the nickname "The Children's Man" because he took great pleasure in tossing the babies of his victims in the air, catching them with the point of his spear. By the end of the tenth century, their reach stretched from Persia to Africa and even west to North America.

For seamen who reveled in their adventurous excursions, it seems logical they would associate their ships with the afterlife journey into the netherworld. And that they did. The bodies of the deceased were either buried on land in a ship or a ship was used as a funeral pyre. For burials, the ship could be an actual one or just an outline of a ship made of stones. The method was probably determined by the person's occupation, status, and wealth.

In a moment, we will take a look at an eyewitness account of one of these fiery funerals, with its human sacrifice—that is as dramatic as the Vikings-lives were, but in order to gain some insight into what they were doing, we must first understand their beliefs.

As with most peoples, the Vikings' funeral practices were closely tied with their religion—the Vanir cult. The Vanir were fertility deities, the best known of which were Odin, Thor, and Freyr. The Vanir were not concerned with justice or morality. Their world was not split into good and evil. Instead, their focus was on power and bringing new life into the world. In the ancient world, life-bringing deities were often worshipped with orgies and sacrifices. With modern Western culture's Puritan background and problems with overpopulation, it is difficult for us to visualize a culture where morality takes a backseat to fertility, but in a harsh world where most infants don't survive childhood and where many adults die in battle, worshipping amoral fertility gods and goddesses becomes more understandable. Although the Nordic religion developed during centuries of limited population, it was actually the eventual overpopulation that forced the Vikings to launch their onslaught on Europe. By then, their religion was deeply rooted.

The reverence of fertility also carried over into their funeral rites. Animals associated with fertility deities—such as horses, pigs and birds—were sacrificed at a funeral. Their remains are found at the sites of the Viking ship burials in Norway and Sweden. Seed corn, hazelnuts, and apples, which are typical symbols of fruitfulness, have also been found.

Myths also associate mead with Odin, the god of the dead. Mead is a liquor made from honey, malt, and spices. It was by stealing mead from some dwarves that Odin passed the gift of oratory and poetic inspiration to the gods and men. The Vikings considered mead to be a magic drink. While some cults—like those of Thor and the Vanir—were more widespread and involved the whole community, the cult of Odin was primarily restricted to the aristocracy.

Every nine years, the Vikings in Sweden flocked to Uppsala for a special religious festival. In the eleventh century, Adam of Bremen wrote, "Of every living thing that is male, they offer nine heads, with the blood of which it is customary to placate gods of this sort. The bodies they hang in the sacred grove that adjoins the temple. Now this grove is so sacred in the eyes of the heathen that each and every tree in it is believed divine because of the death or putrefaction of the victims. Even dogs and horses hang there with men."

Sacrifice was also closely associated with Odin. He is the one who conducts the deceased into the netherworld, either in person or through his messengers, the Valkyries. So that he could gain the knowledge for gods and men, Odin himself was sacrificed by being stabbed by a spear while he was hung from a tree; thus, the sacrifice of humans and animals by piercing and strangulation was often part of religious ceremonies involving him. The human sacrifices at funerals were usually the wife of the deceased or slaves who volunteered for the privilege and treated like royalty or deities until the day of the funeral. The idea was that they would serve their master on his journey to Valhalla. Likewise, the deceased's choicest possessions were burned or buried with him to assist him in his travels.

Many of these images and practices appear in the description of a Viking funeral by an envoy from the Caliph of Baghdad named Ibn Fadlan. His account was translated by A. S. Cook in 1923 and appeared in the *Journal of English and German Philology*. This funeral was for the chief of the Rus, who were the Viking settlers in Russia. It was performed on the Volga River in A.D. 922. The Volga was a primary Viking trading route that ran from Sweden to Baghdad.

> I was told that the least of what they do for their chiefs when they die, is to consume them with fire. When I was finally informed of the death of one of their magnates, I sought to witness what befell. First they laid him in his grave—over which a roof was erected—for the space of ten days, until they had completed the cutting and sewing of his clothes. In the case of a poor man, however, they merely build for him a boat, in which they place him, and consume it with fire. At the death of a rich man, they bring together his goods, and divide them into three parts. The first of these is for his family; the second is expended for the garments they make; and with the third they purchase strong drink, against the day when the girl resigns herself to death, and is burned with her master. To the use of wine they abandon themselves in mad fashion, drinking it day and night; and not seldom does one die with the cup in his hand.
>
> When one of their chiefs dies, his family asks his girls and pages, "Which one of you will die with him?" Then one of them answers, "I." From the time that he utters this word, he is no longer free: should he wish to draw back, he is not permitted. For the most part, however, it is the girls that offer themselves. So, when the man of whom I spoke had died, they asked his girls, "Who will die with him?" One of them answered, "I." She was then committed to two girls, who were to keep watch over her, accompany her wherever she went, and even, on occasion, wash her feet. The

people now began to occupy themselves with the dead man—to cut out the clothes for him, and to prepare whatever else was needful. During the whole of this period, the girl gave herself over to drinking and singing, and was cheerful and gay.

When the day was now come that the dead man and the girl were to be committed to the flames, I went to the river in which his ship lay, but found that it had already been drawn ashore. Four corner-blocks of birch and other woods had been placed in position for it, while around were stationed large wooden figures in the semblance of human beings. Thereupon the ship was brought up, and placed on the timbers above-mentioned. In the meantime the people began to walk to and fro, uttering words which I did not understand. The dead man, meanwhile, lay at a distance in his grave, from which they had not yet removed him. Next they brought a couch, placed it in the ship, and covered it with Greek cloth of gold, wadded and quilted, with pillows of the same material. There came an old crone, whom they call the angel of death, and spread the articles mentioned on the couch. It was she who attended to the sewing of the garments, and to all the equipment; it was she, also, who was to slay the girl. I saw her; she was dark, thick-set, with a lowering countenance.

When they came to the grave, they removed the earth from the wooden roof, set the latter aside, and drew out the dead man in the loose wrapper in which he had died. Then I saw that he had turned quite black, by reason of the coldness of that country. Near him in the grave they had placed strong drink, fruits, and a lute; and these they now took out. Except for his color, the dead man had not changed. They now clothed him in drawers, leggings, boots, and a *kurtak* and *chaftan* of cloth of gold, with golden buttons, placing on his head a cap made of cloth of gold, trimmed with sable. Then they carried him into a tent placed in the ship, seated him on the wadded and quilted covering, supported him with the pillows, and, bringing strong drink, fruits, and basil, placed them all beside him. Then they brought a dog, which they cut in two, and threw into the ship; laid all his weapons beside him; and led up two horses, which they chased until they were dripping with sweat, whereupon they cut them in pieces with their swords, and threw the flesh into the ship. Two oxen were then brought forward, cut in pieces, and flung into the ship. Finally they brought a cock and a hen, killed them, and threw them in also.

Like the rest of the world at that time, the Vikings were very cruel. One of the ways they liked to kill their enemies was by a hideous method called "the blood eagle." The victim's back was split open and his blood-covered lungs were lifted out so that they flapped around like a pair of wings as he struggled to take his last breaths.

The girl who had devoted herself to death meanwhile walked to and fro, entering one after another of the tents which they had there. The occupant of each tent lay with her, saying, "Tell your master, 'I [the man] did this only for love of you.'"

When it was now Friday afternoon, they led the girl to an object which they had constructed, and which looked like the framework of a door. She then placed her feet on the extended hands of the men, was raised up above the framework, and uttered something in her language, whereupon they let her down. Then again they raised her, and she did as at first. Once more they let her down, and then lifted her a third time, while she did as at the previous times. They then handed her a hen, whose head she cut off and threw away; but the hen itself they cast into the ship. I inquired of the interpreter what it was that she had done. He replied: "The first time she said, 'Lo, I see here my father and mother'; the second time, 'Lo, now I see all my deceased relatives sitting'; the third time, 'Lo, there is my master, who is sitting in Paradise. Paradise is so beautiful, so green. With him are his men and boys. He calls me, so bring me to him.'" Then they led her away to the ship.

Here she took off her two bracelets, and gave them to the old woman who was called the angel of death, and who was to murder her. She also drew off her two anklets, and passed them to the two serving-maids, who were the daughters of the so-called angel of death. Then they lifted her into the ship, but did not yet admit her to the tent. Now men came up with shields and staves, and handed her a cup of strong drink. This she took, sang over it, and emptied it. "With this," so the interpreter told me, "she is taking leave of those who are dear to her." Then another cup was handed her, which she also took, and began a lengthy song. The crone admonished her to drain the cup without lingering, and to enter the tent where her master lay. By this time, as it seemed to me, the girl had become dazed; she made as though she would enter the tent, and had brought her head forward between the tent and the ship, when the hag seized her by the head, and dragged her in. At this moment the men began to beat upon their shields with the staves, in order to drown the noise of her outcries, which might have terrified the other girls, and deterred them from seeking death with their masters in the future. Then six men followed into the tent, and each and every one had carnal companionship with her. Then they laid her down by her master's side, while two of the men seized her by the feet, and two by the hands. The old woman known as the angel of death now knotted a rope around her neck, and handed the ends to two of the men to pull. Then with a broad-bladed dagger she smote her between the ribs, and drew the blade forth, while the two men strangled her with the rope till she died.

The next of kin to the dead man now drew near, and, taking a piece of wood, lighted it, and walked backwards towards the ship, holding the stick in one hand, with the other placed upon his buttocks (he being naked), until the wood which had been piled under the ship was ignited. Then the others came up with staves and firewood, each one carrying a stick already lighted at the upper end, and threw it all on the pyre. The pile was soon aflame, then the ship, finally the tent, the man, and the girl, and everything else in the ship. A terrible storm began to blow up, and this intensified the flames, and gave wings to the blaze.

Walt Whitman and President Lincoln's Assassination

Walt Whitman (1819–1892) is considered one of America's greatest poets, primarily for *Leaves of Grass*, which was published in 1855. During the Civil War, he worked as a volunteer nurse in Army hospitals in Washington, D.C. He was then given a job as a clerk in the Indian Department. He often saw Lincoln on the streets of Washington. Although he wasn't actually in the audience of Ford's

Theater on the night when President Lincoln was assassinated, a close friend of his—Peter Doyle—was. He took this witness's statement and wrote this brilliant and striking account of what happened. It was published in his *Memoranda During the War* (1875). The assassination also inspired one of Whitman's most popular poems, "O Captain, My Captain."

> The day, April 14, 1865, seems to have been a pleasant one throughout the whole land—the moral atmosphere pleasant too the long storm, so dark, so fratricidal, full of blood and doubt and gloom, over and ended at last by the sunrise of such an absolute National victory, and utter breaking down of Secessionism—we almost doubted our own senses! Lee had capitulated beneath the apple-tree of Appomattox. The other armies, the flanges of the revolt, swiftly followed. . . . And could it really be, then? Out of all the affairs of this world of woe and passion, of failure and disorder and dismay, was there really come the confirmed, unerring sign of plan, like a shaft of pure light—of rightful rule—of God? . . . So the day, as I say, was propitious. Early herbage, early flowers, were out. (I remember where I was stopping at the time, the season being advanced, there were many lilacs in full bloom. By one of those caprices that enter and give tinge to events without being at all a part of them, I find myself always reminded of the great tragedy of that day by the sight and odor of these blossoms. It never fails.)
>
> But I must not dwell on accessories. The deed hastens. The popular afternoon paper of Washington, the little *Evening Star*, had spattered all over its third page, divided among the advertisements in a sensational manner in a hundred different places, *The President and his Lady will be at the Theater this evening*. . . . (Lincoln was fond of the theater. I have myself seen him there several times. I remember thinking how funny it was that He, in some respects, the leading actor in the greatest and stormiest drama known to real history's stage, through centuries, should sit there and be so completely interested and absorbed in those human jackstraws, moving about with their silly little gestures, foreign spirit, and flatulent text.)
>
> On this occasion the theater was crowded, many ladies in rich and gay costumes, officers in their uniforms, many well-known citizens, young folks, the usual clusters of gas-lights, the usual magnetism of so many people, cheerful, with perfumes, music of violins and flutes—(and over all, and saturating all, that vast vague wonder, *Victory*, the Nation's Victory, the triumph of the Union, filling the air, the thought, the sense, with exhilaration more than all perfumes.)
>
> The President came betimes, and, with his wife, witnessed the play, from the large stage-boxes of the second tier, two thrown into one, and profusely draped with the National flag. The acts and scenes of the piece—one of those singularly written compositions which have at least the merit of giving entire relief to an audience engaged in mental action or business excitements and cares during the day, as it makes not the slightest call on either the moral, emotional, aesthetic, or spiritual nature—a piece, (*Our American Cousin*) in which, among other characters, so called, a Yankee, certainly such a one as was never seen, or the least like it ever seen, in North America, is introduced in England, with a varied fol-de-rol of talk, plot, scenery, and such phantasmagoria as goes to make up a modern popular drama—had progressed through perhaps a couple of its acts, when in the midst of this comedy, or tragedy, or non-such, or

whatever it is to be called, and to off-set it or finish it out, as if in Nature's and the Great Muse's mockery of those poor mimes, comes interpolated that Scene, not really or exactly to be described at all (for on the many hundreds who were there it seems to this hour to have left little but a passing blur, a dream, a blotch)—and yet partially to be described as I now proceed to give it. . . . There is a scene in the play representing a modern parlor, in which two unprecedented English ladies are informed by the unprecedented and impossible Yankee that he is not a man of fortune, and therefore undesirable for marriage-catching purposes; after which, the comments being finished, the dramatic trio make exit, leaving the stage clear for a moment. There was a pause, a hush as it were. At this period came the murder of Abraham Lincoln. Great as that was, with all its manifold train, circling round it, and stretching into the future for many a century, in the politics, history, art, of the New World, in point of fact the main thing, the actual murder, transpired with the quiet and simplicity of any commonest occurrence—the bursting of a bud or pod in the growth of vegetation, for instance. Through the general hum following the stage pause, with the change of positions, came the muffled sound of a pistol shot, which not one hundredth part of the audience heard at the time—and yet a moment's hush—somehow, surely a vague startled thrill—and then, through the ornamented, draperied, starred and striped space-way of the President's box, a sudden figure, a man raises himself with hands and feet, stands a moment on the railing, leaps below to the stage (a distance of perhaps fourteen or fifteen feet) falls out of position, catching his boot-heel in the copious drapery (the American flag), falls on one knee, quickly recovers himself, rises as if nothing had happened (he really sprains his ankle, but unfelt then)—and so the figure, Booth, the murderer, dressed in plain black broadcloth, bareheaded, with a full head of glossy, raven hair, and his eyes like some mad animal's flashing with light and resolution, yet with a certain strange calmness, holds aloft in one hand a large knife—walks along not much back from the footlights—turns fully toward the audience his face of statuesque beauty, lit by those basilisk eyes, flashing with desperation, perhaps insanity—launches out in a firm and steady voice the words, *Sic semper tyrannis* [the motto of Virginia, which means "thus always to tyrants"]—and then walks with neither slow nor very rapid pace diagonally across to the back of the stage, and disappears. . . . (Had not all this terrible scene making the mimic ones preposterous—had it not all been rehearsed, in blank, by Booth, beforehand?)

Approximately 10 percent of America's presidents have been assassinated—Lincoln (1865), Garfield (1881), McKinley (1901), and Kennedy (1963). In addition, assassination attempts were made on another 20 percent: George Washington (1776; though not yet president, he was the country's commander-in-chief), Jackson (1835), Lincoln (1861 and 1864), Theodore Roosevelt (1912; while campaigning for a third term), Franklin Roosevelt (1933; as president elect), Truman (1950), Nixon (1974), Ford (twice in 1975; both times by women), and Reagan (1981). Undoubtedly there were other attempts that have been hushed up. Between 1900 and 1980, there were thirty-two major assassinations in the United States.

A moment's hush, incredulous—a scream—the cry of *Murder*—Mrs. Lincoln leaning out of the box, with ashy cheeks and lips, with involuntary cry, pointing to the retreating figure, *He has killed the President*. . . . And still a moment's strange, incredulous suspense and then the deluge!—then that mixture of horror, noises, uncertainty—(the sound, somewhere back, of a horse's hoofs clattering with speed)—the people burst through chairs and railings, and break them up—that noise adds to the queerness of the scene—there is inextricable confusion and terror—women faint—quite feeble persons fall, and are trampled on—many cries of agony are heard—the broad stage suddenly fills to suffocation with a dense and motley crowd, like some horrible carnival—the audience rush generally upon it—at least the strong men do—the actors and actresses are all there in their play costumes and painted faces, with mortal fright showing through the rouge, some trembling—some in tears—the screams and calls, confused talk redoubled, trebled—two or three manage to pass up water from the stage to the President's box—others try to clamber up—etc., etc., etc.

In the midst of all this, the soldiers of the President's Guard, with others, suddenly drawn to the scene, burst in—(some two hundred altogether)—they storm the house, through all the tiers, especially the upper ones, inflamed with fury, literally charging the audience with fixed bayonets, muskets and pistols, shouting *Clear out! clear out! you sons of bitches*. . . . Such the wild scene, or a suggestion of it rather, inside the playhouse that night.

Outside, too, in the atmosphere of shock and craze, crowds of people, filled with frenzy, ready to seize any outlet for it, come near committing murder several times on innocent individuals. One such case was especially exciting. The infuriated crowd, through some chance, got started against one man, either for words he uttered, or perhaps without any cause at all, and were proceeding at once to actually hang him on a neighboring lamp-post, when he was rescued by a few heroic policemen, who placed him in their midst and fought their way slowly and amid great peril toward the Station House. . . . It was a fitting episode of the whole affair. The crowd rushing and eddying to and fro—the night, the yells, the pale faces, many frightened people trying in vain to extricate themselves—the attacked man, not yet freed from the jaws of death, looking like a corpse—the silent resolute half-dozen policemen, with no weapons but their little clubs, yet stern and steady through all those eddying swarms—made indeed a fitting side-scene to the grand tragedy of the murder. . . . They gained the Station House with the protected man, whom they placed in security for the night, and discharged him in the morning.

And in the midst of that night-pandemonium of senseless hate, infuriated soldiers, the audience and the crowd—the stage, and all its actors and actresses, its paint-pots, spangles, and gas-lights—the life-blood from those veins, the best and sweetest of the land, drips slowly down, and death's ooze already begins its little bubbles on the lips. . . . Such, hurriedly sketched, were the accompaniments of the death of President Lincoln. So suddenly and in murder and horror unsurpassed he was taken from us. But his death was painless.

Major Henry Rathbone was a witness who was even closer to the action. He and his fiancée (who was also his stepsister) had gone to the theater with the president and his wife, and they were all seated together in the Presidential Box when it happened. The following account was part of the testimony he gave at trial of the conspirators. Though it lacks Whitman's polished style, it does provide another glimpse into what happened from someone who was much closer to the action.

> When the second scene of the third act was being performed, and while I was intently observing the proceeding upon the stage, with my back toward the door, I heard the discharge of a pistol behind me, and, looking round, saw through the smoke a man between the door and the President. The distance from the door to where the President sat was about four feet. At the same time I heard the man shout some word, which I thought was "Freedom!" I instantly sprang toward him and seized him. He wrested himself from my grasp, and made a violent thrust at my breast with a large knife. I parried the blow by striking it up, and received a wound several inches deep in my left arm, between the elbow and the shoulder. The orifice of the wound was about an inch and a half in length, and extended upward toward the shoulder several inches [underneath the flesh]. The man rushed to the front of the box, and I endeavored to seize him again, but only caught his clothes as he was leaping over the railing of the box. The clothes, as I believe, were torn in the attempt to hold him. As he went over upon the stage, I cried out, "Stop that man." I then turned to the President; his position was not changed; his head was slightly bent forward, and his eyes were closed. I saw that he was unconscious, and, supposing him mortally wounded, rushed to the door for the purpose of calling medical aid.

President Lincoln lying in state in New York's City Hall.

Gideon Wells, the Secretary of the Navy, wrote in his diary:

> The President had been carried across the street from the theater, to the house of a Mr. Peterson. We entered by ascending a flight of steps above the basement and passing through a long hall to the rear, where the President lay extended on a bed, breathing heavily. . . . I inquired of Dr. H. [Dr. Hall], as I entered, the true condition of the President. He replied the President was dead to all intents, although he might live three hours or perhaps longer.
>
> The giant sufferer lay extended diagonally across the bed. . . . His slow, full respiration lifted the clothes with each breath that he took. His features were calm and striking. I had never seen them appear to better advantage than for the first hour, perhaps, that I was there. After that, his right eye began to swell and that part of his face became discolored. . . . [About seven hours later] The respiration of the President became suspended at intervals, and at last entirely ceased at twenty-two minutes past seven.

Before this fatal night, there were at least two other attempts to take Lincoln's life.[10] Since he ordered that they not be publicized, few people are aware of them. While he was riding home alone one night in 1861, a man shot at him from less than fifty yards away. That bullet missed, but a second assassination attempt in August 1864 came much closer, with the bullet piercing his stovepipe hat.

Lincoln seems to have sensed that something was going to happen to him. He once said, "I feel a presentiment that I shall not outlast the rebellion. When it is over, my work is done."

John Wilkes Booth was the brother of the most famous actor of that time and was himself a very successful and admired actor—especially by women. It's said that in one year alone, he earned more than $30,000—a tremendous amount at that time. Lincoln liked Booth's melodramatic style so much that he actually invited Booth to visit him at the White House. Booth declined. Born in Maryland, Booth's family was Unionist. But for him, the rights of the states were an integral part of independence, and he viewed the Union as something of a dictatorship. He was also a white supremacist who saw slavery as a good thing.

After twelve days on the run, Union soldiers surrounded Booth and an accomplice in a Virginia tobacco barn. The accomplice surrendered, but Booth refused, and the barn was set on fire. As the flames rose, he was shot in the back of the neck. Whether this was due to suicide or a soldier firing against orders is unclear.

Some people believe this wasn't really Booth at all, but another man whose body was passed off as Booth's. The controversy began almost immediately because so much mystery surrounded Booth's autopsy and burial, but it died down about the time the conspirators' trial ended—only to flare up again in 1867, 1898, 1903, 1907, 1937, and various times since then.

Some, including Lincoln's wife, have insisted that President Andrew Johnson was behind the assassination and helped Booth get out of the heavily guarded capital. Others say it was actually Secretary of War Edwin Stanton, and still others have argued Jefferson Davis had a hand in the assassination. Many people just dismiss all this as another bunch of conspiracy theories like those surrounding President Kennedy's murder.

"I am dying. My name is John Wilkes Booth and I am the assassin of President Lincoln. . . . Notify my brother Edwin Booth, of New York City."

—John St. Helen to Finis Bates, 1872

"I am going to die in a few minutes. . . . I killed the best man that ever lived. . . . I am John Wilkes Booth."

—David E. George to Mrs. E. C. Harper, 1900 or 1902[11]

Those who believe Booth wasn't killed disagree on what happened to him after his escape. Some reports said he went to South America. Others

[10] I have one book that says there were more than eighty abortive plots and attempts on his life. Unfortunately, it gives no further information.

[11] There is some confusion on the year. Both of these quotes are from Finis Bates's *The Escape and Suicide of John Wilkes Booth* (1907).

believed that he eventually went to Canada and then on to England, where he married Elizabeth Marshall Burnley—a girlfriend he had prior to the assassination—and that he changed his name to John Byron Wilkes. A few insisted he then went on to India, where he died. But probably the most interesting theory is that he escaped to Kentucky and Tennessee, where in 1872, he married Louisa Payne as "Jno. W. Booth." It's said he abandoned her and made his way to Texas using the name John St. Helen. Then he moved on to Oklahoma, where he assumed the name David E. George and where he committed suicide by poison in 1903.

Apparently George confessed to being Booth the previous year to Mrs. E. C. Harper, the wife of a minister, during a suicide attempt. When she read of his death, she revealed the confession, and newspapers began reporting it. A Memphis lawyer named Finis Bates read about this and went to see the body. Bates insisted George was also St. Helen, who he said had confessed to him thirty-one years earlier that he (St. Helen) was Booth. Bates also said he had a photograph of St. Helen that proved he was Booth and George.

Because of the controversy and because no one claimed the body, the undertaker preserved it. Some months later, Bates bought it, and the corpse was displayed in carnivals around the country as Booth's until it disappeared in 1976. The body was examined by a group of expert medical men and criminologists in 1931, who claimed the fractured leg, broken thumb, and scar on the neck all proved it was the remains of Booth.

Recent attempts to exhume the body buried in Booth's grave for identification have failed, so there may be no definitive answer for a while. However, almost all historians still believe Booth died near that tobacco barn in 1865.

The Booth brothers (l. to r.) John Wilkes, Edwin, and Junius Brutus, Jr.—in Julius Caesar. *Edwin and Junius Jr. were strong supporters of the North.*

Booth's diary was found just after the assassination, and in it the twenty-seven-year-old Shakespearean actor had written, "I struck boldly, and not as the papers say. I walked with a firm step through 1,000 of his friends, was stopped, but pushed on. A colonel was at his side. I shouted, "Sic semper" before I fired. In jumping, broke my leg. I passed all his pickets, rode 60 miles that night, with the bone of my leg tearing the flesh at every jump. I can never repent it, although we hated to kill. Our country owed all her troubles to him, and God simply made me the instrument of His punishment."

Booth really believed he'd done the country a great service and just couldn't understand why he was being chased. "I am here in despair," he wrote. "And why? For doing what Brutus was honored for—what made [William] Tell a hero. And yet I, for striking down a greater tyrant than they ever knew, am looked upon as a common cutthroat. . . . I have too great a soul to die like a criminal. O may He spare me that, and let me die bravely!"

Actually Lincoln's death did more harm to the South than good. General Lee had surrendered five days earlier, so the war was already over. The difficult Reconstruction was about to begin, and Lincoln wanted to make the reunification as smooth and easy as possible. His restoration plan was considered to be too lenient by radical Republicans, and they put forward their own, much harsher, plan. The stage was set for Lincoln's battle with members of his own political party when he was suddenly murdered. Although his successor, Andrew Johnson, held a position similar to Lincoln's, Johnson was a Democrat, and the issue became a battle between the two political parties, resulting in gridlock. Radical Republicans were overwhelmingly reelected to Congress by Northerners in the 1866 election, and they passed a series of acts that forced the South to begin the Reconstruction all over again. With a Republican Congress against him, Johnson was powerless to implement his own plan, so he did his best to hinder them from implementing theirs. They moved to have him impeached, and though the conviction failed by one vote, it effectively put an end to Johnson's interference.[12] The Republicans went ahead with their plan, but the Reconstruction was an abysmal failure. One result was the rise of the Ku Klux Klans (there are several) and similar vigilante-style terrorist organizations. Eventually, the Southern Republican governments disintegrated, leading to the Democratic domination of the South that persists to this day.

Almost all historians agree that the Reconstruction failed miserably, but they disagree over what should have been done instead. Some believe the Republicans should have been conciliatory, whereas others argue that they should have been even tougher and seized stronger control of the South. Either way, it's difficult to say how much different things would be today if Lincoln had not been assassinated.

Four days before his assassination on January 30, 1948, Gandhi explained that his escape from an assassin's bomb the week before "was God's mercy," adding, "I am quite prepared to obey His order when it does come. I talk of leaving Delhi on February 2, but I do not myself feel that I shall be able to go away from here. After all, who knows what is going to happen tomorrow?"

On the night before he was killed, he said, "If I die of disease or even a pimple, it will be your duty to shout to the world from the rooftops that I was a false mahatma. Then my soul, wherever it may be, will rest in peace. But, if an explosion took place as it did last week, or somebody shot at me and I received his bullet on my bare chest without a sigh with Rama's name on my lips, only then should you say I was a true mahatma." The following day he received three bullets in his bare chest and died with Rama's name on his lips.

John Lennon, another pacifist who was assassinated, once commented, "Mahatma Gandhi and Martin Luther King are great examples of fantastic nonviolents who died violently. . . . I'm not sure what it means when you're such a pacifist that you get shot."

---

12 Technically, Johnson was actually impeached. People commonly use the term *impeachment* to refer to booting the president out of office. The term really refers to the House of Representatives bringing charges against the president. Once the House brings the charges, the Senate decides whether or not to convict. Johnson was impeached in the House by a vote of 126 to 47, with all the Republicans voting for impeachment and all the Democrats against. He missed being convicted in the Senate by a vote of 35 to 19—one short of the required two-thirds. In Nixon's case, the House Judiciary Committee voted to recommend three articles of impeachment to the House. Facing almost certain impeachment and conviction, Nixon resigned.

Official DOCUMENTS

THE FBI COURSE IN BOMB-MAKING

According to the FBI, countries like Britain and Germany usually have fewer than forty bombings a year, whereas the United States has more than two thousand. The difference is that almost all of theirs are terrorist bombings, and almost all American bombings are crime related. In America, they usually involve drugs, organized crime, or acts of vengeance. Fortunately, the FBI is very good at catching terrorists and usually gets them before they explode their bombs. Unfortunately, there are an awful lot of criminals in America.

Pipe bombs are the most common type of bomb used in the United States. They are easy to make, and their components are readily available. Many other types of homemade bombs can also be constructed from everyday household products. Interestingly, the FBI teaches people how these bombs are made. Now, this is not to say that the FBI *wants* people to go out and make bombs. Oh, no. They do this to give people some idea what to look for so that they can recognize one of these homemade monstrosities when they see it. One of the instructors who gives this briefing is Special Agent Examiner Wallace Higgins of the Explosives Unit at the Laboratory Division of the FBI. He refers to his seminar as "Bomb Building 101," but points out that what he teaches is "sanitized." In other words, certain specifics are withheld to discourage the attendees from going out and trying to put this information to use. As Higgins puts it, "Don't take the information that I give you and try to build a bomb with it because you will hurt yourself."[13]

The unsanitized information is actually very easy to get a hold of. Bomb-making is illegal, but because of freedom of speech, telling someone how to make a bomb is completely legal. In fact, books that do just that are readily available. With titles like *The Anarchist's Cookbook* and *Kitchen Improvised Blasting Caps*, the FBI estimates more than 130 of these publications are out there. These books—along with such publications as *How I Steal Cars*, *Getting Started in the Illicit Drug Business*, *Techniques of Revenge*, *How to Kill*, *The Poisoner's Handbook*, and *Gunrunning for Fun and Profit*—are easily obtainable by mail order. I've also seen them at gun shows, head shops, and some major chain bookstores. The FBI says they're even available at some libraries.

[13] This warning is so obvious that it seems ridiculous to repeat it, but my publisher insists that I remind you not to try to build any of the devices discussed in this section yourself. The descriptions given here are intended to inform you about bombs, not to encourage you to construct them on your own. Though the information is correct (at least according to the FBI), it is inadequate to build a bomb with. Building your own bomb is A REALLY BAD IDEA—you could put an eye out, or worse.

Because this information is so readily available, people who work in places that are likely bombing targets need to know how to spot all sorts of explosive devices. This is where the FBI's bomb-making course comes in.

What I'm about to present to you are transcripts from a U.S. Nuclear Regulatory Commission conference that was given over three days in November 1989. The transcripts were later published by the U.S. government under the title *Security Training Symposium* (1990). Men and women who work for law enforcement agencies, power companies, and nuclear power plants from all over the country descended on Bethesda, Maryland, to learn about bombs.

The most interesting seminar from our point of view is the one given by Higgins. But before we get into that, it will help to look at an excerpt from the FBI Bomb Data Center publication *Introduction to Explosives*, which was handed out at the conference. After providing information on the different types of explosions and explosives, it has a section on improvised explosives.

> *Improvised Explosives.* When manufactured explosives are not available, it is relatively easy to obtain all of the ingredients necessary to make improvised explosive materials. The list of existing materials and simple chemical compounds which can be employed to construct homemade bombs is virtually unlimited. The ingredients required can be obtained at local hardware or drug stores and are so commonplace that their purchase rarely arouses any suspicion.
>
> Starch, flour, sugar or cellulose materials can be treated to become effective explosives. Powder from shotgun shells or small arms ammunition, match heads, firecracker powder and ammonium nitrate fertilizers can all be accumulated in sufficient volume to create a devastating main charge explosive. To explode or detonate the improvised main charge, some means of initiation is required. The most common methods of ignition of improvised explosives are summarized below.
>
> *Blasting Caps.* Blasting caps, when available, provide the most successful means of causing the complete detonation of improvised explosives.
>
> *Percussion Primers.* Shotgun, rifle or pistol ammunition primers have served as initiators in some bomb assemblies, particularly with explosives that are sensitive to heat.
>
> *Flashbulbs.* Although not explosive by nature, carefully prepared flashbulbs or light bulbs can be used as initiation devices when placed in contact with explosive materials that are sensitive to heat and flame. They can be initiated electrically to provide the necessary heat required to ignite black powder, smokeless powder and other heat-sensitive explosive or incendiary mixtures.
>
> As noted above, improvised main charge explosives are limited only by the materials available and the training and imagination of the bomber. Some main charges are produced by using existing commercial compounds converted to the bomber's tactical use, and in other cases the main charge explosive is chemically formulated and manufactured from materials available from grocery or drug stores.
>
> One of the most widely used improvised main charge explosive [sic] is black powder. Black powder is especially easy to manufacture and, when dry, is also one of the most dangerous explosives to handle because of its sensitivity to sparks, flame or friction.

Other common improvised explosives include:

Match Heads. A main charge consisting of ordinary match heads confined inside a steel pipe will produce an effective explosion. Bombs filled with match heads are extremely sensitive to heat, shock and friction and should always be handled with care.

Smokeless Powder. Smokeless powder, obtained from assembled cartridges purchased for hand reloading, is widely employed as a main charge, particularly in pipe bombs.

Ammonium Nitrate Fertilizer. Fertilizer grade ammonium nitrate mixed with fuel oil makes excellent main charge explosive. A booster is required for detonation unless the prills are pulverized.

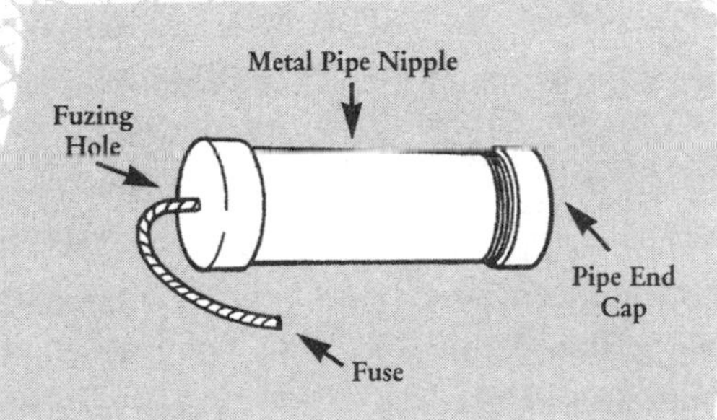

Diagram of a pipe bomb.

Okay, now here are some excerpts from Special Agent Higgins's Bomb Building 101, as he calls it. Unfortunately, we can't see the slides he showed the audience because they are of "a sensitive nature." I'm afraid we'll just have to use our imaginations.

What does the terrorist need to build a bomb? He needs explosives, and he needs an initiator, a blasting cap; he needs a fusing system, and he needs a container for it. The terrorist can't walk in someplace carrying a bomb in his hands and expect to get by the security guard, so he will put it in some kind of container. If he wants to cause personnel damage, he will put shrapnel in the bomb. That is, bolts, nails, beebees [sic], whatever he can find. He will need the tools to put all this together. . . .

As far as explosives, domestically we find that the pipe bomb and the low explosive[14] is very popular. Why? Because anyone can go in any gun store with cash in hand and buy it. You do not need a driver's license. All you have to do is look like you are over 21, pay your money and walk out with a can that has a lot of power in it. There are States that allow a person to walk in with a driver's license, pay the money, and walk out with a case of dynamite and the blasting caps. Simple as that, it's easy to do.

If anyone is looking for high explosives, he can go and buy them. It's as simple as that: Pay the money, show a driver's license, and get it. He can make it in his own home. Buy the fertilizer, buy the aluminum powder, diesel fuel, and you have a high explosive. All he needs then is one blasting cap. In some cases, he can steal it from the military. That is where you get your best explosives, military explosives. They have a high brisance, or shattering effect.

You don't need an initiator for a low explosive. All you need is a spark. You can use a flashbulb, lightbulb, anything, an element that fires these model rockets. You do not need a blasting cap. For high explosives you need a blasting cap.

There are two types of blasting caps, non-electric and electric. Non-electric uses a fuse system that you light. The powder train burns, just like you see in the movies with John Wayne. The blasting cap goes and sets off the high explosive. That is not very common in improvised bombs. The most common is the electric blasting cap or the exploding bridge wire. You need electricity to set them off.

On an electric fusing system, you need the basic requirements for a DC circuit. You need a power source, you need a conductor, you need a load. That's all you need. To control that circuit you need one other thing, and that is switches. We will get heavily into switches, but let's go into power sources first. What kind of power sources are we going to talk about here? Batteries. Batteries come in all shapes and sizes, big ones, little ones. All you need is a battery that has sufficient power to set off a blasting cap. Some of the smaller ones like the ones that fit in your ear or watch do not have enough power to set off a blasting cap.

So you need something that has enough power in it to set off a blasting cap. A bomber's choice is usually a 9-volt transistor battery. Why, I do not know. Maybe it is just more reliable and always fires. This is a 6-volt battery. It is a flatpack. It is in every roll of film that you buy from Polaroid. It is thin, lightweight, and it has enough power to set a blasting cap off.

Next, you need the conductors. Wire or a printed circuit board, anything that conducts electricity. Wire comes in all shapes, sizes, colors, and gauges. Next you need a load. In this case, it is an electric blasting cap. This is a military-type blasting cap. It is very powerful and it will set off any type of explosive that can be set off with an electric blasting cap. My favorite part is when we get to the switches. Switches can be made of anything that anyone could probably think of to use.

We will [now] talk about clocks, clocks that are either mechanical or electrical. How does a bomb maker make a timing device or a switch out of a clock? He takes one wire and hooks it to the base of the clock. Next, he will drill a hole in the face of that clock and insert a screw and attach a wire to it. He will probably take off the hour hand or the minute hand, whichever he wants to operate on. One gives him 12 hours and the other one gives him 1 hour.

This is part of a pipe bomb shrapnel from the FBI publication, Introduction to Explosives.

I have one here to show you that is wired up, only this one is wired to the bell. When the clapper hits the bell, it goes off. No drilling in this. This is a little electronic egg timer. It makes a beep. It makes a beep that has sufficient current in it, so that if it is amplified just a little bit, it will set a blasting cap off. The bomb maker just has to pull the back off, cut out the beeper, put in a small amplifying circuit, and he can create a timer that will time up to 99 hours.

Another type of switch is a vibration switch. This type of switch is sold in an electronic warehouse store for house wiring so that a person can wire an area in his/her house where an excess type of vibration will set the alarm off. Another type is a mercury switch, which can be bought at Radio Shack or any electronic warehouse, or it can be made. The mercury switch has a little ball of mercury and two electrodes embedded in the glass container. When the mercury rolls over and makes contact with those two electrodes, the current flows. It can be carried in one position, move it, set it down, and somebody else comes along, moves it, and that will set the bomb off. A mercury switch can be homemade, with a test tube, a plug, two contacts, and some mercury. It is a very simple switch. It is an antidisturbance switch, has no time factor. In other words, it is waiting for somebody to disturb it and it will go off.

A photoelectric switch is another type that can be bought. With a little modification to the circuitry, it can make a bomb go off when the ambient light is disturbed. When the light source changes the ambient light and [it] either gets lighter or it gets darker, the circuitry can be set so that it will set the bomb off. We will go through some of these circuits after you understand what the switches are like, and you will get an idea how the circuitry works.

There are a lot of other electronic components. There are transistors, silicone control rectifiers, which have different functions than electronics, but in bomb making they are basically just switches that control the circuit in a bomb. By combining a resistor and a capacitor, you can make a timing circuit that will detonate a bomb. There are other integrated circuits that can be built. One is the popular 555 circuit. There are several other types of circuits that can be designed to not set off the bomb for years. It can be set at a predestined time in the future and it will function at years, months, minutes later. There are electrochemical switches, E cells that are nothing but timers. They work under the premise that when an electrode deplates and plates onto the other electrode at a timed sequence, when it is through deplating, a current will either flow or be interrupted and set the bomb off. There also are sound-activated switches. The concept is similar to that used for the "dancing flower" that they have out in the stores right now. That's a sound-activated switch that makes the flower jump around. A bomb can be built so that a normal voice talking over it will set it off.

There are other switches that are proximity switches, and they work off magnetic induction—in other words, if a person walks toward the location or the bomb, that person will change the magnetic field and that will set the bomb off. These are just some of the options that bomb builders have if they use their imagination and they will.

Relays can be used in building bombs. They can hold a circuit open until the battery decays, releasing the contact inside the relay which will fire the bomb.

An altimeter, quite commonly used in aircraft, can be purchased in a good automotive store in the United States or in Europe. An altimeter for a vehicle will cost about $30.00. An altimeter can be modified so that a change in altitude will make it set off a bomb. Where would we use one of these? In an aircraft. That would probably be one of the few places you would use an altimeter switch.

Radio-controlled devices are becoming more and more popular. They are complicated to build, but a reliable system can be built for about $130.00. A person can go to a hobby shop and buy a FUTABA or any other brand device that is used for radio control of model airplanes. With a little ingenuity, a person can build a reliable radio-controlled device. Granted, it doesn't have a long-distance range only about a quarter of a mile. But a terrorist can be a quarter of a mile away from his target when the bomb goes off. A reliable radio-controlled system can be built. However, if one is not careful about the way he builds one of these it can be fatal and unhealthy because, when turned on, the receiver sometimes has a little slap in the servo, a little current goes through. Here's another type of radio control. This one is encoded and decoded. In other words, it operates on a frequency on which there are other radios working. Unless it receives a certain code before the transmission is received, it doesn't work. If it receives that code, the receiver turns on. This device can be tailored to reception in a bomb. Again though, it is tricky because the bomber could be delivering it to a target site and somebody could key a radio on the same frequency and inadvertently set off the bomb. That can be unhealthy.

I have a couple of radio-controlled devices that were confiscated in some raids. These are not sophisticated, they get back to the basics. This is a switch. How does it operate? What is it? It's two tin can lids with nail holes in them and a piece of paper between. What happens if somebody pushes on the tin can lid or steps on it? It completes the circuit. It can be hooked to a bomb.

This is another one that is made with common, ordinary clothespins. Clothespins are not as popular nowadays, but you can still buy them. They can be wired in about five different ways. They can be set for pressure release, pressure, or time—several different ways to wire a clothespin and have it function as a switch. Another favorite of "dopers" who are trying to guard marijuana fields and their drug stash is a simple mouse trap, which can act as a switch. All one has to do is make a contact for the wire to come down on and a contact for it to function against. Current will flow to the bomb.

I have a device that was found on an aircraft; it was found under the seat of an aircraft. It is a sheet explosive, with circuitry that consists of a resistor, an E cell, one transistor, and a blasting cap. Not a very bulky circuit. The device was placed under the seat of an aircraft, a passenger got on that flight and sat down. When they sat down, they made contact with a pressure switch, which caused the current to flow into the E cell, the E cell starts deplating, and when it is through deplating, the current flows through the transistor and fires the blasting cap. The passenger inadvertently sat on a bomb.

I have a diagram of an altimeter switch that was hooked into a fairly complicated circuit with power source and explosive. Altimeter switches are mostly used in aircraft.

Those are some of the basic electrical circuits that you will find. A person who knows nothing about electronics can go to an electronics store or buy a book and learn everything he needs to know to be able to build a DC circuit and adapt it to firing a bomb. My telling you this is not any type of security violation because all the information is out there in simple books for anyone to read.

One thing that a bomb maker has to consider is a container for the bomb. Domestically, the most popular is the pipe. It is easy to buy; it's cheap; it provides a lot of fragmentation. The pipe can be purchased in different sizes to hold as much explosive as the bomb maker wants to put in it. It can be fired in several ways. It can be fired nonelectric or electric. The whole firing circuit can be placed inside the pipe container; the end caps can be screwed down and the bomb placed. Even if it is found, the bomb technician that has to work on it has a big problem. It is not easy to get in that pipe and get the explosives and firing train out.

Secretary of State James Baker justified the U.S. alliance with Syria, by saying, "We have problems with their support of terrorism, but we share a common goal."

The reasons why the pipe bomb is probably so popular: it is cheap and provides a lot of fragmentation. About 30 pounds of dynamite can be placed in a common briefcase with a firing circuit. It would be very easy to carry on the streets of Washington, D.C. and nobody would ever question the carrier. Letter bombs can be made with a sheet explosive, a thin explosive, and some type of switch, a power source that is thin. For example, a Polaroid battery and some kind of switch that makes contact when the secretary sticks the letter opener in to open it up. An antidisturbance type of switch would not work in this type of package because of the handling it receives en route. It would need to be a switch that is activated by the individual opening the letter or package.

Containers can come in all shapes and sizes; carry-on baggage or a pocketbook may be used for an aircraft. An umbrella can be a bomb very easily; all the circuitry and explosives can be inside the umbrella. In fact, in one case, it was. It hung in the hallway of a building for several days before somebody discovered it. Fortunately, it didn't go off.

When a bomb maker builds a bomb, there is no manual for it and there is no quality control for it. Terrorist organizations don't have quality control. They try to make the bombs reliable, but it is not 100 percent. Airports have a lot of suitcases, and a suitcase can be a bomb container. We are trying to detect explosives in suitcases. There will be no simple answer for our problem with bombs at the airport. There will be no one simple machine that solves the problems of explosives at airports. It will be a system.

Pretty creepy, ay? A bomb can be disguised as just about anything. I have to wonder how they found out the umbrella was really a bomb. It seems as if it would take an expert to spot bombs like that, and even with this course, I wonder if your average Joe working in a nuclear power plant knows enough to spot those exploding umbrellas. I certainly hope so.

Special Agent Higgins goes on to explain that terrorists probably wouldn't be dumb enough to try to smuggle a bomb into a heavily guarded facility. It's much easier to just smuggle in the blasting cap and the explosives in small amounts. Then using items that are already in the facility, they will put the bomb together at the site. He added, "Even if you have the best security in place, don't rely on it." He also stressed, "If you suspect it's a bomb, it's a bomb. Don't touch it. . . . If the bomb goes off, your quality of life has suddenly changed, and it's not going to be very good if you live." So if you happen to find a mysterious umbrella in your office, call the FBI. Their phone number is (202) FBI-BOMB.

In another seminar at the same conference, FBI chemist Dr. Dean Fetterolf talked about a couple of the *Bomb-Making For Fun and Profit*-type books I mentioned earlier.

> These books will tell you how to make non-nitrogen containing explosives [which can't be detected by nitrogen-based bomb detectors]. With $12.85 and a trip to the hardware store, you can buy some acetone, you can buy some sulfuric acid drain cleaner; you can go to the beauty parlor and get some hydrogen peroxide that is used in bleaching your hair; you mix those together on your kitchen stove at home and you can make an explosive called triacetone triperoxide that contains no nitrogen has a detonation velocity almost equivalent to PETN[15] and has been used in various parts of the world.
>
> One of the common things where we first heard about this was in the Middle East. They would mix up this stuff and pour it into Coke cans and leave the Coke or Pepsi cans or beer cans lying on the streets. Little children would come along—and what do they do when they see a can—they kick it. This stuff is extremely shock sensitive. It is a primary explosive. If you mix it up at home on your stove, which I don't recommend that you do, when you try to scrape it out of the pan, you have a problem.

Dr. Fetterolf also told of how "five-year-old Erin Bower was walking through K Mart with her mother. She reached up on the shelf and grabbed one of these pump-type toothpaste tubes and it detonated. She lost part of her left hand, some injuries to her left eye, and had some shrapnel wounds in her stomach. Just another concealment device, considerably different than anything you've seen so far."

Makes you glad the FBI is good at capturing terrorists, doesn't it? Now if we can just do something about all those criminals.

Naval Discipline

Maintaining order in the military is very important. Here is how the U.S. Navy did it in 1848. This list of punishments for delinquent squids appeared in Horace Greeley's *The Tribune Almanac for the Years 1838 to 1868* (1868).

For bad cooking	12 strokes of the whip
For stealing a major's wig	12 strokes of the whip
For skulking	12 strokes of the whip
For running into debt on shore	12 strokes of the whip
For tearing a sailor's frock	9 strokes of the whip
For filthiness	12 strokes of the whip

[15] PETN (pentaerythritol tetranitrate) is used in detonating cords. If you light one end of a five-mile cord of PETN, the flame will reach the other end one second later. It is also used as a booster.

For striking a schoolmaster	12 strokes of the whip
For drunkenness and breaking into the liquor closet	12 strokes of the whip
For noise at quarters	6 strokes of the whip
For bad language	12 strokes of the whip
For dirty and unwashed clothes	12 strokes of the whip
For being out of hammock after hours	12 strokes of the whip
For throwing overboard the top of a spittoon	6 strokes of the whip
For taking bread out of oven	9 strokes of the whip
For neglecting mess utensils	12 strokes of the whip
For taking clothes on shore to sell	12 strokes of the whip
For skylarking (running up and down the rigging of a ship)	6 strokes of the whip
For being naked on deck	9 strokes of the whip

I must admit, I don't know why they whipped sailors more for taking bread out of the oven than for tossing the spittoon lid overboard. I have to wonder what punishments they would have meted out for some of the offenses in the Tailhook scandal. Here is a list of chapter headings from the Pentagon's report on abuses at the Navy's Tailhook Association convention in 1991: "Streaking," "Mooning," "Ballwalking," "Leg Shaving," "Belly/ Navel Shots," "Chicken Fighting," and "Butt Biting." I guess streaking would be the same as being naked on deck. At least at Tailhook, they didn't take the bread out of the oven.

The Army of the Netherlands is a bit unusual in that its soldiers belong to a union called the VVDM. As a result, Dutch grunts only salute during ceremonies, get overtime pay for unpleasant duties like KP, can wear sneakers instead of combat boots when on maneuvers, and their hair can be any length as long as they wear a hairnet around heavy machinery.

Survival Under Atomic Attack

There are two basic types of nuclear explosions: atomic and hydrogen. An atomic explosion is created by splitting the nuclei of certain heavy atoms, whereas in a hydrogen explosion, the nuclei of certain light atoms are combined. The first hydrogen bomb was exploded in 1952. Hydrogen bombs—also known as thermonuclear bombs—are much more powerful than atom bombs. The most powerful hydrogen bomb yet detonated had a yield of fifty-seven megatons (or equivalent to fifty-seven million tons of TNT). It was set off by the Soviets in 1961, and the shockwave circled the globe three times. They claimed to have a 100-megaton bomb. Although most of today's nuclear bombs yield less than one megaton, this is made up for by the tremendous quantities of these bombs that are ready for use. You can destroy a lot more with ten one-megaton bombs than you can with one ten-megaton bomb.

There are other types of nuclear weapons, some combining both fission and fusion to improve efficiency. Clean bombs are designed to create a minimum amount of radiation, whereas dirty bombs—like the neutron bomb—create maximum radiation with the least amount of blast, killing living things but leaving buildings and equipment intact.

The terms *strategic* and *tactical* refer more to how the bomb is used rather than the type of bomb. Nuclear weapons used on cities or a military installation would be strategic, and one used on a battlefield would be tactical. Obviously, tactical nukes would tend to have a lower yield than strategic ones. For the most part, strategic nukes would be delivered by missiles or bombers, whereas tactical nukes could be fired from artillery or left like a land mine when retreating.

More than a third of a million people were killed by the two nuclear bombs dropped on Japan in 1945. Since then, more than 1,800 nuclear explosions have occurred on earth (about half of them set off by the United States). They were tests, of course, but there has been thought of using them against an enemy.

- In 1950, President Truman publicly announced that he was considering using nuclear weapons in Korea.
- Then in 1954, Secretary of State John Foster Dulles offered to give three atomic bombs to France to use at Dienbienphu in Vietnam, but the French refused.
- In 1958, President Eisenhower got the Joint Chiefs of Staff to commit themselves to a plan to use nukes if the Chinese tried to occupy two islands—Quemoy and Matsu—that lie just off the Chinese coast.
- Three years later in 1961, the Joint Chiefs of Staff recommended to Kennedy that they should be used if the Chinese tried to do anything about the proposed U.S. occupation of Laos. Instead, Kennedy decided not to occupy Laos.
- America came to the brink of nuclear war during the Cuban missile crisis in 1962.
- General Westmoreland, in his memoirs, revealed that the use of tactical nuclear weapons was considered when Khe Sanh was under siege in 1968.
- H. R. Haldeman wrote in his memoirs that within months of taking office, President Nixon and Secretary Kissinger began secretly threatening the North Vietnamese with their use. They also secretly said this to the Soviets and the Chinese. This went on at least until the December 1972 bombings of Hanoi. Other sources reveal plans were drawn up to use nuclear devices on rail lines and on the Ho Chi Minh trail.
- It's reported that during the Cold War, NATO buried tactical nukes in what was then West Germany so that if the Soviets invaded from East Germany, these bombs could be set off from a remote location.
- It seems the British thought about launching some Polaris nuclear missiles at Argentina during the 1982 Falklands War.
- It recently was revealed that President Reagan strongly believed throughout his administration that the United States was on the verge of fighting a nuclear battle with the Soviet Union. He further believed that in accordance with biblical prophecy, the "Evil Empire" would invade Israel, that America and the Soviets would nuke it out at Armageddon, and that Jesus would then descend from heaven. So while Soviet Premier Gorbachev was talking about trying to save the world from nuclear holocaust by eliminating these weapons, Reagan thought they were a good thing and necessary to fulfill prophecy and bring about Christ's return.
- And General Norman Schwarzkopf testified before a Senate committee that the United States threatened to nuke Iraq

during the Persian Gulf war if they used chemical weapons.

And then there were the accidents. It is known that the Navy had a policy of covering up nuclear accidents in order to avoid frightening the public (and, no doubt, embarrassing themselves). A May 8, 1984, directive from Admiral William Crowe, then commander in chief in the Pacific, ordered commanders "to recover or remove, if at all practical, all evidence of the nuclear weapon accident or significant incident as expeditiously as possible" and "a denial should characterize the accident or incident as a non-nuclear event."

Here are some storage instructions of warheads and torpedoes from the British Admiralty that really inspire confidence in their handling of these weapons: "It is necessary for technical reasons that these warheads should be stored with the top at the bottom, and the bottom at the top. In order that there may be no doubt as to which is the top and which is the bottom, for storage purposes, it will be seen that the bottom of each head has been labeled with the word TOP."

Although many of these incidents are probably still considered very, very secret, a few have made it into the press. Here are some I've run across.

- In 1957, a hydrogen bomb fell out of an Air Force bomber near Albuquerque, New Mexico. Turbulence had caused the navigator to grab the bomb release mechanism to keep from falling. The nuclear portion of the bomb didn't explode, but the conventional portion did, creating a crater twelve feet deep and twenty-five feet across. The only casualty was a cow. The Air Force wouldn't confirm this accident until 1981, when they said only minor radioactivity was detected at the site. Though the military refused to say, it's thought the bomb had an explosive yield of 10 megatons, or about 625 times that of the Hiroshima bomb.
- In 1966, three hydrogen bombs fell on Palomares, Spain, after an Air Force bomber crashed into a refueling plane. A fourth bomb fell into the Mediterranean. The built-in safety devices kept the bombs from incinerating most of southern Spain, but the village was showered with plutonium and uranium particles. Antonian Flores, who was six years old at the time, said, "One of the bombs made a huge crater in our back yard. We played with the debris until they told us it was dangerous." The Air Force tried to clean up the town by burning crops, killing animals, and removing 2,000 tons of topsoil.
- In 1979, an apparent computer malfunction at the North American Air Defense Command (NORAD) headquarters sent out an alert that a missile attack was underway from Soviet submarines. The error took about six minutes to be discovered. The president had not yet been notified, but ten U.S. and Canadian F-106 fighters took off to intercept the nonexistent Soviet bombers, while nuclear missile bases were put on alert. The Air Force said no B-52 bombers took off. During an 18-month period around this same time, NORAD had 151 false alarms caused by computer errors—4 of which put bomber and missile crews on alert. Just a few years later, a Stanford University computer-operations specialist

filed a lawsuit to prevent the United States from hooking up a computer system that would automatically launch nuclear missiles in response to a warning of a Soviet attack.

- In 1983, a solor storm caused the Soviet Early warning satellites to indicate the Soviet Union was under a massive attack by the United States.
- And on January 25, 1995, Russian President Boris Yeltsin was notified that a ballistic missile, possibly from a submarine, was rising over the Norwegian Sea. He had only four minutes to decide whether or not to retaliate. He decided not to. It turned out to be a Norwegian meteorological rocket. Moscow had been informed of the launch, but the word hadn't been passsed on to senior military officials.

And then there are the legitimate concerns of terrorists using nuclear weapons. This risk is emphasized by the many incidents where the smugglers of nuclear components have been caught. But let's not get into that.

Ever since the bombs were dropped on Hiroshima and Nagasaki, people have worried about having one of these horrors dropped on them. Since the demise of the Soviet Union, this threat has become more nebulous, making it a bit more difficult for people to focus their fears.[16] As a result, their fears have diminished somewhat even though the threat has probably increased because of the increase in countries that have the bomb and the advances in technology that enable a bomb to be made from fissionable material the size of a beer can, while a bomb that can level a city can now be made to fit into a knapsack. But during the Cold War, the threat seemed much more immediate.

Partly in response to these fears, the government implemented programs to teach people how they could protect themselves in the event of a nuclear attack. Early efforts downplayed the risks. One amazing example of this is the pamphlet *Survival Under Atomic Attack*. Published by the U.S. government in 1950, this official booklet proclaims, "You can SURVIVE. You can live through an atom bomb raid and you won't have to have a Geiger counter, protective clothing, or special training in order to do it." And then it goes on to give such advice as, "After an air burst, wait a few minutes then go help to fight fires. After other kinds of bursts wait at least 1 hour to give lingering radiation some chance to die down."

Discussing the role of the IRS in a nuclear attack, the Internal Revenue Service Handbook *(1976) says, "During a state of national emergency resulting from enemy attack, the essential functions of the Service will be as follows: (1) assessing, collecting, and recording taxes. . . ."*

Here's some more of its sage advice on how you can "SURVIVE" atomic destruction.

What are Your Chances?

If a modern A-bomb exploded without warning in the air over your home town tonight, your calculated chances of living through the raid would run something like this:

[16] As of 1997, Russia and the United States still had about seven thousand strategic (or long rang) warheads each. Roughly half of these could be launched with a few minutes notice.

Should you happen to be one of the unlucky people right under the bomb, there is practically no hope of living through it. In fact, anywhere within one-half mile of the center of explosion, your chances of escaping are about 1 out of 10.

On the other hand, and this is the important point, from one-half to 1 mile away, you have a 50/50 chance.

From 1 to 1½ miles out, the odds that you will be killed are only 15 in 100. And at points from 1½ to 2 miles away, deaths drop all the way down to only 2 or 3 out of each 100. Beyond 2 miles, the explosion will cause practically no deaths at all.

Naturally, your chances of being injured are far greater than your chances of being killed. But even injury by radioactivity does not mean that you will be left a cripple, or doomed to die an early death. **Your chances of making a complete recovery are much the same as for everyday accidents.** These estimates hold good for modern atomic bombs exploded without warning.

What about Super Bombs?

Do not be misled by loose talk of imaginary weapons a hundred or a thousand times as powerful. All cause destruction by exactly the same means, yet one 20,000-ton bomb would not create nearly as much damage as 10,000 two-ton bombs dropped a little distance apart. This is because the larger bombs "waste" too much power near the center of the explosion. . . .

To be more specific, a modern atomic bomb can do heavy damage to houses and buildings roughly 2 miles away. But doubling its power will extend the range of damage to only about 2½ miles. In the same way, if there were a bomb 100 times as powerful, it would reach out only a little more than 4½, not 100 times as far.

And remember: All these calculations of your chances of survival assume that you have absolutely no advance warning of the attack.

Just like fire bombs and ordinary high explosives, atomic weapons cause most of their death and damage by blast and heat.

* * *

What about Radioactivity?

In all stories about atomic weapons, there is a great deal about radioactivity.

Radioactivity is the only way—besides size—in which the effects of A or H bombs are different from ordinary bombs. But, **with the exception of underwater or ground explosions, the radioactivity from atomic bursts is much less to be feared than blast and heat.**

Radioactivity is not new or mysterious. In the form of cosmic rays from the sky, all of us have been continually bombarded by radiation every hour and day of our lives. We all have also breathed and eaten very small amounts of radioactive materials without even knowing it. For over half a century, doctors and scientists have experimented and worked with X-rays and other penetrating forms of energy. **Because of all this experience, we actually know much more about radioactivity and what it does to people than we know about infantile paralysis, colds, or some other common diseases.**

* * *

What about "Radiation Sickness"?

Should you be caught upstairs or in the open at the time of a bombing, you might soak up a serious dose of explosive radioactivity. Even so, the first indication that you had been pierced by the rays probably wouldn't show up for a couple of hours. Then you most likely would get sick at your stomach and begin to vomit. However, you might be sick at your stomach for other reasons, too, so vomiting won't always mean you have radiation sickness. The time it would take you to get sick would depend on how strong a dose you got. The stronger the dose, the quicker you would get sick. **For a few days you might continue to feel below par and about 2 weeks later most of your hair might fall out. By the time you lost your hair you would be good and sick. But in spite of it all, you would still stand better than an even chance of making a complete recovery, including having your hair grow in again.**

Where is the Best Place to Go?

. . . If you live in a State where there is danger from sudden storms like cyclones or hurricanes, you may have a "cyclone cellar" or something similar. If so, you have a shelter that will give excellent protection against atomic bombs.

[People soon realized this wasn't quite true, and they began building bomb shelters.]

"All you have to do [to protect yourself from radiation] is go down to the bottom of your swimming pool and hold your breath."

—David Miller, Department of Energy spokesperson

What about Lingering Radioactivity?

Knowing how to protect yourself from blast, heat, and explosive radioactivity, only one major problem remains: That is how to avoid harm from lingering radioactivity.

Explosive radioactivity bursts from the bomb at the time of explosion and lasts for only little more than a minute.

Lingering radioactivity remains for a longer time, from a few minutes to weeks or months, depending on the kind of radioactive material. Lingering radioactivity may become a danger when atomic bombs are exploded on the ground, underground, or in the water. Air bursts leave no dangerous lingering radioactivity.

Most lingering radioactivity comes from leftover bomb wastes, or "ashes," technically called fission products. They consist of countless billions of fragments, or pieces, of atoms split up in the explosion. Smaller, and usually less dangerous, amounts of lingering radioactivity may be thrown off by scattered atoms of uranium or plutonium that fail to split up when the bomb goes off.

These totally invisible radioactive particles act much the same as ordinary, everyday dust. When present in any real quantity, they are scattered about in patches and contaminate, or pollute, everything they fall on, including people. While they can be removed easily from some surfaces, they stick very tightly to others. It is practically impossible to get absolutely all of them out of household corners and cracks. Most of the time, it is far easier to prevent pollution than it is to remove it.

What about Radioactive Clouds?

In spite of the huge quantities of lingering radioactivity loosed by atomic explosions, people fortunately are not very likely to be exposed to dangerous amounts of it in most atomic raids.

Since high-level bursts do the greatest damage, that is the kind we can expect most often. **When atomic weapons are exploded in mid-air, the violent, upward surge of super-hot gasses and air quickly sweeps practically all the radioactive ashes and unexploded bits of bomb fuel high into the sky. Most of them are carried harmlessly off in the drifting bomb clouds. High-level explosions definitely will not create "ashes of doom", where no man dares enter and no plant can grow. In fact, they will leave very little radioactivity on the ground, even near the point of explosion. Firefighters and rescue teams can move promptly toward the center of destruction with little danger of facing harmful radiation.**

And regardless of all you may have heard or read concerning the dangers of radioactive clouds, after the first minute and a half there is actually little or nothing to fear from those produced by high-level bursts. While most of the radioactive materials swept up into the sky eventually fall back to earth, they are so widely and so thinly spread that they are very unlikely to offer any real dangers to humans. Thousands of bombs would have to be set off in the air before serious ground contamination would be found over really large areas. There was no ground-level pollution of any importance following either of the two Japanese atomic bombings.

It was said earlier that 15 percent of the Japanese A-bomb deaths or injuries were caused by radioactivity. But not one of them was caused by the lingering kind. Explosive radioactivity caused them all. . . .

And remember that an air burst will leave no lingering radioactivity of importance, so after a few minutes it will be safe to get out and help fight fires or to help people who may need it.

What about Protecting Yourself from Lingering Radioactivity?

While attempting to avoid exposure to the bomb's blast, heat, and explosive radioactivity, also do what you can to keep from being showered by radioactive waste materials. Inside a shelter or building there is little or nothing to fear from this source. But if caught out-of-doors, try to grab hold of something to cover yourself with when you fall to the ground. **A board or some sheets of newspaper might help, but a raincoat would be better.** The object is, of course, to keep radioactive dust and raindrops off your body and clothing. When it's safe to get up, throw away your covering.

Always do what you can to help other people. There is no chance of your being harmed by radioactivity from the bodies of others, even if they have radiation injuries. . . .

If you have walked through rubble from a ground burst or water from an underwater burst, be sure to change at least your outer garments and shoes. Outer clothes will automatically serve as a "trap" for most of the radioactivity you may accidentally pick up. By taking them off you will remove most of the contamination. If the clothing is heavily contaminated, it is best to bury it.

You also should manage to take a bath or shower, if you have been in an area of lingering radioactivity. It is important that all radioactive materials be removed as soon as possible from your body, and bathing is the only practical means of getting rid of them. You won't need special cleaning compounds. Warm water and soap are ideal. . . .

If there is a radiological defense man handy, have him check you with his meter after you've finished your clean-up. Should he find your body still radioactive, again scrub yourself from head to foot. Then do it a third time if necessary. You can remove practically all of the radioactivity if you keep at it.

Remember all this is necessary only for persons who have come in contact with radioactive materials in heavily contaminated areas.

* * *

What about Radioactivity in the House?

A few simple steps will go a long way toward keeping your house from being contaminated by lingering radioactive wastes scattered about in some bombings. . . .

Keep all windows and doors closed for at least several hours after an atomic bombing. . . . Keep your cat or dog indoors. And when you come in from outside, leave your shoes at the door, for their soles are likely to be covered with radioactive dusts. . . . **Take these precautions, but don't worry. There isn't much chance really dangerous amounts will pile up in the house.** . . .

What about Food and Water?

. . . Food and utensils that were in closed drawers or tight cupboards will be all right.

If it was an air burst, don't worry about the food in the house. It will be safe to use.

Be careful of drinking water after atomic explosions. . . . If you have to use city water before you get official information, boil it. Boiling won't remove radioactivity, but the chances that your water supply will be radioactive are pretty slim. Boiling will kill most germs that may get into damaged water mains.

So there you have it. You're now prepared to survive nuclear warfare. Think you can handle it?

Actually, it's very hard to believe that, after five years of intensively studying the effects of atomic bombs and radiation at Hiroshima, Nagasaki, and various tests involving military personnel as human guinea pigs, the government didn't have a better idea of the dangers.

"My fellow Americans. I am pleased to tell you I just signed legislation which outlaws Russia forever. The bombing begins in five minutes."

—President Ronald Reagan during a sound check for a live radio show, 1984

In one of the tests in 1953, U.S. soldiers were placed near the explosion to test how well they could function after a blast. Sergeant Reason Warehime was one of fifty soldiers who were in a trench two miles from ground zero. They wore no protective gear. "The first thing I saw," he later reported, "was a real bright light like a flashbulb going off in my face, but it stayed on. It was so bright that even with sunglasses on, my hands over my eyes, and my eyes closed, I could actually see the bones in my hands. I felt as if someone was hugging me really tight, and my whole body was being compressed. All of a sudden, I heard an awful noise and felt an intensely hot wind blowing and the ground rocking like an earthquake. The dust was so thick I could not see the man right next to me. The air was so hot that it was difficult to breathe. . . . Since the fireball was directly over our heads, there is no doubt in my mind that we were in the 'stem' of the mushroom cloud."

A voice over a loudspeaker ordered them to advance toward ground zero. The sandbags along the top of their trench were on fire. On reaching a bunker that was just over a mile from ground zero, they found eight men. "Those guys were sick as dogs and heaving their guts out," he said. Soon they began finding spots where the sand had melted into glass. After reaching the crater, they turned back and eventually were picked up by two radiation specialists in full protective gear. On the way back, Warehime and some of his companions started throwing up. A few months later, all of his hair fell out, his teeth began to rot, and he was diagnosed as sterile. Eventually, he developed cataracts, lung cancer, his bones became brittle, and he had to use crutches to get around. Even though radiation is known to cause these things, in the 1980s, the Veterans Administration insisted his problems weren't caused by this bomb and denied disability to him and many others like him. An estimated 250,000 military personnel were exposed to radiation in experiments between 1946 and the 1970s. Many additional civilians were also used as guinea pigs in radiation tests. Very few have ever received any compensation for or assistance with the permanent damage caused to them.

Warehime was exposed to a forty-three-kiloton (not megaton) bomb. It turned out to be almost twice as powerful as the physicists had calculated it would be and was about twice as powerful as those used on Hiroshima and Nagasaki. Its radiation cloud spread across the nation from Nevada, fogging undeveloped film as far away as New Jersey.

A Dire Warning Against the Railroads

Whenever change occurs, there always seems to be someone offering dire predictions of the adverse impact that change will have on society. Unfortunately (or perhaps, fortunately), the future is not quite so easy to predict. As a result, the warnings often fall quite wide of the mark.

Such was the case when future-president Martin Van Buren wrote a letter to President Andrew Jackson warning of the terrible impact the railroads were going to have on the canal system unless they were immediately stopped. Here is that letter.[17] (The emphasis is his.)

Dear President Andrew Jackson:

The canal system of this country is being threatened by the spread of a new form of transportation known as railroads. The federal government must preserve the canals for the following reasons:

One—If canal boats are supplanted by railroads, serious unemployment will result. Captains, cooks, drivers, repairmen and lock tenders will be left without means of livelihood, not to mention the numerous farmers now employed in growing hay for horses.

Two—Boat builders would suffer and tow-line, whip and harness makers would be left destitute.

Three—Canal boats are absolutely essential to the defense of the United States. In the

[17] A copy of this letter was given to me for inclusion in this book by historian Carl Chafin.

event of the expected trouble with England, the Erie Canal would be the only means by which we would move the supplies so vital to waging modern war.

As you may well know, Mr. President, railroad carriages are pulled at the enormous speed of 15 miles per hour by engines which in addition to endangering life and limb of passengers, roar and snort their way through the countryside *setting fire to crops*, scaring the livestock and frightening women and children. The Almighty certainly never intended that people would move at such breakneck speed.

Signed—Martin Van Buren, Governor of New York, April 1829

Jackson, of course, ignored these warnings, but he did promptly appoint Van Buren as his secretary of state. Seven years later, Van Buren was elected the eighth president of the United States.

A Spy Reveals How Easy It Was to Steal U.S. Secrets

Many will remember Christopher Boyce from the book and movie, *The Falcon and the Snowman*. He was the Falcon. As an employee for TRW, he was given access to CIA secrets, which he began selling to the KGB through his friend, Andrew Daulton Lee—the Snowman. The secrets included NSA code ciphers, information on spy satellites called Rhyolite and Argus, and on a satellite communications system called Pyramider.

They were arrested in January 1977 and both found guilty of espionage and conspiracy. Boyce was sentenced to forty years and Lee was sentenced to life, with both becoming eligible for parole in about 1995. Boyce escaped from prison in 1980 and wasn't captured again until a year and a half later. Because of this, his sentence was extended to sixty-eight years.

On April 18, 1985, Boyce appeared before the U.S. Senate Permanent Subcommittee on Investigations Committee on Governmental Affairs. I received a copy of the statement he made as part of my training as an intelligence officer for the U.S. Air Force. This is what he told the senators.

In early 1975 at the age of twenty-one, I took my first stumbling steps towards the KGB. I was a totally naive amateur. I lacked even the most rudimentary skills this Subcommittee would associate with espionage. But even today I am still astounded at how easy the thing was to begin and, given the security system, how near impossible it was to prevent. Regardless of expensive and elaborate security systems, I suggest that espionage arrests are made mainly when beginners make artless, blundering mistakes. . . .

On April 28, 1977, at the age of twenty-four, I was convicted on eight counts of violating the espionage statutes and given a sentence of forty years. My boyhood friend and codefendant, Andrew Daulton Lee, was convicted in a separate trial on twelve counts of espionage and sentenced to life imprisonment. . . .

I don't think I need to recount a long narrative of what we did. Suffice it to say that from March 1975 through December 1976, I removed or photographed a sizeable number of classified documents from the highly secret "black vault" of

TRW, a CIA contractor in Redondo Beach, California and sent them on with Daulton to the KGB in Mexico City. I was able to obtain those documents through my position as a specially cleared TRW employee, working in the black vault, located in building M4. On more than a dozen occasions I removed documents from TRW and photographed them. On approximately six occasions, probably more, I personally photographed documents while within the vault itself. Daulton, in turn, delivered and sold the documents to KGB agents working out of the embassy in Mexico City. The documents pertained in part to the existence and operation of then highly secret intelligence satellites. . . .

Obviously, neither the government's clearance procedures nor the company's security procedures worked very well. In fact, the company's security procedures were of great help to me in compromising a CIA project to the Russians. There are some obvious reasons why.

Let me begin with the question of clearances. In 1975, when I sent Daulton off with the first classified documents to the Soviets, neither of us was a professional spy, to say the least. We knew as much about espionage as we did about hieroglyphics. On my part, I was not even a professional or longstanding member of the intelligence community. After dropping out of college, I went to work at TRW in July 1974. My only prior interest in the intelligence community had been one of suspicion and distrust. At twenty-one, in an era of Vietnam, assassinations, Chile, and Richard Nixon's resignation, I had a strong distaste for government. I considered the CIA as, if anything, the enemy. When I came to TRW I had no idea that my work would, in any way, involve the CIA.

"The Agency [CIA] is not an intelligence agency. It is a covert action agency whose role is to overthrow governments. Disinformation is a major part of its covert action role. The American people are the primary target of its lies."

—Ralph McGehee, who worked with the CIA for twenty-five years

"Have we gone beyond the bounds of reasonable dishonesty?"

—A CIA memo

I got the job through what one might call the "ole boy network." My father, a former FBI agent who then worked in security at another large defense contractor, was a friend of Mr. Regis Carr, also a former FBI agent, and then manager of TRW security for Top Secret contracts. It was Mr. Carr who hired me.

I started at TRW as a general clerk making approximately $140 per week. I was immediately given what is known as a "Confidential" clearance. Almost immediately my supervisors submitted my name for receipt of a Secret, then a Top Secret clearance, then access to two Special Projects, and, finally, access to NSA codes. By December all those clearances had been approved and I was assigned to the "black vault," which I subsequently learned to be one of the most secret and classified areas of work at TRW. It was only then that I learned that I would be working on a Special Project involving the CIA.

I was assigned, with my immediate supervisor, to monitor and process secret communications traffic between the CIA, TRW, and other CIA contacts around the world. My work included daily contact with the intelligence satellite program. . . .

I've been told that in other espionage cases, there were some obvious "red flags" of potential security violators which went unnoticed in background investigations and by co-workers: heavy financial indebtedness, sudden affluence, alcoholism, disgruntlement.

What was my red flag? Using those indicators, probably none. I was the oldest son in a well-respected, stable, upper middle class, Catholic family. My father had a fine reputation in professional positions of trust. I had performed moderately well in school. While my background investigations were underway, I heard that friends of my parents had been contacted as references. Speaking as adults, they told the investigators that I was the courteous, bright, responsible son of a good family, exactly as they were expected to say. This was the extent of the investigation, as best as I can tell.

What the investigators never sought was the Chris Boyce who moved in circles beyond the realm of parents, teachers, and other adult authority figures. To my knowledge, they never interviewed a single friend, a single peer, during the entire background investigations.

Had they done so, the investigators would have interviewed a room full of disillusioned longhairs, counterculture falconers, druggie surfers, several wounded paranoid vets, pot-smoking, anti-establishment types, beaded malcontents generally, many of whom were in trouble. In 1974 I believe that the majority of young people of my generation could not be considered politically reliable by ClA standards. . . . Had Mr. Carr even bothered to query his own sons, my high school classmates, they could have easily told him far more than the government's entire background investigation did. . . .

I might add that the only thing I was asked to do to get these clearances was to fill out a few forms. Although, at the time, my little sister was polygraphed before she went to work at a 7-Eleven, I was never polygraphed. . . .

To continue—I was never given a subject interview. A year later, after I had already started sending TRW/CIA documents to the KGB, I was given access to yet another Special Project after merely signing a few more forms. No additional background investigation was done to my knowledge.

On the question of physical security at TRW's black vault, I can answer it simply and quickly: there was none. In my view, and I believe in the eyes of my fellow workers there, security was a joke, certainly nothing to be taken seriously.

The FBI mug shot of Christopher Boyce, also known as the Falcon, who sold CIA secrets to the KGB.

Take, for example, our project security manager, whom we regularly referred to as our "token hippie." On lunch breaks, when not drinking with us or others at the local bars, he would often be skateboarding around the neighborhood. Sometimes he returned the worse for wear, with bruises and torn pants. On one occasion, he told me he wanted the security atmosphere in M4 to be as unintrusive as that on a college campus. . . .

I suppose most people view security regulations as something that should be held in awe by employees. That was clearly not the case at TRW. A number of employees made phony security badges as pranks. My immediate supervisor once made a security badge with a monkey's face on it and, to everyone's amusement, used it to come in and out of the building. . . .

Aside from badges, there was almost no supervision over access to the building and the vault. Although my comings and goings at building M4 were logged by the security guards, there was nothing to stop me from entering at any time during the day or night. . . . I remember laughing about this with a girl I knew who was a bank teller. She used to tell me that Security Pacific would never allow their employees to open and enter their vaults at will, unsupervised, at any time.

Controls on access beyond the black vault area here hardly much better. As part of my courier duties I made deliveries to the ClA facility. Although I had no clearance or authorization to do so, on occasion I wandered into their code room. Once I recall talking to a female employee inside the vault there. On a clipboard hanging on the wall beside her was a list of all the code words for every station on their circuit. Because I was naturally curious about everything that went on there, I began to note all the "handles." She caught me reading it, paused to flip the board over, and just smiled. I do recall that one employee did ask me to leave because I was unauthorized.

Within the TRW vault, management had effectively "compartmentalized" security away. By making the vault such a highly secret area those of us inside had been given, in effect, total autonomy. We worked under our own set of rules, or more accurately, lack of rules. We brought in an uncleared company locksmith and altered the numbers on the vault tumblers by half clicks to prevent unauthorized access by our superiors. We did not want them trespassing on our private preserve. We regularly partied and boozed it up during working hours within the vault. Bacardi 151 was usually stored behind the crypto machines. Under security regulations we were required to destroy the code cards for the machines daily in a destruction blender. We chose instead to throw the code cards towards, but not necessarily in, canvas bags in the corner. We used the code destruction blender for making banana daiquiris and mai-tais. Although only about eight people had authorized clearances to the vault, often many non-cleared members of our "club", so to speak, would be in the vault for libations. On occasion the Project Security Manager would join us for a drink on the house.

Part of our informal duties included frequent runs to the liquor store with "orders" from various employees throughout the building. We used the satchel for classified material as a cover to bring in their peppermint schnapps, rum, Harvey Wallbanger mix, what have you, along with our stout malt, back into M4. In doing so I sometimes used the satchel to take classified documents out. To return the documents, I used packages, potted plants, and camera cases. Packages and briefcases were never searched by the guards. On one occasion I needed to return a rather large ream of documents that I had taken out earlier in the satchel on a Rhyolite beer run. I went to a floral shop and bought two large clay pots about two feet tall. I put the ream of documents in one after wrapping them in plastic, covered it with dirt and then stuck bushy plants in both pots. I brought one of the plants into the building myself and asked the security guard to carry the plant holding the documents back into the building. He obliged.

A more severe security breach regularly entered our vault over the encrypted teletype link from Langley. Routinely we would receive from the CIA communications operators misdirected TWXs on other contractors' projects. We were not cleared for these projects and there was no accountability for the misdirected TWXs we received other than a lackadaisical request to "destroy" typed from the Langley communications operators. . . .

I remember only two government inspections in the vault during the entire time I was there. It amazed me that even though we were using all this highly secret equipment that belonged to the government, the government wasn't even around to oversee it. . . .

I distinctly remember one of the two government inspections. The code cards for the crypto machines came in checkbook-style binders sealed in clear plastic envelopes. The envelopes were to be unsealed and the binders removed only at the beginning of the month they were to be used. We were given books of these codes sometimes five months in advance of their date use, despite obvious security risks. I was amazed that NSA would let half a year's worth of their codes sit anywhere out of their possession.

At the time of the inspection, I had been unsealing some of these "future" codes, removing them, and photographing them. I would reseal the plastic with the heat from an iron or with glue and then replace them in the vault. They were all packaged in an official established manner. The inspector came across one code binder that I had replaced upside down and face down, and then resealed. Once tampered with, the plastic envelopes never looked quite the same, despite my botched efforts at resealing them. He noticed it, looked puzzled, but instead complained about some other relatively insignificant missing item—one that no one could remember. He had looked closely at the displaced code card binder, but chose to pass over the broken seal. . . .

Convicted Soviet spy John Walker has a peculiar notion of what patriotism is. "I am very patriotic," he told the FBI. "I've only committed one crime in my life."

There was little, if any, outside influence over our day-to-day activities. We were project security and we viewed security as a joke because we could easily circumvent it by our insulation from the usual management controls. What little security we saw was ineffective and incompetent. If we had been strictly supervised, perhaps I would have thought twice before acting as I did. Instead I decided that the intelligence community was a great bumbling, bluffing deception. . . .

I think, even in these responsible times, that if not carefully monitored, the intelligence community of any Western nation can be, potentially, a threat to an open society. But there is nothing "potential" about the KGB. That state apparatus not only threatens every open society, but it crushes open societies. That is the distinction I could not see at a rebellious twenty-one. It is a distinction which Americans must see. . . .

When I was at TRW, I and several hundred other relatively fresh employees were given a group talk on the perils of espionage. A clean-cut, all-American type addressed us from the podium. Here I sat with the KGB monkey already on my back, surrounded by all these young people who were being fed totally inaccurate and inappropriate descriptions of espionage. . . .

It was surreal. A government spokesman, automatically accepted by everyone as competent, stood there entertaining all those naive, impressionable youngsters around me with tales of secret adventure, intrigue, huge payoffs, exotic weaponry, seduction, poisons, hair-raising risks, deadly gadgetry. It was a whole potpourri of James Bond lunacy, when in fact almost everything he said was totally foreign to what was actually happening to me.

Where was the despair? Where were the sweaty palms and shakey [sic] hands? This man said nothing about having to wake up in the morning with gut-gripping fear before steeling yourself once again for the ordeal of going back into that vault. How could these very ordinary young people not think that here was a panacea that could lift them out of the monotony of their everyday lives, even if it was only in their fantasies? None of them knew, as I did, that there was no excitement, there was no thrill. There was only depression and a hopeless enslavement to an inhuman, uncaring foreign bureaucracy. I hadn't made myself count for something. I had made my freedom count for nothing. . . .

For whatever reason a person begins his involvement, a week after the folly begins, the original intent and purpose becomes lost in the ignominy of the ongoing nightmare.

Yes, only a minuscule portion of work in the intelligence community might approach the popular media image. It's mostly white collar types analyzing obscure and otherwise useless information. James Bond is about as much like your average intelligence worker as Indiana Jones is like your average archeologist.

Alternative VIEWS

Geronimo Tells His Side of the Story

Geronimo was one of the most feared Native Americans who ever lived, and he belonged to what was considered one of the most violent tribes—the Apaches. His name in Apache was Goyathlay or Goyakla, which means "He Who Yawns." Here, in the words of the famous "bloodthirsty savage" himself, is his version of how his battles against the whites began.

About the time of the massacre of "Kaskiyeh" (1858)[18] we heard that some white men were measuring land to the south of us. In company with a number of other warriors I went to visit them. We could not understand them very well, for we had no interpreter, but we made a treaty with them by shaking hands and promising to be brothers. Then we made our camp near their camp, and they came to trade with us. We gave them buckskin, blankets, and ponies in exchange for shirts and provisions. We also brought them game, for which they gave us some money. We did not know the value of this money, but we kept it and later learned from the Navajo Indians that it was very valuable.

Every day they measured land with curious instruments and put down marks which we could not understand. They were good men, and we were sorry when they had gone on into the west. They were not soldiers. These were the first white men I ever saw.

About ten years later some more white men came. These were all warriors. They made their camp on the Gila River south of Hot Springs. At first they were friendly and we did not dislike them, but they were not as good as those who came first.

After about a year some trouble arose between them and the Indians, and I took the warpath as a warrior, not as a chief. I had not been wronged, but some of my people had been, and I fought with my tribe; for the soldiers and not the Indians were at fault.

Not long after this some of the officers of the United States troops invited our leaders to hold a conference at Apache Pass (Fort Bowie). Just before noon the Indians were shown into a tent and told that they would be given something to eat. When in the tent they were attacked by soldiers. Our chief, Mangus-Colorado, and several other warriors, by cutting through the tent, escaped; but

18 The Chiricahua—the band of Apaches that Geronimo belonged to—were peacefully camped near Janos, Mexico, trading with the Mexicans when Mexican troops suddenly launched a surprise attack on them, killing many of his people. Geronimo was away at the time and returned to find his mother, wife, and three children dead. He was chosen as a war chief after this massacre. They found revenge a year later in a two-hour battle with the Mexican troops.

most of the warriors were killed or captured.[19] Among the Bedonkohe Apaches killed at this time were Sanza, Kladetahe, Niyokahe, and Gopi.[20] After this treachery the Indians went back to the mountains and left the fort entirely alone. I do not think that the agent had anything to do with planning this, for he had always treated us well. I believe it was entirely planned by the soldiers.

From the very first the soldiers sent out to our western country, and the officers in charge of them, did not hesitate to wrong the Indians. They never explained to the Government when an Indian was wronged, but always reported the misdeeds of the Indians. Much that was done by mean white men was reported at Washington as the deeds of my people.

"Almost every war between the Indians and the whites has been occasioned by some injustice of the latter towards the former."
—Benjamin Franklin, 1786

"War usually springs from a sense of injustice. The best possible way to avoid war is to do no act of injustice. When we learn that the same rule holds good with Indians, the chief difficulty is removed. But it is said that our wars with them have been almost constant. Have we been uniformly unjust? We answer unhesitatingly, yes."
—Report of the Commissioner of Indian Affairs

The Indians always tried to live peaceably with the white soldiers and settlers. One day during the time that the soldiers were stationed at Apache Pass I made a treaty with the post. This was done by shaking hands and promising to be brothers. Cochise and Mangus-Colorado did likewise. I do not know the name of the officer in command, but this was the first regiment that ever came to Apache Pass. This treaty was made about a year before we were attacked in a tent, as above related. In a few days after the attack at Apache Pass we organized in the mountains and returned to fight the soldiers. There were two tribes—the Bedonkohe and the Chokonen Apaches, both commanded by Cochise. After a few days' skirmishing we attacked a freight train that was coming in with supplies for the Fort. We killed some of the men and captured the others. These prisoners our chief offered to trade for the

---

19 Geronimo's memory seems to be a bit hazy concerning this incident, probably because he received this information second or third hand. In October of 1860, a man named John Ward beat his half Native American son in a drunken rage, causing the boy to run away. He later reported to Fort Buchanan near Tucson that Chief Cochise had kidnapped the boy and stolen some of his cattle. Lt. George Bascom and a force of fifty-four of his men went to Apache Pass in the heart of Chiricahua territory and requested a meeting with Cochise (not Mangus-Colorado). When Cochise arrived with his brother, two nephews, a woman, and two children, they were shown to a tent, which was then surrounded by soldiers. Accused of a kidnapping he had no knowledge of, Cochise immediately protested his innocence. He was then told that he would be held as their prisoner until the boy and cattle were handed over. He quickly drew his knife and sliced a hole in the tent. Leaping through it, the tall, knife-wielding chief dashed through the startled soldiers and escaped before they could react. The others were held as hostages. As the editor of Tucson's *The Star* described it, "It appears that Cochise and his tribe had been on the warpath for some time and he with a number of subordinate chiefs was brought into the military camp at Bowie under the promise that a treaty of peace was to be held, when they were taken into a large tent where handcuffs were put on them. Cochise, seeing this, cut his way through the tent and fled to the mountains; and in less than six hours had surrounded the camp with from three to five hundred warriors but the soldiers refused to make fight."

20 Apparently these were among those that were later killed.

Indians whom the soldiers had captured at the massacre in the tent. This the officers refused, so we killed our prisoners, disbanded, and went into hiding in the mountains.[21] Of those who took part in this affair I am the only one now living.

In a few days troops were sent out to search for us, but as we were disbanded, it was, of course, impossible for them to locate any hostile camp. During the time they were searching for us many of our warriors (who were thought by the soldiers to be peaceable Indians) talked to the officers and men, advising them where they might find the camp they sought, and while they searched we watched them from our hiding places and laughed at their failures.

After this trouble all of the Indians agreed not to be friendly with the white men any more. There was no general engagement, but a long struggle followed. Sometimes we attacked the white men—sometimes they attacked us. First a few Indians would be killed and then a few soldiers. I think the killing was about equal on each side. The number killed in these troubles did not amount to much, but this treachery on the part of the soldiers had angered the Indians and revived memories of other wrongs, so that we never again trusted the United States troops.

* * *

"If I were an Indian, I often think I would greatly prefer to cast my lot among those of my people [who] adhered to the free open plains, rather than submit to the confined limits of a reservation, there to be the recipient of the blessed benefits of civilization."

—Lieutenant Colonel George Custer, My Life on the Plains, *c. 1873*

Perhaps the greatest wrong ever done to the Indians was the treatment received by our tribe from the United States troops about 1863. The chief of our tribe, Mangus-Colorado, went to make a treaty of peace for our people with the white settlement at Apache Tejo, New Mexico. It had been reported to us that the white men in this settlement were more friendly and more reliable than those in Arizona, that they would live up to their treaties and would not wrong the Indians.

Mangus-Colorado, with three other warriors, went to Apache Tejo and held a council with these citizens and soldiers. They told him that if he would come with his tribe and live near them, they would issue to him, from the Government, blankets, flour, provisions, beef, and all manner of supplies. Our chief promised to return to Apache Tejo within two weeks. When he came back to our settlement he assembled the whole tribe in council. I did not believe that the people at Apache Tejo would do as they said and therefore I

21 Chiefs Cochise and Mangus-Colorado (Cochise's father-in-law) and their warriors began ambushing stagecoaches, killing the Mexicans and capturing three white men to trade for the hostages. Meanwhile, the soldiers captured three more Apaches. When Lt. Bascom refused to negotiate, Cochise, in frustration and to show he meant business, dragged one of his captives to death behind his horse while the soldiers watched. Lt. Bascom still refused to talk, so they killed the other two captives. In revenge, the soldiers hanged the six Apache men, including Cochise's brother. This prompted Cochise and the Apaches to try to chase the whites out of their territory. It's estimated they killed 150 whites and Mexicans in the next two months. As historian Frederick W. Turner III put it, "The Cochise wars were on, and for ten years the chief made whites in Arizona and New Mexico wish they had questioned that Mr. Ward more closely."

opposed the plan, but it was decided that with part of the tribe Mangus-Colorado should return to Apache Tejo and receive an issue of rations and supplies. If they were as represented, and if these white men would keep the treaty faithfully, the remainder of the tribe would join him and we would make our permanent home at Apache Tejo. I was to remain in charge of that portion of the tribe which stayed in Arizona. We gave almost all of our arms and ammunition to the party going to Apache Tejo, so that in case there should be treachery they would be prepared for any surprise. Mangus-Colorado and about half of our people went to New Mexico, happy that now they had found white men who would be kind to them, and with whom they could live in peace and plenty.

No word ever came to us from them. From other sources, however, we heard that they had been treacherously captured and slain.[22] In this dilemma we did not know just exactly what to do, but fearing that the troops who had captured them would attack us, we retreated into the mountains near Apache Pass.

During the weeks that followed the departure of our people we had been in suspense, and failing to provide more supplies, had exhausted all of our store of provisions. This was another reason for moving camp. On this retreat, while passing through the mountains, we discovered four men with a herd of cattle. Two of the men were in front in a buggy and two were behind on horseback. We killed all four, but did not scalp them; they were not warriors. We drove the cattle back into the mountains, made a camp, and began to kill the cattle and pack the meat.

Before we had finished this work we were surprised and attacked by United States troops, who killed in all seven Indians—one warrior, three women, and three children. The Government troops were mounted and so were we, but we were poorly armed, having given most of our weapons to the division of our tribe that had gone to Apache Tejo, so we fought mainly with spears, bows, and arrows. At first I had a spear, a bow, and a few arrows; but in a short time my spear and all my arrows were gone. Once I was surrounded, but by dodging from side to side of my horse as he ran I

---

22 In January of 1863, Chief Mangus-Colorado received word that Captain Edmond Shirland wanted to discuss peace. His men feared a trap and insisted on sending fifteen warriors with him for his protection. As they reached the soldier's camp, they were met by an interpreter who said the chief must enter the camp alone. The chief insisted they raise a flag of truce over the camp first. When that was done, his men turned back and he went on alone. As he neared the camp, a dozen soldiers leapt out of hiding and aimed their cocked rifles at him. Daniel Conner, a prospector traveling with the soldiers explained, "We hurried Mangus off to our camp at old Fort McLean and arrived in time to see General West come up with his command. The general walked out to where Mangus was in custody to see him, and looked like a pigmy beside the old chief, who also towered above everybody about him in stature. He looked careworn and refused to talk and evidently felt that he had made a great mistake in trusting the paleface on this occasion."

Two soldiers were designated to guard him for the night. One soldier later reported that he heard General West tell the guards to shoot the chief if he tried to escape, saying, "I want him dead or alive in the morning. Do you understand? *I want him dead.*" Conner later saw the guards tormenting the old chief, who was in his seventies, as he tried to sleep by heating their bayonets in the fire and making him flinch by applying the hot metal to his feet and legs. He endured this several times and then, according to Conner, he sat up and "began to expostulate in a vigorous way by telling the sentinels in Spanish that he was no child to be playing with. But his expostulations were cut short . . . when both sentinels promptly brought down their minié muskets to bear on him and fired, nearly at the same time, through his body." The guards emptied their pistols into him. One soldier took his scalp, while another cut off his head, boiled the flesh off his skull and later sold it. The chief's skull was later put on display in the Smithsonian. This renewed the desire of Cochise, Geronimo, and the Apache warriors to rid their territory of the whites and hostilities escalated.

escaped. It was necessary during this fight for many of the warriors to leave their horses and escape on foot. But my horse was trained to come at call, and as soon as I reached a safe place, if not too closely pursued, I would call him to me. During this fight we scattered in all directions and two days later reassembled at our appointed place of rendezvous, about fifty miles from the scene of this battle.

"After we resolved our conflict with the villainous English, the next were the Indians, who had some absurd philosophy that since they were here before us, they had some claim upon the land. Setting the antecedent to Nazi purging, we proved to those dunderheads the correctness in the Aristotelian aphorism, 'Possession is nine-tenths of the law.' If you have any doubts, if you're ever in Miami, drive to the one-tenth: the Seminole Indian Reservation, the mosquito-ridden, agriculture-resistant Everglade swamps."

—Lenny Bruce

About ten days later the same United States troops attacked our new camp at sunrise. The fight lasted all day, but our arrows and spears were all gone before ten o'clock, and for the remainder of the day we had only rocks and clubs with which to fight. We could do little damage with these weapons, and at night we moved our camp about four miles back into the mountains where it would be hard for the cavalry to follow us. The next day our scouts, who had been left behind to observe the movements of the soldiers, returned, saying that the troops had gone back toward San Carlos Reservation.

A few days after this we were again attacked by another company of United States troops. Just before this fight we had been joined by a band of Chokonen Indians under Cochise, who took command of both divisions. We were repulsed, and decided to disband.

After we had disbanded our tribe the Bedonkohe Apaches reassembled near their old camp vainly waiting for the return of Mangus-Colorado and our kinsmen. No tidings came save that they had all been treacherously slain. Then a council was held, and as it was believed that Mangus-Colorado was dead, I was elected Tribal Chief.

For a long time we had no trouble with anyone. It was more than a year after I had been made Tribal Chief that United States troops surprised and attacked our camp. They killed seven children, five women, and four warriors, captured all our supplies, blankets, horses, and clothing, and destroyed our tepees. We had nothing left; winter was beginning, and it was the coldest winter I ever knew. After the soldiers withdrew I took three

Geronimo with his sixth wife and his children at Fort Sill, Oklahoma.

warriors and trailed them. Their trail led back toward San Carlos.

The Chiricahua were confined on a reservation in 1872, but five years later when they were about to be moved to another, more desolate reservation, Geronimo and his people ran off into Mexico. A year after that, he was arrested while visiting a reservation in New Mexico. He remained at peace for four years until 1881 when he began making raids on both sides of the border. It was two years before General George H. Crook captured him again and returned him to the reservation. In 1885, he and his men began making raids again. The following year they surrendered to General Nelson A. Miles and were shipped to Florida and Alabama as prisoners of war. There, the unfamiliar climate and disease wiped out one fourth of the band. After eight years, what was left of the Chiricahua were moved to Fort Sill in Oklahoma. By then, Geronimo was a celebrity. He attended the St. Louis World's Fair and was at Theodore Roosevelt's inauguration. He died at Fort Sill of pneumonia in 1909.

Escape to Alcatraz

A group of Native American activists seized Alcatraz, an island in the San Francisco Bay, for the third time in November 1969. Four activists had previously occupied this former prison site for three hours in March 1964, invoking an 1868 treaty turning abandoned federal properties over to the Native Americans. On November 9, 1969, fourteen activists again landed on the island for nineteen hours. Returning about two weeks later, seventy-eight activists seized the island and more joined them. By the end of the month, they numbered almost six hundred. They remained on the island for about a year and a half until they were forcibly evicted in June 1971. They issued the following proclamation delineating their claim to the island:

Proclamtion:
To the Great White Father
and All His People

We, the native Americans, re-claim the land known as Alcatraz Island in the name of all American Indians by right of discovery.

We wish to be fair and honorable in our dealings with the Caucasian inhabitants of this land, and hereby offer the following treaty:

We will purchase said Alcatraz Island for twenty-four dollars ($24) in glass beads and red cloth, a precedent set by the white man's purchase of a similar island about 300 years ago. We know that $24 in trade goods for these 16 acres is more than was paid when Manhattan Island was sold, but we know that land values have risen over the years. Our offer of $1.24 per acre is greater than the 47¢ per acre that the white men are now paying the California Indians for their land. We will give to the inhabitants of this island a portion of that land for their own, to be held in trust by the American Indian Affairs and by the bureau of Caucasian Affairs to hold in perpetuity—for as long as the sun shall rise and the rivers go down to the sea. We will further guide the inhabitants in the proper way of living. We will offer them our religion, our education, our life-ways, in order to help them achieve our level of civilization and thus raise them and all their white brothers up from their savage and unhappy state. We offer this treaty in good faith and wish to be fair and honorable in our dealings with all white men.

We feel that this so-called Alcatraz Island is more than suitable for an Indian Reservation, as determined by the white man's own standards. By this we mean that this place resembles most Indian reservations in that:

1. It is isolated from modern facilities, and without adequate means of transportation.
2. It has no fresh running water.
3. It has inadequate sanitation facilities.
4. There are no oil or mineral rights.
5. There is no industry and so unemployment is very great.
6. There are no health care facilities.
7. The soil is rocky and non-productive; and the land does not support game.
8. There are no educational facilities.
9. The population has always exceeded the land base.
10. The population has always been held as prisoners and kept dependent upon others.

Further, it would be fitting and symbolic that ships from all over the world, entering the Golden Gate, would first see Indian land, and thus be reminded of the true history of this nation. This tiny island would be a symbol of the great lands once ruled by free and noble Indians. . . .

United States Tried for War Crimes
Hiroshima and *Nagasaki*

When it comes to war crimes, one usually thinks of Nazis and the Holocaust. We don't normally associate them with the United States. But not only has the United States been tried for war crimes, it has actually been found guilty. Not once, but several times. And not always by our enemies.

War crimes are violations of the rules of war. The idea is to limit the cruelty and destructiveness of war. The rules of war form the oldest portion of international law and basically fall into four categories: (1) the status of combatants, (2) the conduct of hostilities, (3) conduct during the occupation, and (4) conduct during a truce, armistice and toward neutral nations.

The rules of war specify such things as the type and extent of damage that can be inflicted, the amount of suffering that can be caused, and who can engage in combat and other military activities. For instance, professional soldiers can legally kill enemy soldiers in battle, but they may not kill prisoners or civilians. Prisoners who escape and are recaptured cannot be punished. Civilians and soldiers disguised as civilians cannot kill the enemy even in battle unless they are "volunteer corps" (that is, partisans or guerrillas) that abide by rules governing what they can and cannot do. Pillaging by soldiers or civilians is illegal, and private property cannot be confiscated. Attacking or bombarding unprotected towns, buildings, or dwellings is prohibited, as is the use of poison gas and biological weapons. And the enemy has the right to try all war crime suspects.[23]

Any war crime is considered to be an extremely serious offense. As the U.S. basic field manual says, "All war crimes are subject to the death penalty, although a lesser penalty may be imposed."

---

23 Some of this may sound like a liberal interpretation of the law, but I compiled this information from the *Encyclopedia Americana*, *Encyclopedia Britannica*, and the *World Book Encyclopedia*.

The rules of war have changed considerably throughout history. It was once accepted practice for a conquering army to plunder a captured city and kill every man, woman, and child they could find. In fact, the laws governing warfare that are mentioned in the Bible state:

> When thou comest nigh unto a city to fight against it. . . And the Lord thy God hath delivered it into thine hands, thou shalt smite every male thereof with the edge of the sword [i.e. kill the prisoners.]: But the women, and the little ones, and the cattle, and all that is in the city, even all the spoil thereof, shalt thou take unto thyself; and thou shalt eat the spoil of thine enemies, which the Lord thy God hath given thee. . . . But of the cities of these people, which the Lord thy God doth give thee for an inheritance [as opposed to attacking cities in other countries], thou shalt save alive nothing that breatheth [including women and children]. (Deuteronomy 20:10, 13-14, 16)

But it also adds that while besieging a city, they shouldn't destroy any of the enemy's fruit-bearing trees, saying, "thou mayest eat of them, and thou shalt not cut them down (for the tree of the field is man's life)" (Deuteronomy 20:19).

In later periods, instead of massacring the vanquished, they were taken as slaves. In 1179, Pope Alexander III requested that the practice of enslaving prisoners be restricted to non-Christians. During the previous century, the Church proclaimed the "Truce of God," which forbid fighting on certain days. Violators were excommunicated. Those enemies of other religions who violated God's truce by attacking on these days were severely punished for their "treachery."

Technically, the very first war crimes trial was that of Sir William Wallace in 1305. This was dramatized in the movie *Braveheart*, with actor Mel Gibson as Wallace. Wallace was executed in London for treason and for waging a war of extermination against English towns "sparing neither age nor sex, monk nor nun."

Today, the core of the international law governing warfare is the Hague Regulations of 1907 though this has since been refined by various international conventions, such as the Geneva Prisoner of War Convention of 1929. These laws were agreed to and signed by most countries and are generally accepted as being binding on all nations.

The question of whether or not the atomic bombing of Hiroshima and Nagasaki were legal has been raised off and on over the passing years. This especially applies to Nagasaki. Since before the bombings Japan was already preparing to surrender, many feel the destruction of Hiroshima was more than enough to convince Japan to the immediate and unconditional surrender the Allies were seeking. So was the destruction of Nagasaki really necessary?

It's estimated 100,000 people died at Hiroshima on August 6, 1945. Seventy-five hours later, another 74,000 were killed at Nagasaki. But these figures include only those who perished in the initial blasts. Many more people died soon afterward from radiation sickness, and others would die years later from leukemia, pernicious anemia, and other radiation-related diseases. Current estimates calculate the total number of deaths so far from the two blasts at more than 340,000 people.

"This is the greatest thing in history!"

—President Harry Truman on receiving news that the nuclear bomb had successfully exploded over Hiroshima

Dr. Tatsuichiro Akizuki was working in a Nagasaki hospital some two miles from ground zero when the bomb hit. He later described what he witnessed in his book *Nagasaki 1945* (1981), saying:

> Out in the yard, brown-colored smoke or dust cleared little by little. I saw figures running. Then, looking to the southwest, I was stunned. The sky was as dark as pitch, covered with dense clouds of smoke; under that blackness, over the earth, hung a yellow-brown fog. Gradually the veiled ground became visible, and the view beyond rooted me to the spot with horror. All the buildings I could see were on fire. . . . To say everything burned is not enough. It seemed as if the earth itself emitted fire and smoke, flames that writhed up and erupted from underground. The sky was dark, the ground was scarlet, and in between hung clouds of yellowish smoke. . . . It seemed like the end of the world.

Dr. Akizuki set about getting those who were still alive out of the hospital because the roof was on fire. While the three-story building was still standing, some were trapped under fallen beams and rubble inside.

Soon victims burned by the flash began stumbling onto the hospital grounds. Dr. Akizuki said, "Half-naked or stark naked, they walked with strange, slow steps, groaning from deep inside themselves as if they had traveled from the depths of hell. They looked whitish; their faces were like masks." They reeled about holding their heads with their hands. Their clothes had been burned off them in the flash and they were all asking for water because their throats had been singed. Temperatures for a mile around the epicenter of the blast had instantly shot up to between 1,000°F and 6,000°F.

Within a few hours, victims of a different appearance began to arrive at the hospital. "The crowd of ghosts which had looked whitish in the morning were now burned black. Their hair was burnt; their skin, which was charred and blackened, blistered and peeled." And the severity of the victims' injuries kept increasing. Those closer to the blast that weren't vaporized or instantly killed had their facial features burned off, their eyes melted in their sockets, and the patterns of their clothing were tattooed on their flesh.

There wasn't much the doctor could do for the people who came to the hospital since the wind from the blast that had swept through the building had carried off the instruments and medications.

Right after the bombing of Hiroshima, garbled reports of the devastation spread across Japan. The Japanese Cabinet tried to find out what had happened. Most didn't believe the amazing stories they were hearing. American Army Chief-of-Staff General George C. Marshall later said, "What we did not take into account was that the destruction would be so complete that it would be an appreciable time before the actual facts of the case would get to Tokyo."

Actually, the decision to drop the second bomb had essentially been made already. As early as July 16, Major General Leslie Groves, commander of the Manhattan Project, was convinced it was necessary to drop two bombs—one to demonstrate the bomb's tremendous destructive power and the second to prove that we had more than one bomb. Groves and the civilian leaders of the Manhattan Project had convinced Truman that two Japanese cities would have to be wiped out in order to end the war. Nagasaki was chosen over the other two potential targets of Kokura and Niigata.

Five days after Nagasaki was bombed, Japan submitted to the unconditional surrender that America was insisting on. America's conventional bombing of Japan continued right up until surrender was finalized, killing more than 15,000 people after the Nagasaki bombing.

"We have grasped the mystery of the atom and rejected the Sermon on the Mount."

—General Omar Bradley, 1948

On August 15, Emperor Hirohito announced Japan's defeat over the public address systems. It was the first time the Japanese people had ever heard his voice. As the people gathered around the loudspeakers with their heads bowed in reverence, Hirohito explained that "the enemy has begun to employ a new and most cruel bomb, the power of which to do damage is indeed incalculable, taking the toll of many innocent lives."

The primary justification given for the bombings is that it hastened the end of the war and saved American lives that would have been lost in an invasion of Japan. But Massachusetts Institute of Technology history professor John W. Dover points out that America was not actually on the brink of invasion when the bombs were dropped in August. November 1 was the earliest that the preliminary assault on Kyushu, Japan's southernmost island, was scheduled, while an invasion of Tokyo and the Kanto area on the main island wouldn't have taken place until March 1946. And it's likely the war would have ended without an invasion. The United States had been pushing for the Soviets to enter the Pacific War and knew that they soon would, and indeed they did so two days after Hiroshima.

According to the U.S. Strategic Bombing Survey report, published by the government in 1946, "Based on detailed investigation of all the facts and supported by the testimony of the surviving Japanese leaders involved, it is the Survey's opinion that certainly prior to 31 December 1945, and in all probability prior to 1 November 1945, Japan would have surrendered even if the atomic bombs had not been dropped, even if Russia had not entered the war, and even if no invasion had been planned or contemplated." One member of the survey team also reported that the emperor and the Supreme War Direction Council had secretly decided to end the war on June 20, 1945, and it was just the "usual bureaucratic lags" that prevented them from suing for peace immediately. That same month, U.S. leaders found out from decoded messages that Japan had started making overtures to the Soviets about negotiating their surrender.

But the whole idea of the bombs saving American lives is brought a little more into perspective when it's realized that almost 200,000 men, women, and children were dead within days of these two attacks and that this is about twice as many people as all the American soldiers who lost their lives in the entire Pacific War. In addition, Dr. Dover points out that the bomb victims included Koreans, Chinese, Southeast Asian students, British and Dutch POWs, European priests, and more than a thousand visiting Americans of Japanese descent who were prevented from returning to the United States by the unexpected attack on Pearl Harbor. There were also twelve U.S. navy pilots killed in Hiroshima.[24]

Dr. Dover suggested some other reasons for targeting Japan in his article, which was published in the August 1995 issue of *Technology Review*:

> While it was fear of a Nazi bomb that originally propelled the Manhattan Project, it now is known that U.S. planners had identified Japan as the prime target for the atomic bomb as early as 1943—a year or more before it became clear that Germany was not attempting to build such a weapon. One reason for this shift of target was the fear that if the bomb didn't work, sophisticated German scientists and engineers might be able to disassemble it and figure out how to build their own. (No one worried that the Japanese had this capability.). . .
>
> [J. Robert] Oppenheimer [director of the Manhattan Project] also confided that after Germany's surrender on May 8, 1945, he and his fellow scientists intensified their efforts out of concern that the war might end before they could finish. . . .
>
> Sheer visceral hatred abetted the targeting of Japan for nuclear destruction. . . . "Remember Pearl Harbor—Keep 'em Dying" was a popular military slogan from the outset of the war, and among commentators and war correspondents at the time it was a commonplace that the racially and culturally alien Japanese were vastly more despised than their German allies.
>
> U.S. leaders also had postwar politics on their minds—both global and domestic. Documents declassified since the 1960s make it unmistakably clear that from the spring of 1945, top-level policymakers hoped that the bomb would dissuade Stalin from pursuing Soviet expansion into Eastern Europe and elsewhere. Some individuals closely involved with the development of the bomb (such as Arthur Compton, Edward Teller, and James Conant) further argued that the new weapon's very horrendousness compelled its use against a real city, so that the postwar world would understand the need to cooperate on arms control. At the same time, shrewd readers of the domestic political winds in the United States warned that if the Manhattan Project ended with nothing dramatic to show for its efforts, the postwar Congress surely would launch a hostile investigation into the huge disbursal of secret funds.

Dr. Dover goes on to explain how the United States and the League of Nations strongly condemned Japan's bombing of Chinese cities in 1937 and the Spanish Civil War bombing of Guernica by the fascists (immortalized by Picasso's famous mural), but that just a few years later, Britain and the United States were fire-bombing German cities and carpet-bombing Dresden, where more than 100,000 people were killed. When Italy bombed cities in the Ethiopian war and Germany bombed Rotterdam in Holland, Coventry in England, and a few other cities, Roosevelt

[24] The United States has yet to officially acknowledge this.

described this as "inhuman barbarism that has profoundly shocked the conscience of humanity," yet these were small compared to the large-scale British and American attacks on German cities. The United States continued to use this strategy against Japan with the carpet-bombings of Tokyo and sixty-three other Japanese cities. Dr. Dover says, "The atomic bombings were simply a more efficient way of terrorizing enemies and destroying a newly legitimized target of war: civilian morale."

"We sure liberated the hell out of this place."

—An American soldier in the ruins of a French village in 1944

"It became necessary to destroy the town in order to save it."

—Attributed to an American Army major explaining the bombing and shelling of Ben Tre, South Vietnam, on February 8, 1968

"In order to win the city, it was necessary to demolish it."

—Conquistador Juan Rodríguez de Escobar talking about the destruction of the Aztec capital city, 1521

The nuclear bombings were brought up at the Tokyo War Crimes Trial that followed the war. This trial of the Japanese leaders was comparable to the trial of the Nazi leaders at Nuremberg. The most famous defendant at the Tokyo trial was General Hideki Tojo, who had been Japan's prime minister during the war. Of the twenty-five defendants tried by the Allies, seven (including Tojo) were given death sentences, sixteen were sentenced to life in prison, and two received other prison sentences.

In 1971, Princeton University published a book by Richard Minear, titled *Victor's Justice*, which shows that this trial was little more than a kangaroo court where the defendants were prevented from receiving a fair trial through such devious means as the judges interpreting the rules of evidence liberally when the prosecution presented its case, but changing to a conservative interpretation for the defense's portion of the trial, and then becoming liberal again with the prosecution's rebuttal. "The Tokyo tribunal found Tojo guilty and sentenced him to death by hanging. It is my contention that he was legally innocent," he wrote. Minear believes this was primarily a political trial for the purpose of corroborating "our convictions about the dastardly and criminal nature of Japan's wartime leadership and policies." Evidently this was also apparent at the time, for on January 11, 1949, the *Washington Post* said, "It is more and more evident to us that the good name of justice, let alone of the United States, had been compromised . . . in Tokyo."

There is overwhelming evidence the Japanese committed many war crimes—the Bataan Death March and the horrendous medical experiments immediately come to mind—but how responsible the Japanese leadership was for these crimes is uncertain. The thing is, the Tokyo tribunal didn't really focus on conventional war crimes. Instead, it primarily dwelt on the legally dubious idea of Japanese aggression even though Japanese colonialism was not that much different from American and British colonialism in the nineteenth century. Minear said, "The trial was a kind of morality play, a reaffirmation of a world-view that had been one factor in the making of World War II. To the extent that this world-view was itself invalid, the Tokyo trial was harmful rather than helpful. It prolonged our immersion in the unreal world of our dreams."

But be that as it may, when the question of the nuclear bombings was raised by the defense, the tribunal determined the evidence was inadmissible.

Despite this, three of the Tribunal's eleven justices did mention it. Justice Jaranilla of the Philippines felt that it was okay to use these devices of mass destruction because they shortened the war and saved Allied lives, adding, "If the means is justified by the end, the use of the atomic bomb was justified."

Justice Pal of India, on the other hand, did not agree with this. Recalling Germany's war crimes of World War I, he wrote:

> The Kaiser Wilhelm II was credited with a letter to the Austrian Kaiser Franz Joseph in the early days of that war, wherein he stated as follows: "My soul is torn, but everything must be put to fire and sword; men, women and children, and old men must be slaughtered and not a tree or house be left standing. With these methods of terrorism, which are alone capable of affecting a people as degenerate as the French, the war will be over in two months, whereas if I admit considerations of humanity it will be prolonged for years. In spite of my repugnance I have therefore been obliged to choose the former system." This showed his ruthless policy, and this policy of indiscriminate murder to shorten the war was considered to be a crime. . . .

"I can't understand how all this can happen. It's enough to make one lose one's faith in God!"

—Eva Braun in a letter to a friend written during the siege of Hitler's bunker and the bombing of Berlin, April 1945

> In the Pacific war under our consideration, if there was anything approaching what is indicated in the above letter of the German Emperor, it is the decision coming from the Allied Powers to use the atom bomb. . . . If any indiscriminate destruction of civilian life and property is still illegitimate in warfare, then, in the Pacific war, this decision to use the atom bomb is the only near approach to the directives of the German Emperor during the first world war and of the Nazi leaders during the second world war. Nothing like this could be traced to the credit of the present accused [the Japanese leaders then on trial].

Twelve years after the Tokyo War Crimes Trial, Justice Röling of the Netherlands compared the bombings to the Holocaust when he said, "from the Second World War above all two things are remembered: the German gas chambers and the American atomic bombings."

Brigadier General Telford Taylor, who was involved in the Nuremberg War Crimes Trial, said, "The rights and wrongs of Hiroshima are debatable, but I have never heard a plausible justification of Nagasaki. It is difficult to contest the judgment that Dresden and Nagasaki were war crimes, tolerable in retrospect only because their malignancy pales in comparison to Dachau, Auschwitz, and Treblinka." In other words, even though he considered the annihilation of Nagasaki a war crime, at least it wasn't as bad as the horrendous war crimes of the Nazis.

At least one trial directly dealt with the bombings: the Shimoda case, which was tried in the District Court of Tokyo. On December 7, 1963, the court determined that the destruction of both Hiroshima and Nagasaki were in fact illegal acts.

Whether U.S. officials were guilty of war crimes in these instances or not, it is obvious that when it comes to war crimes, there is a significant advantage in winning the war, since the officials of the losing country are tried and often executed, whereas the victors are immune from prosecution. If those U.S. officials accused of war crimes had been tried by the Japanese as international law demands, I think there's little doubt what that trial's outcome would have been. And herein lies the problem with international law. In the absence of a world government, who gets to interpret the law, who determines who goes to trial and who doesn't, who forces the accused country to heel? Unless forced to submit, no country willingly allows other countries to sit in judgment of it. This especially applies to the United States. I just cannot see the United States or its leaders ever submitting to anyone else's judgment without a fight.

Until the United States makes itself subject to international law, maybe it shouldn't insist that other countries be subject to it. But this then raises the question: what should be done in cases like the Holocaust or the Khmer Rouge's genocide in Cambodia?

Revolutionary War Crimes

There is little doubt that atrocities are committed in every war. One common crime is the murder of prisoners who are in custody and no longer a threat. It is tempting for soldiers who have watched their friends die to exact revenge on their captives. (Remember the movie *Breaker Morant*, 1979, based on the true story of the Australian who was tried and executed for just that reason during the Boer War?)

The Revolutionary War was no exception. On May 29, 1780, Banastre Tarleton and his British Legion charged into battle against a regiment of Virginian infantry under Colonel Abraham Buford on the border between the two Carolinas. Though Buford had almost four hundred men, they were quickly overrun by the British, and he decided to surrender. They raised the white flag, but the man holding it was quickly shot. On seeing they weren't going to be allowed to surrender, Buford's men took up their arms again, but they were all killed. "Not a man was spared," wrote surgeon Robert Brownfield. "[Tarleton's men] went over the ground plunging their bayonets into everyone that exhibited any signs of life."

Shortly following this massacre, some patriots decided to take some revenge, as is revealed in the following account by one young militiaman:

> I was invited by some of my comrades to go and see some of the Tory prisoners. We went to where six were standing together. Some discussion taking place, I heard some of our men cry out, "Remember Buford," and the prisoners were immediately hewed to pieces with broadswords. At first I bore the scene without any emotion, but upon a moment's reflection, I felt such horror as I never did before nor have since, and, returning

to my quarters and throwing myself upon my blanket, I contemplated the cruelties of war until overcome and unmanned by a distressing gloom from which I was not relieved until commencing our march next morning before day by moonlight. I came to Tarleton's camp, which he had just abandoned leaving lively rail fires. Being on the left of the road as we marched along, I discovered lying upon the ground something with the appearance of a man. Upon approaching him, he proved to be a youth about sixteen who, having come out to view the British through curiosity, for fear he might give information to our troops, they had run him through with a bayonet and left him for dead. Though able to speak, he was mortally wounded. The sight of this unoffending butchered boy . . . relieved me of my distressful feelings for the slaughter of the Tories, and I desired nothing so much as the opportunity of participating in their destruction.

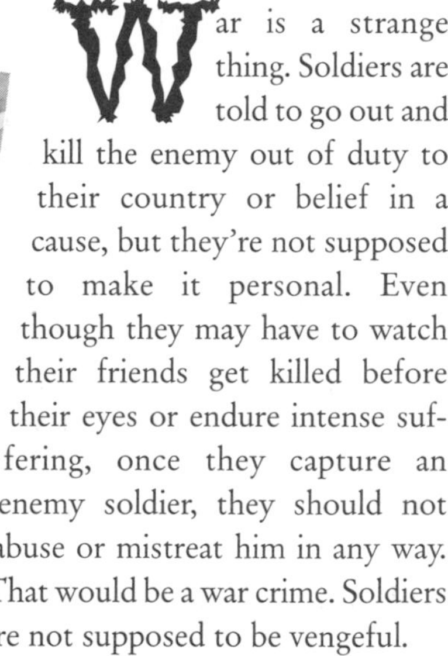

American propaganda poster from 1944.

One Swedish officer named Karl Gustav Tornquist, who was serving with the French navy in the area at the time, reported that at one beautiful estate, the floor of one room was covered with the broken pieces of plaster figurines. In their place in the cupboard were five human heads. While in a nearby room, "a pregnant woman was found murdered in her bed through several bayonet stabs. The barbarians had opened both of her breasts and written above the bed canopy: 'Thou shalt never give birth to a rebel.'" The baby that had been ripped from her womb was found outside hanging from a tree.

Being Friendly with the Enemy

War is a strange thing. Soldiers are told to go out and kill the enemy out of duty to their country or belief in a cause, but they're not supposed to make it personal. Even though they may have to watch their friends get killed before their eyes or endure intense suffering, once they capture an enemy soldier, they should not abuse or mistreat him in any way. That would be a war crime. Soldiers are not supposed to be vengeful.

This is very difficult considering the amount of propaganda a government puts out during the war to stir up hatred against an enemy. One role of propaganda is to dehumanize the enemy. This is often accomplished by encouraging prejudices and presenting the enemy as being subhuman. During World War II, the Japanese were referred to as Japs or Nips, and they were caricatured as being unfeeling, unthinking robots for their government who all looked alike and had thick glasses and buck teeth. Such racist propaganda was even common in publications like *Time* magazine, which said, "The ordinary unreasoning

Jap is ignorant. Perhaps he is human. Nothing . . . indicates it."

Unfortunately, encouraging prejudices also has the side effect of stirring up animosity against anyone who resembles the enemy. For example, during World War II, even loyal Americans were rounded up and put in prison camps without a trial, losing everything they owned, just because of their Japanese ancestry. (Sounds a bit like Nazi Germany, doesn't it? It's interesting that General Eisenhower, Admiral Nimitz, and many others were not barred from positions of trust during World War II because of their German ancestry.) Then in Vietnam, the United States was there ostensibly to save the South Vietnamese from communism, but even the South Vietnamese were called gooks and treated as being inferior. Similarly, during the Persian Gulf War, the proclaimed purpose was to defend Saudi Arabia from invasion and to liberate Kuwait, while back in America, the hatred against the Iraqis became so heated that many Arab-American businesses—including those belonging to Americans of Saudi Arabian and Kuwaiti ancestry—were attacked and had their windows smashed.

Once the war is over, the propaganda stops, and the enemy often becomes a friend and ally. Although the government usually has a fairly easy time changing gears into a friendly mode, the citizens, who have been subjected to the barrage of propaganda, sometimes even maintain those fostered prejudices throughout the rest of their lives.

Ideally, soldiers should be able to put their feelings behind them once the fighting stops, but it's not that easy. The passage of time helps, making it easier to be friendly with the enemy. Still, it took Alex Haley—the author of *Roots*—more than thirty years to get over his "fear and hatred of the Japanese." In 1977, he was being interviewed for a Japanese television show when he and the interviewer began talking about the war. They suddenly discovered they had both fought on Manus Island and had come very close to killing each other. After a teary embrace, Haley explained that he was "overwhelmed by this simple truth: We need each other more than we need to fight each other." It must be a strange experience to suddenly be face to face with somebody you never met before, but had once tried to kill.

Occasionally, former enemies even get together for reunions. Toward the end of World War II, five thousand U.S. marines spent eighteen months trying to kill off a small group of Japanese on the island of Saipan. They slowly whittled down the group until the remaining forty-four Japanese soldiers finally surrendered in 1945 with the commander of the group, Captain Sakae Oba, handing over his sword to a young Army officer named Howard Kurgis, who later retired as a brigadier general. In 1986, Kurgis and three of his men had a reunion with Oba in Los Angeles. Oba said of Kurgis, "I came to see him as a friend."

In 1977, American veterans of the 70th Infantry Division began having reunions in Germany with Waffen SS veterans of the 6th Mountain Division every two years, despite protests from Jewish leaders. One of the Americans justified the reunions saying the atrocities were committed by another branch of the SS, whereas those he had fought during the war were just ordinary soldiers. Another American, Delyle Omholt, explained that "we sit around the table and drink their beer, and hopefully have a good time."

This is not a new phenomenon. Just before the start of World War II, Germany's Luftwaffe reconstituted the Richthofen Geschwader

(Wing). Baron Manfred von Richthofen, better known as the Red Baron, was the famous ace who shot down eighty planes in World War I before he was killed. Richthofen's eightieth victim, Second Lieutenant D. G. Lewis of Britain, survived being shot down, and in 1938 he was invited to visit the reestablished Richthofen fighter wing. Unfortunately, I don't know how he felt about this or if he accepted the invitation.

Something of a similar circumstance occurred to Major General Adolf ("Dolfo") Galland, who was Germany's General of Fighters and one of the top aces of World War II, having shot down 104 Allied aircraft. Galland was shot down by a young American pilot named Jim Finnegan. In 1982, Galland visited Finnegan in San Francisco, where he showed his badly scarred knee to Finnegan's four-year-old grandson, saying, "See what your grandfather did to me?" While he was there, Galland also met with his pen pal, U.S. Colonel Ed Rudka. Rudka's cousin and two of his buddies were killed in air battles with Galland's elite fighter unit.

Sometimes bouts of friendliness break out during wartime, much to the chagrin of some commanding officers. One of the most famous incidents of this happened during World War I on Christmas of 1914.

The British General Headquarters had issued an message stating, "It is thought possible that the enemy may be contemplating an attack during Xmas or New Year. Special vigilance will be maintained during these periods." Despite this, some of the troops were overcome by the Christmas spirit.

What happened next was described by British Gunner Herbert Smith of the 5th Battery, Royal Field Artillery, in a letter he wrote at the time.

On Christmas Eve there was a lull in the fighting, no firing going on at all after 6 P.M. The Germans had a Christmas tree in the trenches, and Chinese lanterns all along the top of a parapet. Eventually the Germans started shouting, "Come over, I want to speak to you." Our chaps hardly knew how to take this, but one of the "nuts" belonging to the regiment got out of the trench and started to walk towards the German lines. One of the Germans met him about half-way across, and they shook hands and became quite friendly. In due time the "nut" came back and told all the others about it. So more of them took it in turns to go and visit the Germans. The officer commanding would not allow more than three men at a time.

I went out myself on Christmas Day and exchanged some cigarettes for cigars, and this game has been going on from Christmas Eve till midnight on Boxing Day [the day after Christmas] without a single round being fired. The German I met had been a waiter in London and could use our language a little. He says they didn't want to fight and I think he was telling the truth as we are not getting half so many bullets as usual. I know this statement will take a bit of believing but it is absolutely correct. Fancy a German shaking your flapper as though he were trying to smash your fingers, and then a few days later trying to plug you. I hardly know what to think about it, but I fancy they are working up a big scheme so that they can give us a doing, but our chaps are prepared, and I am under the impression they will get more than they bargained for.

In 1888, Otto von Bismark decided to establish a German colony in Samoa and sent a fleet of ships to take over this group of South Pacific islands. They shelled the native villages—destroying some American property—and later ripped down an American flag. In response, the United States sent a fleet of ships to protect the Americans. As the two groups of warships prepared to fight it out in a Samoan harbor, a hurricane suddenly struck the islands, destroying both fleets. The German and American sailors found themselves frantically trying to save each others' lives. Both countries soon forgot their grievances, but if that hurricane had hit just a few days later, it's very likely the United States and Germany would have gone to war.

British Second Lieutenant Cyril Drummond of the 135th Battery, Royal Field Artillery, saw what was going on, but didn't seem to mind. In fact, he found it all rather intriguing.

> On Boxing Day we walked up to the village of St. Yvon where the observation post was. I soon discovered that places where we were usually shot at were quite safe. There were the two sets of front trenches only a few yards apart, and yet there were soldiers, both British and German, standing on top of them, digging or repairing the trench in some way, without ever shooting at each other. It was an extraordinary situation.
>
> In the sunken road I met an officer I knew, and we walked along together so that we could look across to the German front line, which was only about seventy yards away. One of the Germans waved to us and said, "Come over here." We said, "*You* come over here if you want to talk." So he climbed out of his trench and came over towards us. We met, and very gravely saluted each other. He was joined by more Germans, and some of the Dublin Fusiliers from our own trenches came out to join us. No German officer came out, it was only the ordinary soldiers. We talked, mainly in French, because my German was not very good and none of the Germans could speak English well. But we managed to get together all right. One of them said, "We don't want to kill you, and you don't want to kill us, so why shoot?"
>
> They gave me some German tobacco and German cigars—they seemed to have plenty of those, and very good ones too—and they asked whether we had any jam. One of the Dublin Fusiliers got a tin of jam which had been opened, but very little taken out, and he gave it to a German who gave him two cigars for it. I lined them all up and took a photograph.

An interesting view from the other side is provided by German Lieutenant Johannes Niemann of the 133rd Royal Saxon Regiment.

> We came up to take over the trenches on the front between Frelinghien and Houplines, where our regiment and the Scottish Seaforth Highlanders were face to face. It was a cold starry night and the Scots were a hundred or so meters in front of us in their trenches where, as we discovered, like us they were up to their knees in mud. My Company Commander and I, savoring the unaccustomed calm, sat with our orderlies round a Christmas tree we had put up in our dugout.
>
> Suddenly, for no apparent reason, our enemies began to fire on our lines. Our soldiers had hung little Christmas trees covered with candles above the trenches and our enemies, seeing the lights, thought we were about to launch a surprise

attack. But, by midnight it was calm once more. Next morning the mist was slow to clear and suddenly my orderly threw himself into my dugout to say that both the German and Scottish soldiers had come out of their trenches and were fraternizing along the front. I grabbed my binoculars and looking cautiously over the parapet saw the incredible sight of our soldiers exchanging cigarettes, schnapps and chocolate with the enemy. Later a Scottish soldier appeared with a football which seemed to come from nowhere and a few minutes later a real football match got underway. The Scots marked their goal mouth with their strange caps and we did the same with ours. It was far from easy to play on the frozen ground, but we continued, keeping rigorously to the rules, despite the fact that it only lasted an hour and that we had no referee. A great many of the passes went wide, but all the amateur footballers, although they must have been very tired, played with huge enthusiasm. Us Germans really roared when a gust of wind revealed that the Scots wore no drawers under their kilts—and hooted and whistled every time they caught an impudent glimpse of one posterior belonging to one of "yesterday's enemies." But after an hour's play, when our Commanding Officer heard about it, he sent an order that we must put a stop to it. A little later we drifted back to our trenches and the fraternization ended.

The game finished with a score of three goals to two in favor of Fritz against Tommy.

At the British headquarters, the commanders were very displeased, and soon all the units that had engaged in this unmilitary behavior were transferred to other parts of the front.

At the other end of the spectrum are those who were once friends or who are relatives, but end up fighting against each other on the battlefield. This was very common, of course, during the Civil War. Families were divided, and many of the officers had gone to West Point together or fought alongside one another during the Mexican War from 1846 to 1848.

It also happened during the Revolutionary War. This war wasn't just the British against the Americans. There were also the American Loyalists (or Tories) who fought with and supported the British. Even Ben Franklin found himself on the opposite side from his son, William, while Loyalist General Timothy Ruggles was opposed by his wife, brothers, and some of his children. And of Loyalist judge David Ogden's five sons, three were Loyalists and two were Patriots.

One Loyalist officer who fought at the Battle of Bennington[25] in 1777 later said that:

> a little before the Royalists gave way, the Rebels pushed with a strong party on the Front of the Loyalists where I commanded. As they were coming up I observed a Man fire at me, and, crying out: "Peters, you damned Tory, I have got you," he rushed on me with his Bayonet, which entered just below my left Breast, but was turned by the Bone. By this time I was loaded and I saw that it was a Rebel Captain, and old Schoolfellow & Playmate, and a Couzin of my Wife's. Tho' his Bayonet was in my Body, I felt regret at being obliged to destroy him.

25 This battle was fought near Walloomsac, New York, but it was named after Bennington, Vermont, because that's where the British, Hessian, and the loyalist troops were heading before they were forced to turn back.

A Child's View of War

Sometimes children are not aware of the horrors of war. Perhaps they do not yet understand the possibility of their own death or are not aware of the dangers. Whatever the reason, a child can have a very different view of war. An interesting example of this comes from George Macbeth's *A Child of War*. Here he describes what it was like growing up while the Germans were bombing London during 1940.

> In the morning, I would walk along Clarkehouse Road with my eyes glued to the pavement for shrapnel. It became the fashion to make a collection of this, and there were few days when I came home without a pocketful of jagged, rusting bits, like the unintelligible pieces from a scattered jigsaw of pain and violence.
>
> Of course we didn't see them as this at the time. They were simply free toys from the sky, as available and interesting as the horse chestnuts in the Botanical Gardens, or the nippled acorns in Melbourne Avenue.
>
> It must have been about this time that the British Restaurants were opening, with their austerity jam roll and meat balls; and our own meals were beginning to rely rather more on rissoles and home-made apple sponge. But my mother was always a good manager, and I have no sense of any sudden period of shortage or of going hungry.
>
> Sweets were the great loss. There was no longer an everlasting, teeth-spoiling fountain of sherbet and liquorice, or of Boy Blue cream whirls, or of Cadbury's Caramello. Sweets were hard to come by, and then limited to a fixed ration.
>
> One of the worst casualties was chocolate. The traditional division into milk and plain disappeared, and an awful intervening variety known as Ration Chocolate was born, issued in semi-transparent grease-proof wrappers, and about as appetizing as cardboard. In spite of a lifelong sweet tooth, I could never eat it.

Native Americans Versus Western Civilization

When I entered the school I had no thought but that I would spend my life in a tepee and hunt buffalo as my father had. Even by the time I was ready to leave, I had no more than a vague idea of what lay ahead for me, but a magic door had been opened that would take me from the ABC's to calculus; from a tepee lighted with buffalo oil burning in a clay dish to the electric lights in a penthouse; from messages sent through puffs of smoke made by a blanket over a campfire to a swift interchange by telephone; from the horse to the superjet; and lastly, perhaps more significantly, from the arrow to the hydrogen bomb. . . .

I met Thomas Edison and Alexander Graham Bell, and many others who impressed me as great people, but pride in them and their achievements has not overawed me, for I am not convinced that the comforts and advancements which they brought into the world have made people more content and happy than the Indians were through the centuries on the mountains, prairies, and deserts of the primeval, virgin continent.

—Chief Red Fox (1870–c.1971), Sioux, nephew of Chief Crazy Horse

Only to the white man was nature a "wilderness" and only to him was the land "infested" with "wild" animals and "savage" people. To us it was tame. Earth was bountiful and we were surrounded with the blessings of the Great Mystery. Not until the hairy man from the east came and with brutal frenzy heaped injustices upon us and the families that we loved was it "wild" for us. When the very animals of the forest began fleeing from his approach, then it was that for us the "Wild West" began.

—Chief Luther Standing Bear (1868–1939), Oglala Sioux

"God has not been preparing the English speaking and Teutonic peoples for a thousand years for nothing. . . . He has given us the spirit of progress to overwhelm the forces of reaction throughout the earth. He has made us adept in government that we may administer government among savage and senile peoples. . . . And of all our race He has marked the American people as His chosen nation to finally lead in the redemption of the world."

—Senator Albert J. Beveridge, 1900

Nothing the Great Mystery placed in the land of the Indian pleased the white man, and nothing escaped his transforming hand. Wherever forests have not been mowed down, wherever the animal is recessed in their quiet protection, wherever the earth is not bereft of four-footed life—that to him is an "unbroken wilderness."

But, because for the Lakota there was no wilderness, because nature was not dangerous but hospitable, not forbidding but friendly, Lakota philosophy was healthy—free from fear and dogmatism. And here I find the great distinction between the faith of the Indian and the white man. Indian faith sought the harmony of man with his surroundings; the other sought the dominance of surroundings.

In sharing, in loving all and everything, one people naturally found a due portion of the thing they sought, while, in fearing, the other found need of conquest.

For one man the world was full of beauty; for the other it was a place of sin and ugliness to be endured until he went to another world, there to become a creature of wings, half-man and half-bird.

Forever one man directed his Mystery [i.e. God] to change the world He had made; forever this man pleaded with Him to chastise his wicked ones; and forever he implored his God to send His light to earth. Small wonder this man could not understand the other.

But the old Lakota was wise. He knew that man's heart, away from nature, becomes hard; he knew that lack of respect for growing, living things soon led to lack of respect for humans, too. So he kept his children close to nature's softening influence.

—Chief Luther Standing Bear

From Wakan Tanka, the Great Spirit, there came a great unifying life force that flowed in and through all things—the flowers of the plains, blowing winds, rocks, trees, birds, animals—and was the same force that had been breathed into the first man. Thus all things were kindred, and were brought together by the same Great Mystery.

Kinship with all creatures of the earth, sky, and water was a real and active principle. In the animal and bird world there existed a brotherly feeling that kept the Lakota safe among them. And so close did some of the Lakotas come to their feathered and furred friends that in true brotherhood they spoke a common tongue.

The animals had rights—the right of man's protection, the right to live, the right to multiply, the right to freedom, and the right to man's indebtedness—and in recognition of these rights the Lakota never enslaved an animal, and spared all life that was not needed for food and clothing.

This concept of life and its relations was humanizing, and gave to the Lakota an abiding love. It filled his being with the joy and mystery of living; it gave him reverence for all life; it made a place for all things in the scheme of existence with equal importance to all.

The Lakota could despise no creature, for all were of one blood, made by the same hand, and filled with the essence of the Great Mystery. In spirit, the Lakota were humble and meek. "Blessed are the meek, for they shall inherit the earth"—this was true for the Lakota, and from the earth they inherited secrets long since forgotten. Their religion was sane, natural, and human.

—Chief Luther Standing Bear

[Speaking to a missionary:] Brother, listen to what we say. There was a time when our forefathers owned this great island. Their seats extended from the rising to the setting sun. The Great Spirit had made it for the use of the Indians. He had created the buffalo, the deer, and other animals for food. He made the bear and the beaver, and their skins served us for clothing. He had scattered them over the country, and taught us how to take them. He had caused the earth to produce corn for bread. All this he had done for his red children because he loved them. If we had any disputes about hunting grounds, they were generally settled without the shedding of much blood: but an evil day came upon us; your forefathers crossed the great waters and landed on this island. Their numbers were small; they found friends, not enemies; they told us they had fled from their own country for fear of wicked men, and come here to enjoy their religion. They asked for a small seat; we took pity on them, granted their request, and they sat down among us; we gave them corn and meat; they gave us poison in return. The white people had now found our country, tidings were carried back, and more came among us; yet we did not fear them, we took them to be friends; they called us brothers; we believed them and gave them a larger seat. At length their number had greatly increased; they wanted more land; they wanted our country. Our eyes were opened, and our minds become uneasy. Wars took place; Indians were hired to fight against Indians, and many of our people were destroyed. They also brought strong liquors among us: it was strong and powerful, and has slain thousands.

Brother, our seats were once large, and yours were very small; you have now become a great people, and we have scarcely left a place to spread our blankets; you have got our country, but are not satisfied; you want to force your religion upon us.

"Maybe we should not have humored them [the Native Americans when they asked to live on reservations]. . . . Maybe we should have said, 'No, come join us. Be citizens along with the rest of us.'"

—President Ronald Reagan answering questions in Moscow

Brother, continue to listen. You say that you are sent to instruct us how to worship the Great Spirit agreeably to his mind, and if we do not take hold of the religion which you white people teach, we shall be unhappy hereafter; you say that you are right, and we are lost; how do we know this to be true? We understand that your religion is written in a book; if it was intended for us as well as you, why has not the Great Spirit given it to us, and not only to us, but why did he not give to our forefathers the knowledge of that book, with the means of understanding it rightly? We only know what you tell us about it; how shall we know when to believe, being so often deceived by the white people?

Brother, you say there is but one way to worship and serve the Great Spirit; if there is but one religion, why do you white people differ so much about it? Why do you not agree, as you can all read the book?

Brother, we do not understand these things; we are told that your religion was given to your forefathers, and has been handed down from father to son. We also have a religion which was given to our forefathers, and has been handed down to us their children. We worship that way. It teacheth us to be thankful for all the favors we receive; to love each other, and to be united. We never quarrel about religion.

Brother, the Great Spirit has made us all; but he has made a great difference between his white and red children; he has given us a different complexion, and different customs; to you he has given the arts; to these he has not opened our eyes; we know these things to be true. Since he has made so great a difference between us in other things, why may we not conclude that he has given us a different religion according to our understanding; the Great Spirit does right; he knows what is best for his children; we are satisfied.

Brother, we do not wish to destroy your religion, or take it from you; we only want to enjoy our own.

Brother, you say you have not come to get our land or our money, but to enlighten our minds. I will now tell you that I have been at your meetings, and saw you collecting money from the meeting. I cannot tell what this money was intended for, but suppose it was for your minister, and if we should conform to your way of thinking, perhaps you may want some from us.

Brother, we are told that you have been preaching to white people in this place; these people are our neighbors, we are acquainted with them; we will wait a little while and see what effect your preaching has upon them. If we find it does them good, makes them honest, and less disposed to cheat Indians, we will then consider again what you have said.

Brother, you have now heard the answer to your talk, and this is all we have to say at present. As we are going to part, we will come and take you by the hand, and hope the Great Spirit will protect you on your journey, and turn you safe to your friends.

—Chief Red Jacket, Seneca, 1805

[The missionary refused to shake Chief Red Jacket's hand, explaining "that there was no fellowship between the religion of God and the works of the devil, therefore, he could not join hands with them." Smiling politely, the Seneca chiefs departed.]

"It was wholly impossible to avoid conflicts with the weaker race, unless we were willing to see the American continent fall into the hands of some other strong power; and even had we adopted such a ludicrous policy, the Indians themselves would have made war on us."

—President Theodore Roosevelt, The Winning of the West, *1889*

Soon after our return home, news reached us that a war [the War of 1812] was going to take place between the British and the Americans.

Runners continued to arrive from different tribes, all confirming the reports of the expected war. The British agent, Colonel Dixon, was holding talks with, and making presents to, the different tribes. I had not made up my mind whether to join the British or remain neutral. I had not discovered yet one good trait in the character of the Americans who had come to the country. They made fair promises but never fulfilled them, while the British made but few, and we could always rely implicitly on their word. . . .

Why did the Great Spirit ever send the whites to this island to drive us from our homes and introduce among us poisonous liquors, disease, and death? They should have remained in the land the Great Spirit allotted to them. But I will proceed with my story. My memory, however, is not very good since my late visit to the white people. I have still a buzzing noise in my ears. . . .

On my arrival at the village I was met by the chiefs and braves and conducted to the lodge which was prepared for me. After eating, I gave a full account of all that I had seen and done. I explained to my people the manner in which the British and Americans fought. Instead of stealing upon each other and taking every advantage to kill the enemy and save their own people as we do, which with us is considered good policy in a war chief, they march out in open daylight and fight regardless of the number of warriors they may lose. After the battle is over they retire to feast and drink wine as if nothing had happened. After which they make a statement in writing of what they have done, each party claiming the victory and neither giving an account of half the number that have been killed on their own side. . . .

We can only judge of what is proper and right by our standard of what is right and wrong, which differs widely from the whites', if I have been correctly informed. The whites may do wrong all their lives and then if they are sorry for it when about to die, all is well, but with us it is different. We must continue to do good throughout our lives. If we have corn and meat, and know of a family that have none, we divide with them. If we have more blankets than we absolutely need, and others have not enough, we must give to those who are in want.

—Chief Black Hawk, Sauk, 1833

"Were it possible to introduce among the Indian tribes a love for exclusive property, it would be a happy commencement of the business."

—Secretary of War Henry Knox to President George Washington, 1789

[Charles Eastman, a.k.a. Ohiyesa, had never seen a white person when his uncle gave him this description:]

The greatest object of their lives seems to be to acquire possessions—to be rich. The desire to possess the whole world. For thirty years they were trying to entice us to sell them our land. Finally the outbreak (Minnesota, 1862) gave them all, and we have been driven away from our beautiful country.

They are a wonderful [i.e., amazing] people. They have divided the day into hours, like the moons of the year. In fact, they measure everything. Not one of them would let so much as a turnip go from his field unless he received full value for it. . . .

I am also informed, but this I hardly believe, that their Great Chief (President) compels every man to pay him for the land he lives upon and all his personal goods—even for his own existence—every year! (This was his idea of taxation.) I am sure we could not live under such a law. . . .

In war they have leaders and war-chiefs of different grades. The common warriors are driven forward like a herd of antelopes to face the foe. It is on account of this manner of fighting—from compulsion and not from personal bravery—that we count no *coup* on them.

—The uncle of Charles Alexander Eastman, a.k.a. Ohiyesa, Santee Sioux, c. 1870. Eastman didn't see a white person until he was sixteen years old. He went on to become a physician after graduating from Dartmouth College and Boston University

Hear me, people: We have now to deal with another race—small and feeble when our fathers first met them, but now great and overbearing. Strangely enough they have a mind to till the soil and the love of possession is a disease with them. These people have made many rules that the rich may break but the poor may not. They take their tithes [taxes] from the poor and weak to support the rich and those who rule. They claim this mother of ours, the earth, for their own and fence their neighbors away; they deface her with their buildings and their refuse. That nation is like a spring freshet that overruns its banks and destroys all who are in its path.

—Chief Sitting Bull, a.k.a. Tatanka Yotanka, Hunkpapa Sioux, 1877

The more I consider the condition of the white men, the more fixed becomes my opinion that, instead of gaining, they have lost much by subjecting themselves to what they call the laws and regulations of civilized societies.

—Chief Tomochichi (c. 1650–1739), Creek

In the government you call civilized, the happiness of the people is constantly sacrificed to the splendor of empire. Hence the origin of your codes of criminal and civil laws; hence your dungeons and prisons. We have no prisons, we have no pompous parade of courts; we have no written laws; and yet judges are as highly revered among us as they are among you, and their decisions are as much regarded.

Property, to say the least, is well-guarded, and crimes are as impartially punished. We have among us no exalted villains above the control of our laws. Daring wickedness is here never allowed to triumph over helpless innocence. The estates of widows and orphans are never devoured by enterprising swindlers. In a word, we have no robbery under the color of the law.

—Joseph Brant, a.k.a. Thayendanegea, Mohawk, 1807

"With regard to the narrative enclosed [on the death of Colonel William Crawford by Native Americans], I subjoin some observations with regard to the animal, vulgarly called Indians. . . . What use do these ringed, streaked, spotted and speckled cattle make of the soil? Do they till it? Revelation said to man, 'Thou shalt till the ground.' This alone is human life. . . . I would as soon admit a right in the buffalo to grant lands, as in Killbuck, the Big Cat, the Big Dog, or any of the ragged wretches that are called chiefs and sachems. What would you think of going to a big lick . . . and addressing yourself to a great buffalo to grant you land? . . . I am so far from thinking the Indians have a right to the soil, that not having made a better use of it for many hundred years, I conceive they have forfeited all pretense to claim, and ought to be driven from it."

—Henry Brackenridge, a prominent citizen of Pittsburgh (then a frontier village), 1782

The sight of your cities pains the eyes of the red man. But perhaps it is because the red man is a savage and does not understand.

There is no quiet place in the white man's cities, no place to hear the leaves of spring or the rustle of insects' wings. Perhaps it is because I am a savage and do not understand, but the clatter only seems to insult the ears.

The Indian prefers the soft sound of the wind darting over the face of the pond, the smell of the wind itself cleansed by a midday rain, or scented with piñon pine. The air is precious to the red man, for all things share the same breath—the animals, the trees, the man.

Like a man who has been dying for many days, a man in your city is numb to the stench.

—Chief Seattle (1786-1866), Suqwamish and Duwamish

[Speaking to the Lord Lieutenant of a French colony in Newfoundland:] I am Master of my Condition and mine. I am Master of my own Body. I have the absolute disposal of my self, I do what I please, I am the first and the last of my Nation, I fear no Man, and I depend only upon the Great Spirit. Whereas thy Body, as well as thy Soul, are doomed to a dependence upon thy great Captain, thy Vice-Roy disposes of thee, thou hast not the liberty of doing what thou hast a mind to; thou art afraid of Robbers, false Witnesses, Assassins, etc., and thou dependest upon an infinity of Persons whose Places have raised them above thee.

—Chief Adario, a.k.a. Kondiaronk, Huron, late 1600s

When one examines the history of American society one notices the great weakness inherent in it. The country was founded in violence. It worships violence and it will continue to live violently. Anyone who tries to meet violence with love is crushed, but violence used to meet violence also ends abruptly with meaningless destruction.

—Vine Deloria, Jr., Sioux, 1969

As a child I understood how to give; I have forgotten this grace since I became civilized. I lived the natural life, whereas I now live the artificial. Any pretty pebble was valuable to me then; every growing tree an object of reverence. Now I worship with the white man before a painted landscape whose value is estimated in dollars! Thus the Indian is reconstructed, as the natural rocks are ground to powder and made into artificial blocks which may be built into the walls of modern society.

—Charles Alexander Eastman, 1911

"Civilization directs us to remove as fast as possible that natural growth from the lands."

—Revolutionary War General Benjamin Lincoln, 1792

"My family, I believe, have cut down more trees in America than any other name!"

—President John Adams

"It's unfair that it remain empty and unspoiled."

—Developer Hugh Stone, when permits for his subdivision were delayed

---

When I was a youth, the country was very beautiful. Along the rivers were belts of timberland, where grew cottonwood, maple, elm, ash, hickory, and walnut trees, and many other kinds. Also there were many kinds of vines and shrubs. And under these grew many good herbs and beautiful flowering plants.

In both the woodland and the prairie I could see the trails of many kinds of animals and could hear the cheerful songs of many kinds of birds. When I walked abroad, I could see many forms of life, beautiful living creatures which *Wakanda* [the Great Spirit] had placed here; and these were, after their manner, walking, flying, leaping, running, playing all about.

But now the face of all the land is changed and sad. The living creatures are gone. I see the land desolate and I suffer an unspeakable sadness. Sometimes I wake in the night, and I feel as though I should suffocate from the pressure of this awful feeling of loneliness.

—Anonymous, Omaha

I am an old woman now. The buffaloes and blacktail deer are gone, and our Indian ways are almost gone. Sometimes I find it hard to believe that I ever lived them.

My little son grew up in the white man's school. He can read books, and he owns cattle and has a farm. He is a leader among our Hidatsa people, helping teach them to follow the white man's road.

He is kind to me. We no longer live in an earth lodge, but in a house with chimneys, and my son's wife cooks by a stove.

But for me, I cannot forget our old ways.

Often in summer I rise at daybreak and steal out to the corn fields, and as I hoe the corn I sing to it, as we did when I was young. No one cares for our corn songs now.

Sometimes in the evening I sit, looking out on the big Missouri. The sun sets, and dusk steals over the water. In the shadows I seem again to see our Indian village, with smoke curling upward from the earth lodges, and in the river's roar I hear the yells of the warriors, and the laughter of little children as of old.

It is but an old woman's dream. Then I see but shadows and hear only the roar of the river, and tears come into my eyes. Our Indian life, I know, is gone forever.

—Buffalo Bird Woman, a.k.a. Waheenee, Hidatsa

Our ideas will overcome your ideas. . . . What is important is that we have a superior way of life. We Indians have a more human philosophy of life. We Indians will show this country how to act human. Someday this country will revise its constitution, its laws, in terms of human beings, instead of property. . . . What is the ultimate value of a man's life? That is the question.

—Vine Deloria, Jr., Sioux, 1971

"I don't feel we did wrong in taking this great country away from them [Native Americans]. Our so-called stealing of this country from them was just a matter of survival. There were great numbers of people who needed new land, and the Indians were selfishly trying to keep it for themselves."

—John Wayne

So thanks to my mother's courage and foresight, I didn't have to grow up as a reservation Indian, cruelly trapped and systematically abused. Instead, I would grow up with many of the opportunities available to white Americans—and I would learn firsthand about American racism.

—Russell Means, Oglala Sioux, 1995

Just as the pharaoh ignored Moses, the U.S. government did not hear my forebears. I say to my nation and to all indigenous peoples: To hell with the pharaoh! Let us embrace the ideals of our ancestors. Let us show the white man how to find peace of mind by living in harmony with the universe. Let us show him how to honor and protect our Grandmother [Earth]. Let *us* go.

—Russell Means, 1995

Firsthand ACCOUNTS by Famous People

Wyatt Earp Tells of the Shoot-Out at O.K. Corral[26]

There never was a shoot-out at the O.K. Corral. There was a shoot-out, but it actually took place in a vacant lot about a quarter of a block away from the rear of the O.K. Corral. Of course, "the Shoot-Out at O.K. Corral" sounds much better than "the Shoot-Out in the Vacant Lot Between Harwood's House and Fly's Lodging House," so I guess someone decided to change it. "O.K. Corral" has more of a Western ring to it. Personally, I think "the Gunfight in Tombstone" sounds pretty good, but there's no point trying to change it now.

The famous gunfight took place in Tombstone, which is in the southeast corner of Arizona, on October 26, 1881. Cochise had died in 1874, and by 1875 most of the Apaches were confined on reservations, though Geronimo and his small band of Chiricahua jumped the reservation periodically over the next decade. The town of Tombstone[27] was a year old when the Earps arrived there in November of 1879. At that time, its population was about 900, almost double what it was just two months previously. It doubled again in the next two months. By the time of the shoot-out, Tombstone's population had shot up to about 5,000. This was because of the tremendous influx of money from nearby silver mines, which would eventually yield $40 million.

Partially because of lingering hostilities from the Civil War, there was considerable friction between the townspeople and country folk. The country people were ranchers, cowboys, rustlers, and bandits who were primarily Southerners, mostly from Texas. The townspeople, on the other hand, were largely Northerners who came there to advance themselves and create an Eastern-type society where they were at the top. They wanted things nice, orderly, and quiet. The cowboys, on the other hand, were drunken, rowdy, hell-raisers, who came in off the range to party. They wanted to get drunk, find a prostitute, and shoot up the place. Thrown into this were also the mining and gambling factions. But in

26 When it comes to the Earps and the gunfight, there is a tremendous amount of erroneous information in circulation, making it awfully difficult to sort out what really happened. In order to ensure this piece was as accurate as possible, I sought out the aid of Carl Chafin, who is an expert on Tombstone. I am very grateful for his assistance. A truly complete, accurate, and authoritative book on the Earps and the shoot-out has yet to be published, but I understand one by Jeff Morey on the gunfight and one by Casey Tefertiller on Wyatt Earp's life will soon be released.

27 There were actually two Tombstones. The first appeared in November 1878 on a nearby hill, but as the town grew, it was moved to its present location about four months later.

many ways, the Tombstone fight was a carryover of the Civil War.

The Earps were townspeople. Wyatt, Virgil, Morgan, Warren, and James Earp came to Tombstone with their wives to get ahead and establish themselves at the top of society. Wyatt, Virgil, and Morgan had all previously worked in law enforcement, and they continued to do so in Tombstone. After Tombstone's city marshal was killed by rustler/bandit William "Curly Bill" Brocius, Virgil took the position. Virgil was also a deputy U.S. marshal. Both Wyatt and Morgan worked as occasional policemen and Wyatt was planning on running for county sheriff in the next election.

The pay of policework was adequate, but it still was not uncommon for those in law enforcement to also work in gambling establishments to supplement their income. This is what the Earps did. Wyatt primarily considered himself a saloonkeeper since he had a piece of the gambling concession at the Oriental Saloon. James, the oldest of the Earps, was also a saloonkeeper, and Warren was primarily a laborer, though he did do a little policework for Virgil while he was in Tombstone. Warren was away from Tombstone at the time of the shoot-out. James was there, but he didn't play a part in it. Morgan was primarily riding shotgun on the Wells Fargo stage to Benson at the time.

"The less you bet, the more you lose when you win."

—Wyatt's creed

And then there was John "Doc" Holliday. Doc was a former dentist, who, when he discovered he was slowly dying from tuberculosis, headed out west and turned to gambling to make a living. In those days, gambling was considered an honorable profession, and successful gamblers were highly respected. Doc was successful, but he was also temperamental, belligerent, and an alcoholic, in addition to having a quick temper. He became involved because he was a close friend of Wyatt's, and he'd had a few altercations with the rustlers himself.

Tombstone's gang of criminals, which they called "the cowboys," primarily rustled cattle in Mexico to sell in Arizona and New Mexico, and rustled cattle in Arizona and New Mexico to sell in Mexico. The head of the outlaws was Old Man Clanton, that is, until he was killed by Mexicans near the border. Then Curly Bill Brocius and Johnny Ringo took over. The gang, which numbered about two hundred outlaws, committed many other types of crimes besides stealing cattle and horses. Sometimes when they needed money, they would hold up a stage. There were about a half dozen such robberies during the cowboys' heyday, and Wells Fargo almost stopped service to the area, which would have been disastrous for Tombstone.

One manager of a mine near Galeyville, Arizona, wrote a letter to the governor describing several of their crimes—which included robbing a saloon, murdering Mexicans, and ambushing a Mexican pack train carrying coin and bullion—and the failure of the courts to punish them. He went on to say, "The cow-boys frequently visit our town and often salute us with an indiscriminate discharge of fire arms, and after indulging in a few drinks at the saloons, practice shooting at the lamps, bottles, glasses etc., sometimes going to the length of shooting the cigar out of one's mouth; this of course produces a nervous feeling among visitors especially."

After Curly Bill was released from jail for the Marshal White shooting, he decided to celebrate in Charleston and Contention—two mining camps about ten miles west of Tombstone—by making a minister dance in his church and by making all the people in one saloon dance for half an hour stark naked. His wild behavior continued for another six months until he was shot in the jaw by another cowboy. That really dampened his spirits.

The cowboys quickly began having run-ins with the Earps and often made threats on the Earps' lives. At one point, Wyatt's horse was stolen. When he found it several months later, it was in the possession of cowboy Billy Clanton. The Earps also found six mules stolen from a U.S. Army post at the ranch of cowboys Tom and Frank McLaury, just after the McLaurys changed the "U.S." brands. And about a month before the shoot-out, the Earps arrested Frank Stilwell and "Pete Spence"[28] for holding up a stagecoach. Spence was a friend of the Clantons. Stilwell was a tough character, who, according to the *San Francisco Chronicle*, was "implicated in the ritual killing of an old man named Horton, whose brains were beaten out with stones at the Brokow Mine, south of Tombstone." One has to wonder what is meant by "ritual killing." Stilwell was released on technicalities. At one point, he was also a deputy of the county sheriff, John Behan.

Sheriff Behan was an ardent supporter of the cowboys, partly because it made his job much easier if he got along with them, but the main reason was that they were against the Earps.[29]

Behan didn't like the Earps—especially Wyatt. And Wyatt didn't like Behan. When Democrat Behan first ran for sheriff of the newly formed Cochise County, Republican Wyatt started to run against him, but Behan made Wyatt a deal that if Wyatt didn't run, he would make Wyatt his deputy and allow Wyatt to run unopposed in the following election. Wyatt agreed, but after Behan won the election, he made someone else deputy. But this was just the start. There was also a woman.

"To kill your man seems a way of winning your spurs, as it were, and establishing yourself on a proper footing in the community."

—William Henry Bishop

Behan's mistress, the beautiful nineteen-year-old Josephine Marcus transferred her affections to Wyatt. Behan had convinced Josephine to come from San Francisco to Tombstone and take care of his son by offering to marry her, but he actually had no intention of going through with it. They were living together in Tombstone, which would make

[28] "Pete Spence" was an alias. His real name was Elliot Larkin Ferguson.

[29] According to Doc Holliday, "He [Behan] has always stood in with the rustlers and taken his share of their plunder, and in consequence he is in their power, and must do as they say. This is shown by the fact that he has five Rustlers under him as deputies. One of these men is Johnny Ringo, who jumped on the stage of the variety theater in Tombstone one night about three weeks ago [in April 1882], and took all the jewels from the proprietor's wife in full view of the audience." About the cowboys, he said, "They ran the country down there and so terrorized the country that no man dared say anything against them."

her his common-law wife, but she soon realized he was a womanizer and left him. There's evidence she was a high-class call girl for a short while before becoming involved with Wyatt.

At the time, Wyatt was married to his second wife, Mattie, but again, their exact relationship is unclear. It's likely they were living together as well and just referring to themselves as "married" when it was convenient. Actually, couples living together were quite common on the frontier. Doc Holliday was also living with his girlfriend, "Big Nose Kate" Fisher, who was a dance hall girl and prostitute. But whether or not Wyatt and Mattie had a marriage certificate, they were together for about eight years.

Josephine linked up with Wyatt at about the time Behan became sheriff, and this may have been the reason he didn't make Wyatt his deputy. Wyatt later married Josephine[31] and they remained together until his death in 1929.

Behan and the Clantons set about framing Doc Holliday—and by implication the Earps—for an attempted stagecoach robbery in which two men were killed. This was in spite, or perhaps because, of the fact that the Earps captured one of the criminals, whom Behan later allowed to escape. A short while after this, the Earps arrested Behan's deputy and the Clantons' friend, Stilwell, for holding up another stage. This prompted more threats against the Earps.

At the time of the gunfight, Wyatt was thirty-three years old, Virgil was thirty-eight, Morgan was thirty, and Doc was thirty. They went up against the Clanton brothers, Ike (age thirty-four) and Billy (nineteen), and the McLaury brothers, Frank (thirty-three) and Tom (twenty-eight). Ike and Tom arrived in Tombstone the day before the fight and the other two the following morning.

The night before the gunfight, Doc got into an argument with Ike. According to Wyatt, Ike had made a secret deal with him to help him catch three stagerobbing cowboys in exchange for the reward money. When Ike let this slip to Doc, Doc promptly berated him for his treachery. Virgil broke up the argument after a few minutes and a very upset Ike wandered off to spend the rest of the night drinking and playing poker. The morning found Ike armed and threatening to kill some Earps and Holliday. Several people woke up Wyatt and Virgil telling them of this.

This is the point at which we'll begin Wyatt's account of what happened. It comes from Wyatt's testimony at a hearing that was held afterward to determine if the Earps had actually murdered Billy Clanton and the McLaury brothers in cold blood as the cowboys claimed. The best transcripts that survive of this hearing are from Tombstone's newspaper, the *Daily Nugget*. This newspaper was actually pro-Behan and anti-Earp—the town's other paper, the *Epitaph*, was on the Earps' side—but despite the anti-Earp bias, the *Daily Nugget*'s transcripts are the most complete record of the hearing.

The shoot-out lasted about thirty seconds, during which time more than thirty bullets were fired in several waves. When things settled down again, Billy Clanton and both McLaurys were dead, and Virgil and Morgan were wounded. And it

---

30 Today, people commonly believe a couple must live together for three or seven years before they have a common-law marriage. This is not true. A couple has a common-law marriage just as soon as they agree to live together as if they were married. That is, as long as there's nothing that would legally prevent such a marriage, like one of them being underage or already married. The law was the same back then.

31 Josephine claimed this was in about 1888, but a record of the marriage has yet to be found.

wasn't over yet. The war between the Earps and the cowboys continued on for several more months.

Here is what Wyatt testified happened on the day of the gunfight.[32]

I got up the next day, October 26th, about noon. Before I got up, Ned Boyle came to me and told me that he met Ike Clanton on Allen Street near the telegraph office and that Ike was on it, that he said that as soon as those damned Earps make their appearance on the street today the ball will open; that Ike said "We are here to make a fight and we are looking for the sons-of-bitches!" I laid in bed some little time after that; got up and went down to the Oriental Saloon.

Harry Jones came to me after I got up and said, "What does all this mean?" I asked him what he meant. He says, "Ike Clanton is hunting you Earp boys with a Winchester rifle and six-shooter." I said, "I will go down and find him and see what he wants." I went out and at the corner of Fifth and Allen I met Virgil Earp, the marshal. He told me how he heard that Ike Clanton was hunting us. I went down Allen Street and Virgil went down Fifth and then Fremont Street. Virgil found Ike Clanton on Fourth near Fremon, in an alleyway.

He walked up to him and said, "I heard you were hunting for some of us." I was coming down Fourth Street at the time. Ike Clanton then threw his Winchester around toward Virgil. Virgil grabbed it and hit Clanton with his six-shooter and knocked him down. Clanton had his rifle and his six-shooter in his pants. By that time I came up, Virgil and Morgan Earp took his rifle and six-shooter and took them to the Grand Hotel after examination, and took Ike Clanton before Justice Wallace.

Before the examination, Morgan Earp had Ike Clanton in charge, as Virgil Earp was out. A short time after I went to Wallace's Court and sat down on a bench, Ike Clanton looked over to me and said, "I will get even with all of you for this. If I had a six-shooter now I would make a fight with all of you." Morgan Earp then said to him, "If you want to make a fight right bad'll, I'll give you this!" at the same time offering Ike Clanton his own (Ike's) six-shooter.

Ike Clanton started to get up and take it, and Campbell, the Deputy Sheriff, pushed him back in his seat, saying he would not allow any fuss. I never had Ike Clanton's arms at any time, as he stated. . . .

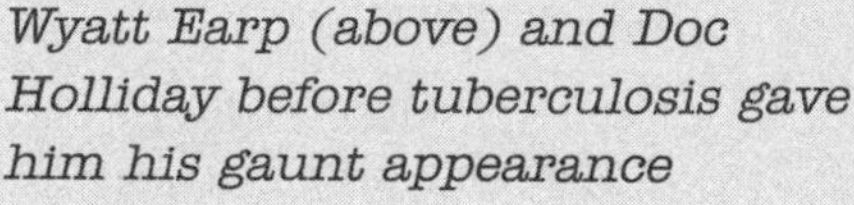

Wyatt Earp (above) and Doc Holliday before tuberculosis gave him his gaunt appearance

32 Wyatt had a very good lawyer. He had Wyatt read a written statement in court so Wyatt couldn't be cross-examined.

I was tired of being threatened by Ike Clanton and his gang. I believed from what they said to me and others, and from their movements that they intended to assassinate me the first chance they had, and I thought that if I had to fight for my life with them I had better make them face me in an open fight. So I said to Ike Clanton, who was then sitting about eight feet away from me. "You damned dirty cow thief, you have been threatening our lives and I know it. I think I would be justified in shooting you down any place I would meet you, but if you are anxious to make a fight, I will go anywhere on earth to make a fight with you, even over the San Simon among your own crowd!"

"All right," he replied, "I will see you after I get through here. I only want four feet of ground to fight on!"

I walked out and just then outside of the courtroom near the Justice's office, I met Tom McLaury. He came up to me and said to me, "If you want to make a fight I will make a fight with you anywhere." I supposed at the time that he had heard what had just transpired between Ike Clanton and myself. I knew of his having threatened me, and I felt just as I did about Ike Clanton, that if the fight had to come, I had better have it come when I had an even show to defend myself. So I said to him, "All right, make a fight right here!" And at the same time slapped him in the face with my left hand and drew my pistol with my right. He had a pistol in plain sight on his right hip in his pants, but made no move to draw it. I said to him, "Jerk your gun and use it!" He made no reply. I hit him on the head with my six-shooter and walked away, down to Hafford's Corner. I went into Hafford's and got a cigar and came out and stood by the door.

"Dark and high the war clouds were piling. Forked hatreds snaked flamingly across the blind gloom, and vengeance threatened in rumbling thunder growls. The red deluge was about to burst. Nothing could hold back the storm."

—Walter Noble Burns, Tombstone, *1928*

Pretty soon after, I saw Tom and Frank McLaury and William Clanton. They passed me and went down Fourth Street to the gunsmith shop. I followed down to see what they were going to do. When I got there, Frank McLaury's horse was standing on the sidewalk with his head in the door of the gunsmith shop. I took the horse by the bit, as I was deputy city marshal, and commenced to back him off the sidewalk. Tom and Frank McLaury and Billy Clanton came to the door. Billy Clanton laid his hand on his six-shooter. Frank McLaury took hold of the horse's bridle. I said, "You will have to get this horse off the sidewalk." Frank McLaury backed him off on the street. Ike Clanton came up about that time and they all walked into the gun shop. I saw them in the gunsmith shop changing cartridges into their belts. They came out of the shop and walked along Fourth Street to the corner of Allen. I followed them as far as the corner of Fourth and Allen Streets, and then they went down Allen Street and over to Dunbar's Corral.[33]

Virg Earp was then City Marshal; Morgan Earp was a special policeman for six weeks or two months, wore a badge and drew pay. I had been sworn in Virgil's place, to act for him while Virgil

33 Owned by Dunbar and Behan.

was gone to Tucson to Spence's and Stilwell's trial. Virgil had been back several days but I was still acting. I knew it was Virgil's duty to disarm those men. I expected he would have trouble in doing so, and I followed up to give assistance if necessary, especially as they had been threatening us, as I have already stated.

About ten minutes afterwards, and while Virgil, Morgan, Doc Holliday and myself were standing on the corner of Fourth and Allen Streets, several person's said, "There is going to be trouble with those fellows," and one man named Coleman said to Virgil Earp, "They mean trouble. They have just gone from Dunbar's Corral into the O.K. Corral, all armed. I think you had better go and disarm them." Virgil turned around to Doc Holliday, Morgan Earp and myself and told us to come and assist him in disarming them.

Morgan Earp said to me, "They have horses, had we not better get some horses ourselves, so that if they make a running fight we can catch them?" I said, "No, if they try to make a running fight we can kill their horses and then capture them."

We four started through Fourth to Fremont Streets. When we turned the corner of Fourth and Fremont we could see them standing near or about the vacant space between Fly's Photograph Gallery[34] and the next building west. I first saw Frank McLaury, Tom McLaury, Billy Clanton and Sheriff Behan standing there. We went down the left-hand side of Fremont Street.

When we got within about 150 feet of them I saw Ike Clanton and Billy Claiborne and another party. We had walked a few steps from there when I saw Behan leave the party and come toward us. Every few steps he would look back as if he apprehended danger. I heard Behan say to Virgil "Earp, For God's sake, don't go down there, for you will get murdered!" Virgil Earp replied, "I am going to disarm them," he being in the lead. When I and Morgan came up to Behan he said, "I have disarmed them." When he said this, I took my pistol, which I had in my hand, under my coat, and put it in my overcoat pocket.[35] Behan then passed up the street, and we walked on down.

We came up on them close; Frank McLaury, Tom McLaury, and Billy Clanton standing all in a row against the east side of the building on the opposite side of the vacant space west of Fly's photograph gallery. Ike Clanton and Billy Claiborne and a man I did not know[36] was standing

34 Fly had built a photography studio behind his boarding house. They were actually in the lot between Fly's Lodging House and Harwood's house to the west. At the hearing, a distinction usually wasn't made between Fly's boarding house and his photography studio. Both were usually referred to as the photograph gallery.

It's interesting that more emphasis wasn't placed on this because the cowboys were waiting right outside Doc's window. Doc and Kate had taken a room in Fly's Lodging House, and it seems obvious the cowboys were waiting to ambush Doc. Ike had spent the morning looking all over town for the Earps with unpleasant and disappointing results, so he apparently turned his attention to Doc. It's likely he and his friends thought he could provoke Doc into fighting them even though they outnumbered him, or at least they would give him a rough time. They probably didn't expect to be confronted by Doc *and* the Earps. Kate and Mrs. Fly saw the beginning of the fight through the window the cowboys were facing, but Mrs. Fly ducked for cover when a bullet went through the window just above their heads.

35 Wyatt normally carried his gun in his coat pocket. He is trying to show here that he wasn't expecting a fight.

36 This may have been either Wes Fuller or Billy Allen. Or Wyatt may have said someone else was there to explain the shot he thought he heard coming from between Fly's two buildings.

in the vacant space about halfway between the photograph gallery and the next building west.[37]

"When they got to the corner of Fly's building, they had their six-shooters in their hands, and Marshal [Virgil] Earp said, 'You sons-of-bitches, you've been looking for a fight, and you can have it!' And then he said, 'Throw up your hands.'"

—Billy "the Kid" Claiborne, cowboy

I saw that Billy Clanton and Frank and Tom McLaury had their hands by their sides, Frank McLaury's and Billy Clanton's six-shooters were in plain sight.[38] Virgil said, "Throw up your hands, I have come to disarm you!" Then Billy Clanton and Tom McLaury [sic, Frank] commenced to draw their pistols. At the same time, Tom McLaury threw his hand to his right hip, throwing his coat open like this, (showing) and jumped behind a horse.

I had my pistol in my overcoat pocket, where I had put it when Behan told us he had disarmed the other parties. When I saw Billy Clanton and Frank McLaury draw their pistols, I drew my pistol. Billy Clanton leveled his pistol at me, but I did not aim at him. I knew that Frank McLaury had the reputation of being a good shot and a dangerous man, and I aimed at Frank McLaury. The first two shots were fired by Billy Clanton and myself, he shooting at me, and I shooting at Frank McLaury. I do not know which shot was fired first. We fired almost together. The fight then became general.[39]

After about four shots were fired, Ike Clanton ran up and grabbed my left arm. I could see no weapon in his hand, and thought at the time he had none, and so I said to him, "The fight had commenced. Go to fighting or get away," at the same time pushing him off with my left hand. He started and ran down the side of the building and disappeared between the lodging house and photograph gallery.[40]

My first shot struck Frank McLaury in the belly. He staggered off on the sidewalk but fired one shot at me. When we told them to throw up their hands Claiborne held up his left hand and then broke and ran. I never seen him afterwards until late in the afternoon.[41] I never drew my

---

37 Basically, what you have was a bunch of very upset cowboys looking for a showdown. They'd had little or no sleep, and a couple of them had been hit over the head with guns. The Clantons and McLaurys had just finished off a bottle of whiskey as Sheriff Behan approached them the first time.

38 The vacant lot was only 15 to 18 feet wide. When the fight began, the antagonists were standing only about five or six feet apart. They could almost have reached out and touched each other.

Virgil wanted to disarm or arrest the cowboys and wasn't expecting serious trouble. He was caught completely unprepared when the fighting started. Having given his shotgun to Doc, he was carrying Doc's cane in his shooting hand.

It seems the cowboys were also taken by surprise since Ike would have surely taken one of the two rifles that were on the horses to arm himself if he expected the fight.

39 The cowboys were trying to focus blame on Doc Holliday by claiming he fired the first shot. They claimed the almost simultaneous second shot was fired by Morgan.

40 Actually, Ike went to Fremont Street, through the lodging house, out the back and off toward Allen Street, which runs parallel to Fremont. The O.K. Corral is on Allen Street.

41 Sheriff Behan had followed the Earps into the vacant lot. When the shooting started, he grabbed Billy Claiborne, and they jumped into the narrow passageway between Fly's Lodging House and Fly's Photographic Gallery.

pistol or made a motion to shoot until after Billy Clanton and Frank McLaury drew their pistols. If Tom McLaury was unarmed, I did not know it, I believe he was armed and fired two shots at our party before Holliday, who had the shotgun, fired and killed him. If he was unarmed, there was nothing in the circumstances or in what had been communicated to me, or in his acts or threats, that would have led me even to suspect his being unarmed.[42]

I never fired at Ike Clanton, even after the shooting commenced, because I thought he was unarmed. I believed then, and believe now, from the acts I have stated and the threats I have related and the other threats communicated to me by different persons as having been made by Tom McLaury, Frank McLaury, and Ike Clanton, that these men last named had formed a conspiracy to murder my brothers, Morgan and Virgil, Doc Holliday and myself. I believe I would have been legally and morally justified in shooting any of them on sight, but I did not do so, nor attempt to do so. I sought no advantage when I went as deputy marshal to help disarm them and arrest them. I went as a part of my duty and under the directions of my brother, the marshal, I did not intend to fight unless it became necessary in self-defense and in the performance of official duty. When Billy Clanton and Frank McLaury drew their pistols, I knew it was a fight for life, and I drew in defense of my own life and the lives of my brothers and Doc Holliday.

Tom and Frank McLaury and Billy Clanton after the shootout. Their bodies were placed on display in a hardware store window.

Although this is what Wyatt said happened, his account might not be completely accurate because Behan and the cowboys were doing all kinds of lying—trying to railroad the Earps and Holliday to the gallows.

In another account of the shootout by Wyatt that was published in the *San Francisco Examiner* on August 2, 1896, he gave a few more details of the fight.

The four newcomers and Ike Clanton stationed themselves on a fifteen foot lot between two buildings in Fremont Street and sent us word if we did not come down and fight they would waylay and kill us. So we started down after them—Doc Holliday, Virgil, Morgan and I. As we came to the lot they moved back and got their backs against one of the buildings.

"I'm going to arrest you boys," said Virgil.

For answer their six-guns began to spit. Frank McLaury fired at me and Billy Clanton at Morgan. Both missed. I had a gun in my overcoat pocket

42 The cowboys claimed he was unarmed, but several witnesses saw him firing. Wyatt believed Wes Fuller picked up Tom's gun after the fight.

and I jerked it out at Frank McLaury, hitting him in the stomach. At the same time Morgan shot Billy Clanton in the breast. So far we had the best of it, but just then, Tom McLaury, who had got behind his horse fired under the animal's neck and bored a hole right through Morgan sideways. The bullet entered one shoulder and came out at the other.

"I got it, Wyatt," said Morgan.

"Then get behind me and keep quiet," I said—but he didn't.

By this time bullets were flying so fast I could not keep track of them. Frank McLaury had given a yell when I shot him and made for the street, one hand over his stomach. Ike Clanton and Billy Clayton [sic, Claiborne] were shooting fast[43] and so was Virgil, and the two latter made a break for the street. I fired a shot which hit Tom McLaury's horse and made it break away, and Doc Holliday took the opportunity to pump a charge of buckshot out of a Wells Fargo shotgun into Tom who promptly fell dead. In the excitement of the moment, Doc Holliday didn't know what he had done and flung away the shotgun in disgust, pulling his six-shooter instead.

Then I witnessed a strange spectacle. Frank McLaury and Billy Clanton were sitting in the middle of the street, both badly wounded, emptying their six-shooters like lightning. One of them shot Virgil through the leg and he shot Billy Clanton. Then Frank McLaury started to his feet and staggered across the street, though he was full of bullets. On the way he came face to face with Doc Holliday.

"I got ye now, Doc," he said.

"Well, you're a good one if you have," said Holliday with a laugh.

With that they both aimed. But before you can understand what happened next I must carry the narrative back half a minute.

After the first exchange in the lot Ike Clanton had gotten into one of the buildings from the rear and when I reached the street he was shooting out of one of the front windows. Seeing him aim at Morgan I shouted: "Look out, Morg, you're getting it in the back!"

Morgan wheeled around and in doing so fell on his side. While in that position he caught sight of Doc Holliday and Frank McLaury aiming at each other. With a quick drop he shot McLaury in the head. At the same instant McLaury's pistol flashed and Doc Holliday was shot in the hip.

That ended the fight. Ike Clanton and Billy [Claiborne] ran off and made haste to give themselves up to the sheriff, for the citizens were out a hundred strong to back us up.

There are many accounts of the gunfight by various witnesses, and they all disagree with one another. There are even conflicts between Wyatt's two accounts of what happened. But of all the accounts, Wyatt's seem to be the most accurate.

Here is a listing of who fired and at what as presented in Bob Boze Bell's *The Illustrated Life and Times of Doc Holliday* (2nd edition, 1995). Billy Clanton's six shots didn't hit anyone. Frank McLaury fired four shots—the first hit Virgil in the right calf, the second hit Wyatt's coat, the third was at Morgan but hit the ground, and the fourth glanced off Doc's holster taking a little skin off his hip. Assuming Tom McLaury had a pistol, he fired two or three times, hitting Morgan once. This bullet entered Morgan's back

[43] Actually, neither Ike nor Billy Claiborne fired any shots. Both had run away by this time. It was Billy Clanton and the McLaurys who were still shooting.

just below the left shoulder blade, passed through and exited about the same position below the right shoulder blade, taking off part of a vertebra on the way.

Wyatt probably let loose with five bullets. The first struck Frank McLaury in the belly. Ike grabbed him and a shot went into the ground. The third was at the withers of the horse Tom McLaury was hiding behind. The fourth was at Frank McLaury. And his final shot was toward the landing between Fly's Lodging House and Photographic Gallery. Wyatt thought he heard a shot from that direction and was returning fire, but what he probably heard was the back door of the lodging house slamming as Ike ran out.

Morgan probably fired five times—the first four at Billy Clanton. The first one hit Billy in the chest, and one other went through his right wrist. The fifth shot hit Frank McLaury in the head, just below the right ear. Virgil fired four times. The first missed Frank McLaury, and of the three fired at Billy Clanton, one hit his stomach. Doc fired a blast from the shotgun that hit Tom McLaury in the right side just below his armpit as the horse he was hiding behind ran away and he tried to hold onto it. Doc then pulled his pistol, firing two shots at Billy Clanton, both of which missed, and then one at Frank McLaury, though it's uncertain whether or not he hit him in the chest.

Exactly how accurate all this is remains uncertain, but it's probably the best listing so far. There is still a lot of controversy and conflicting evidence, and a detailed analysis of the shoot-out has yet to be published.

News of the gunfight flashed all across the country, prompting President Arthur to threaten to impose martial law if the citizens of Cochise County didn't put an end to all the lawlessness.

Predictably, the cowboy faction was upset by the shoot-out and claimed it was cold-blooded murder. Behan saw this as an opportunity to get rid of the Earps. Behan and the cowboy faction claimed the cowboys were trying to surrender when the Earps and Doc gunned them down. They said the Earps and Doc fired five shots before the cowboys began trying to fight back. The Earps and Doc were arrested, and the hearing was a result.

The hearing, which lasted thirty days, was held before Judge Wells Spicer, who ruled it was justifiable homicide, saying, "I . . . cannot resist the firm conviction that the Earps acted wisely, discreetly and prudentially to secure their own self-preservation—they saw at once the dire necessity of giving the first shot to save themselves from certain death . . . ; it was a necessary act done in the discharge of official duty."

The San Francisco Examiner *blamed the fight on Doc, saying, "Now comes Doc Holliday, as quarrelsome a man as God ever allowed to live on earth. . . . Doc Holliday is responsible for all the killings, etc., in connection with what is known as the Earp-Clanton imbroglio in Arizona. He kicked up the fight, and Wyatt Earp and his brothers 'stood in' with him, on the score of gratitude. Everyone in Tombstone conversant with the circumstances deprecates the killing of the McLowerys [sic] and Clanton. It's produced a feud that has driven the Earps from Arizona and virtually made outlaws of them."*

Of course, the cowboys were not pleased with this decision, and they decided to do away with the Earps themselves. Judge Spicer, the mayor, and a couple others were also marked for death. An attempt was made to assassinate the mayor, but he escaped. Then exactly eight weeks after the gunfight, Virgil was ambushed, and four shotgun blasts were fired at him. He was shot in the left arm and thigh and fortunately survived, but he lost the use of that arm. Morgan was not so lucky.

One night in March 1882, Morgan was shot in the back while he was bending over a pool table. The shots were fired through a window in the billiard hall's backdoor and one struck the far wall just above Wyatt's head. The other shattered Morgan's spine before lodging in a bystander. Morgan died. At the coroner's inquest, Pete Spence's wife Maria implicated the stagecoach robbers—Spence and Frank Stilwell—Florentine Cruz, Hank Swilling, and someone named Fries.[44] Though it wasn't revealed at the time, the real person behind the shootings of Virgil and Morgan was Texas lawyer William McLaury, Frank and Tom's brother. He hired these men to do it.

Three days after the murder, while escorting Morgan's casket on the train to California, Wyatt and Doc spotted Stilwell at the Tucson train station. Wyatt chased after him with a shotgun, catching up with him about twenty yards in front of the engine. Stilwell turned and grabbed the barrel of the shotgun. In the struggle, Wyatt blasted him. Apparently, Doc then emptied his pistol into him for good measure. At this point, Wyatt and Doc became vigilantes and set off to deal with the rest of the culprits on their own.

This was at 7 P.M., though the body wasn't found until the next morning. In the meantime, Wyatt, Doc, Warren Earp, Sherm McMasters, Texas Jack, and Turkey Creek Johnson—all heavily armed—headed back to Tombstone, where Wyatt began liquidating his assets.

Hearing of Stilwell's death, Sheriff Behan swore in many of the cowboys as deputies to hunt for Wyatt and Doc. This posse included Ike Clanton, Phin Clanton, and Johnny Ringo. By then, Wyatt's group was off hunting for Pete Spence. When they found Spence's camp, Spence wasn't there, but Florentine Cruz (a.k.a. Indian Charlie)[45] was, and they promptly filled him with lead.

"When any of you fellows have been hunted from one end of the country to the other, as I have been, you'll understand what a bad man's reputation is built on."

—Doc Holliday

Behan's posse gave up and turned back, but the following day, Wyatt and his men found Curly Bill at one of the cowboy camps. Wyatt promptly gave him both barrels from his shotgun, practically cutting Curly Bill in half. They then had a shoot-out with eight other cowboys who were nearby.[46]

Wyatt and Doc's vigilante spree lasted less than a week, and they headed off to Albuquerque, New

44 This was probably Fritz Bode.

45 Apparently Cruz was of Mexican and Native American descent.

46 Johnny Ringo was killed three and a half months later, when Doc and Wyatt were far away. He was found with a bullet in his head and one bullet fired from his gun. The official cause of death is listed as suicide, but this is unlikely since he was partially scalped. Some have suggested Frank Leslie was hired by Wells Fargo to kill Ringo. Others think rancher Henry Hooker had Lou Cooley do it. It's also possible William Downing did it because he believed Ringo stole a couple of his mules and was fooling around with his twenty-year-old daughter. Whatever happened, it's interesting that a month before he was killed, Ringo was living with Sheriff Behan.

Mexico, to be out of the range of Arizona law. In the end, while the gunfight and the vendetta made the Earps famous, it had a very negative effect on their lives. Virgil lost the use of his left arm and Morgan was killed. The Earps were also forced to quickly liquidate their assets in Tombstone, which included all or partial interest in about ten mines, plus eight lots in town that they owned. And it almost got them tried for murder.[47]

The Red Baron Describes Being Shot Down

Baron Manfred von Richthofen (1892–1918) was the top ace of World War I. At a time when airplanes were rickety and pilots very poorly trained—most having spent only a few hours in the air before they were sent into battle—a pilot had to shoot down five aircraft to become an ace. Rittmeister (Captain) Richthofen had a confirmed total of eighty in less than fifteen months. Between seventy-five and ninety-one Allied airmen were killed by him in dogfights and many more soldiers in bombing runs.

Richthofen is closely associated with his blood-red Fokker triplane, though he wasn't the only German to fly a red triplane. Actually, he did not begin using his triplane until August 1917, by which time he already had shot down sixty planes. Before that, he usually flew a red two-winged Albatros. His red planes earned him the nicknames "Red Baron," "Red Dragon," "Red Devil," and "Red Knight." He eventually became the commander of Germany's first fighter wing. The squadrons were called "flying circuses" because they were periodically moved around the front. Most planes were camouflaged, but Richthofen's flying circus was noted for its brightly colored planes.

Even though Richthofen was famous for his flying skill, he crashed on his first solo flight. A few months later, before his first kill, he crashed again. Both times he was uninjured, but the second time, his plane was totally destroyed. He almost crashed again when he followed his first kill to the ground. Later, describing this encounter, he wrote:

> I was so close to him that I was afraid I would ram into him. Then, suddenly, the opponent's propeller turned no more. Hit! The engine was shot up and the enemy had to land on our side, as it was out of the question for him to reach his own lines. I noticed the machine making swaying movements that [indicated] something was not quite right with the pilot. Also the observer was no longer to be seen, his machine-gun pointed unattended up in the air. Therefore, I had hit him and he was lying on the floor of the fuselage.

The plane went out of control, but the pilot revived long enough to safely land at a German airfield. The British observer was already dead, and the pilot died soon afterwards. Richthofen was so excited about his kill that he closely followed the British plane all the way down and almost wiped out his Albatros in a very rough landing.

[47] For those who love movies, *Tombstone* (1993), starring Kurt Russell and Val Kilmer, and *Wyatt Earp* (1994), starring Kevin Costner and Dennis Quaid, are both excellent films. Though they both contain many inaccuracies, *Tombstone* is the more accurate of the two. But both are definitely worth seeing.

American Captain J. H. Hedley was riding in a plane piloted by a Canadian named Makepeace on January 6, 1918, when at 15,000 feet, they came under German attack. Makepeace suddenly put the plane into a steep dive to evade their attackers, and Hedley flew right out of his seat into the open sky. When Makepeace finally pulled out of his dive, Hedley landed on the plane's tail. Apparently, he was caught in a suction created by the dive and was pulled along with the aircraft. Grabbing hold of the tail, he was eventually able to drag himself back into his seat.

Though Richthofen quickly became a master of the sky, he had other brushes with death that almost put an end to his career. Once he was even shot in the head. It occurred on July 6, 1917, between Ypres and Armentières in France just as he was about to attack an English two-seated F.E. airplane that had turned and was flying to attack him. The gunner in front was Second Lieutenant Albert Woodbridge, and the pilot seated behind him was Captain Douglas Cunnell. According to British reports, it was forty German aircraft against six British. Woodbridge later described the fight, saying:

> Two of them came at us head on, and I think the first one was Richthofen. I recall there wasn't a thing on that machine that wasn't red, and God, how he could fly! I opened fire with the front Lewis [machine gun], and so did Cunnell with the side gun. Cunnell held the F.E. to her course and so did the pilot of the all-red scout. Gad, with our combined speeds we must have been approaching each other at somewhere around 250 miles an hour.
>
> Thank God, my Lewis didn't jam. I kept a steady stream of lead pouring into the nose of that machine. He was firing also. I could see my tracers splashing along the barrels of his Spandaus and I knew the pilot was sitting right behind them. His lead came whistling past my head and ripping holes in the bathtub.
>
> Then something happened. We could hardly have been twenty yards apart when the Albatros pointed her nose down suddenly. Zip, and she passed under us. Cunnell banked and turned. We saw the all-red plane slip into a spin. It turned over and over and round and round. It was no manœuvre. He was completely out of control.

Suddenly, more Germans dove at them, and they were too busy to see if he crashed. They were credited with shooting down four other planes, but not this one. Captain Cunnell was killed six days later.

Now, here's Richthofen's dramatic account of the experience.

> Suddenly, something struck me in the head. For a moment, my whole body was paralyzed. My arms hung down limply beside me; my legs flopped loosely beyond my control. The worst was that a nerve leading to my eyes had been paralyzed and I was completely blind.
>
> I felt my machine tumbling down—falling. At the moment, the idea struck me, "This is how it feels when one is shot down to his death." Any moment, I waited for my wings to break off. I was alone in my bus. I didn't lose my senses for a moment.
>
> Soon I regained power over my arms and legs, and was able to grip the wheel. Mechanically, I cut off the motor, but what good did that do?

One can't fly without sight. I forced my eyes open—tore off my goggles—but even then I could not see the sun. I was completely blind. The seconds seemed like eternities. I noticed I was still falling.

From time to time, my machine had caught itself, but only to slip off again. At the beginning I had been at a height of 4,000 yards, and now I must have fallen at least two to three thousand yards. I concentrated all my energy and said to myself, "I must see—I must—I must see."

Whether my energy helped me in this case, I do not know. At any rate, suddenly I could discern black-and-white spots, and more and more I regained my eyesight. I looked into the sun—could stare straight into it without having the least pain. It seemed as though I was looking through thick black goggles.

The first thing I did was to look at the altimeter. I had no idea where I was. Again I caught the machine and brought it into normal position and continued gliding down. Nothing but shell holes were below me. A big block of forest came before my vision, and I recognized that I was within our lines.

If the Englishman had followed me, he could have brought me down without difficulty, but, thanks to God, my comrades protected me. At the beginning, they could not understand my fall.

First, I wanted to land immediately, for I didn't know how long I could maintain consciousness and my strength; therefore, I went down to fifty yards but could not find amongst the many shell holes a spot for a possible landing. Therefore, I again speeded up the motor and flew to the east at a low height. At this, the beginning, I got on splendidly, but, after a few seconds I noticed that my strength was leaving me and that everything was turning black before my eyes. Now it was high time.

I landed my machine without any particular difficulties, tore down a few telephone wires, which, of course, I didn't mind at the moment. I even had enough strength left in me to get up and to try to get out of the plane. I tumbled out of the machine and could not rise again—I was weak.

Some soldiers who had been watching the fight quickly rushed to his aid. Finding him lying in some thorns, they quickly bandaged his head, and an ambulance soon arrived. The bullet had glanced off his skull without penetrating it. He explained, "I had quite a good-sized hole—a wound of about ten centimetres in length. At one spot, as big as a dollar, the bare white skull bone lay exposed. My thick Richthofen skull had proved itself bullet proof." There were also several bone splinters in the wound. After suffering from a headache for several days, he fully recovered.

Actually, dogfights were not as dangerous as balloon busting. This was probably the most dangerous mission these early fighter pilots faced. Observation balloons—or as the Germans called them, "gas bags" and "flying sausages"—were used to see what the enemy was doing behind their lines. They were heavily protected by antiaircraft artillery, and sometimes scouts patrolled nearby. They were also very flammable. A balloon buster had to fly low and come up at the balloon from below, firing incendiary ammunition into it. Then he had to quickly turn to escape from the shock wave and heat as the gas bag burst into a ball of flame rising into the sky. The balloon's observer would parachute to the ground.

Richthofen never tried shooting down one of these tethered flying sausages, but he did go up in one to see what that was like, and he wrote about his experience.

> The day I flew it was absolutely calm. In a heavy wind it is very easy for one to become seasick. On command the balloon is released by many men and goes up into the air at a rather fast rate. One stands within a small basket beneath [the balloon] and takes in the whole area. I have always believed that one sees much more from inside the "eye of the army," as these airships are often called. I saw frightfully little. It is about the same as in an aeroplane when I climb to 1,000 metres. . . .
>
> The most interesting aspect of all about a captive balloon, of course, is when the thing is attacked and the crewman must jump out: the famous leap into the unknown. The decision is made relatively easily, as the Gasnulle [gas bag] above him slowly begins to burn and, if he decides not to jump out, he is surely doomed. Then the "unknown" is preferred to certain death. The situation is not at all so uncertain, however, as there is rarely an accident connected with it.

Although Richthofen didn't go balloon busting, some of his men did. The following account comes from observer Bernard Oliver, who was in one of these gas bags along with an unnamed officer he calls "Officer No. 3" when they came under attack. It happened in the summer of 1918.

"I decided to dive at her [a Zeppelin] . . . firing a burst straight into her as I came. I let her have another burst as I passed under her and then banked my machine over, sat under her tail and flying along underneath her pumped lead into her for all I was worth. . . . As I was firing, I noticed her to begin to go red inside like an enormous Chinese lantern. She shot up about 200 feet, paused, and came roaring down straight on to me before I had time to get out of the way. I nose-dived for all I was worth, with the Zeppelin tearing after me. . . . I put my machine into a spin and just managed to corkscrew out of the way as she shot past me, roaring like a furnace . . . then proceeded to fire off dozens of green Very lights in the exuberance of my feelings."

—Lieutenant W. J. Tempest, Royal Flying Corps, 1915

> Soon after reaching our observation height about 4,000/5,000 feet, we were informed on the telephone to look out for Richthofen's flying circus, who had attacked one of us. Very soon we noticed the fourth one north of us in flames, then the third one went down. It was a cloudy day so the planes could easily hide. All was quiet for a while, we settled down and got to work. Suddenly machine-gun bullets were flying all around in all directions. I saw one of the red-marked planes of Richthofen's, very close to us. Looking to my officer for orders to get out, I found myself alone! . . . Like a shot, I was over the side, closed my eyes and dropped into space. On my downward journey I opened my eyes and, behold, the pilot of the plane was flying very close to me waving his hand. I gladly waved back. I landed on the edge of a hop field.
>
> As I was heavier than Officer No. 3, I had passed him on the way down. He landed in a stream of dirty water and the wind in the chute carried him quite a way through it. Yes! I think I

may have smiled a little to see him! A motor car from the section soon picked us up and No. 3 Officer said, on arriving back at camp, "You heard me tell you to jump?" "Yes, Sir," I replied.

For years there was a great deal of controversy about how Richthofen met his end. Canadian pilot Captain A. Roy Brown believed he'd shot down the Red Baron, while several Australian gunners firing from the ground also claimed the credit. Conclusive evidence that he was actually downed by the gunners was finally presented by Dale M. Titler in his book, *The Day the Red Baron Died* (1970). Unfortunately, the controversy is much too complex to deal with here so I'll have to refer you to Titler's excellently researched book. Instead, I want to focus on Richthofen's final moments.

On April 21, 1918, Richthofen was chasing Second Lieutenant Wilfred May when he broke one of his own rules. In his *Air Combat Operations Manual*, he had written, "One should never obstinately stay with an opponent . . . when the battle lasts until it is . . . on the other side [behind enemy lines] and one alone is faced by a greater number of opponents." He persisted in chasing May and was in turn pursued by Captain Brown.

May later said, "Had I known it was Richthofen—I should have passed out on the spot!" He didn't know it was Richthofen, but he did know he was in trouble and was desperately trying to escape.

> I kept dodging and spinning down until I ran out of sky and had to hedge-hop along the ground. Richthofen was firing continually and the only thing that saved me was my poor flying! I didn't know what I was going to do and I don't suppose Richthofen could figure this out either. . . . I started up the Somme Valley at a very low altitude with Richthofen close on my tail. I went around a curve in the river just near the corbie, but Richthofen beat me to it by cutting over a hill and at that point I was a sitting duck, too low down between the banks to turn away. I felt he had me cold and I had to restrain myself from pushing the stick forward and disappearing into the river. I was sure this was the end. . . . Looking up I saw one of our machines directly behind.

After firing into Richthofen's plane, Brown saw Richthofen glance over his shoulder and veer slightly. Thinking he'd hit him, Brown banked away. A few seconds later, Richthofen, flying just above the ground right behind May, came into the sights of the Australian gunners. Richthofen turned in a semicircle and suddenly dove to the ground. From when Brown left Richthofen's tail, to the crash, was slightly more than sixty seconds.

There is still some uncertainty over which of the gunners actually hit him and how many times he was hit. Even the various official medical reports disagree on the details of his wounds though they all focus on a chest wound as the cause of death. Apparently, there were other wounds in the abdomen and knees.

The gunners who thought they hit him include Gunner William Evans, Gunner Robert Buie, Sergeant Cedric Popkin, and Sergeant-Major Alfred Franklyn. All were Australians except Franklyn, who was a British soldier temporarily attached to an Australian field battery. There's no way to know who actually delivered the fatal blow though evidence seems to point to Evans and Buie. Richthofen may have been hit by more than one gunner. As he flew through the barrage of Australian gunfire, it's interesting he didn't receive more wounds than he did.

One of the witnesses to his demise was Gunner R. L. Clifford Hunt, who said:

> I claim that, apart from Gunner Evans, I was the nearest to the ill-fated airman.
>
> Gunner Evans was 20 to 30 yards from my end gun and on slightly higher ground. I could see Evans clearly although my attention was directed mainly at the German airman. I saw Richthofen as clearly as I would see any man at 30 to 40 feet and at that moment the camouflage net [disguising their position] flapped violently. He banked sharply over the battery and I looked directly into the cockpit. I don't think the flapping net attracted his attention—it would have been too late then. He realized his danger when on top of the enemy post, banked, and completely exposed himself. It was then that Evans fired his fatal burst—at point-blank range.
>
> I did not notice Richthofen's actions when struck. His plane immediately regained an even keel and went into a shallow dive—until it crashed.

Nearby was another eyewitness—Sergeant Horrie Hart—who reported seeing the following:

Baron Manfred von Richthofen wearing his Pour le Mérite, which is also known as "the Blue Max."

> Across the valley of the Somme the planes approached the ridge that rises sharply and upon which our battery's guns were mounted. As they passed over the infantry lines in the distance, the German triplane fired on the plane in front and I heard a single machine gun fire from the ground. Both planes were only 150 feet above the ground and by this time the red plane had so gained upon the British pilot that it was only a matter of moments before the German pilot would be victorious. The watchers, and I was one, held their breaths as the two planes flew directly toward the two Lewis guns of Buie and Evans, which were mounted close to each other on high ground behind the battery of 18-pounders. I was standing with the others below the ridge at Bonnay, on lower ground and forward of the two machine guns, against a protective ridge under which the dugouts were built. Buie and Evans were less than 50 yards away.
>
> The planes were so close together that the gunners had to hold their fire until the British plane passed. Evans's gun, more at an angle, opened fire first. Buie held his fire momentarily because Evans appeared to be in his line of sight. The German plane was then so near that the body of the pilot was clearly visible. The plane bore frontally, practically into the muzzle of Buie's gun and after the first burst of fire the plane shook, splinters flew from it and it veered—drifted in an arc northward out of control—and gradually reached the ground. It crashed about 500 yards from the battery position.

Gunner Robert Buie gave this account of what happened.

> I can still remember seeing Richthofen clearly. His helmet covered most of his head and face and he was hunched in the cockpit aiming over his guns at the lead plane. It seemed that with every burst he leaned forward in the cockpit as though he were concentrating very intently on his firing. Certainly he was not aware of his dangerous position or the close range of our guns. His position was much as a strafing attack would appear, and had he not been so intent upon shooting down Lieutenant May, he could easily have maneuvered his machine and fired upon us, had he been so inclined. Richthofen and his men frequently strafed our trenches to the east.
>
> At 200 yards, with my peep sight directly on Richthofen's body, I began firing in steady bursts. His plane was bearing frontal and just a little to the right of me, and after 20 rounds I knew the bullets were striking the right side and front of the machine, for I clearly saw fragments flying.
>
> Still Richthofen came on, firing at Lieutenant May with both guns blazing. Then, just before my last shots finished at a range of 40 yards, Richthofen's guns stopped abruptly. The thought flashed through my mind—I've hit him!—and immediately I noticed a sharp change in engine sounds as the red triplane passed over our gun position at less than 50 feet and still a little to my right. It slackened speed considerably. The propeller slowed down and the engine sound disappeared, although the machine still appeared to be under control. Then it veered a bit to the right and then back to the left and lost height gradually, coming down near an abandoned brick kiln, 400 yards away on the Bray-Corbie Road.

The British gave Canadian pilot Captain Roy Brown credit for the kill and awarded him a medal, while the Australians gave Evans and Buie credit. The Australians buried Richthofen with full military honors.

The Red Baron was just eleven days short of his twenty-sixth birthday when he was shot from the sky.

The Sacking of the White House

Dolly Madison is not a cupcake. Well . . . Dolly Madison is a brand of cupcakes, but one that is named after the wife of President James Madison. But then, I'm sure you already knew that. Although people generally think of her as one of the most popular first ladies, few realize she and President Madison barely escaped becoming prisoners of war when the British invaded Washington, D.C. Having missed capturing the president and his wife, the British proceeded to sack the White House and set the Capitol on fire. All this, of course, happened during the War of 1812.

This turbulent period and their escape from the White House were described by Dorthea "Dolly"[48] Madison herself in letters to her friends. I find it particularly interesting because I've heard several intelligent people make the comment that the United States has never been

[48] Sometimes her nickname is spelled "Dolley."

invaded by a foreign power. Obviously, they were unaware of this invasion.

During World War II, California, Oregon, and Washington were all attacked by the Japanese. On February 23, 1942, the Bankline Oil Refinery at Glorieta in Southern California was hit by thirteen shells fired from a Japanese submarine, causing damage to one oil well. Then on June 21, the harbor defenses of the Columbia River in Washington State were shelled by a Japanese submarine. The next day, the military depot at Fort Stevens, Oregon, was shelled. On September 9, a Japanese warplane launched from a submarine dropped a total of four incendiary bombs on Mt. Emily and near Brookings in Oregon. It was a successful attempt to start forest fires, but the fires caused little damage. Twenty days later, the plane again bombed Mt. Emily, while the sub sank two tankers off the coast. In early 1944, a German reconnaissance aircraft flew over New York City taking photos of possible bombing targets. After British code breakers revealed this to the United States, waves of bombers were sent to destroy the German aircraft plants where they were building long-range bombers. The Japanese air attack on San Francisco—which was used as an excuse to confine Americans of Japanese ancestry in internment camps—never actually happened.

Most historians now agree that the war actually began because the United States wanted to expand into Canada to the north, Native American land to the west, and the Floridas to the south. It's all really complicated, but I'll try to simplify it the best I can. We don't need an in-depth analysis here.

At that time, Canada belonged to Britain and the Floridas to Spain. In order to invade Canada, the United States needed to start a war with Britain. When war was declared, three reasons were given.

First, the United States blamed Britain for interfering with American shipping. While Britain was fighting Napoleon, the United States took advantage of its neutrality to increase its shipping. In fact, American shipping quadrupled in about a dozen years, until Britain and France declared blockades against each other. Although these weren't directed at the United States, they did have a serious effect on American shipping. The United States tried all sorts of things to get Britain to end its blockade of France. The British finally did—two days before the United States declared war on Britain. The U.S. government didn't hear about this major concession until after the war began. Even if they had, they probably would have gone ahead with the war anyway. After they did hear about it, they rejected British attempts to stop the hostilities.

The second reason America said it declared war was that it objected to Britain's impressment of American sailors into the British Navy. Because many British deserters found work on American ships, Britain insisted they had the right to take them back. Some of these deserters had phony papers saying they were American, and inevitably, some real Americans were taken by mistake.

The final reason (and here's the Canada/Native American connection) was that America claimed Britain was inciting Native Americans into making sporadic attacks along the frontier. In 1807, a Shawnee chief named Tecumseh tried to put together a Native American confederation to protect themselves from a U.S. invasion and prevent the United States from taking away any more of their land. British agents in Canada were sympathetic because of their lucrative fur trading with the Native Americans. Because of the sporadic Native American attacks, in 1811, future-president General William Henry Harrison invaded Native American territory to intimidate them. Instead, Harrison's men received a thrashing at Tippecanoe Creek. Back in the United States, people were calling for vengeance. Since some British arms were found on Native Americans killed in the battle, the United States decided to blame Britain.

The United States was also looking for excuses to take the Floridas from Spain. As the *Encyclopedia Americana* put it:

> War with England also promised benefits to the South, which eyed greedily Spain's possessions in East and West Florida. A portion of the latter, to which the United States laid dubious claim as included in Louisiana, had already been occupied without Spain's consent. In the spring of 1812 an agent of the United States stirred up a revolt against Spanish authority in East Florida and led United States troops into the province at the invitation of the insurgents. His too transparent operations were disavowed in Washington, but Southerners expected that a declaration of war against Great Britain, with which Spain was now allied, would be the signal for the seizure of the remainder of the Floridas.

Thus began the War of 1812.

After Napoleon was defeated in Europe in 1814, releasing thousands of British troops to fight in America, the United States was suddenly forced to forget about taking Canada and begin to worry about defending the United States from invasion. It was on August 24, 1814, that the British invaded Washington, D.C., and sacked the White House. President James Madison and First Lady Dolly Madison barely escaped. President Madison took over direct command of the armed forces. This was the only instance of a president facing gunfire in battle and actively assuming his role as commander in chief of the armed forces.

Many New Englanders were so against the War of 1812 that they seriously considered seceding from the Union.

Dolly Madison's account of what happened comes from *Memoirs and Letters of Dolly Madison* (1886). This first excerpt is from her letter to President Madison's former private secretary, Edward Coles, and is dated May 12, 1813. It shows how many people feared an attack more than a year before it actually happened.

> And now if I could I would describe to you the fears and alarms that circulate around me. For the last week all the city and Georgetown (except the Cabinet) have expected a visit from the enemy, and were not lacking in their expressions of terror and reproach. Yesterday an express announced the pause of a frigate at the mouth of the Potomac. The commander sent his boats to examine a Swedish ship that lay near, but our informer was too frightened to wait for further news. We are making considerable efforts for defense. The fort is being repaired, and five hundred militia, with perhaps as many regulars, are to be stationed on the Green, near the Windmill, or rather Major Taylor's. The twenty tents already look well in my eyes, who

have always been an advocate for fighting when assailed, though a Quaker. I therefore keep the old Tunisian sabre within reach. One of our generals has discovered a plan of the British,—it is to land as many chosen rogues as they can about fourteen miles below Alexandria, in the night, so that they may be on hand to burn the President's house and offices. I do not tremble at this, but feel hurt that the admiral (of Havre de Grace memory) should send me word that he would make his bow at my drawing room very soon.

When the attack finally did come, the first lady waited until the last minute to abandon the White House. In a letter written to her sister that she started the day before, she talks about what was happening just before she had to flee in face of the enemy.

To Anna.

Tuesday, August 23, 1814

Dear Sister,—My husband left me yesterday morning to join General Winder. He inquired anxiously whether I had courage or firmness to remain in the President's house until his return on the morrow, or succeeding day, and on my assurance that I had no fear but for him, and the success of our army, he left, beseeching me to take care of myself, and of the Cabinet papers, public and private. I have since received two despatches [sic] from him, written with a pencil. The last is alarming, because he desires I should be ready at a moment's warning to enter my carriage, and leave the city; that the enemy seemed stronger than had at first been reported, and it might happen that they would reach the city with the intention of destroying it. I am accordingly ready; I have pressed as many Cabinet papers into trunks as to fill one carriage; our private property must be sacrificed, as it is impossible to procure wagons for its transportation. I am determined not to go myself until I see Mr. Madison safe, so that he can accompany me, as I hear of much hostility towards him. Disaffection stalks around us. My friends and acquaintances are all gone, even Colonel C. with his hundred, who were stationed as a guard in this inclosure [sic]. French John (a faithful servant), with his usual activity and resolution, offers to spike the cannon at the gate, and lay a train of powder, which would blow up the British, should they enter the house. To the last proposition I positively object, without being able to make him understand why all advantages in war may not be taken.

Wednesday Morning, twelve o'clock.

Since sunrise I have been turning my spy-glass in every direction, and watching with unwearied anxiety, hoping to discover the approach of my dear husband and his friends; but, alas! I can descry only groups of military, wandering in all directions, as if there was a lack of arms, or of spirit to fight for their own fireside.

Three o'clock.—Will you believe it, my sister? we have had a battle, or skirmish, near Bladensburg, and here I am still, within sound of the cannon! Mr. Madison comes not. May God protect us! Two messengers, covered with dust, come to bid me fly; but here I mean to wait for him. . . . At this late hour a wagon has been procured, and I have had it filled with plate and the most valuable portable articles, belonging to the house. Whether it will reach its destination, the "Bank of Maryland," or fall into the hands of British soldiery, events must determine. Our kind friend, Mr. Carroll, has come to hasten my departure, and in a very bad humor with me, because I insist on waiting until the large picture of General Washington is secured, and it requires to be unscrewed from the wall. This process was found too tedious for these perilous moments; I have ordered the frame to be broken, and the canvas taken out. It is done! and the precious portrait placed in the hands of two gentlemen of New York, for safe keeping. And now, dear sister, I must leave this house, or the retreating army will make me a prisoner in it by filling up the road I am directed to take. When I shall again write to you, or where I shall be tomorrow, I cannot tell!

DOLLY

Memoirs and Letters of Dolly Madison was edited by Dolly Madison's grand-niece, who chose to remain anonymous. The rest of the story is best told by her, as she undoubtedly heard it from Dolly herself.

"At what point shall we expect the approach of danger? By what means shall we fortify against it? Shall we expect some transatlantic military giant, to step the Ocean, and crush us at a blow? Never! All the armies of Europe, Asia and Africa combined, with all the treasure of the earth . . . could not by force, take a drink from the Ohio, or make a track on the Blue Ridge, in a trial of a thousand years."

—Abraham Lincoln, 1838

Hoping and fearing, Mrs. Madison lingered on at the President's house for Mr. Madison's return, until the British officers were actually at the threshold, and the moment could be no longer delayed. She had secured the public papers and the Declaration of Independence, and was being hurried out to the waiting carriage by Mr. De Peyster and Mr. Barker, when her eye was attracted by the valuable portrait of General Washington hanging on the wall, this being one of the few adornments of the White House at that time, and an excellent likeness of the adored first President. She felt she could not leave it, and at the risk of capture herself, resolved to save it, if possible. After much valuable time spent in trying to unfasten the great frame from the wall, the servants were obliged to break the outside edge with an axe, keeping the entire canvas, however, quite uninjured. . . . "I lived a lifetime in those last moments," she tells a friend afterwards, "waiting for Madison's return, and in an agony of fear lest he might have been taken prisoner! Anna, too, was away, I hardly knew where." . . .

John Sioussa, the French porter, was the last to leave the house, and after seeing Mrs. Madison safely off, he took a macaw, which had been much petted by her, to the house of a friend, Colonel Taylor; then locking the house carefully, he deposited the key with the Russian Minister, Mr. Dashoff, whose house was protected by his country's flag, and went to Philadelphia. All the afternoon, parties of straggling soldiers, on their way to Georgetown, with vagrant negroes pilfered in many directions, in spite of the efforts of faithful servants. Mad with disappointment at the escape of the President and his wife, "whom they wanted to capture and show in England," the enemy broke open the doors of the White House, and ransacked it from cellar to attic, finding nothing of value, in the way of trophies, except a small bundle of pencil notes received by Mrs. Madison from her husband when he was with the troops, and which she had inadvertently rolled together, and left in her table drawer. To everything else in the house, furniture, wines, provisions, and family stores of all kinds, which had cost Mr. Madison twelve thousand dollars, together with an excellent library, the torch was applied. Fire for the purpose was procured at a small beer-house opposite the Treasury, and common soldiers, together with negroes, and thieves of all grades, did what they could to pillage and destroy. The White House was not so large and complete as it is now. The east room, which had served Mrs. Adams for a drying-room, was bare and unfurnished; the whole house was plain, unfinished, and totally destitute of ornament; the front vestibule had not then been added, and the grounds were uninclosed [sic], and entirely uncultivated.

Nothing but the lateness of the hour and the threatening storm prevented the troops from firing the War Department. The promised reinforcement had failed to come, filling the minds of the officers with vague and timorous apprehension, and they resolved to evacuate the next day. Constant rumors and frights had unnerved the stoutest hearts, and the unhappy citizens of Washington flying from a foreign foe rendered the situation of those who could not leave even more distressing. All the vehicles had been pressed into the service, and valuables scattered in every direction for safety.

An English narrator states that "the most tremendous hurricane ever remembered by the inhabitants broke over Washington the day after the conflagration. Roofs of houses were torn off and carried up into the air like sheets of paper, while the rain which accompanied it was like the rushing of a mighty cataract rather than the dropping of a shower. This lasted for two hours without intermission, during which time many of the houses spared by us were blown down, and thirty of our men, with as many more of the inhabitants, were buried beneath the ruins. Two cannons standing upon a bit of rising ground were fairly lifted in the air and carried several yards to the rear."

Long before day Mrs. Madison and her sleepless companions bade farewell to their hospitable friend and started forth to the place appointed by Mr. Madison for a meeting. Consternation and despair were at their height; the whole region filled with frightened people and straggling soldiers, roaming about and spreading alarms that the enemy was coming now this way, now that, making no place safe. As the day wore on the storm burst upon the forlorn refugees, as they traveled slowly, and with great difficulty, through roundabout lanes and roads to the little tavern in the middle of an apple orchard, sixteen miles from Washington, where Mr. Madison had promised to join them. Here the drenched, tired travelers were very inhospitably received; the house was crowded with refugees, who, frightened and miserable, worked themselves up into a feeling of anger and reproach against Mr. Madison and herself, declaring them to be the cause of their present troubles, and refusing them entrance. With evening came another furious thunder-storm, and common humanity made them open the doors to the poor shivering women, who were afraid to leave the neighborhood for fear of missing their friends. . . . Nervous and intensely anxious, Mrs. Madison waited on in breathless impatience for the promised relief, too unhappy to feel the discomforts around her; until late in the night her fears were relieved by the approach of Mr. Madison with the friends who had accompanied him the night before. He looked careworn and weary, and after a somewhat scant meal of such food as had been left in the overcrowded tavern, he yielded to his wife's entreaties and sought forgetfulness in sleep.

During that time General Ross hastily evacuated the town; victors and vanquished alike victims of imaginary perils: the one superstitiously fearful of the violent, almost tropical, storms to which they were unused, and credulous of vague reports of reinforcements on the other side; while the American troops were still too scattered and frightened to distinguish the false from the true in the rumors of murder and rapine that were flying in all directions.

Toward midnight a courier, breathless from fatigue and excitement, warned the President that the enemy had discovered a clue to his hiding-place, and were even now on their way hither. Yielding to the entreaties of his wife and friends he sought refuge in a miserable little hovel in the woods, where the boughs moaned and sobbed around him, and the storm expended itself in dismal sighs through the tall trees; here he spent the remainder of the night, expecting at any moment to hear the tread of the British soldiers as they passed, or perhaps halted and searched for the coveted prisoner.

Mrs. Madison had promised to disguise herself and seek safety further on; so attended only by Mr. Duvall and one soldier she started out at the first dawn of day, leaving her carriage to her companions and taking a small wagon. Before they had gone very far, however, the news reached them that Washington was evacuated, and joyfully retracing their steps, after a weary ride they reached the Long Bridge, only to find it burned at both ends. Forgetting her disguises she appealed to an officer standing by to take her across the river in the one remaining boat, but was curtly refused, not daring, as she said, "to let an unknown woman into the city." No alternative was left but to explain who she was, and after some doubt and demur on his part the frail little craft landed them safely on the other side. There she found her former home in ruins, and the smoke still rising from the heaps of blackened timber that greeted her on every side; the streets were as deserted and quiet as the forests through which she had just passed, and sick at heart she turned away, and in a strange carriage drove to the house of her sister, Mrs. Cutts, to await the return of Mr. Madison.

After the British captured Washington, D.C., British Admiral Cockburn assembled his officers and men in the House of Representatives. Taking the Speaker's seat, he said, "Gentlemen, the question is: Shall this harbor of Yankee Democracy be burned? All in favor of burning it will say aye!" The soldiers yelled a unanimous "Aye!" and he said, "Light up!"

"The memory of the burning of Washington cannot be obliterated. It can never be thought of by an American, and ought not to be thought of by an enlightened Englishman, except with deplorable shame and mortification. History cannot record it as a trophy of war for a great nation. The metropolis at that time had the aspect of a straggling village, interspersed here and there by a handsome public building, and with a scattered population of not more than eight thousand inhabitants; fortresses there were none, and but a few mounted cannon."[49]

Late in the day, the news reached the President in his hovel that the enemy had retreated to their shipping; and he, too, turned his steps toward the city and rejoined his wife. . . .

Many houses were offered to the President on his return to Washington, and for a year he rented a building called the Octagon, owned by Colonel Taylor, and there it was that the treaty of peace was signed. Afterwards he removed to the northwest corner of Pennsylvania Avenue and Nineteenth Street, to a large house, which had previously been occupied by the Treasury Department.

The White House was repaired only in time for Mr. Monroe.

Earlier in the war, when the United States invaded Canada and captured York (now Toronto), the U.S. forces had set the Parliament Building of Upper Canada on fire. It was in retaliation for this that the British put the U.S. Capitol Building and the White House to the torch.

When the war ended, the United States and Britain both agreed to give up all the territory gained during the war and the borders returned to where they were at the start. None of the various reasons the United States had listed as causing the war were discussed. These issues just resolved themselves on their own over the following few years. Since Britain was no longer at war, they no longer needed blockades or impressments. The United States had occupied part of Florida during the war and was able to buy the rest from Spain soon afterwards.

Also during the war, the British made Chief Tecumseh a brigadier general in their army, and he was largely responsible for many of their early successes. It's said he was repeatedly shot as he continued to lead his men in battle. A group of Kentuckians later skinned the body they thought was Tecumseh's, but the actual body was never found. In the end, the war destroyed the power of the Native Americans to the Northwest and the South.

Jack London Witnesses the 1906 San Francisco Earthquake

Jack London (1876–1916) was the author of the classics *The Call of the Wild* and *White Fang*. He was born in San Francisco, the illegitimate son of a traveling astrologer. As a child, poverty forced him to work ten-hour days in a canning factory for ten cents an hour. At the age of fourteen he borrowed money to buy a small boat and began joining in raids on privately owned oyster fields. His education came primarily from books. At the age of nineteen he began high school, and the following year he attended a semester at the University of California. In 1897, he left for the Klondike to take part in the gold rush there. On returning to San Francisco, he tried to make a living at writing, but with little luck until his adventure stories set in the Yukon began to be published. These were a tremendous success. An active socialist with Marxist leanings, he claimed he wrote only for money, saying, "if I

[49] This may be a quotation, taken from one of Dolly Madison's letters.

could have my choice about it, I never would put pen to paper—except to write a socialist essay to tell the bourgeois world how much I despise it." But this didn't slow him down, for he wrote close to fifty books in seventeen years. After enduring a divorce, continuing financial difficulties, failing health and his heavy drinking, he finally committed suicide with an overdose of morphine.

On April 18, 1906, the earthquake hit at 5:13 A.M. It overturned stoves and oil lamps starting numerous fires and causing gas mains to explode. The water mains were also damaged, so the firemen had little water with which to combat the flames. The fires raged for four days, destroying more than 28,000 buildings—the majority of what was then America's ninth largest city. The disaster claimed 700 lives, and 225,000 people were suddenly homeless. The damage amounted to $500 million. If this same quake happened today, the damage would be about $135 billion.

In comparison, the 1989 San Francisco earthquake killed seventy people and caused $6 billion in damage, while the two quakes that hit Los Angeles's San Fernando Valley in 1994 killed sixty-one and cost $20 billion. The 1906 quake is still considered to be the worst disaster to hit a North American city—at least, so far. And of all natural disasters, only 1992's Hurricane Andrew cost more at about $30 billion.

But as far as earthquakes go, it could be considered a minor one compared to the 1201 earthquake in Upper Egypt or Syria that killed a million people. Even the 1995 earthquake in Kobe, Japan, killed more than 5,500 people and cost over $100 billion. In fact, there have been at least seventy-nine earthquakes dating back to A.D. 365 that have killed more people than the 1906 San Francisco quake. Although many of these were not as powerful, there have been stronger ones that have caused fewer fatalities.

In California, two continental plates are moving past each other at the rate of around two inches a year. In 1906, this built-up pressure was released, causing the ground to jump as much as twenty-one feet in just a few seconds.

Jack London was at his farm in Glen Ellen when the quake hit and knocked down his barn. He quickly set off for the city to see the devastation. His account of what he saw appeared two and a half weeks later in the May 5 issue of *Collier's Weekly.*

San Francisco is gone! Nothing remains of it but memories and a fringe of dwelling houses on the outskirts. Its industrial section is wiped out. Its social and residential section is wiped out. The hotels and the palaces of the nabobs, are all gone. Remains only the fringe of dwelling houses on the outskirts of what was once San Francisco.

Within an hour after the earthquake shock the smoke of San Francisco's burning was a lurid tower visible a hundred miles away. And for three days and nights this lurid tower swayed in the sky, reddening the sun, darkening the sky, and filling the land with smoke.

On Wednesday morning at a quarter past five came the earthquake. A minute later the flames were leaping upward. In a dozen different quarters south of Market Street, in the working-class ghetto, and in the factories, fires started. There was no opposing the flames. There was no organization, no communication. All the cunning adjustments of a twentieth-century city had been smashed by the earthquake. The streets were humped into ridges and depressions and piled with debris of fallen walls. The steel rails were twisted into perpendicular and horizontal angles. The telephone and telegraph systems were disrupted. And the great water mains had burst. All the shrewd contrivances and safeguards of man had been thrown out of gear by thirty seconds' twitching of the earth crust.

By Wednesday afternoon, inside of twelve hours, half the heart of the city was gone. At that time I watched the vast conflagration from out on the bay. It was dead calm. Not a flicker of wind stirred. Yet from every side wind was pouring in upon the city. East, west, north, and south, strong winds were blowing upon the doomed city. The heated air rising made an enormous suck. Thus did the fire of itself build its own colossal chimney through the atmosphere. Day and night this dead calm continued, and yet, near to the flames, the wind was often half a gale, so mighty was the suck.

The edict which prevented chaos was the following proclamation by Mayor E. E. Schmitz:

The Federal Troops, the members of the Regular Police Force, and all Special Police Officers have been authorized to KILL any and all persons found engaged in looting or in the commission of any other crime.

I have directed all the Gas and Electric Lighting Companies not to turn on gas or electricity until I order them to do so; you may therefore expect the city to remain in darkness for an indefinite time.

"I request all citizens to remain at home from darkness until daylight of every night until order is restored.

I warn all citizens of the danger of fire from damaged or destroyed chimneys, broken or leaking gas pipes or fixtures, or any like cause."

Wednesday night saw the destruction of the very heart of the city. Dynamite was lavishly used, and many of San Francisco's proudest structures were crumbled by man himself into ruins, but there was no withstanding the onrush of the flames. Time and again successful stands were made by the fire fighters, and every time the flames flanked around on either side, or came up from the rear, and turned to defeat the hard-won victory. . . .

At nine o'clock Wednesday evening I walked down through miles and miles of magnificent buildings and towering skyscrapers. Here was no fire. All was in perfect order. The police patrolled the streets. Every building had its watchman at the door. And yet it was doomed, all of it. There was no water. The dynamite was giving out. And at right-angles two different conflagrations were sweeping down upon it.

At one o'clock in the morning I walked down through the same section. Everything still stood intact. There was no fire. And yet there was a change. A rain of ashes was falling. The watchmen at the doors were gone. The police had been withdrawn. There were no firemen, no fire engines, no

San Francisco after the 1906 earthquake and fire.

men fighting with dynamite. The district had been absolutely abandoned. I stood at the corner of Kearny and Market, in the very innermost heart of San Francisco. Kearny Street was deserted. Half-a-dozen blocks away it was burning on both sides. The street was a wall of flame. And against this wall of flame, silhouetted sharply, were two United States cavalrymen sitting on their horses, calmly watching. That was all. Not another person was in sight. In the intact heart of the city two troopers sat on their horses and watched.

Surrender was complete. There was no water. The sewers had long since been pumped dry. There was no dynamite. Another fire had broken out further uptown, and now from three sides conflagrations were sweeping down. The fourth side had been burned earlier in the day. In that direction stood the tottering walls of the Examiner Building, the burned-out Call Building, the smoldering ruins of the Grand Hotel, and the gutted, devastated, dynamited Palace Hotel.

The following will illustrate the sweep of the flames and the inability of men to calculate their spread. At eight o'clock Wednesday evening I passed through Union Square. It was packed with refugees. Thousands of them had gone to bed on the grass. Government tents had been set up, supper was being cooked, and the refugees were lining up for free meals.

At half-past one in the morning three sides of Union Square were in flames. The fourth side, where stood the great St. Francis Hotel was still holding out. An hour later, ignited from top and sides, the St. Francis was flaming heavenward. Union Square, heaped high with mountains of trunks, was deserted. Troops, refugees, and all had retreated.

It was at Union Square that I saw a man offering a thousand dollars for a team of horses. He was in charge of a truck piled high with trunks from some hotel. It had been hauled here into what was considered safety, and the horses had been taken out. The flames were on three sides of the square, and there were no horses.

Also, at this time, standing beside the truck, I urged a man to seek safety in flight. He was all but hemmed in by several conflagrations. He was an old man and he was on crutches. Said he: "Today is my birthday. Last night I was worth thirty thousand dollars. I bought five bottles of wine, some delicate fish, and other things for my birthday dinner. I have had no dinner, and all I own are these crutches."

I convinced him of his danger and started him limping on his way. An hour later, from a distance, I saw the truckload of trunks burning merrily in the middle of the street.

On Thursday morning, at a quarter past five, just twenty-four hours after the earthquake, I sat on the steps of a small residence of Nob Hill. With me sat Japanese, Italians, Chinese, and Negroes—a bit of the cosmopolitan flotsam of the wreck of the city. All about were the palaces of the pioneers of Forty-nine. To the east and south, at right-angles, were advancing two mighty walls of flame.

"Those who survived the San Francisco earthquake said, 'Thank God, I'm still alive.' But, of course, those who died, their lives will never be the same again."

—Representative Barbara Boxer, after the 1994 earthquake

I went inside with the owner of the house on the steps of which I sat. He was cool and cheerful and hospitable. "Yesterday morning," he said, "I was worth six hundred thousand dollars. This morning this house is all I have left. It will go in fifteen minutes." He pointed to a large cabinet. "That is my wife's collection of china. This rug upon which we stand is a present. It cost fifteen hundred dollars. Try that piano. Listen to its tone. There are few like it. There are no horses. The flames will be here in fifteen minutes."

Outside, the old Mark Hopkins residence, a palace, was just catching fire. The troops were falling back and driving refugees before them. From every side came the roaring of flames, the crashing of walls, and the detonations of dynamite.

I passed out of the house. Day was trying to dawn through the smoke pall. A sickly light was creeping over the face of things. Once only the sun broke through the smoke pall, blood-red, and showing a quarter its usual size. The smoke pall itself, viewed from beneath, was a rose color that pulsed and fluttered with lavender shades. Then it turned to mauve and yellow and dun. There was no sun. And so dawned the second day on stricken San Francisco.

Using large amounts of dynamite, the flames were finally subdued three days later. This was the seventh time San Francisco was swept by fire. The other six times were all between 1849 and 1851. The city quickly rebuilt itself and was almost back to normal within a year.

Mark Twain in Another San Francisco Earthquake

Jack London wasn't the only famous author to witness and write about San Francisco's instability. Half a century earlier, in 1863, Mark Twain was in San Francisco during one of the "big ones." He described the experience in *Roughing It* (1872).

A month afterward I enjoyed my first earthquake. It was one which was long called the "great" earthquake, and is doubtless so distinguished till this day. It was just after noon, on a bright October day. I was coming down Third Street. The only objects in motion anywhere in sight in that thickly built and populous quarter were a man in a buggy behind me, and a streetcar wending slowly up the cross street. Otherwise, all was solitude and a Sabbath stillness. As I turned the corner, around a frame house, there was a great rattle and jar, and it occurred to me that here was an item!—no doubt a fight in that house. Before I could turn and seek the door, there came a really terrific shock; the ground seemed to roll under me in waves, interrupted by a violent joggling up and down, and there was a heavy grinding noise as of brick houses rubbing together. I fell up against the frame house and hurt my elbow. I knew what it was, now, and from mere reportorial instinct, nothing else, took out my watch and noted the time of day; at that moment a third and still severer shock came, and as I reeled about on the pavement trying to keep my footing, I saw a sight! The entire front of a tall four-story brick building in Third Street sprung outward like a door and fell sprawling across the street, raising a dust like a great volume of smoke! And here came the buggy—overboard went the man, and in less time than I can tell it the vehicle was distributed in small fragments along three hundred yards of street. One could have fancied that somebody had fired a charge of chair rounds and rags down the thoroughfare. The streetcar had stopped, the horses were rearing and plunging, the passengers were pouring out at both ends, and one fat man had crashed halfway through a glass window on one side of the car, got wedged fast, and was squirming and screaming like an impaled madman. Every door, of every house, as far as the eye could reach, was vomiting a stream of human beings; and almost before one could execute a wink and begin another, there was a massed multitude of people stretching in endless procession down every street my position commanded. Never was solemn solitude turned into teeming life quicker.

Of the wonders wrought by "the great earthquake," these were all that came under my eye; but the tricks it did, elsewhere, and far and wide over the town, made toothsome gossip for nine days. The destruction of property was trifling—the injury to it was widespread and somewhat serious. . . .

One woman who had been washing a naked child ran down the street holding it by the ankles as if it were a dressed turkey. . . .

The plastering that fell from ceilings in San Francisco that day would have covered several acres of ground. For some days afterward, groups of eyeing and pointing men stood about many a building, looking at long zigzag cracks that extended from the eaves to the ground. Four feet of the tops of three chimneys on one house were broken square off and turned around in such a way as to completely stop the draft. A crack a hundred feet long gaped open six inches wide in the middle of one street and then shut together again with such force as to ridge up the meeting earth like a slender grave.

Charles Dickens Witnesses a Death by Guillotine

One of the more memorable symbols of the French Revolution and the Reign of Terror that followed is the guillotine. This instrument of execution is named for a member of the Revolutionary assembly, Dr. Joseph Guillotin, who in 1789, lobbied the French government for the adoption of a humanitarian form of capital punishment. However, he did not invent the contraption that came to bear his name, nor even design it. Earlier versions had been occasionally used in Scotland, England, Germany, Italy, and Southern France from the thirteenth century through the mid-seventeenth century. It's said that even farther back in time the Ancient Persians also had a beheading machine and one German woodcut from 1593 even depicts St. Matthew—Christ's apostle and the author of one of the gospels—being executed by an early guillotine. The well-known French version was actually developed by Dr. Antoine Louis at the behest of the Legislative Assembly, who ordered him to come up with an apparatus that would meet Dr. Guillotin's criteria. The result was initially called the *louisette* and *la petite louison*, but *guillotine* eventually won out.

Prior to the advent of the guillotine, decapitation was a privilege reserved for the aristocracy. At Guillotin's encouragement, this relatively painless method of execution was adopted for all criminals as something of a democratic killing device. It was adopted in 1792—just in time for the Reign of Terror during which 35,000 to 40,000 people lost their lives, including Queen Marie Antoinette. The architect and mastermind behind the Terror, was Robespierre, who wanted to eliminate the corrupt and aristocratic elements from French society. All this backfired on him when other government leaders began to feel death breathing down their necks. Robespierre and his supporters were sent to the guillotine and were among the last to die in the Reign of Terror that they created.

Madame Ducrest, in her book, *Secret Memoirs of the Court of the Empress Josephine*, mentions how Guillotin also came to regret his creation, saying:

> M. Guillotin, a learned physician, had invented . . . the instrument of death which he deemed best calculated to abridge the sufferings of the culprits condemned to forfeit their lives by the sentence of severe but just laws. His invention was laid hold of for the purpose of *dispatching* a greater number of victims. That was the expression used by a member of the Convention.
>
> M. Guillotin, whom I have known in his old age was inconsolable for what he considered as an involuntary blemish in his existence. His venerable countenance bore the impress of a settled gloom, and his hair of a snowy whiteness afforded a clear indication of his mental sufferings. He had aimed at relieving the sorrows of human nature, and he unintentionally contributed to the destruction of a greater number of human beings. Had they been put to death in a less expeditious manner, the people might have been soon wearied out by those executions, which they showed the same eagerness to behold as they would have done a theatrical representation.

Charles Dickens was able to see one of these infamous contraptions in action in Rome on March 8, 1845. The unnamed condemned man was to be executed for robbing and murdering a Bavarian countess who was on her way to Rome as a pilgrim. Dickens described what he witnessed in *Pictures from Italy* (1846).

> The beheading was appointed for fourteen and a half o'clock, Roman time: or a quarter before nine in the forenoon. I had two friends with me; and as we did not know but that the crowd might be very great, we were on the spot by half-past seven. The place of execution was near the church of San Giovanni decolláto (a doubtful compliment to Saint John the Baptist) in one of the impassable back streets without any footway, of which a great part of Rome is composed—a street of rotten houses, which do not seem to belong to anybody, and do not seem to have ever been inhabited, and certainly were never built on any plan, or for any particular purpose, and have no window-sashes, and are a little like deserted breweries, and might be warehouses but for having nothing in them. Opposite to one of these, a white house, the scaffold was built. An untidy, unpainted, uncouth, crazy-looking thing of course: some seven feet high, perhaps: with a tall, gallows-shaped frame rising above it, in which was the knife, charged with a ponderous mass of iron, all ready to descend, and glittering brightly in the morning sun, whenever it looked out, now and then, from behind a cloud.
>
> There were not many people lingering about; and these were kept at a considerable distance from the scaffold, by parties of the Pope's dragoons. Two or three hundred foot-soldiers were under arms, standing at ease in clusters here and there; and the officers were walking up and down in twos and threes, chatting together, and smoking cigars.

At the end of the street, was an open space, where there would be a dust-heap, and piles of broken crockery, and mounds of vegetable refuse, but for such things being thrown anywhere and everywhere in Rome, and favoring no particular sort of locality. We got into a kind of wash-house, belonging to a dwelling-house on this spot; and standing there in an old cart, and on a heap of cart-wheels piled against the wall, looking, through a large grated window, at the scaffold, and straight down the street beyond it, until, in consequence of its turning off abruptly to the left, our perspective was brought to a sudden termination, and had a corpulent officer, in a cocked hat, for its crowning feature.

"Where would Christianity be if Jesus got eight to fifteen years, with time off for good behavior?"

—New York State Senator James H. Donovan on capital punishment

---

Nine o'clock struck, and ten o'clock struck, and nothing happened. All the bells of all the churches rang as usual. A little parliament of dogs assembled in the open space, and chased each other, in and out among the soldiers. Fierce-looking Romans of the lowest class, in blue cloaks, russet cloaks, and rags uncloaked, came and went, and talked together. Women and children fluttered, on the skirts of the scanty crowd. One large muddy spot was left quite bare, like a bald place on a man's head. A cigar-merchant, with an earthern pot of charcoal ashes in one hand, went up and down, crying his wares. A pastry-merchant divided his attention between the scaffold and his customers. Boys tried to climb up walls, and tumbled down again. Priests and monks elbowed a passage for themselves among the people, and stood on tiptoe for a sight of the knife: then went away. Artists, in inconceivable hats of the middle-ages, and beards (thank Heaven!) of no age at all, flashed picturesque scowls about them from their stations in the throng. One gentleman (connected with the fine arts, I presume) went up and down in a pair of Hessian-boots, with a red beard hanging down on his breast, and his long and bright red hair, plaited into two tails, one on either side of his head, which fell over his shoulders in front of him, very nearly to his waist, and were carefully entwined and braided!

Eleven o'clock struck; and still nothing happened. A rumor got about, among the crowd that the criminal would not confess; in which case, the priests would keep him until the Ave Maria (sunset); for it is their merciful custom never finally to turn the crucifix away from a man at that pass, as one refusing to be shriven, and consequently a sinner abandoned of the Savior, until then. People began to drop off. The officers shrugged their shoulders and looked doubtful. The dragoons, who came riding up below our window, every now and then, to order an unlucky hackney-coach or cart away, as soon as it had comfortably established itself, and was covered with exulting people (but never before), became imperious, and quick-tempered. The bald place hadn't a straggling hair upon it; and the corpulent officer, crowning the perspective, took a world of snuff.

Suddenly, there was a noise of trumpets. "Attention!" was among the foot-soldiers instantly. They were marched up to the scaffold and formed round it. The dragoons galloped to their near stations too. The guillotine became the center of the wood of bristling bayonets and shining sabers. The people closed round nearer, on the flank of the soldiery. A long straggling stream of men and boys, who had accompanied the procession from the prison, came pouring into the open space. The bald spot was scarcely distinguishable from the rest. The cigar and pastry-merchants resigned all thoughts of business, for the moment, and abandoning themselves wholly to pleasure, got good situations in the crowd. The perspective ended, now, in a troop of dragoons. And the corpulent officer, sword in hand, looked hard at a church close to him, which he could see, but we, the crowd, could not.

After a short delay, some monks were seen approaching to the scaffold from this church; and above their heads, coming on slowly and gloomily, the effigy of Christ upon the cross, canopied with black. This was carried round the foot of the scaffold, to the front, and turned towards the criminal, that he might see it to the last. It was hardly in its place, when he appeared on the platform, barefooted; his hands bound; and with the collar and neck of his shirt cut away, almost to the shoulder. A young man—six-and-twenty vigorously made, and well shaped. Face pale; small dark mustache; and dark brown hair.

He had refused to confess, it seemed, without first having his wife brought to see him; and they had sent an escort for her, which had occasioned the delay.

He immediately kneeled down, before the knife. His neck fitting into a hole, made for the purpose, in a cross plank, was shut down, by another plank above; exactly like the pillory. Immediately below him was a leathern bag. And into it his head rolled instantly.

The executioner was holding it by the hair, and walking with it round the scaffold, showing it to the people, before one quite knew that the knife had fallen heavily, and with a rattling sound.

When it had traveled round the four sides of the scaffold, it was set upon a pole in front—a little patch of black and white, for the long street to stare at, and the flies to settle on. The eyes were turned upward, as if he had avoided the sight of the leathern bag, and looked to the crucifix. Every tinge and hue of life had left it in that instant. It was dull, cold, livid, wax. The body also.

There was a great deal of blood. When we left the window, and went close up to the scaffold, it was very dirty; one of the two men who were throwing water over it, turning to help the other lift the body into a shell, picked his way as through mire. A strange appearance was the apparent annihilation of the neck. The head was taken off so close, that it seemed as if the knife had narrowly escaped crushing the jaw, or shaving off the ear; and the body looked as if there were nothing left above the shoulder.

Nobody cared, or was at all affected. There was no manifestation of disgust, or pity, or indignation, or sorrow.

Public beheadings like this one continued in France until 1939. The last execution by guillotine, also in France, was in 1977. They abolished capital punishment four years later.

Ignorance & INTELLIGENCE

Unusual Uses for Mummies

From 3000 B.C. to A.D. 500, the ancient Egyptians mummified literally millions of bodies. Tombs and caves were so packed with them that many bodies were just taken to the desert and buried in the sand. Because of the dry climate, virtually every body was preserved whether it was embalmed or not. Giovanni Belzoni, an early Egyptologist, wrote in 1821 what it was like to enter an Egyptian tomb.

> Of these tombs many people could not withstand the suffocating air which often causes fainting. . . . Surrounded by bodies, by heaps of mummies in all directions; which, previous to my being accustomed to the sight, filled me with horror. The blackness of the walls, the faint light given by candles or torches for want of air, the different objects that surrounded me, seeming to converse with each other, and the Arabs, with candles or torches in their hands, naked and covered with dust, themselves resembling living mummies, absolutely formed a scene that cannot be described. . . .
>
> I sought a resting place, found one and contrived to sit; but when my weight bore on the body of a dead Egyptian, it crushed it like a band box. Naturally I had recourse to my hands to sustain my weight, but they found no better support; so that I collapsed together among the broken mummies with such a crash of bones, rags and wooden cases as kept me motionless for a quarter of an hour, waiting until it subsided again. I could not remove from the place, however, without increasing it and every step I took I crushed a mummy in some place or another. . . . Thus I proceeded from one cave to another, all full of mummies piled up in various ways, some standing, some lying and some on their heads.

Hundreds of thousands of mummies were lost underwater when the Aswan Dam was built. Mummies were once so plentiful they were sold by the ton or by the graveyard.

And it was not only people, they also mummified all sorts of animals—from cows and crocodiles to scorpions and insects. Certain cities were devoted to specific animals. So when an Egyptian cat died, it might be brought to one of the cities devoted to cats, where it would be prepared for the afterworld. In 1888, an estimated 300,000 mummified cats were found at Beni Hassan. They were promptly scooped up with tractors, sold at the price of $18.43 per ton, and shipped to England where they were ground up for fertilizer.

Cat mummies weren't alone in receiving such irreverent treatment. Of the multitude of humans who were embalmed and mummified, only a minute fraction of them survive in museums. In the late nineteenth century, millions of human mummies were used as fuel for locomotives in Egypt, where wood and coal was scarce and mummies plentiful. When Mark Twain saw this on his trip through Egypt, he claims he heard an engineer call out, "Damn these plebeians, they don't burn worth a cent! Pass out a King!"

The Egyptians also used them as fertilizer and even to thatch the roofs of their houses. The wood from the coffins was used by poor Egyptians as firewood to cook on. Some Italian homes were even paneled with such coffin wood. Renaissance painters sometimes mixed mummy powder into their paints, believing it would help keep their colors bright. And then during the 1860s, American and Canadian companies bought shiploads of mummies and used their linen wrappings to make wrapping paper. Production was halted after a cholera epidemic was traced to this paper.

These weren't the only innovative uses these preserved corpses were put to. Beginning in around 1100, mummies were in great demand as a type of medicine throughout Europe and the Middle East. At first, it was the resin sealing the mummies that was used. One Arab doctor wrote that it was "sold for a trifle. I purchased three heads filled with the substance." Eventually, the mummies themselves were ground up for medicine. "Where any difficulties arise from procuring bitumen," explained a Cairo doctor, "corpses may be substituted in their stead." By the fifteenth century, the citizens of Cairo were boiling mummies in water and scooping off the oil that floated on top to sell to the French.

Some mummy powder was just a phony mix of pitch and herbs. That was probably the safest since it hadn't even been near a dead body. The worst type was from unscrupulous suppliers who dried out the bodies of beggars, criminals and those who died from diseases, for sale as genuine mummies. Some of these had been dead only a couple of years before they were ground up for powder.

In the seventeenth century, the European medical community insisted Egyptian mummy powder was just the thing to cure a wide variety of ailments. Since it was supposed to stop bleeding, mummy cream was rubbed into wounds. It was also thought to be good for numerous internal ailments, so doctors had their suffering patients mix mummy powder into their food or tea. It was prescribed for bruises, fractures, paralysis, migraines, epilepsy, coughs, nausea, disorders of the liver and spleen, and cases of poisoning. Throughout Europe, people kept it on hand and would take it as we take aspirin today.

In seventeenth-century Scotland, a pound of mummy could be bought for 8 shillings. During the 1970s, an ounce could be bought in New York City occult shops for $40.

Eventually, doctors began to suspect mummy powder was not quite as effective as everyone thought. Seventeenth-century French surgeon Ambrose Paré wrote that, "not only does this wretched drug do no good to the sick . . . it causes them great pain in their stomachs, gives them evil-smelling breath, and brings on serious vomiting which is more likely to stir up the blood and worsen hemorrhaging than to stop it." He insisted the only thing mummies were good for was as fishing bait.

Take Some Lice and Call Me in the Morning

Everyone knows that the medical community once had a fondness for leeches and bloodletting.

Well, here are some other interesting medical cures not offered today.

> For a plague sore—cut a live pigeon in half and apply half to the sore to draw out the venom.
>
> For headache—apply the noose of a hanged man.
>
> For gout—take raspings from a hanged man's skull.
>
> As a snuff—snort moss from a hanged man's skull.
>
> As an unguent—apply baby's fat.
>
> For satyriasis (the male version of nymphomania)—"leape into a great vessel of cold water or put nettles in the codpiece."

Other unusual medicines were made from lice, the stale of a lizard, preparations of toad, unicorn's horn (which was usually rhinoceros horn or narwhal's tusk), bezoar (a stone supposedly found in the stomach of an Asian goat), bowels cut from a live mole, and various exotic dungs. Valuable gems were grated and consumed, as were solutions of gold.

For two centuries after Spanish doctor Nicolas Monardes published *Joyful News Out of the New Found World* (1577) extolling the medicinal qualities of tobacco, tobacco was prescribed by doctors to treat a wide variety of ailments that included headaches, toothaches, arthritis, stomachaches, wounds, and bad breath.

Early in the twentieth century, rattlesnake venom was used to treat epilepsy. Then in the 1950s, as many as a million healthy children and young men were given relatively high, localized doses of radiation to the brain for such conditions as inflamed tonsils, hearing difficulties, ringworm of the scalp, and acne. These patients received as much or more radiation than Hiroshima and Nagasaki survivors received to the same tissues. The treatment caused brain cancers and other serious problems. Presidential assistant Christine Varney said that at the time it "was considered good medical practice and effective treatment." It makes one wonder what treatments currently in use today will seem just as harebrained in the future. After watching the effects of chemotherapy, I nominate it as a prime candidate.

Oil of swallows was popular into the 1600s for restoring sunken sinews. One recipe for preparing it said, "Take young swallows out of their nests, by number twelve, rosemary tips, bay leaves, of each a handful; cut off the long feathers of the swallows, wings and tails, put them into a stone mortar and lay the herbs upon them and beat them all to pieces, guts, feathers, bones and all. . . . "

Viper's flesh was used in several medicines and as an antidote to poison, while viper wine was thought to be an aphrodisiac. The recipe for viper wine read, "Take six live vipers . . . and some spirit. Digest for six months without heat then strain off the wine."

In the seventeenth century, one of King Charles II's physicians devised an interesting invention called the stomach brush. The user would drink warm water or spirits to loosen the crud supposedly lining the stomach walls. The brush was then dipped in alcohol and slowly lowered down the victim's throat by turning its wire handle. Once in the stomach, it was pulled up and down to brush the stomach clean. If used twice a week, it was said to considerably extend the user's life.

Sir Hans Sloane—a doctor to the rich and famous of his time, whose patients included the buccaneer Sir Henry Morgan—highly recommended drinking a glass of water containing fifty live millipedes twice a day to aid digestion.

All this did little for the prestige of the medical profession. In 1832, when James Marion Sims announced he intended to become a physician, his father—a hotelkeeper and the sheriff of Lancaster, South Carolina—exclaimed, "It is a profession for which I have the utmost contempt. There is no science in it. There is no honour to be achieved in it, no reputation to be made, and to think that *my* son should be going round from house to house through this country with a box of pills in one hand and a squirt in the other, to ameliorate human suffering is a thought I never supposed I should have to contemplate!"

Legal Prosecutions of Animals

From the ninth to the twentieth centuries, the Roman Catholic Church excommunicated almost every type of animal. In 1225, eels were booted out of the Church. In 1386, at Falaise, France, a sow was expelled, and in 1389, at Dijon, a horse was ostracized. An ox was banished in 1405. Rats and bloodsuckers were ousted at Bern, Switzerland, in 1451. In Delemont, in 1906, a Swiss dog was one of the last animals to be excommunicated. Somehow cats seemed to have avoided this disgrace, an odd circumstance given the Church's belief that all cats were in cahoots with Satan.

Cats didn't escape the long arm of the law during this period, though. Not only were they sentenced to death in witch trials, they also appeared in nonoccult-related litigations. In fact, all kinds of animals were involved in legal proceedings as plaintiff, defendant, or even as witness.

Apparently, this originally came out of the idea that animals are intelligent and therefore responsible for their actions. Animal trials date at least as far back as Plato (c. 427 B.C.–c. 347 B.C.), for in his book *The Laws*, he wrote, "If a beast of burden or any other animal shall kill anyone, except while the animal is competing in the public games, the relatives of the deceased shall prosecute it for murder."

As the *Encyclopedia Britannica* explains, "In Western Europe procedure against animals was settled both in ecclesiastical and civil courts; in all cases they were provided with counsel, were duly summoned to appear, exceptions were taken in their favor were considered, and their sentences sometimes commuted on the grounds of relative youth, exiguity of body, or a reputation for respectability: a she-ass condemned to death in France in 1750 was pardoned because of good character."

In Lavegny, France, in 1457, a sow and her six piglets were hauled into court for having murdered and partially eaten a child. Although the sow was sentenced to death, the piglets were acquitted because of their youth, the bad example set by their mother, and lack of evidence that they took part in her crime.

At one famous trial in Autun, France, in 1522, some rats were charged with feloniously eating and wantonly destroying the province's barley crop and so were ordered to appear in court. When they failed to show, the rats' attorney argued that the summons was too specific. He insisted that all the rats in the diocese should be summoned and that the summonses should be read from the pulpits of all the parishes in the area. The court agreed and another hearing was scheduled. When the rats again failed to appear, the defense attorney explained that the rats really did want to come to court, but were afraid to leave their holes and make the long journey because of the vigilance of the plaintiffs' cats. He added that the rats would appear if the plaintiffs posted bonds under heavy penalties that the cats would not molest his clients. The judges thought this was fair, but the plaintiffs refused to be responsible for the behavior of their cats, so the case was adjourned without setting a date for another hearing, which in effect ended the case in the rats' favor. The attorney, named Bartholomew Chassenée, went on to become a famous French lawyer.

Animal trials were actually quite common. E. P. Evans's book *The Criminal Prosecution and Capital Punishment of Animals* (1906) contains a list of 191 such trials dating from 824 to the year his book was published. Domestic animals were brought before the criminal courts, and if convicted, they suffered capital punishment. Wild animals were subject to the ecclesiastical courts and were subject to banishment, death by exorcism, or excommunication. "Nor was the latter a light punishment," wrote Robert Chambers in *The Book of Days* (1862–1864). "We all know how St. Patrick exorcised the Irish reptiles into the sea; and St. Bernard, one day, by peevishly saying, 'Be thou excommunicated' to a blue-bottle fly, that annoyed him by buzzing about his ears, unwittingly destroyed the flies of a whole district."

The ecclesiastical trials of wild animals were taken very seriously and were extremely complex affairs. In one case against some insects at St. Julien, France, in 1487, the community offered to set aside a large piece of fertile land solely for the insects' use, reserving the right to flee there in time of war or distress and to work the mines on the property as long as care was taken not to disturb the insects. A complete topographical survey was conducted that included documenting all the plants on the site. After several months of delays, the insects' counsel rejected the proposal saying the land was not suitable for his clients. The court then appointed some experts to examine the place. Unfortunately, the records of this case were damaged by rats or insects, so it's unknown when or how this case ended.

Normally, this is how the process would progress: When the citizens of a district protested that they were being plagued by a certain type of pest, they would file a complaint with the court. The court would then appoint experts to survey the damage. An advocate was appointed to defend the animals, and the court then had to determine

A late-nineteenth-century reconstruction of a fresco illustrating the 1386 execution of a pig. The fresco was on the wall of the Church of the Holy Trinity in Falaise, France, until it was painted over in about 1820.

whether they were clergy or laity since the clergy received special benefits. The pests' attorney would then explain why the defendants should not be summoned. If his argument was unpersuasive, the defendants were served with a summons several times. An officer of the court would proceed to some area where the animals or insects frequented, and he would read the summons in all its formal legalese, usually in Latin, telling them to either stop their abominable behavior or appear in court.

British lawyers like to tell of a trial involving some stolen cows in New South Wales, Australia. The jury's verdict was, "Not guilty if he returns the cows." Infuriated with such a decision, the judge sent them back to deliberate further. After due consideration, they returned with the verdict, "Not guilty—and he doesn't have to return the cows."

An example of this comes from the 1478 trial in Switzerland of a type of beetle they called an inger. The summons read:

> Thou irrational and imperfect creature, the inger, . . . my gracious Lord and Bishop of Lausanne has commanded me in his name to admonish you to withdraw and to abstain. . . . In case, however, you do not heed this admonition or obey this command, and think you have some reason for not complying with them, I admonish, notify and summon you in virtue of and obedience to the Holy Church to appear on the sixth day after this execution at precisely one o'clock after midday at Wifflisburg, there to justify yourselves or to answer for your conduct through your advocate before His Grace the Bishop of Lausanne or his vicar and deputy. Thereupon my Lord of Lausanne or his deputy will proceed against you according to the rules of justice with curses and other exorcisms, as is proper in such cases in accordance with legal form and established practice.

If the offensive creatures failed to appear in court, a judgment was made against them by default and a *monitoire* was issued warning the animals to depart from the district by a certain deadline.

Here is an example of one such judgment. One of the judges began by announcing the case, "The People versus Locusts" and proceeded to declare how the guilt of the accused was clearly proven. He then went on to announce:

> In the name and by virtue of God, the omnipotent, Father, Son and Holy Spirit, and of Mary, the most blessed Mother of our Lord Jesus Christ, and by the authority of the holy apostles Peter and Paul, as well as by that which has made us a functionary in this case, we admonish by these presents the aforesaid locusts and grasshoppers and other animals by whatsoever name they may be called, under main of malediction and anathema to depart from the vineyards and fields of this district within six days from the publication of this sentence and to do no further damage there or elsewhere.

In a case from 1487, processions were made in every parish around Autun, France, for three days to warn some slugs they were about to be accursed if they didn't leave the area. If the pests failed to comply with the court order, the religious leaders would then solemnly proceed with an exorcism.

Of course, things never ran quite as smoothly as all that. Most people have had some experience with today's labyrinthine legal quagmire. Well, the ecclesiastical courts were much worse. The animal's advocate would try every legal trick in the book to delay or prevent the exorcism. And even if the animal was convicted, its attorney could appeal the decision to a higher court where it might be overturned.

If events did reach the point where the exorcism was pronounced, often, instead of "withering off the face of the earth," the depredations of the pests remained the same or got even worse. This was not considered a sign that the verdict was wrong or that the exorcism was faulty. Instead, it was attributed to the malevolence of Satan, who is occasionally permitted by God to harass and annoy His devout parishioners, as in the case of Job.

Some even believed Satan was directly responsible for the depredations in the first place—not the animals. Bartholomew Chassenée insisted that "the anathema then is not to be pronounced against the animals as such, but should be hurled inferentially at the devil, who makes use of irrational creatures to our detriment." Some also felt that since animals were created before man, were allowed to join Noah on the ark, and were entitled to rest on the Sabbath, they should be treated with leniency, tempered with justice.

In 1994, the Philippines' "hanging judge," Maximiano Asuncion, announced that he thought people sentenced to death should have to wrestle poisonous snakes in a giant aquarium where the public could watch.

Of course, all the court costs, expensive religious processions, and numerous ceremonies amounted to quite a bit of money, and it was the community who had to foot the bill. In addition, before the trial could even start, the community had to be totally paid up on all its tithes to the Church. As Robert Chambers aptly put it, "So what with the insects [or pests], the lawyers, and the church, the poor inhabitants must have been pretty well fleeced."

Because this process was expensive and very tedious, some of the country folk resorted to buying unauthorized charms and exorcisms. Unfortunately, if they were caught, they were tried for sorcery. This usually meant being tortured before being burned at the stake.

Sorcery was taken very seriously. Hundreds of thousands of cats were destroyed—usually without a trial—and they were brought to the edge of extinction because of it. In America, the Salem witch trials, which resulted in the deaths of twenty people, also included the executions of two dogs.

In one case in Basle, France, in 1474, a cock was put on trial for having laid an egg. The prosecutor argued that cocks' eggs were particularly valuable for creating various magical concoctions—even more valuable than the philosopher's stone of the alchemists, which was supposed to be able to turn lead into gold. It was believed witches would hatch these eggs, and animals would come out that were extremely harmful to pious Christians and the faith. The defense attorney argued that the cock had no evil intent and that laying the egg was an involuntary act, therefore the cock was innocent of sorcery. He added that there was no record of Satan making contracts with animals. In response to this, the prosecutor pointed out that even though Satan didn't make contracts with animals, he did sometimes possess them, citing Matthew 8:32 where Christ exorcised some demons into some swine who promptly committed suicide by running into the sea. He explained that the pigs' possession was involuntary, but they were still punished with death. The court decided the cock was actually a demon in the form of a cock, and with all due formality, the bird and its egg were burned at the stake.

In criminal trials, such as the one against the pig, it's said some animals were tortured on the rack to elicit a confession. This is not to say that the judges actually expected the animal to confess. They were merely following the form of the law. Sometimes the torture even enabled the judge to be lenient on the creature. Since the animal didn't confess under torture, the judge could then commute a death sentence to whipping, incarceration, banishment, or some other form of punishment.

Animals could also be called as witnesses. For example, a man could kill an intruder in his house and it would be justifiable homicide, but if he lured someone into the house, killed the person, and then claimed that person was an intruder, it would be murder. If such a case came to trial and there were no human witnesses, the accused would not be found innocent unless he brought in one of his animals, like a dog or a cat, that lived in the house and had witnessed the killing. The accused then swore that he was innocent in front of this animal and if the animal didn't speak out against him, he would be judged innocent. The reasoning behind this was the belief that God would cause the animal to talk rather than allow a guilty murderer to escape justice.

Jane Gill was strangled to death on November 3, 1991, in Santa Rosa, California. Her body was discovered in her bedroom along with her dehydrated and starving parrot. After the bird's health returned under the care of a pet shop owner, it began to call out, "Richard, no, no, no!" Gill's business partner was on trial for the murder, and the only Richard in the case was her close friend and former housemate. However, the judge ruled the parrot's testimony was inadmissible.

Now, if you thought the days of animal prosecutions were gone forever, think again. Here are a few more recent cases. In 1991, a judge in Cordoba, Argentina, sentenced a dog to life in prison for killing the three-year-old stepson of its owner. A year later in Mtwara, Tanzania, a goat was sent to jail for seven days after it was found grazing on private property. Then, the year after that, a Kenyan goat went to jail for two days for stealing about $2.25 from a fruit vendor. Also in Kenya in 1993, a shopkeeper carrying four live rats walked into the Busia police station and demanded the offending rodents be incarcerated for ruining his bread supply. "I want these rats put in the cells and charged in court for the damage," he insisted, but, after determining he was sane and sober, the police referred him to the public health officer.

If all that sounds pretty silly to you, wait until you read this: The ancient Greeks had a sort of punishment for inanimate objects that were involved in a murder. In Athens, any such object was publicly condemned and then thrown beyond Athenian boundaries as a form of banishment. As

Plato put it, "If a lifeless thing shall deprive a person of life, provided it may not be a thunderbolt or other missile hurled by a god, but an object which the person may have run against or by which he may have been struck and slain, . . . the culprit shall be put beyond the boundaries, in the same manner as if it were an animal."

In one such case, the object was a bust of the poet Theognis, which fell on a man and killed him. In another case, a statue of a famous athlete was knocked over by the fans of his rivals, killing one of them, so the statue was pitched into the sea . . . after a proper trial, of course.

The idea of the guilt of inanimate objects can be found in other parts of the world as well. E. P. Evans, in his previously mentioned book, wrote:

> Quite recently in China fifteen wooden idols were tried and condemned to decapitation for having caused the death of a man of high military rank. On complaint of the family of the deceased the viceroy residing at Fouchow ordered the culprits to be taken out of the temple and brought before the criminal court of that city, which after due process of law sentenced them to have their heads severed from their bodies and then to be thrown into a pond. The execution is reported to have taken place in the presence of a large concourse of approving spectators and "amid the loud execrations of the masses," who seem in their excitement to have "lost their heads" as well as the hapless deities.

One morning in 1705, an ape who had been the mascot of a ship that wrecked, washed ashore in a rowboat at West Hartlepool in England. The villagers had never seen an ape before, and since England was then at war with France, they assumed the strange creature was a French spy and immediately placed it under arrest. At the ape's court martial, the unfortunate animal was found guilty of espionage and sent to the gallows.

> When the Russian prince Dimitri, the son of Ivan II, was assassinated on May 15, 1591, at Uglich, his place of exile, the great bell of that town rang the signal of insurrection. For this serious political offence, the bell was sentenced to perpetual banishment in Siberia, and conveyed with other exiles to Tobolsk. After a long period of solitary confinement, it was partially purged of its iniquity by conjuration and reconsecration, and suspended in the tower of a church in the Siberian capital; but not until 1892 was it fully pardoned and restored to its original place in Uglich. A like sentence was imposed by a Russian tribunal on a butting ram in the latter half of the seventeenth century.

Not surprisingly, the Roman Catholic Church insisted that it also had the authority to exorcise, anathematize, and excommunicate inanimate objects.

Lost Knowledge Rediscovered

It's generally taught that civilization has gradually progressed through history culminating in today's advanced society. This is not true. Although there has been a general worldwide trend of progression through the ages, knowledge and technology have fluctuated considerably over time. Great advances were made by ancient societies only to be lost, often with centuries passing by before being rediscovered again. In fact, recent archeological finds reveal ancient civilizations were much more advanced than has been previously thought.

"A popular misconception exists that the builders of the pyramids or the cave painters of prehistory were somehow less intelligent than we are," wrote Peter James and Nick Thorpe in their book *Ancient Inventions* (1994).

> This simply isn't true—there is no evidence that the human brain has evolved at all in the last fifty thousand years at least. Modern people are merely benefiting from thousands of years of accumulated knowledge and experimentation, not from increased intellect. . . . These ideas are part of the mistaken view of history best described as temporocentrism—the belief that our own time is the most important and represents a "pinnacle" of achievement. The temporocentric view is a hangover from nineteenth-century ideas of progress. This crude version of Darwinian evolution has led to many misinterpretations of the archeological evidence for ancient technological and cultural achievements.

Our version of history tends to emphasize western civilization as having been the center for the development of human knowledge. It presents European society as the light that brought the rest of the world into the modern age. Actually, there were many societies, such as that of ancient China, that were far more advanced before and during the centuries when Europe was plunged into the backward and superstitious Dark Ages. It was actually a vast influx of knowledge from the Arab world that finally brought Europe out of the Dark Ages.

The Muslims had learned a tremendous amount from their contact with the Greeks, Persians, and Chinese, and they in turn had added many advances of their own. This knowledge included arabic numerals (which probably originated in India), algebra (developed by the Chinese, Persians, East Indians, and later by the Greeks and Arabs), and most of the classical writings from ancient Greece and Rome (which would have been lost if the Arabs hadn't preserved them). Science, astronomy, mathematics, history, literature, philosophy, and medicine were all studied at the many Arab academies and universities, such as those at Baghdad, Cairo, and Cordoba. In Europe, the Renaissance was sparked through knowledge learned from contact with Arab traders and from the libraries and knowledge of refugees who fled the fall of the Byzantine Empire—which was all that remained of Greco-Roman civilization—when the Ottoman Turks took Constantinople in 1453 and renamed it Istanbul.

But it still took centuries for the western world to rediscover knowledge that had long been lost or forgotten in other parts of the world. For example, the Chinese were making things out of aluminum in the third century A.D. Archeologists in 1956 were amazed to find aluminum ornaments in the tomb of a Chinese military commander who had died in A.D. 297. But western civilization with all its knowledge didn't rediscover aluminum until 1827. Another instance is the reaping machine, which was rediscovered in England in 1799, though similar reaping machines were used in Gaul during the first century A.D. In fact, two inventions that were hailed as great achievements of medieval Europe—printing and gunpowder—

were both known centuries earlier in other parts of the world.

Gunpowder was accidentally discovered in the ninth century in China by alchemists who were trying to create an elixir of immortality, and they were soon putting it to many of the same uses that we use it today for. Gunpowder appeared in Europe five centuries later, apparently by way of the Arab world. Printing and movable type appeared simultaneously in Europe in the mid-fifteenth century, though movable type was already being used in Korea a half century earlier and in China by A.D. 1041. In Crete, the Minoans were using rudimentary movable type to stamp hieroglyphics on clay disks in around 1700 B.C. Printing appears to have moved from India to China in the seventh century A.D. China also had one of the earliest encyclopedias, which was gradually built up from the sixth through the first centuries B.C.

Researchers are finding that life long ago was much more complex and advanced than previously thought. The remains of one ancient city consisted of about a thousand brick buildings neatly arranged along narrow streets and courtyards covering around thirty acres. Inside these dwellings, the walls were neatly plastered and decorated with elaborate murals and frescoes. A population of about seven thousand people farmed dozens of different crops, raised herds of cattle, and created a wide variety of crafts, ranging from woven linen to simple metal tools, and from elaborate jewelry to highly polished stone mirrors. All this was taking place at what is now Çatal Hüyük in Turkey about 8,000 years ago. Even though this town is classified as Neolithic, or New Stone Age, its residents were using copper and lead, and one archeologist explained that "the variety of arts and crafts practised at Çatal Hüyük . . . is nearly as great as that of developed civilizations of the Early Bronze Age. Only the arts of book-keeping or writing and music are not represented among the finds."

Babylon, Assyria (both in what is now Iraq), and Egypt all had simple postal systems for mailing clay envelopes containing clay tablets bearing references like "by return of post." It was also at this time that lending banks began appearing in Babylon. By the ninth century A.D., Baghdad's banks were accepting checks and had branches as far away as China. At this time, Baghdad also had a free hospital, pharmacies, thousands of doctors, excellent water and sewage systems, and a paper mill. Archeologists also discovered an electric battery in a tomb near Baghdad that dates from 250 B.C. to A.D. 250. It's still a mystery what it was used for. Batteries weren't reinvented until the Italian Alessandro Volta came along and made one in 1796.

The Etruscans of central Italy were making false teeth and dental bridgework by the seventh and sixth centuries B.C. In India, a few centuries before Christ, more than 120 different surgical instruments—including scalpels, needles, forceps, syringes, and specula—were being manufactured. These were used to perform delicate eye operations, brain surgery, and plastic surgery. The Chinese also knew about the circulation of blood by the second century A.D., though the Europeans didn't figure this out for another fifteen centuries. It also seems the Chinese were extracting sex and pituitary-gland hormones from urine in the second century A.D.—something western medicine didn't discover how to do until 1927. In the tenth century A.D. the Chinese were also inoculating for smallpox. When the West finally discovered in 1717 that the Turks were inoculating for smallpox, initially European doctors didn't believe it would work. That the Romans were aware of bacteria is revealed in this quote by Varro (116–27 B.C.): "Precautions must also be taken in the neighborhood of swamps . . . because there are bred certain minute creatures which cannot be seen by the eyes, which float in the air and enter the body through the mouth and nose and there cause some diseases." Bacteria weren't rediscovered until 1676 when Anton Van Leeuwenhoek happened to see some under a crude microscope, but they were pretty much ignored until 1857 when Louis Pasteur came up with the idea that they might cause some diseases. And then there were the Sudanese, who were using tetracycline 1,400 years before antibiotics were rediscovered.

Contrary to the popular belief that Marco Polo brought spaghetti to Italy from China, the Etruscans were serving pasta in what is now Italy as early as the fourth century B.C. The Greeks and Egyptians also had it.

Some Things Never Change

"These impossible women! How they do get around us! The poet was right: can't live with them, or without them."

—Aristophanes (c. 450 B.C.–c. 385 B.C.)

"A woman is a creature that's always shopping."

—Ovid (43 B.C.- A.D. 18)

Roman women were wearing bikinis by the first century B.C., and the Romans also had apartment blocks, plate glass windows, and toilets that flushed.

Actually, the earliest known indoor toilets with sewage-disposal systems were on the Orkney Islands of Scotland in about 2800 B.C. At about the same time, Egyptians had indoor toilets that were emptied by hand, while outdoor lavatories were being used in the Indus Valley (now India and Pakistan), and soon after in what is now Iraq. By 2700 B.C., the people of the Indus Valley had indoor plumbing with earthen waterpipes. Metal pipes appeared 250 years later in Egypt. The Greeks had showers with piped-in water during the fourth century B.C., and the Chinese had toilet paper by A.D. 589. All these hygienic advances didn't begin appearing in America until about 150 years ago.

Ben Franklin rediscovered lightning rods, saving many buildings from destruction, but the Egyptians were using them on their temples in 212 B.C. and it's possible the Minoans had them in around 1500 B.C. Egyptian temples of the first century A.D. also had coin-operated machines for dispensing holy water.

There is evidence the Nazcans of Peru were going up in hot-air balloons sometime between 500 B.C. and A.D. 900. The western world rediscovered ballooning when a Jesuit priest from Brazil, Father Bartolomeu de Gusmão, demonstrated one in Lisbon, Portugal, in 1709. And it was rediscovered again by the Montgolfier brothers of Paris in 1783.

Diving gear is another rediscovered technology. There is a drawing (c. 1425) from the Hussite Wars of Czechoslovakia showing a diver with flippers, a leather helmet, and an air hose apparently placing some underwater mines constructed of barrels and boxes full of gunpowder. Earlier accounts of similar diving gear date from the eleventh century along the Arabian Gulf and from twelfth-century Germany.

The city of Byzantium (now Istanbul) fended off Islamic invaders using flame-throwers in A.D. 647. The flaming liquid was either pumped through hoses or launched by catapults. According to a thirteenth-century manuscript, the liquid consisted of gasoline, pine and gum resins, sulfur, and saltpeter. In the tenth century, the Arabs were shooting flames of niter and sulfer from copper tubes. Flame-throwers were also being used in China in A.D. 975. The Chinese even had a portable model that consisted of a bamboo tube on a spear filled with enough rocket fuel to shoot flames for about five minutes.

After Robert Fulton, the so-called inventor of the steam engine, mentioned his idea of a steamship to Napoleon, the French emperor exclaimed, "What, Sir? Would you make a ship sail against the wind and currents by lighting a bonfire under her deck? I pray you excuse me. I have no time to listen to such nonsense."

Gasoline[50] was also used in Byzantine and later by the rest of the Arab world to make Molotov cocktails. The egg-shaped pottery or glass vessels often had "Glory" or "Allah" inscribed on them. Actually, these devices could also be considered early hand grenades if they were thrown so that they didn't break open on impact, but exploded. Some looked very similar to pineapple hand grenades. Eventually, they made their way to China, where the Chinese began filling them with gunpowder instead of gasoline. The Chinese had cannons in 1128 and already had mobile artillery by the time the Europeans began making their first rudimentary cannons in the fourteenth century.

The Chinese also used poison gas against their enemies in the fourth century B.C. After digging tunnels underneath the walls of a city they had besieged, they would use bellows to pump the toxic fumes from burning mustard or artemisia through terra-cotta pipes into the city. Even earlier than this, the Chinese and the Egyptians used poison gas to fumigate their homes to rid them of fleas.

Pesticides were being used in China during the third century B.C. They were sprayed on seeds so that they wouldn't be eaten by birds. Different pesticides were sprayed on the ground to kill off insects and weeds before planting and then others on the growing plants to keep animals from eating them and then on the harvest to protect them during storage. One of their pesticides was hydrocyanic acid, which they extracted from crushed cypress leaves.

The Chinese and the Japanese piped in natural gas from miles away for light and heat in the first century B.C., whereas the West's first well for natural gas wasn't drilled until 1821. Around the second century A.D., the Chinese had matchsticks to light their fires with—another innovation that wouldn't appear in the West for over a millennium.

With China's long history of advanced discoveries, it's not surprising this country is also the home of the world's longest running restaurant. Opening for business in 1153, Ma Yu Ching's Bucket Chicken did and still does offer takeout food.

---

50 In some places in the Middle East, unrefined gasoline rises up out of the ground forming pools.

Obviously, a considerable amount of important knowledge was lost at different points in history. Probably the main cause of this was invasion by conquering nations. The Arabs lost a lot to the invading Christians, and the Chinese lost a lot when they were invaded by Mongols and then ruled by a series of puritanical and prudish Mongol emperors. A society could quickly lose several centuries of advancements though an invasion. Of course, such things as revolutions, natural disasters, plagues, and religion also contributed, causing the progression of knowledge and technology to fluctuate and shift around throughout history.

Often, the more powerful invading nations had nothing but contempt for the people they were conquering. As a result, they had little interest in learning anything from the vanquished and had almost no appreciation for the culture they were destroying. A prime example of this is the destruction of the Aztec[51] by the Spanish. The invading Conquistadors, as one historian described them, "were fellows of the lowest sort, rowdies and criminals ejected by their native land, down-and-out Spaniards, the scum of the scum of contemporary Europe. Their sole motive for the expedition was a vulgar lust for gold. . . . The culture of Mexico is to be imagined as being more or less in the same stage as that of the Empire in Rome."

What's usually remembered about the Aztec is that their religion was quite barbarous. The Aztec did sacrifice prisoners of war to their gods. But then, the Romans liked to throw people to lions for entertainment.[52] There was much more to the Aztec than human sacrifice.

The Conquistadors were absolutely amazed when they saw the Aztec capital of Tenochtitlán (now Mexico City) in 1519. No European city could compare to it. Actually, two sister cities, one political and one commercial, they were home to some 250,000 people—a population almost *six times* as large as Spain's largest city, Seville. This magnificent city had massive temples and palaces, huge obelisks, fountains, hospitals, barber shops, saunas, and markets with a tremendous variety of things for sale. Hernán Cortéz wrote that "there are places like apothecaries' shops where they sell medicines ready to be taken, ointments and poultices." Their efficient postal system used speedy couriers who traveled a network of highways coated with stucco, which were so clean the Spaniards said that people could walk on them without getting a bit of dirt on their feet.

Inside, their buildings were decorated with tapestries, paintings, expensive gold work and fragrant cedar ceilings. They also had hot-water systems, hotplates, scent-sprayers, mirrors of polished obsidian, and finely carved plates made of tortoise-shell. They wore splendid woolen cloaks, leather gear, and shoes made of rubber. The women wore skirts and sleeveless blouses. They also wore fine jewelry of silver, gold, and carved jade.

For food, they had a wide variety of dishes, including turkey, fish, shrimp, delicate soups,

---

51 The Aztec referred to themselves as the Mexica, which they pronounced "Mesheeca." This is also how the Spaniards referred to them. Calling them "Aztec" did not become common until the eighteenth century. Although this name is not correct, I have continued to use it to avoid confusion.

52 Of course, our society loves watching violence as well. Only we watch it on television, up close in slow motion with special effects. Admittedly, it's not quite as realistic, but it can be just as explicit. As H. L. Mencken once said, "You must give a good show to get a crowd, and a good show is one with slaughter in it."

spiced dishes, chili, tortillas, waffles, and preserves. Their favorite drink was *chocolatl*—a fine chocolate *crême* that they drank cold with vanilla and other spices. They also had *pulque*—a liquor made of aloe. They smoked tobacco in gilded wooden pipes or as cigars in fine silver holders. They also had a passion for chewing gum, which incidentally, wasn't rediscovered until 1870 by Thomas Adams and again a few years later by William Wrigley, Jr.

Some Things Never Change

"When there is an income tax, the just man will pay more and the unjust less on the same amount of income."

—*Plato (c. 427* B.C.*–c. 347* B.C.*)*

Apparently, the Aztec were the first society to have compulsory education. All boys were required to go to school, though only the daughters of peasants and tradesman were encouraged to go. Their mathematics was advanced enough to have the concept of raising a number to a power (for example, 20^3=8,000) and the concept of zero. In the Old World, the idea of zero was a major advance in mathematics added by the Arabs, and from them it slowly made its way to Europe. For writing, the Aztec used an elaborate system of pictographs. They also had paper, and it's estimated the Aztec government used 480,000 sheets a year. Their books—actually codices—were one long sheet of paper folded accordion- or map-like and printed on both sides with a cover at each end. An Aztec codex could be up to thirteen yards long.

Amazingly, their government was efficient, their police reliable, and there was almost no crime. Criminals were severely punished, but, unlike western society, the rich were punished more harshly than the common people for most crimes. The population was so honest that all the houses were left open without fear of being robbed. The resident simply stuck a reed into the door-mat to show that he or she was out. The courts rarely saw cases involving stolen property. There were no beggars in Aztec society.

Aztec documents show that, like the Europeans, they valued "thrift, compassion, sincerity, carefulness, orderliness, energy, watchfulness, hard work, obedience, humility, grace, discretion, good memory, modesty, courage and resolution," while despising "laziness, negligence, lack of compassion, unreliability, untruthfulness, sullenness, dullness, squandering, deceit, pilfering," in addition to "agitation, disrespect and treachery." Some of the neighboring peoples looked on the Aztec as being prudish because of their hostility to adultery and nudity.

The Aztec capitol, at what is now Mexico City, was on an island in Lake Texcoco that was connected to the mainland by raised roads. Surrounding the island were farms on floating platforms that were anchored by posts to keep them from floating away. They were up to thirty feet wide and three hundred feet long with soil up to four feet deep. These platforms were strong enough to hold a willow tree. The farmer and his family lived in a hut on the platform. Here they grew a wide variety of crops, from tomatoes and avocados to hemp and roses.

The Aztec also had what may have been the most extensive zoological and botanical gardens of the ancient world. Here were a wide variety of animals, including llamas, deer, vicuñas, bison, and poisonous snakes. The larger animals were kept in wooden cages the size of large rooms, whereas animals like snakes were kept in large troughs. One zoo with an aviary specializing in birds of prey required three hundred keepers to maintain it. The birds alone ate five hundred turkeys a day. Another of Montezuma's aviaries had a fresh water lake at its center supplied by an aqueduct. Also with 300 keepers, much of their time was spent rounding up the 250 pounds of fish and large quantities of insects required to feed these birds.

The botanical gardens contained a wide variety of tropical plants and flowers. Among the groves and gardens were ornamental ponds surrounded by marble pavements.

In the sixteenth century, Garcilaso de la Vega described an Inca botanical garden in Peru as it was when the Conquistadors arrived, saying:

> Here were planted the finest trees and most beautiful flowers and sweet-smelling herbs in the kingdom, while quantities of others were reproduced in gold and silver, at every stage of their growth, from the sprout that hardly shows above the earth, to the full-blown plant, in complete maturity. There were also fields of corn with silver stalks and golden ears, on which the leaves, grains, and even the corn silk were shown. In addition to this there were all kinds of gold and silver animals in these gardens, such as rabbits, mice, lizards, snakes, butterflies, foxes and wild-cats; there were birds set in the trees and others bent over the flowers, breathing in their nectar.

Apparently, it was the Aztec botanical gardens that inspired the Europeans to start their first one at Padua in 1545.

When the Conquistadors first saw the Aztec capital, one of Cortéz's lieutenants, Bernal Díaz del Castillo, was prompted to write, "When we saw so many cities and villages built in the water and other great towns on dry land and that straight and level causeway going towards Mexico, we were amazed and said that it was like the enchantments they tell of in the legend of Amadis, on account of the great towers and buildings rising from the water, and all built of masonry. And some of the soldiers even asked whether the things we saw were not a dream."

The Conquistadors, with the help of Native American allies who were enemies of the Aztec, then proceeded to destroy everything they saw in their search for gold. As Díaz del Castillo put it, "Of all these wonders that I then beheld, today it is all overthrown and lost. Nothing is left standing." Though the Aztec culture was annihilated, a few of their descendants still live around Mexico City. They even speak the Aztec language, though their customs and religion are Spanish.

It's terrible what Cortéz and his band of robbers did to the Aztec, but worse acts of treachery were committed by Pizarro and his thugs on the even more advanced Inca in Peru. But in the end, the government of Spain came to rely so much on plundered loot that their empire collapsed as well; though their culture wasn't obliterated in the same way as that of the Aztec. Who knows what incredible wonders were destroyed forever by these greedy, uncomprehending Spaniards who thought themselves so superior.

Archeologists are continuing to discover amazing advances of past civilizations. One has to wonder what other knowledge and inventions were around in ancient times that we have yet to find out about.

Putting Their Wives Up for Sale

Come all you kind husbands who have scolding wives
Who thro' living together are tired of your lives,
If you cannot persuade her, nor good-natur'd make her,
Place a rope round her neck & to market pray take her.

These words, from a song written in about 1696, refer to the practice of divorcing one's wife by selling her off. It's uncertain when and where divorce by sale began, but some say it was going on in England at least as far back as the eighth century A.D. It mostly occurred in rural areas among the lower classes.

Apparently, it stems from three basic ideas. The first was that a woman was essentially the property of her husband. It seems amazing now, but this idea existed in varying degrees until the early twentieth century, when the women's suffrage movement slowly began gaining equal rights for women. It's only recently that women in western society have gained freedom and independence. Before that, unless a woman controlled the purse-strings of an inheritance, found a husband she could dominate, or happened to have a caring and loving husband, then generally her life was just one step above slavery.

The second contributing factor was that many marriages were arranged for social, political, or financial reasons. The idea of romance and marrying for love was developed during the Middle Ages, but it really didn't become widespread until the revival of courtly love in the nineteenth century. Until then, people usually married for more practical reasons, and the husband might find love with a mistress. On rare occasions, especially among the European upper classes, the wife would also have her affairs. Sex in such loveless marriages was primarily for procreative purposes—either to create heirs or so that there would be children to take care of the couple in their old age. Sex for pleasure was more often found with prostitutes.

President Ronald Reagan had a rather strange opinion on the effect the Equal Rights Amendment would have on society. "Human beings are not animals," he insisted, "and I do not want to see sex and sexual differences treated as casually and amorally as dogs and other beasts treat them. I believe this could happen under the ERA." Televangelist, religious leader, and one-time presidential candidate Pat Robertson also has what is, let us hope, a unique view of the amendment. "It is about a socialist, anti-family political movement," he declared, "that encourages women to leave their husbands, kill their children, practice witchcraft, destroy capitalism and become lesbians." The full text of the Equal Rights Amendment says, "Equality of rights under the law shall not be denied or abridged by the United States or by any state on account of sex."

The third idea contributing to this was the common-law marriage. If a couple lives together, they are legally married whether a religious or civil ceremony takes place or not. Many people, especially among the lower classes, had common-law marriages. But if they just couldn't get along, the woman couldn't just leave and go off on her own. Most women were uneducated, and the few jobs available to women wouldn't bring in enough money to support her. So, the easiest way for a disgruntled husband to get rid of his unwanted wife was to find someone else to take her.

All these things combined into the deplorable practice of putting the wife up for sale.

It's uncertain how pervasive the practice was, but it is well documented. The sale was conducted much like a slave or cattle auction. The husband would lead the wife with a halter around her neck into the public marketplace and tie her to a cattle ring. He would then call out to the crowd extolling her virtues and begin the bidding. If only one man was interested, he would usually make a nominal offer. It's said that five shillings and a pot of beer was considered usual. They would then haggle over the price until they came to an agreement. A bill of sale was then produced. One such document read, "I, John Osborne, doth agree to part with my wife, Mary Osborne, and child, to William Serjeant, for the sum of one pound, in consideration of giving up all claims whatever, whereunto I have made my mark as an acknowledgement. Maidstone, Jan. 3, 1815." The bidder would unhitch his new bride and tow her around the marketplace before leading her home.

Here is an eyewitness account of such a sale from a Bristol newspaper dated May 29, 1823.

> This day another of those disgraceful scenes which of late have so frequently annoyed the public markets in this country took place at St. Thomas' market, in this city; a man (if he deserves the name) of the name of John Nash, a drover, residing in Rosemary Street, appeared there leading his wife in a halter, followed by a great concourse of spectators; when arrived opposite the Bell-yard, he publicly announced his intention of disposing of his better half by public auction, and stated that the biddings were then open; it was a long while before anyone ventured to speak, at length a young man who thought it a pity to let her remain in the hands of her present owner, generously bid six d. [pennies]! In vain did the anxious seller look for another bidding, no one could be found to advance one penny, and after extolling her qualities, and warranting her sound, and free from vice, he was obliged, rather than keep her, to let her go at that price. The lady appeared quite satisfied, but not so the purchaser, he soon repented of his bargain, and again offered her to sale, when being bid nine-pence, he readily accepted it and handed the lady to her new purchaser, who, not liking the transfer, made off with her mother, but soon was taken by her purchaser, and claimed as his property, to this she would not consent but by order of a magistrate, who dismissed the case. Nash, the husband, was obliged to make a precipitate retreat from the enraged populace.

Sometimes people tried to prevent these sales. Even the police and judges frowned on this custom and occasionally tried to stop it, but they rarely succeeded. As one magistrate in Ashburn explained in 1818, "Although the real object of my sending the constables was to prevent the scandalous sale, the apparent motive was that of keeping the peace, which people coming to the market in a sort of tumult, would have a tendency to disturb. As to the act of selling itself, I do not think I have a right to prevent it, or even oppose any obstacle to it, because it rests upon a custom preserved by the people of which perhaps it would be dangerous to deprive them by any law for that purpose." So the sales continued.

Another account appeared in the February 26, 1814, issue of the *Statesman*. Apparently, this publication didn't see it as anything out of the ordinary.

Sale of Wives

A gallant son of Mars, of Nottingham, by the name of Linker, already on the wrong side of fifty, still retains the power of getting into the good graces of the belles, although they may not be exactly what are called prudes. The wife of a militia-man named Toone is reckoned in the number of his conquests. Toone being in Nottingham on a furlough, and thinking he had reason to complain of the fidelity of his other half, resolved to get rid of her by auction, trying nevertheless to make as much as possible of his merchandise. The wife who was only a burden to him was exposed for sale in the Swine Market on Saturday evening and set up at auction for threepence, when no other amateur presenting but the noble son of Mars, who was very willing to raise the bid to six-pence, she was delivered to him at that price with an halter around her neck. The numerous spectators admired, without envy, at seeing the amiable spoil delivered into the hands of her amorous purchaser.

Sometimes the disgruntled husband would even run an advertisement in the local newspaper. Here is one from 1796.

To be sold for five shillings, my wife, Jane Hebland. She is stout built, stands firm on her posterns and is sound wind and limb. She can sow and reap, hold a plough, and drive a team, and would answer any stout able men, that can hold a tight rein, for she is damned hard mouthed and headstrong; but if properly managed would either lead or drive as tame as a rabbit. She now and then, if not watched, will make a false step. Her husband parts with her because she is too much for him.—Enquire of the printer.

N.B. All her body clothes will be given with her.

"That . . . man . . . says women can't have as much rights as man, 'cause Christ wasn't a woman. Where did your Christ come from? . . . From God and a woman. Man had nothing to do with him."

—Isabella Van Wagener (a.k.a. Sojourner Truth), 1851

Like cattle, occasionally the woman was even sold by her weight. An example of this comes from the church court records of Thame, Oxfordshire, from 1696.

[Thomas Heath testifies] that he did buy the wife of George Fuller at two pence [per] pound and brought her behind him to a publick house in Thame where she stayed two days and two nights and that he did not see her above one hour in a day while she stayed there . . . and after that he carried her to the White Hart in Benson and that he did sit on the bedside with her both here and at Benson but denies that he had carnal knowledge of her body.

. . . John Pricket of Thame maketh oath that he was not at the bargain making but came time enough to see [the wife of George Fuller] weighed and the money paid which amounted to 29 shilling.

At two pence per pound and with twelve pence in a shilling, this means she weighed 174 pounds. Heath was found guilty in the case and was made to do public penance.

It wasn't just the poor who sold their wives. One well-off cattleman from near London sold his wife for fifty guineas plus the horse the bidder was riding on. Apparently, some churches were even in favor of the practice. It's recorded in the parish of Swadlincote that the parish council ordered a woman to be sold for a florin—which was equal to two shillings or a tenth of a pound—in the Burton-on-Trent market after her husband ran off.

And the custom wasn't just restricted to England. It also occurred in male-dominated societies as far away as what is now Vietnam. One British sailor named Edward Brown escaped from Vietnamese pirates in 1857 and was stranded alone in Cochin-China—now Vietnam, Cambodia, and Laos—for many months before British officials were able to reach him. For much of that time, he was kept in jail for his own protection. He wrote in his book, *Cochin-China, and My Experience of It* (1861), about one prisoner who sold his entire family.

> A most melancholy affair occurred in the jail about this time, that of a prisoner selling his wife.
>
> It appears that this man had been committed four years ago, for having stolen a bag of white rice; and his sentence was, as usual, to remain in prison till further orders.
>
> After he had been here about twelve months, he got permission (through good conduct) to have his wife and family with him. He had three children, two girls and a boy, whose ages varied from two to six years.
>
> His family had not joined him more than six months, when he sold the eldest, a girl six years of age, for fifty thousand cash, or about thirteen dollars. Six months after this, he sold the youngest, a little girl three years of age, for twenty thousand cash, or about five dollars. One year after this, he sold his little boy, five years of age, for the small sum of seventeen thousand cash, or a little more than four dollars; and now he was about to sell his wife. She was a good-looking Cochinese woman; about twenty-seven years of age. He had been married to her, after the Cochinese form, by buying her, ten years ago.
>
> I was present when the poor woman was brought out; she was crying bitterly; and, when her husband spoke to her, she appeared to turn from him in disgust. I pitied her, not merely for her present trouble, but for what she must have suffered on being separated from her children. The day had now arrived when she too must be sold, and for what? not to enable her husband to procure the necessaries of life, but to satisfy his unnatural desire to obtain opium.

"Every argument for the emancipation of the colored man was equally one for that of women; and I was surprised that all Abolitionists did not see the similarity in the condition of the two classes."

—Emily Collins (1818?-1879?)

> Well! to end this mournful affair. The poor woman was handed over to three savage-looking men, one of them receiving a paper, or bill of sale, signed by the husband. They also received a

> bundle of her clothes; and, after paying the purchase-money, they led her away. She was sold for 80,000 cash, or about twenty dollars.

The custom of divorce by sale came to America with the British. "The P'ticular Court" of Hartford, Connecticut, records in 1645, "Baggett Egleston, for bequething his wyfe to a young man is fyned 20 shillings."

Then on March 15, 1736, the following article appeared in *The Boston Evening Post:*

> BOSTON: The beginning of last Week a pretty odd and uncommon Adventure happened in this Town, between 2 men and a certain woman, each one claiming her as his Wife, but so it was that one of them had actually disposed of his Right in her to the other for Fifteen Shillings, this Currency, who had paid only ten of it in part, and refus'd to pay the other Five, inclining rather to quit the Woman and lose his Earnest; but two Gentlemen happening to be present who were Friends to Peace, charitably gave him half a Crown apiece, to enable him to fulfil his Agreement, which the Creditor readily took and gave the Woman a modest Salute wishing her well, and his Brother Sterling much Joy of his Bargain.

Fortunately, the selling of wives doesn't seem to have really caught on in America, but it was still going on in England as late as July 13, 1887, when Abraham Boothroyd of Sheffield sold his wife Clara for five shillings. In 1885, England passed a law making it illegal to sell or kidnap a girl into prostitution if she was under the age of sixteen. Women over the age of sixteen were apparently still fair game. In 1891 it became illegal to keep one's wife imprisoned under lock and key.

Odds & ENDS

Duels Between Women

Dueling, or trial by battle, dates back at least to A.D. 501. Before then, there were two methods of resolving controversies between people: trial by ordeal and trial by oath. It wasn't until the twelfth century that trial by jury was introduced.

With the trial by ordeal, the churchmen and laity would subject the accused to something dangerous, thinking if they were innocent, God would protect them. Here are examples from a medieval document of trial by a red-hot iron and boiling water.

> *The Judgment of the Glowing Iron*
>
> After the accusation has been lawfully made and three days have passed in fasting and prayer, the priest clad in his sacred vestments shall take with the tongs the iron placed before the altar, and singing "The Hymn of the Three Youths,"[53] namely, "Bless Him all His works," he shall bear the iron to the fire and shall say this prayer over the place where the fire is to carry out the judgment: "Bless, O Lord God, this place that there may be for us in it sanctity, chastity, virtue, and victory, and holiness, humility, goodness, gentleness, and plenitude of law and obedience to God the Father and the Son and the Holy Ghost."
>
> After this the iron shall be placed in the fire, and shall be sprinkled with holy water; and while it is heating he shall celebrate mass. But when the priest shall have taken the Eucharist, he shall adjure the man who is about to be tried . . . and cause him to take the communion.
>
> Then the priest shall sprinkle holy water above the iron and shall say, "The blessing of God descend upon this iron for the discerning of the right judgment of God." And straightway the accused shall carry the iron to a distance of nine feet. Finally his hand shall be covered under seal for three days, and if festering blood be found in the track of the iron, he shall be judged guilty. But if, however, he shall go forth uninjured, praise shall be rendered to God.
>
> *The Judgment of Boiling Water*
>
> Having performed the mass the priest shall descend to the place appointed, where the trial itself shall be gone through with; he shall carry with him the book of gospels and a cross and shall chant a moderate litany, and [when finished] he shall exorcise and bless that water before it boils.
>
> After this he shall divest the accused of his garments, and clothe him with clean vestments of

[53] These were the three sons of Israel who King Nebuchadrzzar tossed into a furnace, but they wouldn't burn. (Daniel 3:21–27)

> the church, that is, with the garment of an exorcist or of a deacon—and shall cause him to kiss the gospel and the cross of Christ, [and sprinkle him with the water, and cause him to drink thereof]. Then pieces of wood shall be put under the cauldron, and the priest shall say prayers when the water itself shall begin to grow warm. . . . And that boiling water shall be put down hastily near the fire, and the judge shall suspend that stone, bound to that measure, within that same water, in the accustomed way.
>
> Thus he who enters to be tried by the judgment shall extract it thence in the name of God Himself. Afterward with great diligence his hand shall be wrapped up, signed with the seal of the judge, until the third day; when it shall be viewed and judged of by suitable men.

The ordeal by cold water was where an accused person—often a witch—was thrown into a river or lake. If the accused floated, he or she was considered guilty.

The religious leaders of the day found justification for these methods of trial in the Bible. One example is that of Jonah. To summarize the story, God told Jonah to do something, but instead he sailed away on a ship, so God whipped up a storm. The sailors cast lots and found out that Jonah was the one who God was ticked off at, so they threw him overboard. God wasn't ready to knock him off, so He had a huge fish swallow Jonah for a few days.

Since it was impossible for the religious leaders to find out whether the accused was innocent or guilty, they figured they were placing the matter in God's hands. The ordeals were called "judgments of God."

When given a choice, many defendants chose the trial by oath. Here, the accused's neighbors would swear—at the risk of damning their souls to hell—that the defendant was innocent.

The punishment for committing perjury was to cut off the two fingers the perjurer had held up when taking the oath. It was believed that the same two fingers of the perjurer who died undetected would grow out of the grave seeking to be cut off and that the person's ghost would never rest until this was accomplished.

Realizing that a lot of perjury was being committed—often for a price—King Gundobad of the Burgundians established dueling in A.D. 501, figuring they "might as well risk their bodies as their souls." Gradually, trial by battle became accepted throughout Europe, and it went on to become associated with chivalry and honor.

Dueling is usually thought of as a purely male endeavor, but there were cases where women fought duels. An article describing some of these incidents appeared in *Appleton's Monthly* on April 11, 1874. It was extracted from an article in the German publication *Allgemeine Familien-Zeitung*.

> Duels between women, during the seventeenth and eighteenth centuries, were by no means rare. France, especially, the land *par excellence* of chivalry, furnishes a long list of noteworthy examples.
>
> The first case we shall cite was one which grew out of the gallantries of the famous Duc de (Duke of) Richelieu. A Don Juan of the worst

type, the duke was in the habit of making his secretary the confidant of his intrigues. As it cost him no effort to swear fidelity to Susanna to-day, to Johanna to-morrow, and the next day to sacrifice them both for Mariana; so at the same time, he for a while amused himself at the expense of the Marquise de Nesle and Madame de Polignac. Each of them supposed, of course, that she was sole mistress of his affections.

One morning, as the duke sat over his coffee, his secretary handed him, together with other letters, two that had all the appearance of *billets doux*. These his grace handed back to the secretary, with the request that he would read them. The first one ran thus:

"MON CHER AMI: For three whole days I have not seen you! These long separations rob existence of its value. When shall I see you again?

"As ever, your

"MARQUISE DE NESLE."

"Poor child!" said the duke, smiling. The secretary opened the other note and read:

"It seems an age since I saw you. A horrid dream has made me restless. When shall I see you?

"Faithfully, your

"COMTESSE DE POLIGNAC."

"What time is it?" asked the duke, after giving a moment to reflection.

"Eleven o'clock, your grace."

"Have we any appointments for this afternoon?"

"No, none."

"Very well, write to the two ladies that I hope to have the pleasure of seeing them at my villa this afternoon—the one at two, the other at four o'clock. And let your messenger go at once."

Unfortunately, the secretary inadvertently asked both ladies to come at two o'clock. The consequence was, that they treated his grace to one of the most stormy and painful scenes that could well be imagined.

The following morning Madame de Polignac sent her rival a summons to meet her in single and deadly combat. The Marquise de Nesle accepted the challenge without hesitation, chose the pistol as the weapon, and designated the Bois de Boulogne, of course, as the place of meeting.

They were both punctual. The murderous weapons were loaded, and the distance measured off.

"Fire!" said Madame de Polignac to her antagonist, "but take good care that you do not miss me; if you do, you may be sure I shall not miss you."

The marquise aimed and fired, but the only damage she did was to shoot off two or three little branches of a bush that chanced to be in her range.

"My indignation made my hand unsteady," said she, with a frown.

"Now it is my turn," cried Madame de Polignac.

She took deliberate aim, and shot away a diminutive piece of the marquise's right ear.

The marquise fell to the ground as though she had been shot through the heart, crying out, "Oh, I am wounded! Madame, I pardon you!"

Madame de Saint-Belmont was a masculine sort of woman. Her husband, while in the service of the Duke of Lorraine, fell on the field of honor. After this event, madame determined to manage her own affairs, and especially to look personally after her interests on her landed estates, which were large. She therefore spent much of her time in the saddle, and indeed in the costume of the contemporary dandy. To numberless other adventures and caprices she added that of insisting on fighting a duel with a young man who was enamored of her wit and bright eyes. She rewarded his devotion by forbidding him to approach her, but love is sometimes deaf as well as blind. In this instance it is possible that the cavalier put the seeming invulnerability of the lady down to affectation. Be that as it may, meeting her one day in a wood, where she had alighted to pick some berries, he threw himself at her feet; but, to his protestations of love and devotion, the hard-hearted Madame de Saint-Belmont replied:

"You are challenged. To-morrow I will run my sword through you."

And it was as she said it should be: the young man was killed by the hand of her whom he loved more than life. But hardly had he breathed his last, when his fair antagonist was seized with the keenest remorse. She threw herself upon his dead body and wept bitterly. From that day she was entirely changed; she became very devoted to the Church, heard mass twice daily, wrote three religious tragedies, and gave a large share of her income to different religious orders. Her indignation at the young cavalier was only an inexplicable caprice, she had, in fact, unconsciously loved him, as the sequel fully proved.

A similar but less tragic case is related by Tallemand:

Madame Château-Gay de Murat had a lover in the person of a certain Monsieur de Codières. One day she thought herself justified in believing that he was unfaithful. All his protestations were of no avail. She challenged him to single combat, and, whether he would or no, he was compelled to accept.

De Codières appeared on the ground promptly, and was in an exceedingly gay humor, for he looked upon the affair as simply a jest on the part of his lady-love. He soon, however, became convinced of his error and that she was in furious earnest, for very soon a well-directed thrust came near sending him to the land "whence no traveler returns." From the determined manner in which she attacked him, he saw that he must be on his guard. He determined, therefore, to tire his charming antagonist out, in which endeavor, in the course of half an hour, he was so successful that she let her sword fall from sheer exhaustion. De Codières now placed his weapon against her breast and asked, "Well?"

A look full of love was her only reply, whereupon De Codières dropped his sword and clasped her in his arms.

In consequence of a simple dispute that took place during the course of a performance, the celebrated French actress, Baupré, challenged one of her colleagues, Mdlle. Catharine d'Urlis, to single combat, and furthermore insisted on fighting immediately. In her rage she went to the property-room and brought two swords to the green-room. Mdlle. d'Urlis accepted the challenge, and was severely wounded in the neck.

Colombey mentions a number of duels fought by the dark-eyed daughters of the Iberian Peninsula [Spain and Portugal]. Here the leading *rôle* is played by the *navaja*, the short, dagger-like knife which the Spaniard carries in his belt. In rage and indifference to death no women of the world surpass the Spanish. Their hatred is like a stream of molten lava—it destroys every thing that comes in its way. And with their passionate natures they combine great native cleverness. A single example will suffice to illustrate these characteristic traits:

Two *manolas*—girls of the middle classes—of Madrid contended for the possession of a rich Andalusian. They determined to let a hand-to-hand combat settle the dispute. One bright May morning, therefore, armed with daggers and navajas, and accompanied by their seconds, they drove out at the Alcala gate. The understanding was, that only one of them should return alive. But, just as they reached the spot chosen for the bloody work, they were approached by three policemen, who arrested both principals and seconds.

The manolas laughed disdainfully, and followed good-humoredly to the nearest police-station.

"Señor," said one of the would-be duelists to the officer on duty, "these gentlemen, contrary to all law and right, have wilfully [sic] interfered with our personal liberty."

"That we shall see," replied the *empleado*, with becoming official gravity. "Officer, what charge have you to make against these *señoras?*"

"Señor," replied the policeman, "I had good reasons for believing that the prisoners were about to fight a duel to the death. For that reason we have brought them before your honor that they may be punished according to law."

"If you please, señor," one of the prisoners replied, "we have done nothing, nor were we about to do any thing for which we can be legally punished."

Thereupon the girl pointed out to the astonished official that the law for the suppression of dueling applied to men only, they being specially mentioned in it and they only. The legal erudition of the young girl took the *empleado* completely by surprise, and perplexed him greatly. After a careful examination of the codex, he came to the conclusion that the law did not reach the case under consideration, and he was reluctantly compelled to release the prisoners, but not till he had obtained from them a promise that they would desist from their murderous design.

It is related that two girls in the royal tobacco factory recently had killed each other in a hand-to-hand contest. The mode adopted by the combatants was as romantic as it was barbarous. The antagonists, who were both about twenty years old, and remarkably handsome, repaired, one Sunday morning, accompanied by certain of their comrades, to a village some four or five miles distant, where they breakfasted sumptuously at different tables. The repast ended, they closed the window-curtains, stripped themselves to the waist, and requested their friends to leave the room. Then, at a given signal, they attacked each other with their navajas, and cut, and slashed, and thrust, until both fell to the floor, mortally wounded! When a few minutes had elapsed, their friends reentered the room. Estefania, one of the combatants, had received ten wounds, from which she bled to death in about half an hour. Casilda, her antagonist, died somewhat sooner, from a ghastly wound in the neck.

In this instance the authorities were less scrupulous than in the case of the two manolas. The participants in the horrid tragedy were arraigned and punished.

Undoubtedly, the most colorful female to fight a duel was Mary Read. Born in about 1693 in England and raised as a boy, she joined the military when she was a teenager, serving in the navy and then in both foot and horse regiments. She fought bravely in the War of Spanish Secession. After she fell in love with another soldier, she revealed that she was a woman, and the two were married. They kept a tavern in Holland until her husband died. Dressing again as a man, she joined a regiment, then deserted and caught a ship for the West Indies. When the ship was captured by Captain "Calico Jack" Rackham and his pirates, she joined them. Soon she discovered another woman among the pirates who was also disguised as a man. This was Irishwoman Anne Bonny. These hellcats were two of the bravest and most ferocious pirates in Rackham's crew.

On board one of the many vessels captured by the pirates was a young man that Mary Read fell in love with. His name was Tom Deane. When Deane got into an argument with another pirate, in accordance with the pirates' law, they were slated to go ashore to fight it out. Deane didn't stand much of a chance against the veteran cutthroat, so fearing he would be killed, Mary picked a fight with the pirate and arranged to have her duel first. The two fired pistols at each other, but both missed so she charged him with her sword. Their cutlasses clashed until she finally ran him through. After she'd killed her opponent, she revealed to Deane and the crew that she was a woman. Anne did likewise, and as Anne had been having a secret affair with the captain, they were able to continue as pirates, though now they dressed as women except when in battle.

When they were finally captured, the pirates were taken by surprise, and most were drunk. Anne, Mary and one other pirate were able to hold off the boarding party from the man-of-war, but they were greatly outnumbered. The rest of the pirates had stumbled down into the hold to hide. Mary yelled for the cowards to "come up and fight like men." When they didn't, she fired her pistols down at them, killing one and wounding several others. They were put on trial in Jamaica and sentenced to death in 1720. Mary died in prison from a fever, and Captain Rackham went to the gallows. Anne Bonny's father was a lawyer in the Carolina colony, and his friends secured her release. It's said she returned to South Carolina, but what happened to her after that is unknown.

Dueling didn't quite catch on in America as it did in Europe, but duels were fought in the states. In America's famous most duel, Aaron Burr killed Alexander Hamilton and effectively ended both of their political careers. By the turn of the twentieth century, dueling had essentially vanished from America.

Female Boxing Matches

Boxing is usually considered a man's sport—and perhaps rightly so. The idea of two women trying to beat each other to a pulp just doesn't seem feminine somehow, but this hasn't always been the case. Apparently, boxing matches between women were not all that unusual in the early 1700s. One example of a boxing match being used as a type of duel occurred in 1722 when the following notice of the challenge and its reply were printed in a newspaper in England.

In June 1877, the Dodge City Times *ran a story on a sixty-one-round bare-knuckles prize fight they said took place in Dodge City's Saratoga Saloon. The newspaper reported, "The only injuries sustained by the loser in this fight were two ears chewed off, one eye bursted and the other disabled, right cheek bone caved in, bridge of the nose broken, seven teeth knocked out, one jaw bone mashed, one side of the tongue chewed off, and several other unimportant fractures and bruises."*[54]

CHALLENGE.—I, Elizabeth Wilkinson, of Clerkenwell, having had some words with Hannah Hyfield, and requiring satisfaction, do invite her to meet me upon the stage, and box me for three guineas; each woman holding half a crown in each hand, and the first woman that drops the money to lose the battle.

ANSWER.—I, Hannah Hyfield, of Newgate Market, hearing of the resoluteness of Elizabeth Wilkinson, will not fail, *God willing*, to give her more blows than words, desiring home blows, and from her no favour; she may expect a good thumping!

An advertisement for a bit more professional-sounding bout appeared in London's *Daily Post* on July 17, 1728.

At *Mr. Stokes' Amphitheatre* in Islington Road, this present Monday being the 7 of October, will be a complete Boxing Match by the two following Championesses:—Whereas I, Ann Field, of Stoke Newington, ass-driver, well known for my abilities in boxing in my own defence wherever it happened in my way, having been affronted by Mrs. Stokes, styled the European Championess, do fairly invite her to a trial of the best skill in boxing for 10 pounds, fair rise and fall; and question not but to give her such proofs of my judgment that shall oblige her to acknowledge me Championess of the Stage, to the entire satisfaction of all my friends.

I, Elizabeth Stokes, of the City of London, have not fought in this way since I fought the famous boxing woman of Billingsgate 29 minutes and gained a complete victory (which is six years ago); but as the famous Stoke Newington ass-woman dares me to fight her for the 10 pounds, I do assure her I will not fail meeting her for the said sum and doubt not that the blows which I shall present her with will be more difficult for her to digest, than any she ever gave her asses.

Recently, there has been a revival of female boxing in the United States.

A Dog Is Elected Mayor in California[55]

The residents of one small California town didn't think it odd when they saw their mayor begging for beef jerky, sniffing trees, rolling in the dirt, running after sticks, or even standing around with his tongue hanging out and drooling. That's because their mayor was a Labrador retriever and, though this may or may not be unusual behavior for a politician, it is acceptable when the politician is a dog.

Bosco was elected mayor of Sunol in 1983 and served his community faithfully for eleven years, until his death in 1994. The town—which had a population of about a thousand people at the time of his demise—is thirty miles southeast of San Francisco and fifteen miles north of San Jose.

---

54 In those days, newspapers occasionally made up stories like this as humorous filler.

55 Sunol Journalist Kathy Anderson kindly sent me much of the information on Bosco's tale.

It all began when two Sunol residents—"Honest Paul" Zeiss and Wolf Sauer—were hanging around the Sunol Lounge and got into a lively discussion over who had the most friends in town. This progressed to a discussion of which one of them would be elected mayor if the town ever needed one. Soon they had each launched their campaigns. Not satisfied with either of the two candidates, a third patron of the bar named Brad Leber entered his dog, Bosco "Boss" Ramos, as a candidate.

Campaign fliers were distributed around town, T-shirts appeared, and campaign promises were printed on the front page of *The Sunolian*. According to Brad Leber, Bosco—the founder of the Puplican Party—stood for a bone in every dish, a cat in every tree, and many more fire hydrants. He also pointed out that Bosco didn't drink, smoke, or chase women, though he did sometimes chase cars.

"If we didn't have two parties, we would all settle on the best men in the country and things would run fine. But as it is, we settle on the worst ones and then fight over 'em."

—Will Rogers

When election day finally arrived, Honest Paul landed seven votes and Wolf forty-five, but Bosco was the clear winner with seventy-five. The next day, Wolf declared his intention to run for the position of dogcatcher. News of Bosco's victory was picked up by the wire services, and the story was distributed as far away as China.

A few years later, Bosco was again in the news when he was reported missing after failing to show up for a television interview. Actually, he disappeared several times. Once a couple from the nearby town of Fremont took him and held him in their garage until the publicity surrounding his disappearance prompted them to return the mayor to his grateful constituents. Another time he fell asleep in the back of a van and wound up in Oregon. And then there was the time when an animal control officer picked up His Honor and hauled him off to the pound.

Besides giving interviews to the media, this international celebrity made numerous appearances in parades and presided over Sunol's annual bed races. He also got into some nasty brawls with some of Sunol's other canine residents, and he fathered several illegitimate children. He was serving his sixth term in office when he passed away.

Several hours south of Sunol along the California Coast, about halfway between San Francisco and Los Angeles, is the tourist town of Harmony (population of eighteen) which had a cat named Fred as its mayor. That was until Fred died in 1995 at the age of twenty-two and was buried in the garden across from the glass-blowing studio. Originally a stray that someone dropped off in town, he soon became one of the town's most respected citizens and was unanimously elected mayor. One of the benefits of being mayor was that Fred could sit with customers in the fancy Italian restaurant where he was served his favorite dish—Fettuccini Alfredo. Fred's full name was actually Freddie Cheenie Alfredo. At the time of this writing, Fred's successor is still a kitten and not yet old enough to assume the heavy responsibilities of being mayor of Harmony.

Now, there is a historical precedent for all this. Pliny, the Roman historian who died from volcanic gasses while investigating the eruption of

Mt. Vesuvius in A.D. 79, wrote, "Upon the coast of Affricke inhabit the Ptoeambati and Ptoemphanæ [in what is now Ethiopia]: who have a dog for their king, and him they obey, according to the signs which he maketh by moving the parts of his body, which they take to be his commandments, and religiously they do observe them."

According to legend, in eleventh-century Norway, when the people deposed their king, before leaving he decided to take revenge by forcing them to choose between a slave and a dog as his replacement. They chose the dog. Given the name Saur I, the dog assumed the office complete with a court, bodyguard, and officers. Whenever it rained, his courtiers would carry him so his paws wouldn't get wet. They even had him sign decrees—that is, until he was killed by a wolf. Defending his kingdom, no doubt.

In Iceland, the *Heimskringla* records that after the Upland king Eystein the Bad won a war against the people of Drontheim, he designated his son as their king. Not appreciating this, the people promptly killed the son. He then gave them a choice between having a slave or a dog as king, and the rest of the story is essentially the same as Norway's. This dog king was also named Saur. Similar tales can also be found in Denmark and Hungary.

And then there were instances where dogs were considered sacred by religions in Africa, Tibet, Japan, the Philippines, Sicily, and by some Native Americans, though it's doubtful any of these people actually viewed dogs as gods. Early Chinese writers described how their first temple for dogs was built during the Ch'in dynasty (221-207 B.C.). In Egypt, there was even an entire city dedicated to dogs. Named Cynopolis (or Dogtown), it had hordes of sacred municipal dogs.

"The short memories of American voters is what keeps our politicians in office."

—Will Rogers

More recently, a female rhinoceros in Brazil was elected to São Paulo's municipal council by a landslide 50,000 votes on October 4, 1959. This was in protest against corrupt politics, food shortages, and the high cost of living in Brazil. Several years earlier, in 1954, a goat was elected to the city council of Jaboata, which is also in Brazil. This councilman's name was Smelly.

Menu for a Roman Banquet

Of all the pleasures the Romans indulged in, they were particularly interested in eating. They turned food into a science, with dinner parties being the primary event in their social lives. Roman banquets often lasted all night and included entertainment provided by musicians, dancers, poets, and acrobats. These parties usually had three to five guests and would take place in a formal dining room called the triclinium because they generally contained three couches. Each couch was large enough for three reclining guests. The room would be decorated with flowers because it was thought these would absorb the fumes from the lamps, as well as neutralize the intoxicating properties of the wine.

Guests would arrive early in the afternoon. After removing their shoes, they would lie down on the couches, resting on their left elbows in front of movable tables. All the guests had servants beside them to wash their hands between courses and to ensure their comfort. Some Romans resorted to purging so that they could continue to eat without becoming full.

The meals came in three courses. In about the second century A.D., Juvenal described one meal as consisting of a "huge lobster garnished with asparagus . . . a mullet from Corsica . . . the finest lamprey the Straits of Sicily can purvey . . . a goose's liver, a capon as big as a house, a boar piping hot . . . truffles and . . . apples."

One of the greatest gormandizers of the Roman Empire was the Emperor Vitellius. Distinguished by his gluttony, his reign was otherwise insignificant. It was also very brief, lasting less than a year. He was emperor from A.D. 69 to A.D. 69. But during that short time, he did enjoy himself. That is, until he was murdered by Vespasian's troops. His gormandizing was described by my favorite Roman historian, Suetonius, in *The Life of Vitellius.*

Proper Etiquette

Table manners, on the other hand, have changed a bit over the centuries, as is revealed by these excerpts from Bonvieino da Riva's book, Fifty Table Courtesies *(1290):*

> *"A number of people gnaw a bone and then put it back in the dish—this is a serious offense."*

> *"Refrain from falling upon the dish like a swine while eating, snorting disgustingly and smacking the lips."*

> *"Do not spit over or on the table in the manner of hunters."*

> *"When you blow your nose or cough, turn round so that nothing falls on the table."*

I think Miss Manners would agree with of these recommendations.

> Vitellius always made three meals per day, sometimes four: breakfast, dinner and supper and a drunken revel after all. This load of victuals he could bear well enough, from a custom to which he had inured himself of frequently vomiting. For these several meals he would make different appointments at the houses of his friends on the same day. None ever entertained him at a less expense than 400,000 sesterces [about $200,000]. The most famous was a set entertainment given him by his brother, at which were served up no less than two thousand choice fishes, and seven thousand birds. Yet even this supper he himself outdid at a feast which he gave upon the first use of a dish which had been made for him, and which from its extraordinary size he called "The Shield of Minerva." In this dish were tossed together the livers of charfish, the brains of pheasants and peacocks, with the tongues of flamingoes and the entrails of lampreys, which had been brought in ships of war as far as from the Carpathian Sea and the Spanish Straits.
>
> He was not only a man of insatiable appetite, but he would gratify it at unseasonable times, and with any garbage that came his way. Thus at a sacrifice he would snatch from the fire the flesh and cakes and eat them on the spot. When he traveled, he did the same at inns upon the road, whether the

meat was fresh dressed and hot, or whether it had been left from the day before and was half eaten.

As I'm sure you've noticed, great emphasis was placed on the exotic when it came to preparing the menu. The following one is from the cookbook by Apicius, a glutton who lived about the same time as Jesus Christ:

APPETIZERS
Jellyfish and eggs
Sow's udders stuffed with salted sea urchins
Patina of brains cooked with milk and eggs
Boiled tree fungi with peppered fish-fat sauce
Sea urchins with spices, honey, oil
And egg sauce

MAIN COURSE
Roast parrot
Turtle dove boiled in its feathers
Ham boiled with figs and bay leaves,
rubbed with honey, and baked in pastry crust
Fallow deer roasted with onion sauce, rue,
Jericho dates, raisins, oil and honey
Dormice stuffed with pork and pine kernels
Boiled ostrich with sweet sauce
Flamingo boiled with dates

DESSERT
Hot African sweet-wine cakes with honey
Stoned dates stuffed with nuts and
pine kernels, fried in honey
Fricassee of roses with pastry

Apicius's cookbook also has a recipe for roast pig's testicles. Both human and animal testicles were once wrongly thought to be aphrodisiacs. In fact, the cook of Pope Pius V (1504–1572) was famous for his bull testicle pie.

And for those of you who thought such taste treats were history, the New Hampshire Department of Fish and Game recently published a collection of their favorite dishes in *Cook Wild* (1994). Its three hundred recipes include Moose Fondue, Porcupine Fricassee, Squirrel Soup, Roast Haunch of Beaver, Sweet-and-Sour Wild Pig, Swedish Bear Meatballs, and Chicken-Fried Muskrat. Obviously, good cooking is not a thing of the past.

HOUDINI'S SECRETS

Magicians never like to tell their audiences their secrets, and for good reason. Magic is . . . well . . . magical. Once the secret is revealed, it becomes just a trick. That special element that makes it mysterious is gone and it just seems plain and ordinary. In a way, it's better not to know a magician's secrets. Still, the desire is always there to know how something amazing and mystifying was done. We want to know the secret. We have to know the secret . . . even if it ruins the whole thing.

Well, here we go. I will now reveal the secrets to three of Houdini's most interesting stunts.

Harry Houdini (1874–1926) was the king of magicians. This master showman became a worldwide sensation with such acts as "Walking Through a Brick Wall" and his escape while hanging upside down in the "Chinese Water Torture Cell." George Bernard Shaw once said the three most famous names in history were Jesus Christ, Sherlock Holmes and Harry Houdini.

Houdini, whose real name was Ehrich Weiss, was so good that many people believed he actually had supernatural powers. He often denied that he was doing anything out of the ordinary and once wrote, "I do claim to free myself from the restraint of fetters and confinement, but positively state that I accomplish my performance purely by physical means. My methods are perfectly natural. I do not dematerialize or materialize anything. I simply control and manipulate material things in a manner perfectly well understood by myself and thoroughly accountable for by any person to whom I may elect to divulge my secrets."

Still, people didn't believe him.

Even Sir Arthur Conan Doyle, the creator of Sherlock Holmes, was convinced Houdini was actually a medium pretending to be a magician and even sent him a telegram asking him to acknowledge his occult powers. About the only way he could have convinced everyone would have been if he revealed his secrets. But he couldn't really do that. It would have ruined his show.

It's a good thing he was honest. As one of his friends explained, "He could enter or leave any building or chamber at will, leaving no trace of breakage behind him, and he could open the strongest steel vault. . . . Doubtless Houdini would have wrought even greater havoc in human society had he perfected his genius for illusion to make himself the central figure of a new religious cult. He could have done this without difficulty. Moreover, he was aware of what he could accomplish in setting himself up as the inspired prophet of a new mystical religion."

Unfortunately, when people come up against something that they can't rationally explain, it's sometimes easier to accept a supernatural explanation.

This poster advertising Houdini's show was printed just before his death.

Houdini did actively crusade against spiritualism and mediums by exposing their methods or repeating their performances himself. This is how his "Buried Alive" trick came about. He heard about a fakir who was buried for a certain period of time and was miraculously still alive when they dug him up. Since Houdini didn't think anything supernatural was involved in this, he set about repeating the feat himself. He eventually performed it a number of times.

When he did it, announcements would be posted all over town to attract his audience to where he would be buried alive for an hour. Usually, this was at a plot of land just outside town. Policemen would be there to control the excited crowd and to emphasize the seriousness of the event. Houdini would begin by making a speech, which many in the audience thought might be his last. A hole would then be dug six feet deep into the ground. An ordinary coffin would be inspected and Houdini would climb in. After the lid was screwed closed, the coffin would be lowered into the ground, and the mock grave would be filled in with dirt again.

As time slowly passed, the crowd—including Houdini's managers—would grow uneasy and watch their watches very closely. After about fifty minutes, the workers would set about opening the grave up again and the coffin would be pulled up by ropes. The lid would be unscrewed and a haggard, but very much alive Houdini would emerge to the cheers and obvious relief of the crowd.

In another version of this, Houdini would be sealed inside a galvanized-iron "coffin" that would be lowered into a swimming pool and left underwater. It was in this way that he set his record of ninety-three minutes.

Whereas some people have suggested he somehow smuggled in some sort of breathing apparatus, others thought he somehow escaped before the coffin was buried and reentered it before it was opened again. Both ideas are wrong.

Of course, other magicians have repeated this feat, and some have even broken his record. It's a very dangerous stunt to perform. One man who tried being buried alive a few years ago in Fresno, California, was killed when tremendous weight of the dirt filling the "grave" collapsed the box he was in and crushed him to death. Apparently, he wasn't using a real coffin, as Houdini did.

Houdini's secret was actually quite simple, but it required a lot of concentration and practice. Basically, he trained himself to control his breathing. By taking very slow, short breaths, he would use as little oxygen as possible and thus prolong the amount of time he could remain alive with the limited amount of air inside the coffin. He used to practice by holding his breath underwater, gradually increasing the length of time he could remain under. He also practiced remaining in sealed boxes and controlling his breathing, lengthening the amount of time he felt comfortable and safe with. In addition, coffins come in different sizes and he chose a larger one that would give him a little more air. Even without the threat of the coffin collapsing, this feat was a very dangerous one. Many people tried to talk him out of doing it, but that didn't stop him. He was planning to move it to the stage, where he would have the coffin buried under a ton of dirt, but he died before the start of that tour.

Houdini was, of course, best known for his escapes. Called "the World's Handcuff King and Prison Breaker," it was said "nothing on earth can hold Houdini a prisoner." To prove this, he often accepted challenges. One of these was from a bank safe manufacturer in London, who had a large new safe they were very proud of. Houdini's only requirement was that the safe be delivered to the theater twenty-four hours before the show. This was done, and special supports had to be built under the stage because of the safe's tremendous weight.

The night of the show, the crowd was so large that many people had to be turned away. When the curtain rose, the audience saw the large, formidable safe. Then Houdini came out wearing only a robe over his swimsuit. He explained that this would be dangerous and that he might fail, adding that it wouldn't take long to run out of air inside the safe.

Next he had a committee from the audience come up and examine the safe. This committee included a local doctor and an official from the safe company, who had the only key to the safe. After the committee agreed that no human being could possibly escape from such a safe, Houdini cast off his robe and asked the doctor to give him a medical examination inside the safe to ensure he had nothing concealed about his person. The committee and audience approved and Houdini, the doctor, and an umpire entered the safe, leaving the door half-open. When this was done, the doctor announced that Houdini could not possibly have anything concealed on him and that there was nothing inside the safe. The umpire then stated that the doctor's examination was very thorough. Houdini then shook their hands and stepped back into the safe, which was carefully locked. A large screen was placed around the safe, but it was done in a way that enabled the audience to see if anyone approached the safe.

The audience then waited. After half an hour, people began to get concerned, some shouting that the safe should be opened, but Houdini had left strict instructions with his attendants that the company official with the key should not open the safe unless they heard knocking from inside the safe, which would be his distress signal. Forty minutes into the challenge, one or two women began pleading that Houdini be released. After forty-five minutes had passed, Houdini suddenly pushed back the screen and stepped out before the cheering and amazed audience. The committee then reexamined the still-locked safe and proclaimed that they could not tell how he managed to escape. Everyone was baffled, and many believed it was some sort of miracle. The next day, the newspapers were full of accounts of his mysterious feat.

There are several false stories about how the Great Houdini died. What really happened was that he had just finished a show in Montreal, Canada, when two students from McGill University came to his dressing room to interview him for the school newspaper. When they asked him if he really could withstand a blow to the stomach as he'd claimed, he said he could and started to rise so he could prove it, but one of the students—who was an amateur boxer—punched him before he was prepared and he fell back, badly hurt. He got up, prepared himself, and took another blow. It was later discovered his appendix had been ruptured, causing peritonitis. The infection killed him ten days later in Detroit. His body was shipped to New York in the coffin from his "Buried Alive" stunt.

Actually, it was Houdini's expert knowledge of locks that enabled him to escape. During the twenty-four hours prior to the show, he and his mechanics were able to remove the stiff springs in the safe's locking mechanism and replace them with their own soft springs. Everything appeared normal, but this made the safe easier to open. He then made a three-pronged steel fake key that roughly resembled a small clothespin, which enabled him to open the door from the inside.

It turns out that the person from the audience committee who volunteered to act as umpire with the doctor was Houdini's best friend. He had the fake key attached to the inside of a ring on his finger. Houdini was able to slip it off when they shook hands just before he was locked in the safe. He had actually opened the safe and closed it again within minutes after the screen was put up. He then sat around behind the screen waiting for the audience to work itself up and then made his appearance.

After the show, the safe's original springs were replaced so that everything was back to normal by the time the safe makers retrieved their property.

This challenge greatly increased his fame, and audiences flocked to his shows. It was one of his greatest successes.

Another stunt that drew large audiences was his escape from a packing crate underwater. Like his being buried alive, this was done for publicity. The event would be widely advertised, encouraging the public to appear at a nearby pier or jetty at a specific time. When a large crowd had gathered, two or three local carpenters would begin constructing the crate using normal wood and nails. A hole would be cut into the bottom or lower side to allow the crate to sink faster. When the box was completed, Houdini would address the audience. After the press and public inspected the crate, he would be handcuffed and place inside. The top of the crate would be nailed down and a rope would be tightly tied around the crate, as one would tie a package, but with more knots.

By this time, a ship or tugboat would have appeared near the pier or jetty and its crane would lift the crate up into the air. After the ship had moved out away from the pier, the crate would be lowered. The crowd's excitement would greatly increase as the crate and Houdini sank beneath the water. After a couple of minutes, the crate would be raised with the great escape artist sitting on top of it. The ship would pull alongside the pier again, where the crate would be reinspected and found to be just as it was when Houdini was sealed inside.

So, how did he do it? Like the escape from the safe, this also required a little bit of deception. The handcuffs he used on this occasion were his own and had a secret spring, which, when pressed, would instantly open them. This was done as soon as he was sealed inside the case. As the case was lifted into the air and as the ship moved away from the pier, Houdini would pull out a small pair of nail cutters that he had concealed on him and begin clipping the nails that held one or more boards of the lid in place, probably leaving a few nails until the box was submerged. Once the nails were cut, he would move the boards enough so that he could slip out of the crate. He was an excellent swimmer. Then, sitting on the top of the crate to hold the loose boards in place, the crate would be raised from the water and lowered onto the ship's deck. While everyone's attention was on Houdini, a couple of his workmen would quickly move the crate into a cabin and remove all the cut nails, replacing them with new ones exactly like the originals. By the time the ship was alongside the pier, the crate would be restored and ready for inspection. With all the excitement, everyone would forget about the moments the crate was out of their sight, figuring the escape was already complete by then.

Houdini loved to perform this escape, though it sometimes caused him difficulty with the law. He was stopped several times by police who claimed the crowds were an obstruction and that it was too dangerous because Houdini might drown.

At one performance of this in Liverpool, he knew the police were going to try to stop him. While the crate was being constructed, the constables made their way through the crowd and announced, "Mr. Houdini, we cannot allow you to attempt this thing." As they began removing the construction material, to the disappointment of the crowd, there was suddenly a shout and the crowd quickly moved about fifty yards away where they joined another crowd. It turned out the constables had addressed a double of Houdini, while the real Houdini had actually begun the feat a short distance away from the advertised site. By the time the officers discovered this and reached the actual site, Houdini was already being lowered into the water.

By now, I'm sure what I said earlier about the magic disappearing once the solution is revealed has become apparent. This should not detract from Houdini's prestige or fame, however. He was a master performer and an amazingly talented escape artist. He also accomplished many other feats to wonder at, such as how he was able to escape from a milk can, or how he made an elephant disappear on stage, or how he was able to walk through a brick wall, or how he was able to release himself from a straitjacket while suspended by his feet upside-down off the top of a New York skyscraper, or how he escaped from a Russian prison, or. . . . The list is long and interesting, and there is still more than enough magic left surrounding the Great Houdini.

Victims of HISTORY

Prisoner on a Slave Ship to America

The first slaves brought to America arrived in Virginia on a Dutch warship in 1619. Initially, victims of slavery weren't strictly limited to Africans. Some men and women from England's lower classes sold themselves or were sold as indentured servants to pay for their voyage to America or to pay their debts. One African named Anthony Johnson, who arrived in America in 1622, was by 1651, importing both whites and blacks as indentured servants. By that time, the status of the African as slave had become established. By 1670, all Africans in America were considered slaves unless they could prove otherwise. As the demand for agricultural laborers increased, so did the importation of slaves. Native Americans, Moors, Turks, and Jews were also sold as slaves in seventeenth-century America.

Africa also had slavery, but the system there was considerably different. There, slaves were considered part of the family and were treated as such. A slave's children were regarded as free and equal members of the society. One eyewitness explained, "a slave might marry; own property; himself own a slave; swear an oath; be a competent witness and ultimately become heir to his master. . . . An Ashanti slave, nine cases out of ten, possibly became an adopted member of the family, and in time his descendants so merged and intermarried with their owner's kinsmen that only a few would know their origin." Africa had a wide variety of cultures, and it wasn't unusual for one group to capture people from another as slaves, but these slaves were comparable to the serfs in Europe. African slavery was totally different from the Western version of slavery.

"The African civilization was as advanced in its own way as that of Europe. In certain ways, it was more admirable; but it also included cruelties, hierarchical privilege, and the readiness to sacrifice human lives for religion or profit. It was a civilization of 100 million people, using iron implements and skilled in farming. It had large urban centers and remarkable achievements in weaving, ceramics, sculpture. European travelers in the sixteenth century were impressed with the African kingdoms of Timbuktu and Mali, already stable and organized at a time when European states were just beginning to develop into the modern nation."

—Howard Zinn, A People's History of the United States, *1980*

Once the Europeans began shipping slaves, the Africans began to differentiate between the slaves they kept for themselves and those they traded to the whites. Sometimes the domestic slaves even headed up excursions to capture slaves for export.

Gustavus Vassa experienced both types of slavery. Born in Benin in 1745, he was eleven years old when he was kidnapped by another tribe and made a slave in Africa. Four years later, in 1760, he was sold to white slave traders and shipped to America. He recorded his story in his autobiography, *The Interesting Narrative of the Life of Olaudah Equiano, or Gustavus Vassa the African* (1791).

> The first object which saluted my eyes when I arrived on the coast was the sea, and a slave ship, which was then riding at anchor, and waiting for its cargo. These filled me with astonishment, which was soon connected with terror, when I was carried on board.[56] I was immediately handled, and tossed up to see if I were sound, by some of the crew; and I was now persuaded that I had gotten into a world of bad spirits, and that they were going to kill me. Their complexions too differing so much from ours, their long hair, and the language they spoke (which was very different from any I had ever heard), united to confirm me in this belief.
>
> Indeed, such were the horrors of my views and fears at the moment, that, if ten thousand worlds had been my own, I would have freely parted with them all to have exchanged my condition with that of the meanest slave in my own country. When I looked round the ship too and saw a large furnace or copper boiling, and a multitude of black people of every description chained together, every one of their countenances expressing dejection and sorrow, I no longer doubted of my fate; and, quite overpowered with horror and anguish, I fell motionless on the deck and fainted.
>
> When I recovered a little, I found some black people about me, who I believed were some of those who had brought me on board, and had been receiving their pay; they talked to me in order to cheer me, but all in vain. I asked them if I were not to be eaten by those white men with horrible looks, red faces, and long hair. They told me I was not: and one of the crew brought me a small portion of spirituous liquor in a wine glass; but being afraid of him, I would not take it out of his hand. One of the blacks therefore took it from him and gave it to me, and I took a little down my palate, which, instead of reviving me, as they thought it would, threw me into the greatest consternation at the strange feeling it produced, having never tasted any such liquor before.
>
> Soon after this, the blacks who brought me on board went off, and left me abandoned to despair. I now saw myself deprived of all chance of returning to my native country, or even the least glimpse of hope of gaining the shore, which I now considered as friendly; and I even wished for my former slavery in preference to my present situation, which was filled with horrors of every kind, still heightened by my ignorance of what I was to undergo.
>
> I was not long suffered to indulge my grief; I was soon put down under the decks, and there I received such a salutation in my nostrils as I had never experienced in my life: so that with the loathsomeness of the stench and crying together, I became so sick and low that I was not able to eat, nor had I the least desire to taste anything.

56 Sometimes the chests of the slaves were branded with the name of the company shipping them before being loaded on the ship.

I now wished for the last friend, death, to relieve me; but soon, to my grief, two of the white men offered me eatables; and, on my refusing to eat, one of them held me fast by the hands, and laid me across, I think, the windlass, and tied my feet, while the other flogged me severely.

Father Sandoval, a Catholic priest in the Americas wrote to Brother Luis Brandaon, a Church official in Africa, asking if the enslavement of Africans was legal according to Church doctrine. Brother Brandaon's response, dated March 12, 1610, answered, "Your Reverence writes me that you would like to know whether the Negroes who are sent to your parts have been legally captured. To this I reply that I think your Reverence should have no scruples on this point, because this is a matter which has been questioned by the Board of Conscience in Lisbon, and all its members are learned and conscious men. Nor did the bishops who were in Sao Thome, Cape Verde, and here in Loando—all learned and virtuous men find fault with it. We have been here ourselves for forty years and there have been among us very learned Fathers . . . never did they consider the trade as illicit. Therefore we and the Fathers of Brazil buy these slaves for our service without any scruple."

I had never experienced anything of this kind before; and although, not being used to the water, I naturally feared that element the first time I saw it, yet nevertheless, could I have got over the nettings, I would have jumped over the side, but I could not; and, besides, the crew used to watch us very closely who were not chained down to the decks, lest we should leap into the water: and I have seen some of these poor African prisoners most severely cut for attempting to do so, and hourly whipped for not eating. This indeed was often the case with myself.

In a little time after, amongst the poor chained men, I found some of my own nation, which in a small degree gave ease to my mind. I inquired of these what was to be done with us? They gave me to understand we were to be carried to these white people's country to work for them. I then was a little revived, and thought, if it were no worse than working, my situation was not so desperate.

But still I feared I should be put to death, the white people looked and acted, as I thought, in so savage a manner; for I had never seen among any people such instances of brutal cruelty; and this not only shewn towards us blacks, but also to some of the whites themselves.

One white man in particular I saw, when we were permitted to be on deck, flogged so unmercifully with a large rope near the foremast, that he died in consequence of it; and they tossed him over the side as they would have done a brute. This made me fear these people the more; and I expected nothing less than to be treated in the same manner.

I could not help expressing my fears and apprehensions to some of my countrymen: I asked them if these people had no country, but lived in this hollow place (the ship)? They told me they did not, but came from a distant one.

"Then," said I, "how comes it in all our country we 'never heard of them!'" They told me because they lived so very far off. I then asked where were their women? Had they any like themselves? I was told they had: "And why," said I, "do we not see them?" They answered, because they were left behind.

I asked how the vessel could go? They told me they could not tell; but that there were cloth put upon the masts by the help of the ropes I saw, and then the vessel went on; and the white men had some spell or magic they put in the water when they liked in order to stop the vessel. I was exceedingly amazed at this account, and really thought they were spirits. I therefore wished much to be from amongst them, for I expected they would sacrifice me: but my wishes were vain; for we were so quartered that it was impossible for any of us to make our escape.

While we stayed on the coast I was mostly on deck; and one day, to my great astonishment, I saw one of these vessels coming in with the sails up. As soon as the whites saw it, they gave a great shout, at which we were amazed; and the more so as the vessel appeared larger by approaching nearer. At last she came to an anchor in my sight, and when the anchor was let go I and my countrymen who saw it were lost in astonishment to observe the vessel stop; and were now convinced it was done by magic.

Soon after this the other ship got her boats out, and they came on board of us, and the people of both ships seemed very glad to see each other. Several of the strangers also shook hands with us, black people, and made motions with their hands, signifying I suppose, we were to go to their country; but we did not understand them.

At last, when the ship we were in had got in all her cargo, they made ready with many fearful noises, and we were all put under deck, so that we could not see how they managed the vessel.

But this disappointment was the least of my sorrow. The stench of the hold while we were on the coast was so intolerably loathsome that it was dangerous to remain there for any time, and some of us had been permitted to stay on the deck for the fresh air; but now that the whole ship's cargo were confined together, it became absolutely pestilential.

"Of all the racist claims none has done more mischief or seemed more unanswerable to true believers than the charge that only blacks—among the nation's long-settled minorities—never made it. Despite anti-Semitism Jews made it. So did Italians, the Irish, and others. So why not blacks?

"Blacks, in answer, blame racism. Racist whites resort to malicious talk about black inferiority.

"Both are wrong. Blacks have made it, though maybe not as far as others. And they have made it faster than almost any other minority group ever has once they began the climb up. The climb up didn't begin until relatively recent times, however. The starting date is 1950. In that year, according to the federal census records, about 10 percent of American blacks ranked in the middle class. Just a decade later 18 percent did. By 1970, more than a third of American blacks had joined the American middle class. Professor Richard C. Wade, reviewing these data, concludes: 'The size of this black middle class is large; indeed, no other group has had a success story equal to it.'

"Some other groups, like the Vietnamese, have climbed faster than blacks. But comparing their progress with that of blacks isn't exactly fair. Though they may have started out poor,

they usually didn't start out unskilled. Blacks usually did."[57]

—*Richard Shenkman,* Legends, Lies and Cherished Myths of American History, *1988*

The closeness of the place, and the heat of the climate, added to the number in the ship, which was so crowded that each had scarcely room to turn himself, almost suffocated us. This produced copious perspirations, so that the air soon became unfit for respiration, from a variety of loathsome smells, and brought on a sickness among the slaves, of which many died, thus falling victims to the improvident avarice, as I may call it, of their purchasers.

This wretched situation was again aggravated by the galling of the chains, now become insupportable; and the filth of the necessary tubs, into which the children often fell, and were almost suffocated. The shrieks of the women, and the groans of the dying, rendered the whole a scene of horror almost inconceivable.

Happily perhaps for myself I was soon reduced so low here that it was thought necessary to keep me almost always on deck; and from my extreme youth I was not put in fetters. In this situation I expected every hour to share the fate of my companions, some of whom were almost daily brought upon deck at the point of death, which I began to hope would soon put an end to my miseries. Often did I think many of the inhabitants of the deep much more happy than myself. I envied them the freedom they enjoyed, and as often wished I could change my condition for theirs.

Every circumstance I met with served only to render my state more painful, and heightened my apprehensions, and my opinion of the cruelty of the whites. One day they had taken a number of fishes; and when they had killed and satisfied themselves with as many as they thought fit, to our astonishment who were on the deck, rather than give any of them to us to eat, as we expected, they tossed the remaining fish into the sea again, although we begged and prayed for some as well as we could, but in vain. Some of my countrymen, being pressed by hunger, took an opportunity, when they thought no one saw them, of trying to get a little privately; but they were discovered, and the attempt procured them some very severe floggings.

One day, when we had a smooth sea and moderate wind, two of my wearied countrymen who were chained together (I was near them at the time), preferring death to such a life of misery, somehow made through the nettings and jumped into the sea: immediately another quite dejected fellow, who on account of his illness was suffered to be out of irons, also followed their example; and I believe many more would very soon have done the same if they had not been prevented by the ship's crew who were instantly alarmed.

Those of us that were the most active were in a moment put down under the deck, and there was such a noise and confusion amongst the people of the ship as I never heard before, to stop her, and get the boat out to go after the slaves. However two of the wretches were drowned, but they got the other, and afterwards flogged him unmercifully for thus attempting to prefer death to slavery.

[57] This doesn't mean that African-Americans have achieved equality. There's still a lot of resistance to equality in the United States, and the median African-American family income in 1990 was still only 57 percent that of white families.

In this manner we continued to undergo more hardships than I can now relate, hardships which are inseparable from this accursed trade. Many a time we were near suffocation from the want of fresh air, which we were often without for whole days together. This, and the stench of the necessary tubs, carried off many.

During our passage I first saw flying fishes, which surprised me very much: they used frequently to fly across the ship, and many of them fell on the deck. I also now first saw the use of the quadrant; I had often with astonishment seen the mariners make observations with it, and I could not think what it meant. They at last took notice of my surprise: and one of them, willing to increase it, as well as to gratify my curiosity, made me one day look through it. The clouds appeared to me to be land, which disappeared as they passed along. This heightened my wonder; and I was now more persuaded than ever that I was in another world, and that every thing about me was magic.

At last we came in sight of the island of Barbados, at which the whites on board gave a great shout, and made many signs of joy to us. We did not know what to think of this; but as the vessel drew nearer we plainly saw the harbour, and other ships of different kinds and sizes; and we soon anchored amongst them off Bridge-Town.

Many merchants and planters now came on board, though it was in the evening. They put us in separate parcels, and examined us attentively. They also made us jump, and pointed to the land, signifying we were to go there. We thought by this we should be eaten by these ugly men, as they appeared to us; and, when soon after we were all put down under the deck again, there was much dread and trembling.

This ship eventually landed in America, where Gustavus Vassa was sold to a Virginia planter. Later, he was sold to a British naval officer and then to a Philadelphia merchant who gave him the chance to buy his freedom. He became a ship's steward, which enabled him to see much of the world. He also worked to bring an end to slavery.

The following advertisement from India when it was under British rule appeared in a Calcutta daily newspaper in 1818:

"FEMALES RAFFLED FOR.—Be it known, that Six Fair Pretty Young LADIES, with two sweet and engaging CHILDREN, lately imported from Europe, having roses of health blooming on their cheeks, and joy sparkling in their eyes, possessing amiable tempers and highly accomplished, whom the most indifferent cannot behold without expressions of rapture, are to be raffled for, next door to the British Gallery. Scheme: Twelve Tickets, at 12 rupees each; the highest of the three throws, doubtless, takes the most fascinating, &c. &c."

Letter from the Donner Party

Donner Pass cuts through the Sierra Nevada mountain range in eastern California and is the route from Reno, Nevada, to Sacramento and then on to San Francisco. During the severe winter of 1846–1847 it was the site of the terrible tragedy that gave the pass its name.

In April 1846, a wagon train consisting of twenty covered wagons departed from Illinois led by George Donner and James Reed. In July, they decided to take an untried southern trail around the Great Salt Lake and were delayed in the desert. When the party reached the 7,088-foot pass in late October, a snowstorm had already closed it, and they were forced to set up camp, building crude shelters out of logs, rocks, and hides. One group encamped at Truckee (Donner) Lake. The other group was five miles away at Alder Creek.

They were soon snowbound. When their limited food supply ran out, they were forced to eat their animals, mice, their shoes, and twigs. After many members of the party died of starvation, those remaining began eating the bodies of the dead to survive. In December, seventeen of them set out to seek help, of which seven made it through the pass. Four relief parties returned from January through April to rescue the survivors. Of a total of ninety settlers, only forty-eight made it through alive.

Thirteen-year-old Virginia Reed was the daughter of James Reed, who was one of the party's leaders. She wrote a letter to her cousin Mary on May 16, 1847 describing the ordeal.

> We had to Walk all the time we was a travling up the truckee river we met that and 2 Indians that we had sent out for propessions to Suter Fort thay had met pa, not fur from Suters Fort he looked very bad he had not ate but 3 times in 7 days and thes days with out any thing his horse was not abel to carrie him thay give him a horse and he went on so we cashed some more of our things all but what we could pack on one mule and we started Martha and James road behind the two Indians it was a raing then in the Vallies and snowing on the montains so we went on that way 3 or 4 days tell we come to the big mountain or the Callifornia Mountain the snow then was about 3 feet deep thare was some wagons thare thay said thay had atempted to cross and could not, well we thought we would try it so we started and thay started again with thare wagons the snow was then way to the muels side the farther we went up the deeper the snow got so the wagons could not go so thay packed thare oxons and started with us carring a child a piece and driving the oxons in snow up to thare wast the mule Martha and the Indian was on was the best one so thay went and broak the road and that indian was the Pilot so we went on that way 2 miles and the mules kept faling down in the snow head formost and the Indian said he could not find the road we stoped and let the Indian and man go on to hunt the road thay went on and found the road to the top of the mountain and come back and said they thought we could git over if it did not snow any more well the Woman were all so tirder caring there Children that thay could not go over that night so we made a fire and got something to eat & ma spred down a bufalorobe & we all laid down on it & spred somthing over us & ma sit up by the fire & it snowed one foot on top of the bed so we got up in the morning & the snow was so deep we could not go over & we had to go back to the cabin & build more cabins & stay thare all Winter without Pa we had not the first thing to eat Ma maid arrangements for some cattel giving 2 for 1 in callifornia we seldom thot of bread for we had not had any since [words unreadable] & the cattel was so poor thay could note hadley git up when thay laid down we stoped thare the 4th of November & staid till March and what we had to eat i cant hardley tell you & we had that man & Indians to feed well thay started over a foot

and had to come back so thay made snow shoes and started again & it come on a storme & thay had to come back it would snow 10 days before it would stop thay wated tell it stoped & started again I was a goeing with them & I took sick & could not go—thare was 15 started & thare was 7 got throw 5 Weman & 2 men it come a storme and thay lost the road & got out of provisions & the ones that got throwe had to eat them that Died not long after thay started we got out of provisions & had to put Martha at one cabin James at another Thomas at another & Ma & Elizea & Milt Eliot & I dried up what littel meat we had and started to see if we could get across & had to leve the childrin o Mary you may think that hard to leve theme with strangers & did not now wether we would see them again or not we could hardle get a way from them but we told theme we would bring them Bread & then thay was willing to stay we went & was out 5 days in the mountains Elie giv out & had to go back we went on a day longer we had to lay by a day & make snow shows & we went on a while and coud not find the road & we had to turn back I could go on verry well while i thout we wer giting along but as soone as we had to turn back i coud hadley git along but we got to the cabins that night I froze one of my feet verry bad & that same night thare was the worst storme we had that winter & if we had not come back that night we would never got back we had nothing to eat but ox hides o Mary I would cry and wish I had what you all wasted Eliza had to go to Mr Graves cabin & we staid at Mr Breen thay had meat all the time & we had to kill littel cash the dog & eat him we ate his head and feet & hide & evry thing about him o my Dear Cousin you dont now what trubel is yet a many a time we had on the last thing a cooking and did not now wher the next would come from but there was awl wais some way provided

there was 15 in the cabon we was in and half of us had to lay a bed all the time thare was 10 starved to death there we was hadley abel to walk we lived on litle cash a week and after Mr Breen would cook his meat we would take the bones and boil them 3 or 4 days at a time ma went down to the other caben and got half a hide carried it in snow up to her wast

it snowed and would cover the cabin all over so we could not git out for 2 or 3 days we would have to cut pieces of the loges in sied to make a fire with I coud hardly eat the hides and had not eat anything 3 days Pa stated out to us with providions and then came a storme and he could not go he cash his provision and went back on the other side of the bay to get compana of men and the San Wakien got so hye he could not crose well thay Made up a Compana at Suters Fort and sent out we had not ate any thing for 3 days & we had onely a half a hide and we was out on top of the cabin and we seen them a coming

O my Dear Cousin you dont now how glad i was, we run and met them one of them we knew we had traveled with them on the road thay staid thare 3 days to recruet a little so we could go thare was 20 started all of us started and went a piece and Martha and Thomas giv out & so the men had to take them back ma and Eliza James & I come on and o Mary that was the hades thing yet to come on and leiv them thar did not now but what thay would starve to Death Martha said well ma if you never see me again do the best you can the men said thay could hadly stand it it maid them all cry but they said it was better for all of us to go on for if we was to go back we would eat that much more from them thay give them a littel meat and flore and took them back and we come on we went over great hye mountain as strait as stair steps in snow up to our knees litle James walk the hole way over all the mountain in snow up to his waist he said every step he took he was a gitting nigher Pa and somthing to eat the Bears took the provision the men had cashed and we had but very little to eat when we had traveld 5 days travel we met Pa with 13 men going to the cabins o Mary you do not nou how glad we was to see him we had not seen him for months we thought we woul never see him again he heard we was coming and he made some seet cakes to give us he said he would see Martha and Thomas the next day he went to tow [i.e. in two] days what took us 5 days some of the compana was eating from them that Died but Thomas & Martha had not ate any Pa and the men started with 12 people Hiram O Miller Carried Thomas and Pa caried Martha and thay wer caught in [unreadable word] and thay had to stop Two days it stormed so thay could not go and the Bears took their provision and thay weer 4 days without anything Pa and Hiram and all the men started one of Donner boys Pa a carring Martha Hiram caring Thomas and the snow was up to thare wast and it a snowing so thay could hadley see the way they raped the children up and never took them out for 4 days & thay had nothing to eat in all that time Thomas asked for somthing to eat once those that thay brought from the cabins some of them was not able to come and som would not come Thare was 3 died and the rest eat them thay was 10 days without any thing to eat but the Dead Pa braught Thom and pady on to where we was none of the men was abel to go there feet was froze very bad so they was a nother Compana went and braught them all in thay are all in from the Mountains now but five they was men went out after them and was caught in a storm and had to come back thare is another compana gone thare was half got through that was stoped thare sent to their relief thare was but families got that all of them got we was one

O Mary I have not wrote you half of the truble we have had but I hav Wrote you anuf to let you now that you dont now whattruble is but thank the Good god we have all got throw and the onely family that did not eat human flesh we have left every thing but i dont cair for that we have got through but Dont let this letter dishaten anybody and never take no cutofs and hury along as fast as you can

---

In another famous incident involving cannibalism, Alferd E. Packer murdered and ate five of his hunting companions in Colorado during an 1873 blizzard. At the conclusion to his murder trial, the judge exclaimed, "Stand up, you man-eating son-of-a-bitch, and receive your sentence! There were seven Democrats in Hinsdale County, but you, you voracious, man-eating son-of-a-bitch, you ate five of them. I sentence you to be hanged by the neck until you're dead, dead, dead, as a warning against reducing the Democratic population of the state."

Virginia Reed survived and three years later, at the age of sixteen, she married John Murphy. After spending most of her life in San Jose, California, she died in 1921 at the age of eighty-seven.

Lewis Keseberg was not as fortunate as Virginia Reed. He was one of those who was forced to eat his fellow travelers to keep from dying. He was finally saved by the fourth rescue party. His painful account of what happened appeared in C. F. McGlashan's *History of the Donner Party* (1880). It was the first time he talked about it.

> When my provisions gave out, I remained four days before I could taste human flesh. There was no other resort—it was that or death. My wife and child had gone on with the first relief party. I knew not whether they were living or dead. They were penniless and friendless in a strange land. For their sakes I must live, if not for my own. Mrs. Murphy was too weak to revive. The flesh of starved beings contains little nutriment. It is like feeding straw to horses. I can not describe the unutterable repugnance with which I tasted the first mouthful of flesh. There is an instinct in our nature that revolts at the thought of touching, much less eating, a corpse. It makes my blood curdle to think of it! . . .
>
> For nearly two months I was alone in that dismal cabin. No one knows what occurred but myself—no living being ever before was told of the occurrences. Life was a burden. The horrors of one day succeeded those of the preceding. Five of my companions had died in my cabin, and their stark and ghastly bodies lay there day and night, seemingly gazing at me with their glazed and staring eyes. I was too weak to move them had I tried. The relief parties had not removed them. These parties had been too hurried, too horror-stricken at the sight, too fearful lest an hour's delay might cause them to share the same fate. I endured a thousand deaths. To have one's suffering prolonged inch by inch, to be deserted, forsaken, hopeless; to see that loathsome food ever before my eyes, was almost too much for human endurance. I am conversant with four different languages. I speak and write them with equal fluency; yet in all four I do not find words enough to express the horror I experienced during those two months, or what I still feel when memory reverts to the scene. Suicide would have been a relief, a happiness, a godsend! Many a time I had the muzzle of my pistol in my mouth and my finger on the trigger, but the faces of my helpless, dependent wife and child would rise up before me, and my hand would fall powerless. I was not the cause of my misfortunes, and God Almighty had provided only this one horrible way for me to subsist. . . .
>
> The necessary mutilation of the bodies of those who had been my friends, rendered the ghastliness of my situation more frightful.

Edwin Bryant visited the site of the tragedy with General Kearney in the spring. He described what he saw at one of the camps, saying:

> Near the principal cabins I saw two bodies entire, with the exception that the abdomens had been cut open and the entrails extracted. Their flesh had been either wasted by famine or evaporated by exposure to the dry atmosphere, and they presented the appearance of mummies. Strewn around the cabins were dislocated and broken skulls (in some instances sawed asunder with care, for the purpose of extracting the brains), human skeletons, in short, in every variety of mutilation. A more revolting and appalling spectacle I never witnessed.

This was the most spectacular catastrophe involving settlers moving west, and the nation was shocked by the Donner Party's stories of cannibalism. Donner Pass was named in remembrance of this tragedy, and it is now a popular ski resort.

Captured by Indians

There are many accounts by whites who were captured by Native Americans. One of the most striking is by Fanny Kelly. She was nineteen years old when she was suddenly taken from a wagon train by Sioux warriors, separating her from her family.

It happened in Montana in July 1864, while the Civil War was still raging in the South. During 1863 and 1864, General Alfred Sully had made some punitive attacks on the Sioux in the Dakotas. This prompted the Sioux to send war parties down to raid settlers, stagecoach stations, and wagon trains traveling along the Platte route from Kansas to Idaho, which ran right through the Native American's land.[58] The soldiers of Colorado put most of the blame for these raids on the Southern Cheyennes and Arapahos and began attacking them. In response to these unprompted attacks, some Cheyennes and Arapahos began harassing settlers, stagecoach stations, and wagon trains. It was an excellent example of how the ignorance and prejudice that pervaded the Indian Wars combined to exacerbate the situation.

Fanny Kelly's family was part of a wagon train traveling along the Platte route. Fanny was born in Orillia, Canada, and spent the first ten years of her life there. The 1850s saw a tremendous shift of population into the western territories fueled by stories of amazingly fertile soil, opportunities for rapid advancement, and the easy fortunes to be made. This was a period when many working-class families were living barely above a starvation level, often earning only thirty cents for a full day's work. Fanny wrote, "Whole towns in the Eastern States were almost depopulated" because of "Western fever."

It was at this time that her family headed for Kansas. Eight years later, she married Josiah S. Kelly. His ill health prompted them to seek a change of climate, so the newlyweds and their adopted daughter, Mary—who was actually her sister's child—set out for Idaho on May 17, 1864. Their small wagon train gradually grew to include Mr. Gardner Wakefield, two African-American servants named Frank and Andy, a Methodist minister named Mr. Sharp, Mr. Taylor, Mr. Larimer, his wife, and their eight-year-old boy. Their party totaled seven men, two women, and two children. At Fort Laramie in Wyoming, they were assured the trail was safe and the Native Americans friendly. It wasn't long after this that they ran into the war party. Fanny later wrote of her ordeal in *Narrative of My Captivity Among the Sioux Indians* (1871).[59]

> The 12th of July was a warm and oppressive day. The burning sun poured forth its hottest rays upon the great Black Hills and the vast plains of Montana. . . .
>
> The beauty of the sunset and the scenery around us filled our hearts with joy. Mr. Wakefield's voice was loud and strong as he sang,

[58] The U.S. government agreed this was Native American territory in the Treaty of 1851.

[59] For brevity's sake, I have chosen to use a version of her account that has been polished by an editor to make it more readable and concise.

"Ho for Idaho!" Little Mary's low sweet voice, too, joined in the chorus. She was happy that day, as she always was. She was the star and joy of our whole party.

Without a sound of preparation or a word of warning, the bluffs before us were covered with a party of about two hundred and fifty Indians, painted and equipped for war, who uttered their wild war whoop and fired a signal volley of guns and revolvers into the air.

We had no time to think before the main body halted and sent out a part of their force, which circled round us at regular intervals, some distance from our wagons.

Recovering from the shock our men instantly decided to resist and corralled the wagons. My husband was looked upon as leader, as he was principal owner of the train. We were just a handful, but he was ready to stand his ground.

With all the power I could command, I begged him not to fight but to attempt to make peace with the Indians. "They seem to outnumber us ten to one," I said. "If you fire one shot, they will massacre all of us."

Love for the trembling little girl at my side, my husband, and friends made me strong to protest against anything that would lessen our chance to escape with our lives. Poor little Mary! From the first she had entertained an ungovernable dread of the Indians. In our dealings with friendly savages, I had tried to show how unfounded it was, and persuade her they were harmless, but all in vain. Mr. Kelly bought her beads and many little presents from them which she much admired, but she would always add, "They look so cross at me, and they have knives and tomahawks, and I fear they will kill me."

My husband advanced to meet the chief and demand his intentions.

"What is life? It is the flash of a firefly in the night. It is the breath of a buffalo in the wintertime. It is the little shadow which runs across the grass and loses itself in sunset."

—The last words of Crowfoot, a Blackfoot warrior, 1890

The savage leader immediately came toward him, riding forward and uttering the words "How! how!"

His name was Ottawa, and he was a war chief of the Ogalala band of the Sioux nation. He struck himself on his breast, saying, "Good Indian, me." He pointed to those around him. "Heap good Indian, hunt buffalo and deer."

He assured us of his utmost friendship for the white people. Then he shook hands and his band followed his example, crowding around our wagons, shaking us all by the hand over and over again until our arms ached. They grinned and nodded with every demonstration of good will.

Our only safety seemed to be in delay, in hope of assistance approaching. To gain time, we allowed them to do whatever they fancied.

First, they said they would like to change one of their horses for the one Mr. Kelly was riding, a favorite race horse. Very much against his will, he gave in to their request.

My husband came to me with words of cheer and hope, but oh! what a marked look of despair was upon his face—a look such as I had never seen before.

The Indians asked for flour, and we gave them what they wanted. The flour they emptied upon the ground, saving only the sack. They talked to us partly by signs and partly in broken English. As we were anxious to suit ourselves to their whims and keep things friendly as long as possible, we allowed them to take whatever they desired, and offered them many presents besides.

It was, I have said, extremely warm weather, but the Indians remarked that the cold made it necessary for them to look for clothing, and begged for some from our stock. We gave it to them without the slightest objection. I, in a careless-like manner, said they must give me some moccasins for some articles of clothing that I had just handed them. Very pleasantly a young Indian gave me a nice pair, richly embroidered with different-colored beads.

Our anxiety to stay on good terms with them increased every instant. The hope of help arriving from some quarter grew stronger as the moments passed. Unfortunately, it was our only one.

The Indians grew bolder and more insolent in their advances. One of them laid hold of my husband's gun. Repulsed, he gave up.

The chief at last told us to proceed on our way, promising that we should not be molested. We obeyed, without trusting them.

Soon the wagon train was again in motion. The Indians insisted on driving our herd and grew ominously familiar. My husband called a halt. He saw that we were approaching a rocky glen, in whose gloomy depths he anticipated a murderous attack. Our enemies urged us forward, but we resolutely refused to stir. Finally they asked us to prepare supper. They said they would share it with us and then go to the hills to sleep. The men of our party concluded it would be best to give them a feast.

Each man was soon busy preparing the supper. Mr. Larimer and Frank were making the fire. Mr. Wakefield was getting provisions out of the wagon. Mr. Taylor was attending to his team, Mr. Kelly and Andy were out some distance gathering wood, and Mr. Sharp was distributing sugar among the Indians. Then, suddenly, our terrible enemies threw off their masks and displayed their true natures.

There was a simultaneous discharge of arms. When the cloud of smoke cleared away, I could see the retreating form of Mr. Larimer and the slow motion of poor Mr. Wakefield, for he was mortally wounded.[60]

Mr. Sharp was killed within a few feet of me. Mr. Taylor—I can never forget his face as I saw him shot through the forehead with a rifle ball. He looked at me as he fell backward to the ground. I was the last object that met his dying gaze. Our poor faithful Frank fell at my feet pierced by many arrows.[61] I recall the scene with a sickening horror. I could not see my husband anywhere and did not know his fate. Actually, he and Andy made a miraculous escape but I did not learn this until long afterward.

I had but little time for thought, for the Indians quickly sprang into our wagons, tearing off covers, crushing, and smashing everything that

60 Mr. Larimer survived but was wounded in one of his limbs by an arrow. Mr. Wakefield was hit by three arrows. He was found a quarter of a mile away, still alive. He tried removing the arrows himself but could only get the shafts out. He later died.

61 One arrow pierced both his legs, pinning them together. He was killed by a blow to the head.

stood between them and their plunder. They broke open locks, trunks, and boxes, and distributed or destroyed our goods with great rapidity, using their tomahawks to pry open boxes, which they split up in savage recklessness.

They filled the air with fearful war whoops and hideous shouts. I knew that an indiscreet act on my part might jeopardize our lives. I felt certain that we two women would share death by their hands, but, with as much of an air of indifference as I could command, I kept still, hoping to prolong our lives even if only a few minutes.

I was not allowed this quiet but a moment. With tomahawks in their hands, two of the most savage-looking of the party rushed up into my wagon and seized me. They pulled me violently to the ground, almost breaking my arms and legs. My little Mary, with outstretched hands, was standing in the wagon. I took her in my arms and helped her to the ground.

I turned to the chief, put my hand upon his arm, and implored his protection for my fellow-prisoner and our children. At first he seemed utterly indifferent. Partly in words and partly by signs, he ordered me to remain quiet, placing his hand upon the revolver in his belt as an argument to enforce obedience.

A short distance in the rear of our train a wagon was in sight. The chief immediately dispatched a detachment of his band to capture or to cut it off from us. They rode furiously in pursuit of the small party, which consisted only of one family and a man who rode in advance of the single wagon.

The horseman was almost instantly surrounded and killed by a volley of arrows. The man in the wagon quickly turned his team around and, starting them at full speed, gave the whip and lines to the woman, who held a young child close in her arms. He then went to the back end of his wagon and threw out boxes, trunks, everything that he possessed. His wife meantime gave all her mind and strength to urging the horses forward.

The Indians had by this time come very near. They riddled the wagon cover with bullets and arrows. But the man kept them at bay with his revolver, and finally they left him and rode furiously back to our wagon train.

I was led a short distance from the wagon with Mary and told to remain quiet. I tried to obey. A terrible yearning sprang up in my heart to escape, as I hoped my husband had done. But many watchful eyes were upon me. I realized that any effort then at escape would result in failure, and probably cause the death of all the prisoners.

Mrs. Larimer, with her boy, came to us, trembling with fear. "The men have all escaped and left us to the mercy of the savages." [She didn't know the men had been killed.]

"I do hope they have. What benefit would it be to us to have them here? They would be killed, and then all hope of rescue for us would be at an end."

Her agitation was extreme. Her grief seemed to reach its climax when she saw the Indians destroying her property. It consisted principally of articles belonging to the art of daguerreotype photography. She had indulged in high hopes of fortune from practicing this art among the mining towns of Idaho. As she saw her chemicals, picture cases, and other property being destroyed, she uttered a wild, despairing cry. It brought the chief of the band to us. With gleaming knife, he threatened to end all her further troubles in this world.

My own agony was no less than hers. But the loss of my worldly possessions—a large herd of cattle, groceries, and goods of particular value in the mining regions—I gave no thought to. The possible fate of my husband and the dark, fearful future that loomed before myself and little Mary were the only thoughts that flashed through my mind.

But my poor companion was in great danger. I went to the side of the chief. Assuming a cheerfulness I was very far from feeling, I pleaded successfully for her life, but received no evidences of kindness or relenting that I could then understand. He did present me, however, with a wreath of gay feathers from his own head. I afterward learned it was a token of his favor and protection. He then left us, to secure his own share of plunder.

They were placed under a special guard, while the warriors made a bonfire of whatever they couldn't carry with them. Soon they set out into the wilderness. She was dropping pieces of paper to mark their route and after a while she quietly lowered Mary from the horse they were riding, telling her to hide and then to follow the papers back to the remains of their wagons, figuring her daughter had a better chance there. Later, she tried to escape in the same manner, but when the warriors noticed she was gone, they came back and found her, but not her daughter.[62] They beat her and threatened worse treatment if she tried escaping again. Eventually, they camped for the night. They traveled all the next day and camped again for the night. When she woke up the following morning, she discovered one of the Native Americans had helped Mrs. Larimer and her son safely escape, leaving Fanny alone among her captors.

After traveling nearly three hundred miles, they arrived at the Sioux village. The village was very large since nearly all the Sioux had gathered together because of the war. After making a grand entrance, their plunder was divided among everyone. She became part of the chief's family. It was common practice among Native Americans that when someone in their family died or was killed, they would adopt someone to replace the deceased. Sometimes they even captured men, women, or children for this purpose. Since most of the work fell on the women, Fanny was soon given a number of chores to take care of, and she did her best to settle in to the Native American lifestyle. Fanny says she shared the lodge with the chief's old wife and his three sisters, but more likely they were all his wives.

Soon after her arrival, there was a celebration for their successful raid.

The day of the 25th of July was observed by continual feasting in honor of the safe return of

Fanny Kelly.

[62] Mary went back to the road and waited. A party of three or four soldiers saw her from across a ravine, but thought she might be a decoy set out by the Native Americans to lure them into a trap. As they cautiously started toward her, they spotted some Native Americans and fled, leaving the girl behind. Apparently, the Native Americans also saw her and chased her, shooting her with three arrows. They then clubbed her to death with a tomahawk and scalped her. Her body was found two days later by Mr. Kelly and buried.

the braves. There was a large tent made by putting several together, and here all the chiefs, medicine men, and great warriors met for consultation and feasting. I was invited to attend and was given an elevated seat. The rest of the company all sat upon the ground, mostly cross-legged.

In the center of the circle was erected a pole, with many scalps, trophies, and ornaments fastened to it. Near the foot of the pole several large kettles were placed in a row on the ground. In these the feast was prepared.

Thousands climbed and crowded around for a peep at me. At length the chief arose, in a very handsome costume. He addressed the audience and often pointed to me. I could understand but little of his meaning.

Several others also made speeches. They all sounded the same to me. I sat trembling with fear. I thought they were deliberating upon a plan of putting me to some cruel death to finish their amusement.

Soon a handsome pipe was lit and brought to the chief to smoke. He took it and presented the stem to the north, the south, the east, and the west, and to the sun overhead. Then he uttered a few words, drew a few whiffs, and passed it around through the whole group, who all smoked. The feast throughout was conducted in silence.

The lids were raised from the kettles, which were all filled with dog's meat, made into a sort of stew. My dish was given me, and the absolute necessity of eating it was painful to contemplate. After much urging I tasted it a few times and then resigned my dish. It was passed around with others to every part of the group, who all ate heartily. In this way the feast ended, and all left silently.

By looks and gestures the women told me that I should feel highly honored by being called to feast with chiefs and great warriors and, seeing the spirit in which it was given, I could not but treat it respectfully.

As far as I could understand, the dog feast seems to be a truly religious ceremony. In it the superstitious Indian sacrifices his faithful companion to bear testimony to the sacredness of his vows of friendship for the Great Spirit. He always offers up a portion of the meat to his deity, then puts it on the ground to remind him of the sacrifice and solemnity of the offering. . . .[63]

That night was spent in dancing. It all seemed wild and furious to me. I was led into the center of the circle and assigned the painful duty of holding above my head human scalps fastened to a little pole. The dance was kept up until near morning, when all returned to their lodges. The three kind sisters of the chief were there to lead me to mine.

The next morning the village was packed up and put in motion as the warriors set off for battle, having heard that General Sully's troops were approaching. They could hear the sounds of the battle as they fled. They encamped again that afternoon and waited for word from the warriors. They returned three days later and apparently suffered few casualties in the battle. So they continued on.

This country seemed scarred by countless trails, where the Indian ponies have dragged lodge poles, in the savages' change of camp or hunting. The hatred of the Indian for its occupation by the white man is very bitter. The felling of timber,

63 Dogs were very highly valued, and only the very best were sacrificed for this ceremony.

killing of buffalo, traveling of a wagon train, or any signs of permanent possession by the white man excite deadly hostility. It is the Indians' last hope; if they yield and give up this, they will have to die or ever after be governed by the white man's laws. Consequently they lose no opportunity to kill or steal from and harass the whites.

The game still clings to its favorite haunts, and the Indian must press upon the steps of the white man or lose all hope of independence. Herds of elk proudly stand with erect antlers; the mountain sheep look down from crags that skirt the northern face of the mountains. The black and white-tail deer and antelope are ever present, while the hare and the rabbit, the sage hen, and the prairie chicken are nearly trodden down before they yield to the intrusion of the stranger.

The buffalo, in numberless herds, with tens of thousands in a herd, sweep back and forth, filling the valley as far as the eye can reach; they are valued by the red man because they yield him food, a covering for his tepee, fuel, and clothing. The Big Horn River and mountains and streams beyond are plentifully supplied with various kinds of fish. The country seems to be filled with wolves, which pierce the night air with their howls.

"Something ought to be done about these 'primitive' people who live in various parts of the world, and don't know a thing but to live off what nature provides. You would think they would be civilized and learn to live off each other like us civilized folks do."

—Will Rogers

The Indians felt that the nearness of the troops and their inroads through their best hunting grounds would prove disastrous to them, and soon they were making preparations for battle again. On the 8th of August the warriors set forth on the warpath.

Once again, Fanny could hear the battle sounds as the warriors clashed with General Sully's troops. The village fled, and after a couple of days they entered the Bad Lands. They were so hotly pursued that they had to leave all their belongings behind when they swam across the Yellowstone River. General Sully's men destroyed everything the Sioux left behind and then broke off the attack, unaware that Fanny was being held by the Sioux.

After the attack of General Sully was over, an Indian came to me with a letter to read, taken from a soldier killed by him. The letter stated that the topographical engineer was killed, and that General Sully's men had caught the red devils responsible, cut their heads off, and stuck them upon poles. The soldier had written a friendly letter to his people, but before it was mailed he was numbered with the dead.

Eventually, the warriors returned and a "scene of terrible mourning" took place. Since all of their food was gone and there was no game in the area, starvation soon set in. The Sioux were so enraged they threatened to take their revenge by putting Fanny to death, and the chiefs held a council to determine her fate, among other things.

The next morning I could see that something unusual was about to happen. The sun had scarcely appeared above the horizon when the principal chiefs and warriors assembled in council.

Soon they sent an Indian to me. He asked me if I was ready to die—to be burned at the stake. I told him whenever Wakon-Tonka (the Great Spirit) was ready, he would call for me, and I would be willing to go. He said he had been sent from the council to warn me that it had become necessary to put me to death because my white brothers had killed so many of their young men.

Now the chiefs sat silently around the council fire. The pipe carrier entered the circle, holding in his hand the pipe ready lighted. When all the chiefs and men had smoked, one after another, the pipe bearer emptied the ashes into the fire.

"Chiefs of the great Dakota nation, Wakon-Tonka give you wisdom so that whatever you decide may be just," he said. He bowed respectfully and left the circle.

A moment of silence followed. One of the most aged of the chiefs, whose body was furrowed with the scars of innumerable wounds, arose.

"The palefaces, our eternal persecutors, pursue and harass us relentlessly," he said. "They force us to abandon to them, one by one, our best hunting grounds, and we are compelled to seek a refuge in these Bad Lands, like timid deer. Many of them even dare to come into prairies, which belong to us, to trap beaver and hunt elk and buffalo, which are our property. These faithless creatures, the outcasts of their own people, rob and kill us when they can. Is it just to suffer this without complaining? Shall we allow ourselves to be slaughtered like timid Assiniboines, without seeking to avenge ourselves? Does not the law of the Dakotas say, Justice to our own nation and death to all palefaces?" He pointed to the stake that was being prepared for me. "Let my brothers say if that is just."

"Vengeance is allowable," remarked Mahpeah, an old chief.

Chief Ottawa arose. "Vengeance is the right of the weak and oppressed—and yet it ought to be no greater than the injury received. Why should we put this young, innocent woman to death? Has she not always been kind to us, smiled upon us, and sung for us? Do not all our children love her as a sister? Why, then, should we put her to so cruel a death for the crimes of others, because they are of her nation? Why should we punish the innocent for the guilty?"

How thankful I was when I knew their decision was to spare me. Though my life was miserable, it always became sweet when I felt I was about to part with it.

They continued on their way, hoping to find something to eat. Many of the dogs and horses succumbed to starvation and were promptly eaten. Often they only had grass to eat. She soon became ill and delirious. About this time they were attacked again. This battle lasted for three days, and there were many Sioux casualties. Fanny wrote, "Except when encamped for rest, the tribe pursued their wanderings constantly, sometimes fleeing before the enemy. We were always hungry and tired." As winter set in, the U.S. soldiers returned to their fort.

Eventually, General Sully learned that she was among the Sioux and offered to pay a reward for her release. She was then transferred to a small band of the Oglala Sioux called the Blackfoot (who should not be confused with the much larger tribe also called the Blackfoot). Fanny says they decided to use her to gain entrance to Fort

Sully so that they could kill the garrison of two hundred soldiers. She was able to convince one warrior who had fallen in love with her to deliver a note to the fort warning them of the plan.

She says, the night before they went to the fort, she heard the chief make the following speech:

> Friends and sons, listen to my words. You are a great and powerful band of our people. The inferior race, who have encroached on our rights and territories, justly deserve hatred and destruction. These intruders came among us, and we took them by the hand. We believed them to be friends and true speakers; they have shown us how false and cruel they can be.
>
> They build forts to live in and shoot from with their big guns. Our people fall before them. Our game is chased from the hills. Our women are taken from us or won to forsake our lodges [sic], and wronged and deceived.
>
> It has only been four or five moons since they drove us to desperation, killed our brothers and burned our tepees. The Indian cries for vengeance! There is no truth or friendship in the white man. Deceit and bitterness are in his words.
>
> Meet them with equal cunning. Show them no mercy. They are but few, we are many. Whet your knives and string your bows—sharpen the tomahawk and load the rifle!
>
> Let the wretches die, who have stolen our lands, and we will be free to roam over the soil that was our fathers'! We will come home bravely from battle. Our songs shall rise among the hills, and every tepee shall be hung with the scalp locks of our foes.

Eight chiefs and more than a thousand warriors took her on the two-hundred-mile journey through the December snow to Fort Sully in South Dakota. They arrived on December 12 and prepared for their attack. The eight chiefs led her into the fort, and the fort's gates were closed before the warriors could enter.

"True, the Ogalalas had treated me at times with great harshness and cruelty, yet I had never suffered from any of them the slightest personal or unchaste insult. Let me bear testimony to this redeeming feature in their treatment of me."

—Fanny Kelly

The Native American version of what happened is a bit different. Blackfoot Sioux leader Crawler and Sitting Bull's friends and relatives told a South Dakota historian that Fanny was the prisoner of Oglala warrior Brings-Plenty, who gave her the very respectful name of "Real Woman" and who "used her as his wife." With Sitting Bull's encouragement, Crawler took her away from Brings-Plenty at gun point. Then Sitting Bull and the Blackfeet delivered her to the fort for the reward, but they were all locked out—including Sitting Bull. They had never intended to attack the soldiers, and the misunderstanding stemmed from Fanny Kelly's poor understanding of the Sioux language.

Either way, Fanny was free after more than five months in captivity. The Sioux stayed near the fort, but Fanny refused to visit them, so after two weeks they finally departed, leaving behind presents for her. She was suffering from frostbite and remained under medical care for two months. Her husband had been searching all over for her, and when he heard she was at the fort, he headed straight there. They decided to return to Kansas, where they opened a hotel. In 1870, she was awarded $5,000 by Congress in compensation and in recognition for saving the fort. She died in 1904.

Native American attacks on white settlers have been enlarged to mythic proportions, leading people to believe Native Americans were a major threat to wagon trains. In actuality, between 1840 and 1860, when some 250,000 whites and African-Americans made their way across the Plains, only 362 pioneers died in battles with the Native Americans. At the same time, 426 Native Americans were killed in the same battles. More often, the Native Americans helped the pioneers by giving them directions, showing them water holes, acting as guides and interpreters, buying cloth and guns, and selling food and horses. The threat was sensationalized partly because it made good reading and sold newspapers and magazines, but also because it helped justify the removal of the Native Americans from their lands.

Although not excusing the behavior of the Native Americans in this account, in fairness it must be noted that these settlers entered a war zone and were traveling though enemy territory. Whether or not this made them a legitimate target is a matter for debate. Either way, what happened was truly a tragedy.

The U.S. Army Murders Native Americans

In what may very well be the worst atrocity in American history, the U.S. Army attacked a band of peaceful Native Americans, who were under the protection of a U.S. fort, and butchered them as they huddled under an American flag. Although this was just one of many hideous massacres that occurred during the Indian Wars, the circumstances surrounding this tragedy make it particularly horrible.

For years, Chief Motavato (Black Kettle) was the leading advocate for peace with the U.S. government among the Cheyennes. In 1863, he, Cheyenne Chief Lean Bear, and a number of other chiefs were invited to Washington, D.C., where they met President Lincoln. In Washington, Black Kettle was given a huge U.S. flag and was told that if he flew that flag, no soldier would ever fire at him. He was very proud of this flag and always flew it above his teepee when at a permanent encampment. They were also given some medallions to wear and papers certifying they were friends of the United States.

Then in May of 1864, they were told that about one hundred soldiers with two cannons were heading for their camp. Chief Lean Bear decided to go see them to find out what they wanted. Wearing the medal Lincoln had given him and carrying the papers, they set out. When the soldiers saw the Cheyennes, they lined up in formation. Lean Bear told the others to wait, so as not to frighten the soldiers, and he approached alone. One of the warriors, Wolf Chief, later said:

"I learn from Lieutenant J. J. Jackson that Indians have been in your post for the purpose of making a treaty. The Congress of the Confederate States has passed a law declaring extermination to all hostile Indians. You will therefore use all means to persuade the Apaches or any tribe to come in for the purpose of making peace, and when you get them together kill all the

grown Indians and take the children prisoners and sell them to defray the expense of killing the Indians. Buy whisky and such other goods as may be necessary for the Indians and I will order vouchers given to cover the amount expended. Leave nothing undone to insure success, and have a sufficient number of men around to allow no Indian to escape."

—Confederate Arizona Governor John R. Baylor's instructions to the commander of the Arizona Guards in 1862. This plan never went into effect because the higher Confederate command thought it was too brutal.

Lean Bear told us warriors to stay where we were so as not to frighten the soldiers, while he rode forward to shake hands with the officer and show his papers. . . . When the chief was within only twenty or thirty yards of the line, the officer called out in a very loud voice and the soldiers all opened fire on Lean Bear and the rest of us. Lean Bear fell off his horse right in front of the troops, and Star, another Cheyenne, also fell off his horse. The soldiers then rode forward and shot Lean Bear and Star again as they lay helpless on the ground. I was off with a party of young men to one side. There was a company of soldiers in front of us, but they were all shooting at Lean Bear and the other Cheyennes who were near to him. They paid no attention to us until we began firing on them with bows and guns. They were so close that we shot several of them with arrows. Two of them fell backward off their horses. By this time there was a great deal of confusion. More Cheyennes kept coming up in small parties, and the soldiers were bunching up and seemed badly frightened. They were shooting at us with the cannon. The grapeshot struck the ground around us, but the aim was bad.

Meanwhile, Black Kettle was riding up and down yelling for his people to stop fighting. The warriors were extremely upset, and it took a while to get them to stop, though some chased the soldiers all the way back to Fort Larned in Kansas. Three Cheyennes were killed, including Lean Bear, and many were wounded. Many soldiers were killed, but if Black Kettle hadn't stopped the fighting, all the soldiers would have probably been wiped out since there were five hundred Cheyennes in the area.

Black Kettle then sent a message to Colorado's military commander, Colonel John Chivington, to plead for peace, but Chivington wasn't interested. Chivington, a former Methodist minister, was a racist who believed every single Native American should be wiped out. Such sentiments were very common throughout the frontier at that time. Many people actually believed the statement, "the only good Indian is a dead Indian," and often said so. Chivington was one of them. In fact, the colonel, Colorado's Governor John Evans, and the Indian agent were working together to drive the Native Americans out of Colorado altogether. By starting a war, they hoped to take away the Native Americans' land so that the whites could develop it.

In June 1864, a group of Arapahos murdered a frontier couple and their two children causing the people of Denver to panic. This prompted the U.S. War Department to authorize Chivington to raise a volunteer regiment to temporarily supplement his troops. The Third Colorado Cavalry was to disband after one hundred days. He immediately began sending them out to kill any Native American they saw without asking any questions. His orders to his men were to "kill Cheyennes whenever and wherever found."

Governor Evans issued a circular ordering friendly Cheyennes to stay away from those who were at war and go directly to Fort Lyon in Southern Colorado where their agent would give them provisions and show them where they could safely camp.

As attacks on Native Americans in the area increased, General Sully's punitive attacks on the Sioux in Dakota during the previous year had caused the Sioux to begin their raids along the Platte route. This was when Fanny Kelly was captured. The blame for the Sioux raids landed primarily on the Cheyennes and Arapahos. Some Cheyennes, particularly the dog soldiers, launched a few raids of their own in response to attacks on their people by the Third.

Chief Black Kettle tried to stop Cheyenne raids but was unsuccessful. When two white women and five children captives were brought in, he traded his own horses for four of them so he could return them to their families. It was then that he received the circular, but the war was already underway. Afraid to lead his people across Colorado without protection, he sent a message to Fort Lyon asking the commander, Major Edward Wynkoop, to send someone to lead them in.

Wynkoop was obviously very leery of a trap. He probably wouldn't have risked his 127 men to bring in more than two thousand Cheyennes, Arapahos, and Sioux if it hadn't been for the prospects of releasing the captives. Wynkoop was led to Black Kettle's camp by the two warriors who delivered the message, and his conversations with them on the way apparently had a profound effect on him.

"I felt myself in the presence of superior beings," he later said, "and these were the representatives of a race that I heretofore looked upon without exception as being cruel, treacherous, and bloodthirsty without feeling or affection for friend or kindred."

Wynkoop convinced Black Kettle and six other chiefs to accompany him to Denver to make peace. The chiefs rode into Denver in a wagon with Black Kettle's flag flying over them. The four captives also went with them and were released.

"The only good Indians I ever saw were dead."

—Lieutenant General Philip Sheridan, 1868

Governor Evans wasn't interested in meeting the chiefs. Earlier that day, General Samuel Curtis had sent a telegraph to Colonel Chivington saying, "I want no peace till the Indians suffer more." Evans didn't want peace either since he had just sworn to Washington officials that he needed to raise another regiment to fight Native Americans. If there was peace, he thought he'd be accused of misrepresentation. He also knew his constituents would be very displeased because without this regiment and the Third Colorado Cavalry, all those men would be drafted to fight Confederates in the South. Evans told Wynkoop that the Third was "raised to kill Indians, and they must kill Indians."

As can be expected, the meeting did not go well. The chiefs wanted peace, but Evans and Chivington didn't. Chivington suggested

Wynkoop take the Native Americans to Sand Creek, about forty miles from Fort Lyon, which he did. Shortly after Wynkoop's return to the fort, an officer of Chivington's volunteers, Major Scott Anthony, arrived to relieve Wynkoop of his post for being too friendly with the Native Americans.

Anthony immediately ordered the Native Americans' rations to be cut in half, and when some Arapahos came to the fort to trade buffalo skins, he had his men shoot at them, saying "they had annoyed him enough, and that was the only way to get rid of them."

When Black Kettle heard of all this, he and some Cheyennes went to the fort to meet Anthony. Also at the meeting were several officers who later testified that Anthony had told Black Kettle that his people at Sand Creek were under the protection of the fort. While Anthony was making moves to assure them of his friendliness, he sent off a request for reinforcements.

Back in Denver, the Third's one hundred days were about to expire, and the newspapers were thrashing them as "the bloodless Third" because they had yet to fight a single battle. When Colonel Chivington with six hundred of his men arrived at the fort the next day, they included most of the Third, who were itching for blood. Chivington, himself, was talking of "collecting scalps" and "wading in gore." When several of his officers protested, Chivington yelled, "Damn any man who sympathizes with Indians! I have come to kill Indians, and believe it is right and honorable to use any means under God's heaven to kill Indians." Under threat of court martial, these officers went along but secretly ordered their men only to fire in self-defense.

After dark on November 28, seven hundred soldiers with four howitzers set out for Sand Creek with half-Cheyenne rancher Robert Bent as a guide. Black Kettle's camp now contained some six hundred people. Two thirds of them were women and children, since the warriors were out hunting buffalo, as Major Anthony had suggested to them. In the camp, the people spent almost the entire night celebrating the peace they thought they'd achieved.

Robert Bent's brother, George, who was a trader, was in the camp. In the morning, George was still in bed when he heard people running around. He said:

> From down the creek a large body of troops was advancing at a rapid trot . . . more soldiers could be seen making for the Indian pony herds to the south of the camps, in the camps themselves all was confusion and noise—men, women, and children rushing out of the lodges partly dressed; women and children screaming at sight of the troops; men running back into the lodges for their arms. . . . I looked toward the chief's lodge and saw that Black Kettle had a large American flag tied to the end of a long lodgepole and was standing in front of his lodge, holding the pole, with the flag fluttering in the gray light of the winter dawn. I heard him call to the people not to be afraid, that the soldiers would not hurt them; then the troops opened fire from two sides of the camp.

Ten years after the Sand Creek massacre, Chief Eskiminzin and his band of Aravaipa Apaches sought peace by moving to Camp Grant, an army outpost in the desert north of Tucson, and turned in their weapons. Early in the morning of April 30, 1871, a vigilante group of 146 people from Tucson quietly crept into their camp and began murdering the Native Americans in their sleep with clubs and knives. The camp was soon awakened to the horror, and the assassins began using their guns and rifles. It's estimated one hundred innocent women and children and eight men were massacred, since the rest of the men were out hunting. The surviving women were raped and the children taken into slavery. A trial was arranged, but a jury found the vigilantes innocent.

Soon, hundreds of Cheyenne women and children had gathered for protection under the U.S. flag and a white flag that Black Kettle had run up under it. About this time, Robert Bent came in sight of the camp. He later testified before Congress, saying:

> I saw the American flag waving and heard Black Kettle tell the Indians to stand around the flag, and there they were huddled—men, women, and children. This was when we were within fifty yards of the Indians. I also saw a white flag raised. These flags were in so conspicuous a position that they must have been seen. When the troops fired, the Indians ran, some of the men into their lodges, probably to get their arms. . . . I think there were six hundred Indians in all. I think there were thirty-five braves and some old men, about sixty in all . . . the rest of the men were away from camp, hunting. . . . After the firing the warriors put the squaws and children together, and surrounded them to protect them. I saw five squaws under a bank for shelter. When the troops came up to them they ran out and showed their persons to let the soldiers know they were squaws and begged for mercy, but the soldiers shot them all. I saw one squaw lying on the bank whose leg had been broken by a shell; a soldier came up to her with a drawn saber; she raised her arm to protect herself, when he struck, breaking her arm she rolled over and raised her other arm, when he struck, breaking it, and then left her without killing her. There seemed to be indiscriminate slaughter of men, women, and children. There were some thirty or forty squaws collected in a hole for protection; they sent out a little girl about six years old with a white flag on a stick; she had not proceeded but a few steps when she was shot and killed. All the squaws in that hole were afterwards killed, and four or five bucks outside. The squaws offered no resistance. Every one I saw dead was scalped. I saw one squaw cut open with an unborn child, as I thought, lying by her side. Captain Soule afterwards told me that such was the fact. I saw the body of White Antelope [a seventy-five-year-old chief] with the privates cut off, and I heard a soldier say he was going to make a tobacco pouch out of them. I saw one squaw whose privates had been cut out. . . . I saw a little girl about five years of age who had been hid in the sand; two soldiers discovered her, drew their pistols and shot her, and then pulled her out of the sand by the arm. I saw quite a number of infants in arms killed with their mothers.

"Although wrongs have been done me I live in hopes. I have not got two hearts. . . . Now we are together again to make peace. My shame is as big as the earth, although I will do what my friends advise me to do. I once thought that I was the only man that persevered to be the friend of the white man, but since they have come and cleaned

out our lodges, horses, and everything else, it is hard for me to believe white men any more."

—Chief Black Kettle

Lieutenant James Connor testified that this was accurate, adding:

> In going over the battleground the next day I did not see a body of man, woman, or child but was scalped, and in many instances their bodies were mutilated in the most horrible manner—men, women, and children's privates cut out, &c; I heard one man say that he had cut out a woman's private parts and had them for exhibition on a stick; I heard another man say that he had cut the fingers off an Indian to get the rings on the hand; according to the best of my knowledge and belief these atrocities that were committed were with the knowledge of J. M. Chivington, and I do not know of his taking any measures to prevent them; I heard of one instance of a child a few months old being thrown in the feedbox of a wagon, and after being carried some distance left on the ground to perish; I also heard of numerous instances in which men had cut out the private parts of females and stretched them over the saddle-bows and wore them over their hats while riding in the ranks.

Through lack of discipline, cowardice and because many of the soldiers were drunk, most of the Native Americans were able to escape the slaughter by hiding until dark and then fleeing. Chivington, in his official report, claimed they'd killed four hundred to five hundred warriors. In actuality, they'd killed 28 men and 105 women and children. Many more were wounded. The soldiers suffered nine dead and thirty-eight wounded, many from accidentally firing across at the soldiers firing from the other side of the camp. (The same thing happened at the Wounded Knee massacre on December 29, 1890, where almost three hundred Native Americans, mostly women and children, were murdered under their white flags by the U.S. Army after most of their weapons had been confiscated. There, twenty-nine soldiers died and thirty-nine were wounded, primarily from the crossfire.)

A week before the massacre, Colonel Chivington justified the murder of Native American babies by saying, "Nits make lice!" This was during a public speech he'd made in Denver in which he advocated killing off all Native Americans and scalping them.

When the soldiers arrived back in Denver, they paraded through the streets proudly showing off their gruesome trophies while the citizens cheered. The government launched three separate investigations, but Colonel Chivington was never charged for what happened. Today, not far from the site of the massacre, there is a town named Chivington.

Black Kettle escaped up a ravine, and along with his badly wounded wife and the other survivors, he trudged fifty miles to the hunting camp where the warriors were. He then went off with a few relatives and some old men. The following summer, government officials came to see him to sign a new treaty because Denver and many new settlements were on land that legally belonged to the Cheyennes and Arapahos. Black Kettle still believed in peace. He told them, "Although the troops have struck us, we throw it all behind and are glad to meet you in peace and friendship. . . .

We are different nations, but it seems as if we were but one people, whites and all." He and several other chiefs signed the treaty agreeing to move onto the Kiowas' land in what is now Oklahoma. The treaty also guaranteed "perpetual peace."

Four years later, Chief Black Kettle and his wife were murdered by George Armstrong Custer and the Seventh Cavalry in the Washita River massacre. This time, of 103 dead Cheyenne, 53 were women and children; only 9 were warriors. General Sheridan, Custer's superior, was pleased that Custer had "wiped out old Black Kettle." Black Kettle died with his hand raised making the sign for peace.

About the massacre at Wounded Knee in 1890, Chief Black Elk said, "I did not know then how much was ended. When I look back now from this high hill of my old age, I can still see the butchered women and children lying heaped and scattered all along the crooked gulch as plain as when I saw them with eyes still young. And I can see that something else died there in the bloody mud, and was buried in the blizzard. A people's dream died there."

At Sand Creek, Colonel Chivington and his men effectively killed or destroyed the power of every Cheyenne and Arapaho chief who sought peace with the whites. The localized conflict was escalated to a more generalized Indian War. When a peace emissary from the U.S. government met with the new leaders of the Cheyenne and told them there were not enough warriors to fight the Army, they said, "We know it. But what do we want to live for? The white man has taken our country, killed all of our game; was not satisfied with that, but killed our wives and children. Now no peace. We want to go and meet our families in the spirit land. We loved the whites until we found out they lied to us, and robbed us of what we had. We have raised the battle ax until death."

The war continued for another twenty-six years.

On the *Titanic* as it Sinks

Everyone knows that the S.S. *Titanic*, a supposedly unsinkable ship, sank just hours after she set out on her first voyage, and the irony of this is often emphasized, but many people have never read any of the dramatic accounts of the doomed ship's passengers and crew who survived the ordeal. That's unfortunate because these accounts really bring home the magnitude of this tragedy and give a sense of what it was like to be there.

Well now, here's a chance find out how it felt when these people suddenly found themselves in the middle of the ocean in the dead of night on a huge ocean liner that was slowly beginning her descent into the briny deep that would soon become her icy graveyard. But before I bring on the accounts, I need to give a little background to the catastrophe.

On April 10, 1912, what was then the world's largest, most powerful ocean liner set out from Southampton, England, heading for New York City at a speed of twenty-two nautical miles per hour. This ship was 11 stories tall, 883 feet long, 92 feet wide, and weighed 46,000 tons. The "Wonder Ship" of the White Star line, she featured sixteen watertight compartments that would prevent her from sinking as long as no more than two of the compartments were breached. Among the more than 2,200 people[64] aboard were some of the world's richest aristocrats who paid what would be more than $55,000 in today's dollars for a first-class suite. In the steerage were more than seven hundred immigrants.

At 11:35 on the night of April 14, the lookouts saw a mountain of ice loom out of the darkness a quarter mile in front of the *Titanic*. The engines were immediately thrown into full speed astern, and the ship turned hard to port (left). As the 200,000-ton iceberg slid along the starboard side of the ship, chunks of ice broke off falling onto the deck. Some passengers even grabbed pieces off the iceberg as it passed and put them in their drinks. Below the waterline, the sideswiping iceberg ripped a three-hundred-foot-long gash in the *Titanic*'s hull. Six of the watertight compartments began flooding. There were only sixteen lifeboats and four canvas collapsibles, the minimum required by regulation and enough to hold a little more than half the people on the ship, though far fewer than that actually survived. By five minutes after midnight, the captain knew his ship only had about ninety minutes left. There was no one to help them. The *Californian*, which was about ten miles away, apparently had its radio off and didn't hear the distress calls. The *Titanic* was essentially all alone, five hundred miles southeast of Newfoundland. The temperature outside was just one degree above freezing, though the water was four degrees below freezing. The water's salinity kept it from turning to ice.

[64] It's unknown exactly how many people were on board because of last-minute changes in the crew and passenger lists.

Harry Senior was a fireman on the *Titanic*. He was below deck when the great ship met the floating mountain.

> I was in my bunk when I felt a bump. One man said, "Hello. She has been struck." I went on deck and saw a great pile of ice on the well deck before the forecastle, but we all thought the ship would last some time, and we went back to our bunks. Then one of the firemen came running down and yelled, "All muster for the lifeboats." I ran on deck, and the Captain said, "All firemen keep down on the well deck. If a man comes up I'll shoot him."
>
> Then I saw the first lifeboat lowered. Thirteen people were on board, eleven men and two women. Three were millionaires, and one was [J. Bruce] Ismay [the Managing Director of the White Star Line].
>
> Then I ran up on to the hurricane deck and helped to throw one of the collapsible boats on to the lower deck. I saw an Italian woman holding two babies. I took one of them, and made the woman jump overboard with the baby, while I did the same with the other. When I came to the surface the baby in my arms was dead. I saw the woman strike out in good style, but a boiler burst on the *Titanic* and started a big wave. When the woman saw that wave, she gave up. Then, as the child was dead, I let it sink too.
>
> I swam around for about half an hour, and was swimming on my back when the *Titanic* went down. I tried to get aboard a boat, but some chap hit me over the head with an oar. There were too many in her. I got around to the other side of the boat and climbed in.

Mrs. D. H. Bishop was in one of the lifeboats launched from the *Titanic* before the ship's stern began to rise out of the water.

We did not begin to understand the situation till we were perhaps a mile or more away from the *Titanic*. Then we could see the rows of lights along the decks begin to slant gradually upward from the bow. Very slowly the lines of light began to point downward at a greater and greater angle. The sinking was so slow that you could not perceive the lights of the deck changing their position. The slant seemed to be greater about every quarter of an hour. That was the only difference.

In a couple of hours, though, she began to go down more rapidly. Then the fearful sight began. The people in the ship were just beginning to realize how great their danger was. When the forward part of the ship dropped suddenly at a faster rate, so that the upward slope became marked, there was a sudden rush of passengers on all the decks towards the stern. It was like a wave. We could see the great black mass of people in the steerage sweeping to the rear part of the boat and breaking through into the upper decks. At the distance of about a mile we could distinguish everything through the night, which was perfectly clear. We could make out the increasing excitement on board the boat as the people, rushing to and fro, caused the deck lights to disappear and reappear as they passed in front of them.

This panic went on, it seemed, for an hour. Then suddenly the ship seemed to shoot up out of the water and stand there perpendicularly. It seemed to us that it stood upright in the water for four full minutes.

Then it began to slide gently downwards. Its speed increased as it went down head first, so that the stern shot down with a rush.

The lights continued to burn till it sank. We could see the people packed densely in the stern till it was gone. . . .

"I cannot imagine any condition which could cause this ship to founder. I cannot conceive of any vital disaster happening to the vessel. Modern shipbuilding has gone beyond that."

—Captain E. I. Smith, the captain of the Titanic, *1912*

As the ship sank we could hear the screaming a mile away. Gradually it became fainter and fainter and died away. Some of the lifeboats that had room for more might have gone to their rescue, but it would have meant that those who were in the water would have swarmed aboard and sunk her.

At 2 A.M., as the bow of the *Titanic* sank, the three huge propellers lifted out of the water, and then one of the funnels toppled over. At 2:10 A.M., the stern had risen about forty-five degrees out of the water. The ship then began to tear in half, allowing a portion of the stern about the size of a twenty-five-story building to rise out of the water almost vertical by 2:18 A.M. Then the bow broke free, causing the stern to shoot upward a bit. At 2:20 A.M., the stern slowly slid beneath the surface, and the two halves glided down into the ocean depths.

One of the last to leave the ship was Colonel Archibald Gracie.

No one at this point had jumped into the sea. If there had been any, both Clinch Smith and I would have known it. After the water struck the bridge forward, there were many who rushed aft, climbed over the rail and jumped, but I never saw one of them.

I was now working with the crew at the davits on the starboard side forward, adjusting them, ready for lowering the Engelhardt boat from the roof of the officers' house to the Boat Deck below. Some one of the crew on the roof, where it was, sang out, "Has any passenger a knife?" I took mine out of my pocket and tossed it to him, saying "Here is a small penknife, if that will do any good." It appeared to me then that there was more trouble than there ought to have been in removing the canvas cover and cutting the boat loose, and that some means should have been available for doing this without delay. Meantime, four or five long oars were placed aslant against the walls of the officers' house to break the fall of the boat, which was pushed from the roof and slipped with a crash down on the Boat Deck, smashing several of the oars. Clinch Smith and I scurried out of the way and stood leaning with our backs against the rail, watching this procedure and feeling anxious lest the boat might have been stove in, or otherwise injured so as to cause her to leak in the water. The account of the junior Marconi operator, Harold S. Bride, supplements mine. "I saw a collapsible boat," he said, "near a funnel, and went over to it. Twelve men were trying to boost it down to the Boat Deck [the highest deck]. They were having an awful time. It was the last boat left. I looked at it longingly a few minutes; then I gave a hand and over she went."

About this time I recall that an officer on the roof of the house called down to the crew at this quarter, "Are there any seamen down there among you?" "Aye, aye, sir," was the response, and quite a number left the Boat Deck to assist in what I supposed to have been the cutting loose of the other Engelhardt boat up there on the roof. Again I heard an inquiry for another knife. I thought I recognized the voice of the second officer working up there with the crew. Lightoller has told me, and has written me as well, that "boat A on the starboard side did not leave the ship," while "B was thrown down to the Boat Deck," and was the one on which he and I eventually climbed. The crew had thrown the Engelhardt boat to the deck, but I did not understand why they were so long about launching it, unless they were waiting to cut the other one loose and launch them both at the same time. Two young men of the crew, nice looking, dressed in white, one tall and the other smaller, were coolly debating as to whether the compartments would hold the ship afloat. They were standing with their backs to the rail looking on at the rest of the crew, and I recall asking one of them why he did not assist.

At this time there were other passengers around, but Clinch Smith was the only one associated with me here to the last. It was about this time, fifteen minutes after the launching of the last lifeboat on the port side, that I heard a noise that spread consternation among us all. This was no less than the water striking the bridge and gurgling up the hatchway forward. It seemed momentarily as if it would reach the Boat Deck. It appeared as if it would take the crew a long time to turn the Engelhardt boat right side up and lift it over the rail, and there were so many ready to board her that she would have been swamped. Probably taking these points into consideration, Clinch Smith made the proposition that we should leave and go toward the stern, still on the starboard side, so he started and I followed immediately after him. We had taken but a few steps in the direction indicated when there arose before us from the decks below, a mass of humanity several lines deep, covering the Boat Deck, facing us, and completely blocking our passage toward the stern.

There were women in the crowd, as well as men, and they seemed to be steerage passengers who had just come up from the decks below. Instantly, when they saw us and the water on the deck chasing us from behind, they turned in the opposite direction toward the stern. This brought them at that point plumb against the iron fence and railing which divide the first and second cabin passengers. Even among these people there was no hysterical cry, or evidence of panic, but oh, the agony of it! Clinch Smith and I instantly saw that we could make no progress ahead, and with the water following us behind over the deck, we were in a desperate place. I can never forget the exact point on the ship where he and I were located, viz., at the opening of the angle made by the walls of the officers' house and only a short distance abaft the *Titanic*'s forward "expansion joint." Clinch Smith was immediately on my left, nearer the apex of the angle, and our backs were turned toward the ship's rail and the sea. Looking up toward the roof of the officers' house I saw a man to the right of me and above, lying on his stomach on the roof, with his legs dangling over. Clinch Smith jumped to reach this roof, and I promptly followed. The efforts of both of us failed. I was loaded down with heavy long-skirted overcoat and Norfolk coat beneath, with a clumsy life-preserver over all, which made my jump fall short. As I came down, the water struck my right side. I crouched down into it preparatory to jumping with it, and rose as if on the crest of a wave on the seashore. This expedient brought the attainment of the object I had in view. I was able to reach the roof and the iron railing that is along the edge of it, and pulled myself over on top of the officers' house on my stomach near the base of the second funnel. The feat which I instinctively accomplished was the simple one, familiar to all bathers in the surf at the seashore. I had no time to advise Clinch Smith to adopt it. To my utter dismay, a hasty glance to my left and right showed that he had not followed my example, and that the wave, if I may call it such, which had mounted me to the roof, had completely covered him, as well as all people on both sides of me, including the man I had first seen athwart the roof. I was thus parted forever from my friend, Clinch Smith, with whom I had agreed to remain to the last struggle. I felt almost a pang of responsibility for our separation; but he was not in sight and there was no chance of rendering assistance. His ultimate fate is a matter of conjecture. Hemmed in by the mass of people toward the stern, and cornered in the locality previously described, it seems certain that as the ship keeled over and sank, his body was caught in the angle or in the coils of rope and other appurtenances on the deck and borne down to the depths below. . . .

The peculiar way in which the *Titanic* is described as hesitating and assuming a vertical position before her final dive to the depths below can be accounted for only on the hypothesis of the sliding of the boilers from their beds. A second cabin passenger, Mr. Lawrence Beesley, a Cambridge University man, has written an excellent book about the *Titanic* disaster, dwelling especially upon the lessons to be learned from it. His account given to the newspapers also contains the most graphic description from the viewpoint of those in the lifeboats, telling how the great ship looked before her final plunge. He "was a mile or two miles away," he writes:

"... when the oarsmen lay on their oars and all in the lifeboat were motionless as we watched the ship in absolute silence—save some who would not look and buried their heads on each others' shoulders.... As we gazed awe-struck, she tilted slightly up, revolving apparently about a center of gravity just astern of amidships until she attained a vertical upright position, and there she remained—motionless! As she swung up, her lights, which had shown without a flicker all night, went out suddenly, then came on again for a single flash and then went out altogether; and as they did so there came a noise which many people, wrongly, I think, have described as an explosion. It has always seemed to me that it was nothing but the engines and machinery coming loose from their place and bearings and falling through the compartments, smashing everything in their way. [It's now known that this sound was actually the ship tearing in half.] It was partly a roar, partly a groan, partly a rattle and partly a smash, and it was not a sudden roar as an explosion would be; it went on successively for some seconds, possibly fifteen or twenty, as the heavy machinery dropped down to the bottom (now the bows) of the ship; I suppose it fell through the end and sank first before the ship. But it was a noise no one had heard before and no one wishes to hear again. It was stupefying, stupendous, as it came to us along the water. It was as if all the heavy things one could think of had been thrown downstairs from the top of a house, smashing each other, and the stairs and everything in the way...."

Launched in 1840, the President *was the largest ship of its time. After leaving New York on its third voyage across the Atlantic, it vanished and was never heard from again.*

But let me now resume my personal narrative. With this second wind under water there came to me a new lease of life and strength, until finally I noticed by the increase of light that I was drawing near to the surface. Though it was not daylight, the clear starlit night made a noticeable difference in the degree of light immediately below the surface of the water. As I was rising, I came in contact with ascending wreckage, but the only thing I struck of material size was a small plank, which I tucked under my right arm. This circumstance brought with it the reflection that it was advisable for me to secure what best I could to keep me afloat on the surface until succor arrived. When my head at last rose above the water, I detected a piece of wreckage like a wooden crate, and I eagerly seized it as a nucleus of the projected raft to be constructed from what flotsam and jetsam I might collect. Looking about me, I could see no *Titanic* in sight. She had entirely disappeared beneath the calm surface of the ocean and without a sign of any wave. That the sea had swallowed her up with all her precious belongings was indicated by the slight sound of a gulp behind me as the water closed over her. The length of time that I was underwater can be estimated by the fact that I sank with her, and when I came up there was no ship in sight. The accounts of others as to the length of time it took the *Titanic* to sink afford the best measure of the interval I was below the surface.

What impressed me at the time that my eyes b eheld the horrible scene was a thin light-gray smoky vapor that hung like a pall a few feet above the broad expanse of sea that was covered with a mass of tangled wreckage. That it was a tangible vapor, and not a product of imagination, I feel well assured. It may have been caused by smoke or steam rising to the surface around the area where the ship had sunk. At any rate it produced a supernatural effect and the pictures I had seen by Dante and the description I had read in my Virgil of the infernal regions, of Charon, and the river Lethe, were then uppermost in my thoughts. Add to this, within the area described, which was as far as my eyes could reach, there arose to the sky the most horrible sounds ever heard by mortal man except by those of us who survived this terrible tragedy. The agonizing cries of death from over a thousand throats, the wails and groans of the suffering, the shrieks of the terror-stricken and the awful gaspings for breath of those in the last throes of drowning, none of us will ever forget to our dying day. "Help! Help! Boat ahoy! Boat ahoy!" and "My God! My God!" were the heart-rending cries and shrieks of men, which floated to us over the surface of the dark waters continuously for the next hour, but as time went on, growing weaker and weaker until they died out entirely.

As I clung to my wreckage, I noticed just in front of me, a few yards away, a group of three bodies with heads in the water, face downward, and just behind me to my right another body, all giving unmistakable evidence of being drowned. Possibly these had gone down to the depths as I had done, but did not have the lung power that I had to hold the breath and swim underwater, an accomplishment which I had practiced from my school days. There was no one alive or struggling in the water or calling for aid within the immediate vicinity of where I arose to the surface. I threw my right leg over the wooden crate in an attempt to straddle and balance myself on top of it, but I turned over in a somersault with it underwater, and up to the surface again.

I espied to my left, a considerable distance away, a better vehicle of escape than the wooden crate on which my attempt to ride had resulted in a second ducking. What I saw was no less than the same Engelhardt, or "surf-boat," to whose launching I had lent my efforts, until the water broke upon the ship's Boat Deck where we were. On top of this upturned boat, half reclining on her bottom, were now more than a dozen men, whom, by their dress, I took to be all members of the crew of the ship. Thank God, I did not hesitate a moment in discarding the friendly crate that had been my first aid. I struck out through the wreckage and after a considerable swim reached the port side amidships of this Engelhardt boat, which with her companions, wherever utilized, did good service in saving the lives of many others.

When I reached the side of the boat I met with a doubtful reception, and, as no extending hand was held out to me, I grabbed, by the muscle of the left arm, a young member of the crew nearest and facing me. At the same time I threw my right leg over the boat astraddle pulling myself aboard, with a friendly lift to my foot given by someone astern as I assumed a reclining position with them on the bottom of the capsized boat. Then after me came a dozen other swimmers who clambered around and whom we helped aboard. Among them was one completely exhausted, who came on the same port side as myself. I pulled him in and he lay face downward in front of me for several hours, until just before dawn he was able to stand up with the rest of us. The moment of getting aboard this upturned boat was one of supreme mental relief, more so than any other until I reached the deck of the hospitable *Carpathia* on the next morning.

One final, rather poignant description of the *Titanic's* last moments comes from Harold Bride, who was the ship's radio operator.

> There were men all around me—hundreds of them. The sea was dotted with them, all depending on their lifebelts. I felt I simply had to get away from the ship. She was a beautiful sight then. Smoke and sparks were rushing out of her funnel. There must have been an explosion, but we heard none. We only saw the big stream of sparks. The ship was turning gradually on her nose—just like a duck that goes for a dive. I had only one thing on my mind—to get away from the suction. The band was still playing. I guess all of them went down. They were playing "Autumn" then. I swam with all my might. I suppose I was 150 feet away when the *Titanic*, on her nose, with her after-quarter sticking straight up in the air, began to settle—slowly.

It's calculated that nine minutes after the stern went under, the bow hit the ocean's floor. The stern descended more slowly, sinking for thirty-six minutes before it finally crashed into the mud over two miles beneath the waves. Debris continued to rain down for several hours.

Some have suggested that if the *Titanic* had struck the iceberg head-on, only two or three of the watertight compartments might have ruptured and the ship might have survived or at least would not have sank so quickly.

The *Californian* clearly saw the signal rockets fired from the *Titanic*, but did not attempt to make her way toward the stricken vessel. The *Carpathia* heard the radio distress calls and arrived on the scene at 3:35 A.M. She stayed in the area picking up lifeboats until 8:30. There were 705 survivors. Estimates of the number of dead range from 1,490 to 1,517—a high proportion of them were from steerage. Third-class passengers were ordered to remain below deck and some were kept there at gunpoint. Of the women and girls on the ship, 97 percent from first class survived, whereas 84 percent from second class and only 55 percent from third class survived, even though there were only 179 females in third class.

Though the British High Court initially found the White Star Line innocent of negligence, this was later reversed on appeal, and the company had to pay heavy damages to the families of several of the deceased. Many maritime safety measures were instituted following this tragedy.

Inside a Nazi Death Camp

The dark shadow of genocide seems to be something that continually haunts human history. Mass killings, liquidations, and total war have been around almost continually since the beginning of recorded history—from the Assyrians to Attila the Hun to the Conquistadors to Bosnia—and some think the Neanderthals may have been among the first victims of genocide.

Of course, the best known incidence in modern times is that of Nazi Germany. Not only is it the best documented occurrence of genocide, it's considered particularly shocking partly because of the methodical ruthlessness of the

Nazis, but also because Germany was and is considered to be one of the world's most civilized countries—having given us Beethoven, Bach, Wagner, Handel, Schopenhauer, Goethe, Nietzsche, and Einstein (though they effectively chased him out).

It's well known that Hitler's "final solution" abruptly ended the lives of between 5.1 and 6 million of Europe's 10 million Jews, but what's often not mentioned is that an additional 6 million "unwanted" people were also executed. Over half of these were Russian POWs.[65] The remainder included gypsies, partisans, communists, religious dissenters (such as the Jehovah's Witnesses, who were dedicated pacifists that refused to serve in the military, join the Nazi party, or salute their flag), homosexuals, prostitutes, and Polish intelligentsia.[66] It also included anyone deemed "antisocial" or a "habitual criminal"—which meant someone who had been to prison and might commit a crime again sometime in the future. The insane, mentally deficient, cripples, and old people were also murdered by doctors and nurses from late 1939 to August 1941 under a program of "mercy-killing" until public outrage forced Hitler to put a stop to it.

"The best way is to shoot anyone who so much as looks like giving trouble."

—Adolf Hitler, July 16, 1941

In the Auschwitz-Berkenau death camp alone, it's estimated that up to 4 million people died—half a million of them from starvation. Rudolf Hoess, the Commandant at Auschwitz, put his estimate at the number gassed at 2 million. He added that Auschwitz became "the largest human slaughterhouse that history has ever known" and that on one occasion more than 9,000 people were gassed and cremated in a single day, though this was an unusual circumstance.

Unlike some of the other camps, at Auschwitz the SS[67] tried to hide from the victims that they were about to be killed. Still, many knew what was happening. Hoess mentioned this in his autobiography, which he wrote while he was in a Warsaw prison in 1947, saying:

> I noticed that women who either guessed or knew what awaited them nevertheless found the courage to joke with the children to encourage them, despite the mortal terror visible in their own eyes. One woman approached me as she walked past and, pointing to her four children who were manfully helping the smallest ones over the rough ground, whispered, "How can you bring yourself to kill such beautiful, darling children? Have you no heart at all?" . . . I remember, too, a woman who tried to throw her children out

65 During the American and British bombing raids on German cities, Himmler issued orders that all Allied airmen shot down were to be considered terrorists, not POWs, and they were to be immediately executed. Because of this order, a number of American and British airmen were shot after surrendering.

66 Over half of Poland's educated people were exterminated, including more than 2,600 Catholic priests. A plan drawn up in the summer of 1940 titled *Orders Concerning the Organization and Function of Military Government in England* contained a list of British intelligentsia the SS planned to "liquidate" on capturing Britain, which included H. G. Wells, Bertrand Russell, J. B. Priestley, C.P. Snow, and Noel Coward. They also planned to ship large numbers of able-bodied men between the ages of seventeen and forty-five to Germany as slave labor.

67 Since the military was geared for fighting battles, not carrying out mass executions, the job of genocide and operating the death camps fell to the SS.

of the gas chamber, just as the door was closing. Weeping, she called out, "At least let my precious children live." There were many such shattering scenes, which affected all who witnessed them.

In a statement Hoess made to Polish authorities, he described the scene inside the gas chamber, explaining:

> It could be observed through the peephole in the door that those who were standing nearest to the induction vents were killed at once. It can be said that about one-third died straight away. The remainder staggered about and began to scream and struggle for air. The screaming, however, soon changed to the death rattle and in a few minutes all lay still. After twenty minutes at the latest no movement could be discerned. . . . The victims became unconscious after a few minutes, according to their distance from the intake shaft. Those who screamed and those who were old or sick or weak, or the small children, died quicker than those who were healthy or young.

The gas they were using was prussic acid, which came in a crystalline powder called Zyklon B. This gas would paralyze the victims' lungs, causing them to suffocate. They would black out from lack of oxygen and pass on into death. Before using Zyklon B, the Nazis usually used truck exhaust, which caused carbon monoxide poisoning. This was not nearly as efficient, and after being gassed, the victims sometimes revived. This didn't happen with Zyklon B.

Apparently, there was only one person who survived being gassed by Zyklon B and that was Sophia Litwinska. Her case is particularly interesting and probably completely unique because she was removed from the gas chamber by the Nazis *after* they had started pumping in the gas. In her testimony for a war crimes trial, she described what happened to her in 1941.

> *What happened on the day before Christmas day?* There was a big selection in Block No. 4, the hospital block. Over 3000 Jewish women had to parade in this selection, which was under the charge of Hoessler. We had to leave our beds very quickly and stand quite naked to attention in front of him and the doctors, Enna and Keonig. All those who could not leave their beds had their numbers taken, and it was clear to us that they were condemned to death. Those whose bodies were not very nice looking or were too thin, or whom those gentlemen disliked for some reason or other, had their numbers taken, and it was clear what that meant. My number also was taken. We stayed in Block No. 4 for a night and the next day were taken to Block No. 18. About half-past five in the evening trucks arrived and we were loaded into them, quite naked like animals, and were driven to the crematorium.
>
> *When you reached the crematorium what happened there?* The whole truck was tipped over in the way they do it sometimes with potatoes or coal loads, and we were led into a room which gave me the impression of a shower-bath. There were towels hanging round, and sprays, and even mirrors. I cannot say how many were in the room altogether, because I was so terrified, nor do I know if the doors were closed. People were in tears; people were shouting at each other; people were hitting each other. There were healthy people, strong people, weak people and sick people, and suddenly I saw fumes coming in through a very small window at the top. I had to

> cough very violently, tears were streaming from my eyes, and I had a sort of feeling in my throat as if I would be asphyxiated.
>
> I could not even look at the others because each of us concentrated on what happened to herself.
>
> *What was the next thing you remember?* At that moment I heard my name called. I had not the strength to answer it, but raised my arm. Then I felt someone take me and throw me out from that room. Hoessler put a blanket round me and took me on a motor-cycle to the hospital, where I stayed six weeks. As the result of the gas I had still, quite frequently, headaches and heart trouble, and whenever I went into the fresh air my eyes were filled with tears. I was subsequently taken to the political department and apparently I had been taken out of the gas chamber because I had come from a prison in Lublin, which seemed to make a difference.

Of course, millions of people weren't so lucky. The job of removing the bodies from the gas chambers, taking the gold from their teeth, and putting them in the crematory ovens fell to the *Sonderkommando*, or "Death Commando," which were Jewish inmates who were forced to do all the dirty work of disposing of the dead.

Rudolf Reder was one of only two Jews who survived the executions at Belzec, which was another of the Nazi's seven extermination camps. He began working there as one of the Death Commando in August 1942 and later wrote, "I heard the doors [of the gas chamber] being locked, the moaning, shouting and cries of despair in Polish and Jewish; the crying of the children and women which made the blood run cold in my veins. Then came one last terrible shout. All this lasted fifteen to twenty minutes, after which there was silence. . . . We pulled out the corpses of those who were alive only a short time ago, we pulled them using leather belts to the huge mass graves while the camp orchestra played; played from morning 'till night."

Hoess wrote in his autobiography about one striking incident he saw while watching these prisoners at their work. "Once when bodies were being carried from a gas chamber to the fire pit, a man of the Special Detachment suddenly stopped and stood for a moment as though rooted to the spot. Then he continued to drag out a body with his comrades. I asked the Capo what was up. He explained that the corpse was that of the Jew's wife."

One of these Death Commandos who was put to work destroying the evidence of previous atrocities ended up being assigned to dig up what was supposed to be his own grave. Leon Wells explained:

> In the middle of June 1943, I was the last one of my family of seven brothers and sisters and parents and grandparents. I was taken into the Death Brigade which the Germans named Sonderkommando 1005. The purpose of this Death Brigade was to erase all traces of Nazi atrocities so that no witnessing of the atrocities could take place after the war. I think it may have started in 1943 when the Nazis saw that their armies were retreating.
>
> We dug up the graves of people that had been killed, burned their bodies, ground their bones, and took out the gold teeth or any gold we found in these ashes. We normally went through about two thousand bodies a day.

It seems that the Germans had been keeping an exact list of how many people had been shot and where they were buried since they had come into east Poland in 1941. In 1942, while at the Janowska camp, I got sick with typhus, and after three days I was taken to the "sands" in the back of the Janowska camp in Lvov to be shot. I dug my own grave, but at the last minute, after my name was called and crossed off the list, I was able to escape. However, I was presumed by the SS to be dead.

A year later in 1943, as a member of the Death Brigade, I was digging up these same graves to burn the bodies, and we could only find 182 of the 183 bodies on the list. I was the 183rd person. For three days we looked for the missing body so as not to leave any traces of these Nazi murders, but after three days we gave up.

"These girls were compelled to clean a latrine—to remove the excrement and clean it. But they received no utensils. To their question: 'With what?' the Nazis replied. 'With your blouses.' The girls removed their blouses and cleaned the excrement with them. When the job was done they received their reward: the Nazis wrapped their faces in the blouses, filthy with the remains of excrement, and laughed uproariously. And all this because 'Jewish England' is fighting against the Führer with the help of the Juden."

—Chaim Kaplan, in his diary on December 16, 1939, about occurrences in the Lodz Ghetto

---

After Germany invaded Poland in 1939, the Nazis created sealed ghettos throughout Poland to act as holding areas for Jews awaiting emigration. When the Nazis changed their policy from emigration to extermination, the ghettos became concentration camps for the Jews until they could be sent to the death camps. The largest of these ghettos was the one in Warsaw, where the population grew from 60,000 to 400,000 people. Treblinka was opened 75 miles away. Equipped with 30 gas chambers, it was capable of murdering 25,000 people a day.

While the Nazis were hard at work trying to wipe out the Jews, many people were working hard to save as many as they could. These rescuers included children as well. Bojena was only nine years old when she began helping Jews in Warsaw. She later said:

> It began because the adults were afraid to read the announcements, the lists of those whom the Nazis were after which were posted around the city. Everybody had at least one relative or friend in the resistance—so we were often sent to find out whether or not they had been discovered and therefore listed. My mother and father made it clear that we—every one of us children—had certain functions to fulfill. Soon I played an important role in the anti-Nazi conspiracy. I was constantly alert. My whole attention was concentrated on the movements of the Germans: how they behaved, what their intentions toward people were . . . and I told father and mother everything. But my real function was taking Jews out of the ghetto and locating hiding places for them. My father had many contacts with the ghetto. When Jews came out to perform a special mission, I would escort them to a prearranged address.
>
> I was a small girl and my head and eyes were always inclined to one side. This came from always having to watch for Germans. People knew

my function but no one betrayed me. I would make believe I lived close to the spot I had to bring the Jews, stopping every now and then in front of a window pane to make sure I was not followed. While executing dangerous functions, a person matures and there is a fast understanding of the adult world. One blink of the eye made it possible to grasp the whole event.

At one point Reichsführer SS Himmler sent various high-ranking SS officers and Nazi leaders to Auschwitz to witness the "final solution" first-hand. According to Hoess, they were all struck by the horror of it. "Some who had previously spoken most loudly about the necessity for this extermination fell silent once they had actually seen the 'final solution of the Jewish question.' I was repeatedly asked how I and my men could go on watching these operations, and how we were able to stand it. . . . Even Mildner [the head of Gestapo in the district where Auschwitz was located] and [Adolf] Eichmann [the SS 'Jewish specialist'] who were certainly tough enough, had no wish to change places with me. This was one job which nobody envied me."

After the war, Hoess was asked if he ever considered whether the people he murdered had actually deserved it. He explained:

> Don't you see, we SS men were not supposed to think about these things; it never even occurred to us.—And besides, it was something already taken for granted that the Jews were to blame for everything. . . . We just never heard anything else. It was not just newspapers like the *Stuermer* but it was everything we ever heard. Even our military and ideological training took for granted that we had to protect Germany from the Jews. . . . It only started to occur to me after the collapse that maybe it was not quite right, after I had heard what everybody was saying. . . . We were all so trained to obey orders without even thinking that the thought of disobeying an order would simply never have occurred to anybody and somebody else would have done just as well if I hadn't. . . . You can be sure that it was not always a pleasure to see those mountains of corpses and smell the continual burning.—But Himmler had ordered it and had even explained the necessity and I really never gave much thought to whether it was wrong. It just seemed a necessity.

"In the corner of the square a thin, white-haired man was kneeling, and at his side his daughter, a slim brunette. A fat Gestapo man stopped near them, drew his revolver and killed the Jew. His daughter then leaped to her feet and cried to the Gestapo man in German: 'You scoundrel! What did my father do to you that you shot him?'

"The Gestapo man flew at her, hit her and threatened to kill her, too. The girl looked at him with a penetrating gaze. When he turned away, avoiding her eyes, she insulted him again, called him a mean coward who shot defenseless people, and shouted that he dared not look into her eyes.

"'Look straight into my eyes, you coward,' she cried, 'and shoot! These eyes will pursue you and haunt you all your life!'

"The Gestapo man winced, turned away from the girl, as if to muster his courage, and after a moment aimed his revolver at her and shot her."

—Anonymous eyewitness at Tarnow in Poland, July 28, 1942

After the war, Hoess was arrested by the British and handed over to the Americans. After testifying at the Nuremberg trials, he was turned over to the Poles, who tried and executed him in 1947.

While researching this section, almost every discussion of the Nazi death camps that I read raised the question of whether the U.S. government knew about them, and if so, why weren't the camps or the railway lines running to them bombed. They all come to the conclusion that the United States did know.

Reports of atrocities began coming out of Germany shortly after the first slaughter took place in 1941, but it was a while before they were "authenticated." On June 13, 1942, the news wire service UPI reported that Nazi Propaganda Minister Joseph Goebbels said Germany "would carry out a mass 'extermination' of Jews in reprisal for the Allied air bombings of German cities" and that "the Jews would be exterminated throughout Europe 'and perhaps even beyond Europe' in retaliation against the heavy air assaults."

Throughout the war, the media routinely reported on the Holocaust, but it usually buried the stories in the back pages. For instance, in 1944, The *New York Times* had a four-inch story on page 12 on the extermination of 400,000 Hungarian Jews. It wasn't until after the war that it all became front-page news. Perhaps an explanation for this is that stories of German atrocities had been reported during World War I that turned out to be Allied propaganda and no one wanted to believe these reports were true until they were forced to by the overwhelming evidence.

But that applies only to the general public. Jewish groups were providing detailed information to the Allied governments and asking that something be done. In December 1942, the Allies issued a joint declaration condemning extermination. In late 1944, a detailed report of what was going on at Auschwitz with statistics, maps and diagrams was made by Rudolf Vrba and Fred Wetzler, two Jews who escaped from Auschwitz. Vrba had been a prisoner there from 1942 to April 1944. Their report was given to Churchill, Roosevelt, and the Pope, but nothing was done about it.

When the War Refugee Board specifically asked the U.S. War Department to bomb the mass-extermination equipment at Auschwitz, they replied that they wouldn't because it would be "an unwarranted diversion of planes needed elsewhere." This was despite the fact that bombing was being carried out fifty miles away, that there were industrial production facilities near the camp, and that it would have saved the lives of hundreds of thousands of Jews.

The prisoners in Auschwitz were even hoping they'd be bombed. "Our greatest anticipation was when the air raids were on," said Celia Rosenberg, who was there at the time. "It would have been our pleasure to be bombed. It never occurred to us to be afraid." The bombs never came.

David S. Wyman claims, in *The Abandonment of the Jews* (1984), that American leaders, and especially the state department, didn't want to save the Jews because they were afraid the Jews would end up in America.[68] He also blames the

[68] A few months after Kristallnacht, the pogrom when Jewish stores were looted and synagogues were burned, a bill was presented to Congress that would have saved 20,000 Jewish children by allowing them into the United States. Because of pressure from lobbying groups and anti-Semitism in the country, the bill died in committee. Although the president had a chance to save it, he decided against it. Several years later, Congress passed a similar bill allowing British children into the country during Germany's air attacks on Britain.

general public for not speaking up and American Jewish leaders for being too preoccupied with plans for a Jewish homeland in Palestine and not protesting enough.

But then the United States and the rest of world have a history of ignoring genocide. *The Guiness Book of Records* lists the worst genocide by percentage of population as being when Pol Pot and his Khmer Rouge murdered one third of Cambodia's population of 8 million between 1975 and 1979. The victims were primarily their political enemies, Buddhist monks, an Islamic people called the Cham, and just about anyone with an education. After the Vietnamese chased Pol Pot and his thugs into Thailand, the United States, Canada, Western Europe, and Japan supplied the mass murderers with food, shelter, and health care.

Although the atrocities in Bosnia have attracted considerable attention, the massacres of the Hutus by the Tutsis which had been going on since 1971 in Rwanda and Burundi, leaving more than half a million dead didn't get much attention until fifteen years later. Iraq began its campaign of genocide against the Kurds when it was still an ally of the United States. Iraq's atrocities had no effect on the shipments of military weapons it received from America. The Kurds didn't become front-page news until after the Persian Gulf War, when President Bush called on the people of Iraq to rise up against Saddam Hussein. When the Kurds did, the United States failed to provide them any support, and many more were wiped out.

It's estimated that about 40 million were killed in the Soviet Union while it existed, not counting those who died in the "Great Patriotic War." Stalin, a U.S. ally during World War II, was responsible for most of these deaths. And little was done to help the about 13 million Armenians who were exterminated by the Turks during and just prior to World War I. The United States and its allies knew very well what was going on. At the peace conference that concluded the war, all the Armenians' requests were ignored. This holocaust apparently didn't even warrant a war crimes trial.

Hitler, when giving his generals their orders to march on Poland, asserted, "Our strength is in our quickness and brutality. Ghengis Khan had millions of women and children killed by his own will and with a cheerful heart. History sees only in him a great state builder. What weak Western European civilization thinks about me does not matter. . . . I have sent to the east only my 'Death Head' units with the order to kill without mercy all men, women and children of Polish race and language. Only in such a way will we win the vital space that we need. Who still talks nowadays of the extermination of the Armenians?"

China has undoubtedly undergone the worst mass exterminations. Between 1210 and 1219 and then between 1311 and 1340, about 35 million Chinese were wiped out in Mongol invasions each time, for a total of about 70 million. The first of those was by Ghengis Khan. Then about 40 million were massacred in the Sichuan province in 1643-1647 by the bandit leader Zhang Xianzhong, who was known as the "Yellow Tiger."

But the worst may have been in Communist China under Chairman Mao Zedong, who is listed in *The Guiness Book of Records* as holding the record for mass murders. In a report published in 1971, the U.S. Senate Judiciary Committee estimated that from 1949 until the date of the report, between 32.25 and 61.7 million people were killed in China. The *Washington Post*, on July 17, 1994, cited evidence that Mao was responsible for "at least 40 million deaths and perhaps 80 million or more." Compare this to the 42 million deaths that Hitler is blamed for.[69]

Chinese atrocities in places like Tibet continue, and there are numerous reports of children, mostly females, being murdered in state-run nurseries, but all this hasn't deterred the United States from awarding China the most-favored-nation trading status.

[69] That is, 12 million concentration camp deaths and at least 30 million other deaths associated with World War II. It's estimated that a total of 54.8 million people died during World War II.

Weird LITERATURE

Gallows Literature

Public executions were once popular events, drawing huge crowds. In a time when life was harder and people were not as insulated from death, an execution was a major affair for an entertainment-starved population. Most people's lives were surrounded by injustices. This was their chance to see justice being carried out.

This was a real-life drama with the condemned felon as the center of attention. He knew the role he was expected to play since he had probably witnessed several executions himself. Standing on the edge of oblivion, he would often bewail his fate and exhort his audience not to follow the path that had led him to this miserable end. He would confess his evil lifestyle and implore the crowd to live righteously. Of course, this was not always the case. Many criminals went to their deaths defiant and unrepentant. But generally, when faced with the overwhelming uncertainty of the great beyond, most of them quickly discovered religion.

The felon was usually assisted in this by the ministers who visited him in his cell. They would convince him of the necessity of confessing his sins to the public and would often get him to sign a written confession that they would later use in their sermons. Many times these confessions were dictated by the clergymen, or in the cases where the condemned was illiterate, they would write the confession themselves for the condemned man's signature or mark. Usually the convict was glad to tell the ministers whatever they wanted to hear. And he was often assisted in finding something he could blame his crimes on—such as drinking, swearing, and sabbath breaking—easing his guilt somewhat and relieving some of the disgrace he'd cast on his family.

These confessions were also printed up as pamphlets, which also contained a detailed account of their crimes. Sometimes these pamphlets were sold to the crowd at the execution. Known as gallows literature, some of these pamphlets even contained poems and letters by the condemned man. While it's generally impossible to know whether this material was actually written by the felon himself, if it wasn't, it was generally based on the dying man's confession. There are also many ballads written from the criminal's point-of-view, but it's doubtful any of these were written by the person they're attributed to.

Our first example of gallows literature comes from the execution of two pirates. These men, William White and John Rose Archer, were serving under Captain Phillips when they were captured. White was a Massachusetts fisherman working in St. Peters, Newfoundland, when he joined Captain Phillips in 1723. He was drunk at the time, and this was probably his first experience as a pirate. John Rose Archer was on one of the first boats they captured. Since Archer had previously served under Blackbeard, he quickly joined Captain Phillips's crew as their quartermaster. From then, until their capture nine months later, they plundered thirty-four vessels.

When White and Archer were hung, the *Boston News-Letter* reported, "At one end of the gallows was their own dark [pirate] flag, in the middle of which an anatomy, and at one side of it a dart in the heart, with drops of blood proceeding from it; and on the other side an hour-glass." John Rose Archer was about twenty-seven years old, and William White was twenty-two.

Before their deaths, these two pirates made the following declarations with the assistance of two Boston ministers.

> The dying Declarations of John Rose Archer, and William White, on the Day of their Execution at Boston, June 2, 1724, for the Crimes of Pyracy.
>
> First, separately, of *Archer*.
>
> I Greatly bewail my Prophanations of the Lord's Day, and my Disobedience to my Parents.
>
> And my Cursing and Swearing, and my blaspheming the Name of the glorious God.
>
> Unto which I have added, the Sins of Unchastity. And I have provoked the Holy One, at length, to leave me unto the Crimes of Pyracy and Robbery; wherein, at last, I have brought my self under the Guilt of Murder also.
>
> But one Wickedness that has led me as much as any, to all the rest, has been my brutish Drunkenness. By strong Drink I have been heated and hardened into the Crimes that are now more bitter than Death unto me.
>
> I could wish that Masters of Vessels would not use their Men with so much Severity, as many of them do, which exposes us to great Temptations.
>
> And then of *White*.
>
> I am now, with Sorrow, reaping the Fruits of my Disobedience to my Parents, who used their Endeavours to have me instructed in my Bible, and my Catechism.
>
> And the Fruits of my neglecting the publick Worship of God, and prophaning the holy Sabbath.
>
> And of my blaspheming the Name of God, my Maker.
>
> But my Drunkenness has had a great Hand in bringing my Ruin upon me. I was drunk when I was enticed aboard the Pyrate.
>
> And now, for all the vile Things I did aboard, I own the Justice of God and Man, in what is done unto me.
>
> Of both together.
>
> We hope, we truly hate the Sins, whereof we have the Burthen [burden] lying so heavy upon our Consciences.
>
> We warn all People, and particularly young People, against such Sins as these. We wish, all may take Warning by us.
>
> We beg for Pardon, for the Sake of Christ, our Savior; and our Hope is in him alone. Oh! that in his Blood our Scarlet and Crimson Guilt may be all washed away!
>
> We are sensible of an hard Heart in us, full of Wickedness. And we look upon God for his renewing Grace upon us.
>
> We bless God for the Space of Repentance which he has given us; and that he has not cut us off in the Midst and Height of our Wickedness.

We are not without Hope, that God has been savingly at work upon our Souls.

We are made sensible of our absolute Need of the Righteousness of Christ; that we may stand justified before God in that. We renounce all Dependence on our own.

We are humbly thankful to the Ministers of Christ, for the great Pains they have taken for our Good. The Lord reward their Kindness.

We don't despair of Mercy; but hope, thro' Christ, that when we die, we shall find Mercy with God, and be received into his Kingdom.

We with others, and especially the Sea-faring, may get Good by what they see this Day befalling of us.

Declared in the Presence of:

J. W. D. M.

The biblical punishment of "Eye for an eye, tooth for a tooth" is looked on today as being harsh, but its intention was just the opposite. In the time of Moses, slaves were often beaten and killed for minor offenses. Even in England as late as the seventeenth century, a child could be hung for stealing a rag. "Eye for an eye, tooth for a tooth" meant that the punishment should not exceed the crime.

Not all gallows literature or confessions had such religious overtones. The following excerpt is from the dying declaration of one of several pirates who where hung in about 1830 in Cadiz, Spain. It's thought that he may have been one of Captain Gibbs's men. When the British raided Gibbs's Cuban base camp in the summer of 1824, from the burned ships they found there they estimated the murdered crews amounted to about 150 people. Gibbs and most of his men escaped that raid by fleeing into the woods. This pirate apparently was one of these.

In the summer and fall following (1824) we were more fortunate in making prizes; eleven or twelve vessels (mostly American) were captured by us, bound to and from different parts of Europe and the West Indies, and some with valuable cargoes—our place of rendezvous and deposit of goods at that time, was a small island or key in the neighborhood of Cuba; our prizes were generally conveyed there, and after being disburthened of the most valuable part of their cargoes, were sometimes burnt and at other times scuttled, and the crews, if it was thought not necessary otherways to dispose of them were sent adrift in their boats, and frequently without any thing on which they could subsist a single day—nor were all so fortunate thus to escape—"dead men can tell no tales," was a common saying among us, and as soon as we got a ship's crew in our power, a short consultation was held, and if it was the opinion of the majority that it would be better to take life than to spare it, a single nod or wink from our captain was sufficient—regardless of age or sex, all entreaties for mercy were then made in vain—we possessed not the tender feelings to be operated upon by the shrieks and expiring groans of the devoted victims!—there was rather a strife among us, who, with his own hands, should dispatch the greatest number, and in the shortest period of time.

Without any other motives than to gratify a such like hellish propensity (in our intoxicated moments) blood was not unfrequently and unnecessarily shed, and many widows and orphans probably made, when the lives of the unfortunate victims might have been spared, and without the most distant prospect of any evil consequences (as regarded ourselves) resulting therefrom.

Our next example of gallows literature was originally printed as a broadside and is from the hanging of a child molester in Massachusetts that took place during the Revolutionary War.

The Dying Criminal:

POEM, by ROBERT YOUNG, on his own Execution, which is to be on this Day, November 11th, 1779, for RAPE committed on the Body of Jane Green, a Child, eleven years of age, at Brookfield, in the County of Worcester, on the Third Day of September last. Corrected from his own Manuscript.

Attend, ye youth! if ye would fain be old,
Take solemn warning when my tale is told;
In blooming life my soul I must resign,
In my full strength, just aged twenty-nine.

But a short time ago I little thought
That to this shameful end I should be brought;
But the foul fiend, excepting God controuls,
Dresses sin lovely when he baits for souls.

Could you the Monster in true colours see,
His subject nor his servant would you be;
His gilded baits would ne'er allure your minds,
For he who serves him bitter anguish finds.

Had I as oft unto my Bible went,
As on vain pleasures I was eager bent,
These lines had never been compos'd by me,
Nor my vile body hung upon the tree.

Those guilty pleasures which I did pursue,
No more delight—they're painful to my view;
That monster, Sin, that dwells within my breast,
Tortures my soul, and robs me of my rest.

The fatal time I very well remember,
For it was on th' third day of September,
I went to Western, thoughtless of my God,
Though worlds do tremble at his awful nod.

With pot companions did I pass the day,
And afterwards to Brookfield bent my way,
The grand deceiver thought it was his time,
And lead me to commit a horrid crime.

Just after dark I met the little fair,
(O Heav'n forgive, and hear my humble pray'r)
And thou, dear Jane, wilt thou forgive me too,
For I most cruelly have treated you.

I seiz'd th' advantage of the dark'ning hour,
(And savage brutes by night their prey devour)
This little child, eleven years of age,
Then fell a victim to my brutal rage:

Nor could the groans of innocence prevail,
O pity, reader, though I tell the tale;
Drunk with my lust [on] cursed purpose [bent]
Severely us'd th' unhappy innocent.

Her sister dear was to have been my wife,
But I've abus'd her and must lose my life;
Was I but innocent, my heart would bleed
To hear a wretch, like me, had done the deed.

Reader, whoe'er thou art, a warning take,
Be good and just, and all your sins forsake;
May the almighty God direct your way
To the bright regions of eternal day.

A dying man to you makes this request,
For sure he wishes that you may be blest,
And shortly, reader, thou must follow me,
And drop into a vast eternity!

The paths of lewdness, and the base profane,
Produce keen anguish, sorrow fear and shame;
Forsake them then, I've trod the dreary road
My crimes are great, I groan beneath the load.

For a long time on sin should you be bent,
You'll find it hard, like me, [for to] repent;
The more a dangerous wound doth mortify,
The more the surgeon his best skill must try.

These lines I write within a gloomy cell,
I soon shall leave them with a long farewell;
Again I caution all who read the same,
[And] beg they would their wicked lives
   reclaim.

[Last verse illegible]

Our final example is from a pamphlet titled *An Account of the Pirates, with Divers of Their Speeches, Letters, &c. and a Poem Made by One of them*. It took considerable effort to locate this pamphlet, and it's unfortunate I don't have space here to reproduce it in its entirety. But here is a representative section, apparently reprinted for the first time in almost two and a half centuries.

This poem was written by John Fitz-Gerald, a crewman of pirate Captain Low. Originally from County Limerick, Ireland, he was hung—or as the pirates more poetically put it, "he danced on air"—with twenty-six other men on July 19, 1723. He was twenty-one years old.

To mortal Men that daily live,
   in wickedness and sin;
This dying Counsel I do give;
   hoping you will begin
To serve the Lord in Time of Youth
   his Precepts for to keep;
To serve him so in Spir't and Truth,
   that you may Mercy reap.
To you I send my dying Speech,
   a Warning for to be,
The Youths in Chief I do beseech,
   from Wrath to come to flee.
The gracious Precepts of the Lord
   transcend all Wordly Store;
To live in Christ with one Accord,
   and serve him Evermore.
Alas! these Things, slighted have I,
   and turn'd my Back unto;
For which *Fitz-Gerrald* now must die,
   which causes me much Wo.
Wrong doth aloud for Vengeance cry,
   God's Justice will take Place;
To hide from his impartial Eye,
   surpasses human Race.
When Youths do turn their Backs to God,
   and flight his precious Calls;
He over them extends his Rod,
   his Fury on them falls.
In Youthful blooming Years was I,
   when I this Practice took;

Of perpetrating Piracy,
 for filthy Gain did look.
To Wickedness we all were bent,
 our lusts for to fulfill;
To rob at Sea was our Intent,
 and perpetrate all Ill.
The holy Name of our Great God
 we daily did blaspheme;
The purging Blood of our dear Lord,
 of no Effect did deem.
Dear Youths you See my dismal End,
 take Warning now by me;
The Law of God I did offend,
 slighting Eternity.
Slight not the Precepts of the Lord,
 his Sabbaths don't prophane;
In honest Hearts his Word record,
 his Preachers don't disdain.
Your Parents pious Counsels take,
 render them Honour due;
Your Peace with God, befure [sic] to make,
 then bid the World adieu.
Slight its vain Pomps and fading Joys,
 and Lusts of the Flesh also;
Despite not the celestial Joys
 while it is in your View.
Don't covet what is not your own,
 your Lusts for to suffice;
'Twill cause you, when too late, to moan,
 you had such greedy Eyes.
Of all these Things I guilty was,
 the Effects whereof you see;
My utter Ruin prov'd it has,
 an awful Destiny.
I pray the Lord preserve you all,
 and keep you from this End;
O let *Fitz-Gerrald's* great Downfall
 unto your Welfare tend.
I to the Lord my Soul bequeath,
 accept thereof I pray,
My Body to the Earth bequeath,
 dear Friends adieu for aye.

These Lines were put into the Hands of one who frequently visited the Pirates in Prison, by *Fitz Gerrald* himself, the Day before they were executed, with a manifest Desire that they might be disposed of so as would do most Good. The same Person put a paper into the same Hands on the Day of his Execution, which runs after this Manner:

Young Men,

"I desire you all in general to take Warning by me; for you see what a greedy Eye brings a young Man to. Beware how you disobey your Friends. Beware of Drunkenness, for it is the Inlet of all other Sins. I must confess that I was not guilty of Murder, nor of striking Men as others were: But of all other Sins I was guilty, for which, I ask God Pardon. I have been guilty of offending and denying thee the God that is above, in prophaning thy holy Name and Sabbath, and polluting of thy Ordinances, and also committing all the Injuries we were capable of, upon our Neighbours Bodies or Goods in a Manner. I desire you all to obey your Parents, give a good Ear to the Preachers of God, this slighted have I, shun Theft, Drunkenness, Swearing, Evil-speaking, Lying and all evil Frays. So I leave you to God, and the World: And I hope I am provided for a better World, and a glorious heavenly Kingdom."

For the most part, gallows literature vanished with public executions. Though one interesting parallel today might be the videotaped confession of serial killer Ted Bundy. Though he had maintained his innocence throughout his trials, just prior to his death in the electric chair in 1989, he made his last public statement in the form of a videotaped interview with religious broadcaster James Dobson in which he blamed pornography for his crimes (though evidence shows he was actually more interested in detective magazines, cheerleader pamphlets, and physiology texts). This video subsequently became very popular among religious and antiporn groups, selling for a $25 "donation" per copy.

Some Authentic Pirate Songs

Of course everyone knows the immortal lines:

Fifteen men on the dead man's chest—
Yo-ho-ho and a bottle of rum!
Drink and the devil had done for the rest—
Yo-ho-ho and a bottle of rum!

This fragment of a fictional pirate song is from Robert Louis Stevenson's classic pirate novel *Treasure Island*. Although the origin of this fragment is uncertain, it's possible it could have been based on an authentic pirate song, but this will probably never be known.

Unfortunately, most of the seamen's shanties from the heyday of the pirates were never written down. But some were. And among these are a few genuine pirate songs. After considerable research, I was able to dig up a few of these almost forgotten treasures. Many of these songs were sung by honest seamen, as well as pirates.

The first one we'll look at is a fragment which talks of St. Mary's. This was a pirate base on Madagascar in the late 1600s and early 1700s. At that time, Madagascar was something of a pirate colony for the corsairs[70] that haunted the Red Sea, the Persian Gulf, and India's Malabar Coast.

Where is the trader of London town?
His gold's on the capstan
His blood's on his gown
And it's up and away for St. Mary's Bay
Where the liquor is good and the lasses are gay.

This short verse talks of murder, gold, alcohol and women—four basic desires of the pirates. With the possible exception of murder, this is what they dreamed of.

The next song was a humorous shanty sung by French privateers and pirates in the days when the French and English were not getting along very well. Unfortunately, most of the humor is lost in translation. Its title in French is "Le Grand Coureur."

The Great Racer

The corsair, the *Great Racer*, is an
ill-omened ship,
When she sets sail to hunt the English,
The wind, the seas, and the fight, all go
against the French.

[Chorus:] Let's go, lads, cheerily, cheerily,
let's go lads, so gaily!

She comes from Lorient with a good wind
and sea,
She was hauling out on the port tack, sailing
like a fish,
When a squall struck her tophamper an' the
corsair was hulked.

70 Corsair is another word for pirate, though this term is usually used to refer to pirates of the Mediterranean, the Red Sea, and the Indian Ocean. "Buccaneer" usually refers to those pirates of the Caribbean and the West Indies.

We had to re-mast her, an' work like
the devil,
While the job was progressin', there signaled
from starboard,
A fine ship with port-covers on her guns.

An Englishman, in truth, with a double row
of teeth,
Carrier of sudden death, but the Frenchman
has no fear,
Instead of tryin' to escape, we challenge them
to fight.

Their fire it rained upon us, we returned it
shot for shot,
While her beard was singeing, in a great cloud
of smoke,
She sailed away an' soon escaped us.

At the end of six months our prizes amounted
to nothing more than three,
One ship, half sunk an' full of spuds,
The second with slippers for cargo, the third
loaded with manure.

To recuperate from our fights, we had for
our meals,
Dried beans and rancid bacon, vinegar instead
of wine,
Biscuits long since rotten, an' morning cam-
phor instead of coffee.

At the end of this fateful voyage, was our
sinking as we made the port,
In this frightful distress, when each seaman
saw himself lost,
We had to save ourselves, each one the best
way he could.

The captain and his mate saved themselves on
a gun,
The master using the great anchor, the steward
in his grog-tub,
Ah, the wicked, bloody beggar, the robber of
our rations!

You should have seen the cook, with his spoon
an' meat-hook,
He got into his pot, like a horrid stew,
He went like the wind, made land like a
thunderbolt.

For our horrible misfortune, the one responsible was the caulker,
Who, falling from the main-top, over the
forecastle,
Bounced through the galley and smashed up
the ship.

If this story of the *Great Racer* has touched
your hearts,
Have then the good manners to give
generously,
Wine, rum, or beer, an' we shall all be happy.

The next pirate song comes to us by way of Canada, though its use was undoubtedly much more widespread. This one is a bit bloodier and probably more typical of their songs.

Bold Manning

Bold Manning was to sea one day,
And a dreary day it was, too,
As dreary day as ever you see,
All wet with fog and dew.
They spied a large and lofty ship
About three miles ahead.
"Come h'ist up our main-tops'l, boys,
And after her we'll speed!"

He called unto his bosun,
   Whose name was William Craig:
"Oh Craig, oh Craig; come up on deck
   And h'ist up our black flag!"
His bosun was a valiant man,
   His heart was stout and bold.
But when he saw his father's ship,
   He felt his blood run cold.

Now, Manning's ship you all do know,
   That ship of noted fame,
With five hundred seamen and fifty brass guns,
   As brave and crafty fellows
As ever ploughed the main.

[Lines missing]

They ploughed the main all that night
   Until they reached their [the] *Fame*,
And bore right down upon her
   And sheered up alongside.
With his loud-speaking trumpet:
   "Whence come you?" he cried.

"Where are you from?" cries Manning.
   "I pray you tell me true,
For if to me you tell a lie,
   It'll be the worse for you."
"We are the *Fame*, to New York sailed,
   For Liverpool we're bound.
Our captain's name is William Craig,
   A native of that town."

"Oh, no! Oh, no!" cried Manning.
   "These things can never be true!
So heave your main yard to the mast
   And let your ship lay to.
And if you think my orders
   Are not fit to obey,
With grape shot and canister[71]
   I'll sink you where you lay!"

These poor, affrighted seamen,
   Not knowing what to do,
They hove their main yard to the mast
   And let their ship lay to.
These bold and crafty pirates,
   With broadsword in hand,
They went on board of the merchant ship
   And slaughtered every man.

Some they shot and others they stabbed,
   And all of them they drowned,
And most of these poor fellows
   Lay bathing in their blood.
They hunted the ship all over
   And ransacked everything,
Until they came to a female
   In the after mess cabin.

She, not hearing of the murders
   Or knowing what was done,
Played upon her own guitar.
   True sweetily she sung:
"Home, home, sweet, sweet home;
   'Tis for an absent lover that caused me
   to roam."

Some did stomp and some did swear
   They would make her their bride
"Stand back, stand back!" said Manning
   "I'll enter [An end to?] all your strife!"

71 Grapeshot was a cluster of connected iron balls which was shot from a cannon, whereas canister shot was a metal can filled with small shot and scrap metal that scattered when fired.

He boldly rushed upon her,
  Without fear or dread.
He boldly rushed upon this female
  And severed off her head.

These bold and crafty pirates,
  Not caring what they done,
They went on board of the pirate ship
  And boldly crack of dawn [crackéd on?]
With a kag of rum on the capstan,
  So boldly they did sing,
To the mid watch of that night
  You might hear their echoes ring:

  "We pirates lead a merry, merry life
  And a merry, merry life lead we!
  And when a strange sail heaves in sight
  We'll haul her under our lee.
  When the jolly, jolly grog is flowing,
  Light falls [Ri fol?] the dol i day!"

Moving on to something even more picturesque, the next account and song fragment were recorded by Mr. Runciman in about 1880 as he heard it from a crusty old sea dog named Tom Sinnett. Runciman found Sinnett in a seaman's lodging-house in some unspecified port "north of England." Runciman later said, "Tom was not a pleasant-looking man. He had low, brown, and deep-set, cunning eyes. Sometimes he flashed a sudden glance on you, which was a revelation of wickedness, and the hints he dropped made you shudder."

Pirates were actually quite young for the most part. This can be seen in this list of the crew of the pirate ship Adventure *taken from an arrest warrant issued in 1699 by the Governor of Virginia: John Loyd, about 30; Thomas Hughes, about 28; Thomas Simpson, about 10; James Venner, about 20; Tee Wetherly, about 18; Thomas Jameson, 20; William Griffith, about 30; Thomas Davis, about 22; Francis Reade, about 18; and William Saunders, about 15. Very few pirates were older than their late thirties. By then they had either retired or were dead.*

Sinnett told Runciman he sailed from Southampton, England, in 1819 on a French slave ship. The captain of this ship, known as "Captain Hell-Fire," had the unfortunate habit of shooting at the legs of his crewmen when he was drunk, so about halfway through the voyage, the crew mutinied. They ran him through with a marline-spike and tossed him overboard. For their new captain, they chose a Yankee called "Lips." Such nicknames were actually very common among pirates. We tend to know them by their real names or aliases because these are what were used at their trials or in official reports. After plundering numerous ships, they were captured and all were hung in Cuba except Sinnett, who was able to bribe the judges into letting him go.

Runciman recorded Sinnett as saying:

> Aye, sir, I seen a man spin round an' round like a teetotum after a ball had ketched him in the temple; then he lay an' dug at the deck with his heel for half an hour. He knew all the time he was goin'; but couldn't die, an' asked the chaps to club him. . . . A knife wound's a nasty thing. An' I seen a lot of that. One chap dabbed his sticker through

my arm here. Like a flash of fire goin' through you, it was! Aye, but I don't think there's much pain in drowning. They wriggle fer a bit; and then they seem to go sleepy like, and let it come over 'em. . . . Lord, I seen 'em a wriggling and pitching their hands up, one a'ter the other, an' a-squeain' when the sharks got hold on 'em. *Sc—r—r—aunch!* An' a scoot of blood over 20 yards o' water, an' a yell!

At this point in their conversation, Sinnett began to sing an old pirate shanty.

So where they have gone to, there's no one
  can tell,
  Ho, Brandy an' gin an' a bottle o' rum!
But I think we shall meet the poor devils in hell,
  Ho, Brandy an' gin an' a bottle o' rum!
We went o'er the bar on the thirteenth o' May
  Ho, Brandy an' gin an' a bottle o' rum!
The Galloper jump'd an' the sails came away,
  Ho, Brandy an' gin an' a bottle o' rum!

Our final example is an old English ballad that is probably the most representative of the lot.

Of all the lives I ever say,
  A Pirate's be for I.
Hap what hap may he's allus gay
  An' drinks an' bungs his eye.
For his work he's never loth:
  An' a-pleasurin' he'll go;
Tho' certain sure to be popt off,
  Yo, ho, with the rum below!
In Bristowe I left Poll [Polly?] ashore,
  Well stored wi' togs an' gold,
An' off I goes to sea for more,
  A-piratin' so bold.

An' wounded in the arm I got,
  An' then a pretty blow;
Comed home I find Poll's flowed away,
  Yo, ho, with the rum below!

An' when my precious leg was lopt,
  Just for a bit of fun,
I picks it up, on t'other hopt,
  An' rammed it in a gun.
"What's that for?" cries out Salem Dick;
  "What for, my jumpin' beau?
Why, to give the lubbers one more kick!"
  Yo, ho, with the rum below!

I 'llows this crazy hull o' mine
  At sea has had its share:
Marooned three times an' wounded nine
  An' blowed up in the air.
But ere to Execution Bay
  The wind these bones do blow,
I'll drink an' fight what's left away,
  Yo, ho, with the rum below!

"A pirate's life is the only life for a man o' spirit!"

—Phineas Bunch, pirate, c. 1718

Pirate Laws

The rules or laws that the pirates sailed under were called "articles." They were drawn up and agreed upon by the entire company before setting out on a voyage. When a new seaman—usually from a captured ship—decided to "go on account," he was required to sign their articles in order to join them.

Pirates usually destroyed their articles when attacked by a pirate-hunting man-of-war because it contained their signatures and could be used as evidence against them. Some pirate crews put their signatures (or marks) on their articles in a circle so that if they were captured, no one would be able to tell who signed first, enabling them all to claim they'd been forced to sign—a common pirate legal defense when brought to trial. It's also been said they would destroy their articles because they contained something too gruesome or disagreeable that they wouldn't want made public. Apparently, many of the sets of pirate articles that survive today were reconstructed from interviews with the pirates in prison, from trial testimony, or from the forced men who refused to sign.

The following set appears to have survived intact and is reprinted from the 1726 edition of Captain Charles Johnson's *A General History of the Robberies and Murders of the Most Notorious Pyrates.* These articles were drawn up by Captain John Phillips and his crew of pirates at the beginning of their 1723 voyage in the schooner *Revenge*—the same voyage that resulted in the trial of William White and John Rose Archer, whose confession I've included in the "Gallows Literature" section. Their ship was taken by surprise and they didn't have a chance to destroy their articles.

The Articles on Board the *Revenge*.

1. Every Man shall obey civil Command; the Captain shall have one full Share and a half in all Prizes; the Master, Carpenter, Boatswain and Gunner shall have one Share and [a] quarter.
2. If any Man shall offer to run away, or keep any Secret from the Company, he shall be maroon'd with one Bottle of Powder, one Bottle of Water, one small Arm and Shot [usually just enough shot and powder to commit suicide with].
3. If any Man shall steal any Thing in the Company, or game to the Value of a Piece of Eight, he shall be maroon'd or shot.
4. If at any Time we should meet another Marooner (that is, Pyrate), that Man that shall sign his Articles without the Consent of our Company shall suffer such Punishment as the Captain and Company shall think fit.
5. That Man that shall strike another whilst these Articles are in force, shall receive Moses's Law (that is, 40 stripes lacking one) on the bare Back.
6. That Man that shall snap his Arms, or smoak Tobacco in the Hold, without a Cap to his Pipe, or carry a Candle lighted without a Lanthorn [lantern], shall suffer the same Punishment as in the former Article.
7. That Man that shall not keep his Arms clean, fit for an Engagement, or neglect his Business, shall be cut off from his Share, and suffer such other Punishment as the Captain and the Company shall think fit.
8. If any Man shall lose a Joint in Time of an Engagement, he shall have 400 Pieces of Eight, if a Limb, 800.
9. If at any Time we meet with a prudent Woman, that Man that offers to meddle with her, without her Consent, shall suffer present Death.

Bizarre North Korean Propaganda

North Korea's number-one goal has always been reunification with South Korea under one government—theirs. Since they view North and South Korea as just one country, they can't depict the South Koreans as the bad guys in their propaganda. Instead, they say that the southern half of Korea is under occupation and that they're trying to liberate South Korea so South Koreans can be free and happy like the North Koreans.

The primary thing preventing reunification is the U.S. military presence in South Korea, so they paint America out to be the bad guy. The South Korean government is just a puppet government, they say, imposed on the people of South Korea against their will by the United States for its own selfish purposes. With all this as their basic premise, it shouldn't be surprising that America figures prominently in their propaganda. In fact, their attacks on the United States have been nothing short of vitriolic.

According to an article titled "Let Us Intensify the Anti-Imperialist, Anti-U.S. Struggle," written by North Korea's late dictator, Kim Il Sung, the United States is "the most heinous and shameless plunderer known to history," adding that the "U.S. imperialists" have revealed "their true colors as gangsters."

Their propaganda says that because the United States is so evil, conditions in both America and South Korea are horrendous. Kim Il Sung's biography asserts:

> The Yankees and their stooges squander a one-year harvest of the farmers in one night's orgies in gorgeous mansions, while famine is claiming many lives in urban alleys and countryside, with fascism oppressing all things human and progressive everywhere.
>
> This is not all. In olden times, the forefathers of the Yankees organized "Negro-hunting parties," slaughtered peaceful natives at random, and drank water and wine from their skulls. Following this barbarous tradition, the Yankees are engaged in all sorts of hair-raising atrocities in South Korea.
>
> The scoundrels gun down South Korean children and numerous people at will, for the fun of things; they drive their cars over passersby; they

(above:) A North Korean postage stamp publicizing a conference of communist journalists in 1969 showing President Nixon dropping an atomic bomb on a shredded U.S. flag as he is being dismembered by pens. Across the top it says, "Let's cut up U.S. Imperialism all around the world!" (below:) A 1975 North Korean postage stamp commemorating Anti-America Month, with the words next to the U.S. soldier's head reading, "Yankee, son-of-a-bitch!"

shoot at the peasants gathering firewood in the mountains; they break into shops and dwellings, plundering at random and setting them on fire; in broad daylight, they attack and rape women, children and even old women.

The puppet clique prefer to imprison those who punish these atrocities, and they suppress the people who are indignant at the U.S. imperialist wolves.

South Korea is a paradise for plunderers and a hell for the people, people are forced to lead a nightmare life day after day. But the South Korean people never give up the struggle; awakened by the very struggle, they are continuing to build up the revolutionary ranks.

If the blood and tears shed by them were pooled, it would form a river. Everywhere the cries of human suffering can be heard throughout South Korea.

Next to all this, life in North Korea probably doesn't seem quite so bad. Kim Il Sung thought the South Koreans looked to the North as a shining example they could follow to escape from U.S. domination. He wrote, "North Korea is the base of the Korean revolution. The successes of socialist construction there encourage the South Korean people in their anti-U.S., national-salvation struggle and stimulate the preparation of revolutionary forces in South Korea." Ever since the Korean War, North Korea has been insisting the South Koreans were right on the verge of revolting against the U.S. and overthrowing the South Korean government. The predicted revolution hasn't happened, obviously. Nor is it likely to, since South Korea is actually in much better economic shape than the North. (No surprise here.)

Here's an interesting bit of Nazi propaganda from the Deutscher Weckruf und Beobachter *(1940): "Quite a number of people also describe the German classical author Shakespeare, as belonging to English literature, because—quite accidentally born at Stratford-on-Avon—he was forced by authorities of that country to write in English."*

Since North Korea has a closed society and their government has total control of their media, the people of North Korea have no idea how far wrong all this propaganda really is. They've been raised to believe that they owe their "wonderful" lifestyle to Kim Il Sung and the government, which works diligently to protect them from such Western horrors. They're very thankful for this. Since they don't know any better, they have little reason to believe Kim Il Sung or their government would lie to them.

Maybe someday they'll find out what's really been going on.

John Greenleaf Whittier's Poem About Hash

John Greenleaf Whittier (1807–1892) was a Quaker who believed strongly in the abolition of slavery and in nonviolence. For thirty years, he was very active in the antislavery movement. Because he was a pacifist, many considered him a traitor during the Civil War. After the war, he spoke out for an easy reconciliation and against the vengeful reconstruction government that was imposed on the South. This fiery political radical is now primarily remembered as a sentimental New England poet who wrote nostalgically about country life—his most famous poems being "Snow-Bound" and "The Barefoot Boy." During his life, he was considered one of America's greatest poets, but this reputation has diminished somewhat over the ensuing years. This poem about hash and slavery is from *The Panorama*, and Other Poems (1856).

The Haschish

Of all that Orient lands can vaunt
Of marvels with our own competing,
The strangest is the Haschish plant.
And what will follow on its eating.

What pictures to the taster rise,
Of Dervish[72] or of Almeh[73] dances!
Of Eblis,[74] or of Paradise,
Set all aglow with Houri[75] glances!

The poppy visions of Cathay,[76]
The heavy beer-trance of the Suabian;[77]
The wizard lights and demon play
Of nights Walpurgis[78] and Arabian!

The Mollah[79] and the Christian dog
Change place in mad metempsychosis;[80]
The Muezzin[81] climbs the synagogue,
The Rabbi shakes his beard at Moses!

The Arab by his desert well
Sits choosing from some Caliph's daughters,
And hears his single camel's bell
Sound welcome to his regal quarters.

The Koran's reader makes complaint
Of Shitan[82] dancing on and off it;
The robber offers alms, the saint
Drinks Tokay[83] and blasphemes the Prophet.

Such scenes that Eastern plant awakes;
But we have one ordained to beat it,
The Haschish of the West, which makes
Or fools or knaves of all who eat it.

The preacher eats, and straight appears
His Bible in a new translation;
Its angels negro overseers,
And Heaven itself a snug plantation!

The man of peace, about whose dreams
The sweet millennial angels cluster,
Tastes the mad weed, and plots and schemes,
A raving Cuban filibuster[84]!

The nosiest Democrat, with ease,
It turns to Slaver's parish beadle;[85]
The shrewdest statesman eats and sees
Due southward point the polar needle

---

72 Whirling Dervishes are Muslim ascetics who use dancing as a form of meditation and prayer.

73 Almeh are female singers and dancers of Egypt.

74 An evil spirit or the chief of the evil jinn (spirits).

75 The houris are beautiful virgins that are provided to faithful Muslims in Paradise.

76 Cathay is another name for China.

77 The Suabi, or Suebi, were ancient peoples of central Germany.

78 According to German superstition, witches held their sabbaths on Walpurgis Night.

79 A mollah, or mullah, is an Islamic religious teacher or wise man.

80 The transferring of a soul from one body to another.

81 The crier who calls Muslims to prayers from a minaret or part of a mosque.

82 Shittan is a Japanese version of Sanskrit lettering.

83 A Hungarian wine.

84 A pirate.

85 A minor parish official who keeps order during services and waits on the clergyman.

The Judge partakes, and sits erelong
Upon his bench a railing Blackguard;
Decides off-hand that right is wrong,
And reads the ten commandments backward.

O potent plant! so rare a taste
Has never Turk or Gentoo[86] gotten;
The hempen Haschish of the East
Is powerless to our Western Cotton!

George Washington Grew Marijuana

Cannabis was first cultivated around 4000 B.C. in China. Since then, it has been a popular source of fiber. Everything from rope to clothes has been made from it. Even the original drafts of the Declaration of Independence were on hemp paper. But it has also been popular for its medicinal and intoxicating properties. Queen Victoria used it to relieve her period pains, and from 1842 to 1900, nearly half of all the medicine sold in America contained marijuana.

"I'm just here for the drugs."

—First Lady Nancy Reagan at a "Just Say No" rally.

Cannabis was introduced to the New World by the Spaniards prior to 1545. The settlers in Jamestown brought it to Virginia in 1611. It was found to be so useful that in 1762, Virginia awarded bounties to farmers who grew hemp and to manufacturers who converted it into various products. Not stopping there, Virginia also penalized those who didn't produce it.

Although it's uncertain whether the colonists were aware of the plant's medicinal and intoxicating properties, some documents appear to indicate that they were.

Just three years after Virginia was handing out its bounties, George Washington was growing cannabis at Mount Vernon, as can be seen by two entries he made in his diary. For the dates May 12–13, 1765, he wrote, "Sowed Hemp at Muddy hole by Swamp." And then on August 7, 1765, he wrote, "—began to seperate [sic] the Male from the Female Hemp at Do— rather too late."

The second entry seems to indicate he was cultivating marijuana for its medicinal properties. Separating the female from the male plants before they pollinate is done to increase the drug's potency. Although it's possible he wanted to remove one sex because he felt the other produced a better quality of fiber, the phrase "rather too late" indicates he wanted to do it before the females were fertilized—something that would make no difference if he were growing it for fiber, but considerable difference if it was to be used as a drug.

Recreational use of the drug reached America before 1856, for in that year a series of articles written by Fitz Hugh Ludlow about his marijuana-eating experiences were published in *Putnam's Magazine* and then as a book titled *The Hasheesh Eater*. Ludlow was a sixteen-year-old in Poughkeepsie, New York, when he began experimenting with various drugs at the local pharmacy, including chloroform, opiates, and stimulants.

By 1883, hashish houses were established among the opium dens in New Orleans, New York City,

[86] A Hindu.

Boston, Philadelphia, and Chicago. The following year, hashish candy was being sold in Baltimore.

If George Washington were around today, he'd be shocked to find out that not only is hemp illegal, but that many state governments tax it! The government first taxed marijuana (which wasn't illegal at the time) in 1937. To sell marijuana legally, you needed a tax stamp—which the IRS refused to sell. In other words, they use the tax to make marijuana illegal. In 1983, Arizona enacted a new marijuana sales tax. This time the stamps were actually for sale, but there were additional punishments for drug dealers who didn't buy their stamps. By the mid-Nineties, at least twenty-two other states required tax stamps on illegal drugs. As the Alabama Department of Revenue says, "Say 'no' to drugs, but if you don't, buy your stamps."

The father of our country wasn't the only president interested in marijuana—Thomas Jefferson also grew it. And then, of course, there was President Bill Clinton. Since he claims he tried marijuana without inhaling, it might be assumed that he ate some Alice B. Toklas brownies. But either way, *he* definitely knew of the drug's intoxicating properties.

Ben Franklin's Advice on Choosing a Mistress

Dr. Benjamin Franklin—that venerable American patriot, statesman, diplomat, publisher, author, philosopher, scientist, and the inventor of the lightning rod, a stove, several chairs and some glasses—had a passion for sex. As early as 1724, at the age of eighteen, he was already consorting with "low women," and he was still at it in his seventies while he was minister to France. He had at least one illegitimate son, William, whose mother is unknown, but who was raised by Franklin and his common-law wife, Deborah. William went on to be appointed governor of New Jersey in 1762 and later sided with the British in the Revolutionary War.

Born into a poor family, one of seventeen children, Benjamin Franklin was able to attend only two years of school and was largely self-taught. He was later given two honorary doctorates.

Franklin's early views on extramarital affairs is revealed in this letter of advice on choosing a mistress. It is to his friend, Cadwallader Colden of New York. It's not known whether this letter was ever sent or how serious he was.

June 25, 1745

My Dear Friend:—

I know of no Medicine fit to diminish the violent natural inclination you mention; and if I did, I think I should not communicate it to you. Marriage is the proper Remedy. It is the most natural State of Man, and therefore the State in which you will find solid Happiness. Your Reason against entering into it at present appears to be not well founded. The Circumstantial Advantages you have in View by Postponing it, are not only uncertain, but they are small in comparison with the Thing itself, *the being married and settled*. It is the Man and Woman united that makes the complete human Being. Separate she wants his force of Body and Strength of Reason; he her Softness, Sensibility and acute Discernment. Together they are most likely to succeed in the World. A single Man has not nearly the Value he would have in that State of Union. He is an incomplete Animal. He resembles the odd Half of a Pair of Scissors.

If you get a prudent, healthy wife, your Industry in your Profession, with her good Economy, will be a Fortune sufficient.

But if you will not take this Counsel, and persist in thinking a Commerce with the Sex is inevitable, then I repeat my former Advice that in your Amours you should *prefer old Women to young ones*. This you call a Paradox, and demand my reasons. They are these:

1. Because they have more Knowledge of the world, and their Minds are better stored with Observations; their Conversation is more improving, and more lastingly agreeable.
2. Because when Women cease to be handsome, they study to be good. To maintain their Influence over Man, they supply the Diminution of Beauty by an Augmentation of Utility. They learn to do a thousand Services, small and great, and are the most tender and useful of all Friends when you are sick. Thus they continue amiable. And hence there is hardly such a thing to be found as an old Woman who is not a good Woman.
3. Because there is no hazard of children, which irregularly produced may be attended with much inconvenience.
4. Because through more Experience they are more prudent and discreet in conducting an Intrigue to prevent Suspicion. The Commerce with them is therefore safer with regard to your reputation; and regard to theirs, if the Affair should happen to be known, considerate People might be inclined to excuse an old Woman, who would kindly take care of a young Man, form his manners by her good Councils, and prevent his ruining his Health and Fortune among mercenary Prostitutes.
5. Because in every Animal that walks upright, the Deficiency of the Fluids that fill the Muscles appears first in the highest Part. The Face first grows lank and wrinkled; then the Neck; then the Breast and Arms; the lower parts continuing to the last as plump as ever; so that covering all above with a Basket, and regarding only what is below the Girdle, it is impossible of two Women to know an old from a young one. And as in the Dark all Cats are gray, the Pleasure of Corporal Enjoyment with an old Woman is at least equal and frequently superior; every Knack being by Practice capable by improvement.
6. Because the sin is less. The Debauching of a Virgin may be her Ruin, and make her for Life unhappy.
7. Because the Compunction is less. The having made a young Girl *miserable* may give you frequent bitter Reflections; none which can attend making an old Woman *happy*.

8th & lastly. They are so grateful!!!

Thus much for my Paradox. But still I advise you to marry immediately; being sincerely

Your Affectionate Friend,
Benj. Franklin

"Ne'er take a wife till thou hast a house (and a fire) to put her in."

—Benjamin Franklin

When Franklin was sent to France as an ambassador from 1776 to 1785, accompanied by two grandsons, one of them his illegitimate son's illegitimate son, he fit right in with France's sexual openness—much to the chagrin of future-president John Adams, who had trouble dealing with the loose morals of Paris and the common practice of taking mistresses and lovers. Adams also had trouble dealing with Franklin's lifestyle, writing, "The Life of Dr. Franklin was a Scene of continual discipation." Despite all the platitudes in Franklin's *Poor Richard's Almanac*, most of which he took from other sources, Franklin believed in spending money, not saving it, and privately admitted that frugality was "a virtue I could never acquire myself."

Franklin's wife had passed away two years before he went to France, and he was on the prowl. Although his conquests, if there were any, are not documented, there are a series of letters between him and Madame Brillon de Jouy (née Anne-Louise d'Hardancourt) that give insight into his methods of seduction. Her husband was clearly aware of what Franklin was up to because in one of his letters to Franklin he commented, "I am certain that you have just been kissing my wife." But in France at this time, upper-class marriages were arranged solely based on status and monetary concerns. Love was generally sought in extramarital affairs. The general feeling was that, as André Maurois put it, "a faithful husband cuts a ridiculous figure."

Though Franklin was in his seventies and Madame Brillon in her early thirties, this did not slow him down. After all, her husband was in his late fifties, and Franklin was the most famous man in France next to the king, and probably the most popular.

Two days after his arrival in France, John Adams accompanied Franklin to a dinner at the Brillons'. Among the many guests were Madame Brillon's close friend and next-door neighbor, Louis-Guillaume Le Veillard (who Adams mistakenly called Le Vaillant), and the governess for the Brillon's two daughters, Mademoiselle Jupin. In his diary Adams wrote:

> I saw a Woman [Mlle. Jupin] in Company, as a Companion of Madam Brillon who dined with her at Table, and was considered one of the Family. She was very plain and clumsy. When I afterwards learned both from Dr. Franklin and his Grandson, and from many other persons, that this Woman was the *Amie* of Mr. Brillon and that Madam Brillon consoled herself by the *Amitie* of Mr. Le Vaillant, I was astonished that these People could live together in such apparent Friendship and indeed without cutting each others throats. But I do not know the World. I soon saw and heard so much of these Things in other Families and among almost all the great People of the Kingdom that I found it was a thing of course. It was universally understood and Nobody lost any reputation by it.

If Franklin told Adams that Le Veillard was Madame Brillon's lover, he must have believed it. As Adams noted, such an arrangement was quite common. Actually, Madame Brillon was much more conservative than Franklin seems to have realized. Not only was she not having an affair with Le Veillard, she was totally unaware of her husband's affair with their governess. This became apparent more than a year later when she found out about it, and she was furious. But until this happened, Franklin apparently thought she was much more accepting of extramarital affairs. She certainly did not hesitate to flirt with him. In one of her letters to him, she mentions how gossips were criticizing her for "the sweet habit I have of sitting on your lap." In fact, some might say she led him on.

After an apparent religious conversation with her touching on his salvation, she wrote a note to him discussing the seven deadly sins. Listing each of them, she proceeded to explain how he had no problem with the first six, but the seventh one—lust—posed something of a problem for him, though it was something all great men are tainted with. She added, "Go on doing great things and loving pretty women; provided that, pretty and lovable though they may be, you never lose sight of my principle: always love God, America, and me above all."

In reply, Franklin brought up the Ten Commandments, but said there were actually twelve of them, explaining that:

> . . . the first is: increase, multiply and fill the earth; the twelfth (a commandment I enjoin you to obey): love one another. Come to think of it, they are a bit misplaced, and shouldn't the last one be first? . . . But please tell me, my dear casuist, whether to have observed those two commandments religiously (even though they are not in the Decalogue) could not compensate for my having so often failed to respect one of the ten? I mean the one which forbids us to covet our neighbor's wife. A commandment which (I confess) I have consistently violated (may God forgive me) every time I have seen or thought of my kind confessor [i.e. Madame Brillon]; and I fear that I shall never be capable of repenting of this sin, should I even obtain full possession of my confessor's person. . . . But then, why should I be so scrupulous, when you have promised to absolve me even of future sins?

She deftly evaded his seductive reasoning by saying that while this was okay for him, she felt she must hold herself to different standards. And there was also her husband to think of.

> Perhaps there is no great harm in a man having desires and yielding to them; a woman may have desires, but she must not yield. You have kept two very pleasant commandments religiously; you have broken another, one easily violated. . . . My friendship, and a touch of vanity, perhaps, prompt me strongly to pardon you; but I dare not decide the question without consulting that neighbor whose wife you covet, because he is a far better casuist than I am. And then, too, as Poor Richard

Benjamin Franklin while he was an ambassador to France painted by Rosalie Filleul.

would say, "In weighty matters, two heads are better than one."

But then she softens this by adding, "I am as great a sinner as yourself. I have desired to see you, desired to know you, desired your esteem, desired your friendship. . . . And now, I desire that you may love me forever; this desire grows day by day in my heart and it will last all my life. But such is the compassion of God, it is said, that I have not the slightest doubt that all our desires will eventually lead us to Paradise!"

Still, his philandering caused her a bit of jealousy. She also thought the reasoning behind it was unsound. She wrote:

> You ask me for the list of your sins, my dear papa; it would be so long that I dare not undertake such a great work. And yet, you commit only one, but it has so many branches, it is repeated so often that it would take infinite calculations to assess its magnitude. . . . The dangerous system you are forever trying to demonstrate, my dear papa—that the friendship a man has for women can be divided *ad infinitum*—this is something I shall never put up with. My heart, while capable of great love, has chosen few objects on which to bestow it; it has chosen them well, you are at the head of the list. When you scatter your friendship, as you have done, my friendship does not diminish, but from now on I shall try to be somewhat sterner toward your faults.

"By all means marry; if you get a good wife, you'll be happy. If you get a bad one, you'll become a philosopher."

—Socrates

Franklin was not about to limit his attentions to just one woman, especially if she ruled out all chance of a physical relationship. But he wasn't ready to give up all hope yet.

> What a difference, my dear friend, between you and me! You find innumerable faults in me, whereas I see only one fault in you (but perhaps it is the fault of my glasses). I mean this kind of avarice which leads you to seek a monopoly on all my affections, and not to allow me any for the agreeable ladies of your country. Do you imagine that it is impossible for my affection (or my tenderness) to be divided without being diminished? You deceive yourself, and you forget the playful manner with which you stopped me. You renounce and totally exclude all that might be of the flesh in our affection, allowing me only some kisses, civil and honest, such as you might grant your little cousins. What am I receiving that is so special as to prevent me from giving the same to others, without taking from what belongs to you? . . . The sweet sounds brought forth from the pianoforte by your clever hands can be enjoyed by twenty people simultaneously without diminishing at all the pleasure you so obligingly mean for me, and I could, with as little reason, demand from your affection that no other ears but mine be allowed to be charmed by those sweet sounds. . . .
>
> My poor little love, which you should have cherished, it seems to me, instead of being fat and lively (like those of your elegant paintings), is thin and ready to die of hunger for want of the substantial nourishment that his mother inhumanly refuses. And now, also, she wants to cut his little wings, so that he cannot go to seek it elsewhere.

Then, diplomat that he was, he decided to smooth things over by proposing a peace treaty between them.

I imagine that neither of us can gain anything in this war. Consequently, feeling myself to be the weaker, I shall do what ought, in fact, to be done by the wiser: make proposals of peace . . .

> ARTICLE I There must be peace, friendship, and eternal love between Madam B. and Mr. Frank.
>
> ARTICLE II In order to maintain this inviolable peace, Madam B. on her side stipulates and agrees that Mr. F. shall come and see her every time she asks him to.
>
> ARTICLE III That he shall stay at her house as much and as long as it shall please her.
>
> ARTICLE IV That when he is with her, he shall be obliged to take tea, play chess, listen to music or do anything that she may ask him.[87]
>
> ARTICLE V And that he shall love no other woman than her.
>
> ARTICLE VI And the said Mr. F. on his side stipulates and agrees that he shall go to Madam B's as much as he pleases.
>
> ARTICLE VII That he shall stay there as long as he pleases.
>
> ARTICLE VIII That when he is with her he shall do anything he pleases.
>
> ARTICLE IX And that he shall love no other woman as long as he finds her agreeable.[88]

How do you like these preliminaries? Don't they seem to express the true way of thinking and the real intentions of both parties more clearly than most treaties? I am planning to insist heavily on ARTICLE VIII, although without much hope of your consenting to its execution, and also on ARTICLE IX, although I despair of ever finding any other woman I could love with equal tenderness.

Their letters then began to focus on which of them loved the other more, each claiming their love was greater. This prompted Franklin to write:

> It is true that I have often said that I love you too much, and I have told the truth. Judge, by a comparison I am going to make, which of us two loves the most. If I say to a friend: "I need your horses to take a journey, lend them to me," and he replies: "I should be very glad to oblige you, but I fear that they will be ruined by this voyage and cannot bring myself to lend them to anyone," must I not conclude that the man loves his horses more than he loves me? And if, in the same case, I should willingly risk my horses by lending them to him, is it not clear that I love him more than my horses, and also more than he loves me? You know that I am ready to sacrifice my beautiful, big horses.

"Are women books?' says Hodge. 'Then would mine were an almanac to change her every year.'"

—As quoted by Benjamin Franklin

Still impervious to his efforts of seduction, she warned him his continued exertions in this direction were doomed to failure, saying he wanted "a fat, chubby love [i.e., cupid], a love of flesh and bones, spoiled and pampered" but that she was trying "to blunt his little arrows, while giving him full freedom to run by hills and dales and attack

87 [Franklin's footnote] All that he is able to do, of course.

88 [Franklin's footnote] All that he is able to do, of course.

anyone in sight." She then advises him "to fatten up his favorite at other tables than hers, which will always offer too meager a diet for his greedy appetites."

Franklin finally seems to have realized he wasn't going to be able to break down her resistance and at her request their relationship became more like that of a father and a daughter. Still, he must not have given up all his efforts for she later wrote to him:

> If your French is not very pure, it is at least very clear. I give you my word of honor to become your wife in paradise, on condition, however, that you will not ogle the virgins too much while waiting for me; when I choose one for eternity, I want a husband who is faithful; do you hear, my dear papa?
>
> I shall tell Maman [her mother] tonight about your good intentions toward her; I fear, though, that if she plans to oppose my claims on you, it will arouse a kind of jealousy between us. I am willing to yield anything to my mother except you, my good papa.

They had first met in 1777. Four years later, when she was on holiday for her health, Franklin wrote, "I often pass in front of your house. It seems desolate. In olden days, I broke a commandment, by coveting it, together with my neighbor's wife. Today, I don't covet it anymore, so that I am less of a sinner. But as far as the wife is concerned, I still think those commandments very bothersome and I am sorry that they ever were devised. If, in your travels, you ever come across the Holy Father, ask him to rescind them, as given only to the Jews and too much trouble for good Christians."

Madame Brillon was just one of several women who were very close to Franklin. John Adams wrote, "Mr. Franklin who at the age of seventy odd, had neither lost his Love of Beauty nor his Taste for it," explaining that the beautiful, young Mademoiselle de Passy, the daughter of the noble lord of the village of Passy, was "his favorite and his flame and his Love and his Mistress, which flattered the Family and did not displease the young Lady."

Then there was Mademoiselle Geneviève Le Veillard, the daughter of Louis-Guillaume Le Veillard—the man mentioned earlier who Franklin and others thought was Madame Brillon's lover. She sent Franklin a letter saying, "You told me that when you would write that you loved me *a little*, it would mean *a lot*. As for me, I tell you that I love you *a lot*. I hope that you shall not conclude from there that I love you *a little*. For it would be unfair, and I assure you that when I say *a lot*, that is exactly what I mean."

To Madame Helvétius, Franklin wrote, speaking in the third person, "If Notre Dame [this is what he called her] is pleased to spend her days with Franklin, he would be just as pleased to spend his nights with her; and since he has already given her so many of his days, although he has so few left to give, she seems very ungrateful in never giving him one of her nights, which keep passing as a pure loss, without making anyone happy except Poupon [her cat]. Nevertheless, he hugs her very tightly, for he loves her infinitely in spite of her many shortcomings." Eventually, Franklin asked her to marry him, but she turned him down.

There was also the Comtesse d'Houdetot, Madame Foucault, Polly Hewson (who came to France from England with her three children to visit him), and Mademoiselle Chaumont (the daughter of his landlord, whom Franklin affectionately referred to as his "wife"). Undoubtedly, there were many others.

Franklin on Wine

The following humorous piece is from a letter Franklin wrote in about 1784 while he was ambassador to France. Unfortunately, it loses a bit in translation from the French. It was written to Abbot André Morellet, and he signed it as "Abbot" Franklin.

> "*In vino veritas*," says the wise man; "truth is in the wine."
>
> Before Noah, men, having only water to drink, could not find the truth. So they went astray; they became abominably wicked and were justly exterminated by the water which they loved to drink.
>
> This good man Noah, having seen that all his contemporaries had perished by this bad drink, took an aversion to it; and God, to quench his thirst, created the vine and revealed to him the art of making wine from it. With the aid of this liquor he discovered more truth; and since his time the word to divine has been in use, commonly signifying to *discover* by means of wine. . . . Therefore, since this time all excellent things, even the deities, have been called *divine* or *divinities*. [This is a pun on *vin*—the French word for wine—and di*vin*e and di*vin*ities.] . . .
>
> I say this to you as a man of the world, but I will finish, as I began, like a good Christian, by making a religious remark to you, very important, and drawn from the Holy Writ, namely that the Apostle Paul very seriously advised Timothy to put some wine into his water for his health's sake; but that not one of the apostles nor any of the holy fathers have even recommended putting water into wine.

Mark Twain's Speech on Masturbation

Despite having virtually no formal education, Mark Twain (whose real name was Samuel Clemens, 1835–1910) went on to become America's greatest humorist. As the *Encyclopedia Americana* puts it, "Twain liberated humor, raising it to high art. . . . Instead of subduing his humor to seriousness, Twain invaded the citadels of seriousness and freed the humor held captive there." Of course, he is famous for such classics as *The Adventures of Huckleberry Finn*, *The Adventures of Tom Sawyer*, and the children's book *The Prince and the Pauper*, but many people don't know that he also had a taste for ribald humor. The chief example of this is a dinner speech he gave at the Stomach Club in Paris in the spring of 1879, titled "Some Thoughts on the Science of Onanism," in which he definitely invades "the citadels of seriousness."

In Mark Twain's time, masturbation was considered to be very serious behavior that had to be stopped at almost any cost. S. A. D. Tissot (1728–1787) believed semen was more precious than blood and should be used only for procreation. He wrote that masturbation caused everything from pimples, constipation, and hemorrhoids to tumors, bodily decay, and insanity. By masturbation, he meant all nonprocreative sex.

This philosophy became popular with many doctors in the eighteenth and nineteenth centuries. One of these was Sylvester A. Graham (for whom Graham crackers are named because he advocated unsifted flour). In his *Lecture to Young Men* (1834), he wrote on the dangers of excessive sex saying;

> Languor, lassitude, muscular relaxation, general debility and heaviness, depression of spirits, loss of appetite, indigestion, faintness and sinking at the pit of the stomach, increased susceptibilities of the skin and lungs to all the atmospheric changes, feebleness of circulation, chilliness, headache, melancholy, hypochondria, hysterics, feebleness of all the senses, impaired vision, loss of sight, weakness of the lungs, nervous cough, pulmonary consumption, disorders of the genital organs, weakness of the brain, loss of memory, epilepsy, insanity, apoplexy—and extreme feebleness and early death of offspring—are among the too common evils which are caused by sexual excesses between husband and wife.

He recommended having intercourse only once a month and certainly not more than once a week.

"The disease known as clergyman's sore throat *is believed by many eminent physicians to have its chief origin in excessive venery. It is well known that sexual abuse is a very potent cause of throat disease."*

—Dr. J. H. Kellogg, Plain Facts for Old and Young, *1888 (yes, this is the guy the breakfast cereal company was named after)*

To cure the evil of self-pollution, doctors tried everything from applying leeches to the genitals to applying powerful irritants to their patients, who were usually either mental patients or children. Sometimes they made the abusers sleep in a straightjacket or with their hands bound to the bedposts. For females, one Chicago doctor recommended clitoral circumcision, while in 1896 an Ohio doctor recommended removing half an inch to an inch of the dorsal nerves of the penis in males. In 1886, the well-known German neurologist Baron Richard von Krafft-Ebing even reported that he applied a hot iron to a little girl's clitoris to stop her from masturbating. It didn't work.

Apparently Mark Twain realized all this concern over something completely harmless was seriously misplaced. With his ribald sense of humor, it was the perfect topic for him make fun of. Just as Lenny Bruce would later do, Twain was using humor to make a statement about society.

Here is his speech.

> My gifted predecessor has warned you against the "social evil—adultery." In his able paper he exhausted that subject he left absolutely nothing more to be said on it. But I will continue his good work in the cause of morality by cautioning you against that species of recreation called self-abuse—to which I perceive that you are too much addicted. All great writers upon health and morals, both ancient and modern, have struggled with this stately subject; this shows its dignity and importance. Some of these writers have taken one side, some the other. Homer, in the second book of the *Iliad*, says with fine enthusiasm, "Give me masturbation or give me death!" Caesar, in his *Commentaries*, says, "To the lonely it is company; to the forsaken it is a friend; to the aged and impo-

tent it is a benefactor; they that be penniless are yet rich, in that they still have this majestic diversion." In another place this excellent observer has said, "There are times when I prefer it to sodomy." Robinson Crusoe says, "I cannot describe what I owe to this gentle art." Queen Elizabeth said, "It is the bulwark of virginity." Cetewayo, the Zulu hero, remarked that "a jerk in the hand is worth two in the bush." The immortal Franklin has said, "Masturbation is the mother of invention." He also said, "Masturbation is the best policy." Michelangelo and all the other old Masters—old Masters, I will remark, is an abbreviation, a contraction—have used similar language. Michelangelo said to Pope Julius II, "Self-negation is noble, self-culture is beneficent, self-possession is manly, but to the truly great and inspiring soul they are poor and tame compared to self-abuse." Mr. Brown, here, in one of his latest and most graceful poems refers to it in an eloquent line which is destined to live to the end of time—"None know it but to love it, None name it but to praise."

During the Civil War, Mark Twain—then twenty-four years old—served in the Confederate Army for two weeks before he deserted, or as he put it, "resigned."

Such are the utterances of the most illustrious of the masters of this renowned science, and apologists for it. The name of those who decry it and oppose it is legion; they have made strong arguments and uttered bitter speeches against it—but there is not room to repeat them here, in much detail. Brigham Young, an expert of incontestable authority, said, "As compared with the other thing, it is the difference between the lightning bug and the lightning." Solomon said, "There is nothing to recommend it but its cheapness." Galen said, "It is shameful to degrade to such bestial use that grand limb, that formidable member, which we votaries of science dub the 'Major Maxillary'—when they dub it at all—which is seldom. It would be better to decapitate the Major than to use him so. It would be better to amputate the *os fontis* [front bone] than to put it to such a use." The great statistician, Smith, in his report to Parliament, says, "In my opinion, more children have been wasted in this way than in any other." It cannot be denied that the high authority of this art entitles it to our respect, but at the same time I think that its harmfulness demands our condemnation. Mr. Darwin was grieved to feel obliged to give up his theory that the monkey was the connecting link between man and the lower animals. I think he was too hasty. The monkey is the only animal, except man, that practices this science; hence he is our brother; there is a bond of sympathy and relationship between us. Give this ingenious animal an audience of the proper kind, and he will straightway put aside his other affairs and take a whet; and you will see by the contortions and his ecstatic expression that he takes an intelligent and human interest in his performance.

"At noon I observed a bevy of nude native young ladies bathing in the sea, and went and sat down on their clothes to keep them from being stolen. I begged them to come out, for the sea was rising and I was satisfied that they were running some risk. But they were not afraid, and presently went on with their sport."

—Mark Twain in Hawaii, 1866

The signs of excessive indulgence in this destructive pastime are easily detectable. They are these: A disposition to eat, to drink, to smoke, to meet together convivially, to laugh, to joke, and tell indelicate stories—and mainly, a yearning to paint pictures. The results of the habit are: Loss of memory, loss of virility, loss of cheerfulness, loss of hopefulness, loss of character, and loss of progeny. Of all the various kinds of sexual intercourse, this has least to recommend it. As an amusement it is too fleeting; as an occupation it is too wearing, as a public exhibition there is no money in it. It is unsuited to the drawing room, and in the most cultured society it has long since been banished from the social board. It has at last, in our day of progress and improvement, been degraded to brotherhood with flatulence—among the best bred these two arts are now indulged only in private—though by consent of the whole company, when only males are present, it is still permissible, in good society, to remove the embargo upon the fundamental sigh.

My illustrious predecessor has taught you that all forms of the "social evil" are bad. I would teach you that some of those forms are more to be avoided than others; so, in concluding, I say, "If you must gamble away your lives sexually, don't play a Lone Hand too much." When you feel a revolutionary uprising in your system, get your Vendôme Column down some other way—don't jerk it down.

Participants in HISTORY

Opium Dens in America

Although opium has been used for medicinal purposes for at least 6,000 years, it apparently was not used for pleasure until the early seventeenth century when Europeans introduced the idea of smoking it to China. Britain's East India Company became a major importer of opium into China. Even though the Chinese government outlawed it in 1729, it was commonly smuggled into the country by merchant ships that brought it from India to trade for silk, porcelain, and other Chinese products. The opium trade increased tenfold between 1820 and 1840 because of expanded production in India during that period and the ending of East India Company's monopoly on the trade, which allowed many other private merchants to get in on it. When opium addiction became too serious a problem to be ignored, China tried to stop the British from smuggling it in 1839 by seizing 20,000 chests in Canton within just a few days. These chests were valued at $6 million in the currency of that day. This resulted in the Opium War, which the British won after three years of fighting.

Smoking and eating opium came to the United States in the 1850s and 1860s with the Chinese railroad laborers. Soon opium dens were common in every major city in the United States. They could be found in the red-light districts, surrounded by saloons, gambling houses, and brothels. Throughout the 1800s, Americans were able to buy laudanum, morphine, and other opiates legally without a prescription. This came to an end in 1914 with the passage of the Harrison Narcotics Act—the first federal drug control law. Demand for the drug greatly increased when it became illegal and just a decade later it was estimated that one out of every 1,000 people in the United States were opium addicts (or about 100,000 persons). As opium use began to decline, the use of other opiates—primarily heroin—slowly increased and has continued to rise ever since. By the 1960s, one out of every 3,500 were opiate addicts (or about 54,000 persons).[89]

One of the most successful American opium traders was Warren Delano—President Franklin Roosevelt's grandfather. Delano was able to expand his markets while the British were busy fighting the Opium Wars. He was also involved

[89] Of course, when it comes to drug abuse, the government's statistics have to be taken with a grain of salt. Between 1969 and 1972, the Bureau of Narcotics and Dangerous Drugs (the precursor to the DEA) changed the multiplier used in making their estimations twice, so the number of estimated American addicts jumped from 68,088 to 315,000 and then to 559,000. This showed a dramatic rise in drug abuse even though all three figures were based on the same 1969 number of known addicts. Still, the statistics listed here appear to indicate that the prohibition of drugs just made them more popular.

in growing the stuff in Turkey. He once wrote in a letter, "I do not pretend to justify the prosecution of the opium trade in a moral and philanthropic point of view, but as a merchant I insist it has been a fair, honorable and legitimate trade; and to say the worst of it, liable to no further or weightier objections than is the importation of wines, Brandies & spirits into the U. States, England, &c."

One of the most famous opium addicts was Samuel Taylor Coleridge, author of *The Rime of the Ancient Mariner*, one of the most famous poems ever written. He wrote one of his other masterpieces, *Kubla Khan*, while under the influence of opium. The French writer, artist, and filmmaker Jean Cocteau was also an opium addict, as was the French poet Charles-Pierre Baudelaire. Cocteau was able to beat his addiction after about seven years.

The following account of American opium dens was originally written to warn people of the danger of opium. The reporter, writing from prison, is identified only as No. 6606. His story, "A Modern Opium Eater," was published in the June 1914 issue of *The American Magazine*. To my knowledge, it has not been reprinted since then.

The author describes his affiliations with criminals and how writing bad checks landed him in prison for a year, but he was still able to secure opium in the penitentiary. Once on the street again, he returned to his criminal activities. After being arrested for armed robbery, he was back to prison. Since they found opium on him when he was arrested, they put him in rehab, and he goes on to describe the horrors of withdrawals. Although all this is interesting reading, in this history lesson, we focus on the opium use, which he claims led him down the road to ruin.

Five years ago I was editor and manager of a metropolitan daily newspaper. To-day I am a convict serving my second penitentiary sentence—a "two-time loser" in the language of the underworld, my world now. Between these extremes is a single cause—*opium*.

For five years I have been a smoker of opium. For five years there has not been a day, scarcely an hour, during which my mind and body have not been under the influence of the most subtle and insidious of drugs.

Few people in the United States realize the extent to which opium and kindred drugs are being used to-day in this country. You, my reader, may have read of the Federal Government's strict prohibitive law against the importation of smoking opium, and concurred idly and without interest. But do you know that the United States Revenue Service has a roster of over three thousand known users of opium in San Francisco alone? Countless other thousands are unregistered. Every other great city in the country has similar rosters, and numbers its "fiends" by thousands and tens of thousands. Hundreds of cans of the contraband drug are sold daily in New York, Chicago, Denver, New Orleans, Salt Lake, and Portland. The United States army posts have been invaded, and thousands of the wearers of our country's uniform are users of opium, morphine, and cocaine. The severest penalties have not seemed even to check the habit.

Starting at the Presidio in San Francisco with transports returning from the Orient, the drug habit has spread among the enlisted men in the army by leaps and bounds. The reason is easily found. Not one man in a hundred, once he has tested the peace, the mind-ease, the soothed nerves and the surcease from all sorrows, disappointments, and responsibilities that come from a *first* use of opium, ever again has the will-power to deny himself that delightful nepenthe. Opium is like the salary loan shark—a friend to-day, smoothing difficulty and trouble with a free and easy hand. To-morrow it becomes a master, exacting a toll a hundredfold more terrible than the ills it eased.

In 1898, Bayer was advertising cough medicine containing heroin. Similarly, Winslow's Baby Syrup and Kopp's Baby Friend, both of which contained morphine, were very popular in the 1880s. Cocaine was sold to "cure sore throat, neuralgia, nervousness, headache, colds and sleeplessness," whereas cocaine wine was sold "as a sedative allaying nervous fright without perceptive after-effects." In addition to opiates, many patent medicines contained enough alcohol to make them 60 to 80 proof. It's thought that at that time more alcohol was consumed as medicine than as liquor.

My first experience with opium was accidental. As a San Francisco reporter I had specialized in Chinatown and Chinese subjects. Not a licensed guide in the city knew the real Oriental quarter as I knew it. I had taken scores of friends to opium dens on slumming parties, but had never touched a pipe nor been tempted to do so. When I became a newspaper executive and finally attained the chief position of responsibility on the——I naturally spent less time in Chinatown, but I still kept in touch with my news sources, sources that scored many a good "beat" for my paper.

At the time of which I write I was overworked. I was the one experienced newspaper man in an office of "cubs." Every line of copy in our eight- and ten-page sheet passed through my hands. I wrote the more important headlines, planned the "make-up," and in addition directed the efforts of the business office force. In short, I was doing the work of three or four men and the strain was beginning to tell on me. When my day's work was done I was always utterly exhausted. I slept brokenly and sat down to my daily task absolutely unrefreshed. I was approaching a nervous breakdown and knew it, but conditions on my sheet were such that I could see no immediate relief.

One evening I attended an important dramatic opening that I did not care to entrust to any of my inexperienced cubs. From the theater I started for the club where I passed a few hours occasionally. On the street I met a fellow newspaper man, a dramatic critic who, like myself, has since passed into oblivion.

"Take me for a stroll through Chinatown," he asked. "There are some things I want to see first-hand, and you're the one man I know who can get behind their doors."

We went. During our trip my friend suggested a visit to a "hop-joint." I led the way to one little known to ordinary slummers. The mummified Chinese in charge was an old acquaintance of mine and welcomed us warmly. He was smoking opium when we entered and the unventilated cell in which he lived was heavy with the fumes of the drug. I took one deep breath of the pungent sweetish, smoke-laden air. My friend squatted on the bunk chatting with the Chinese. Again and again I inhaled the smoke fresh from the pipe, taking it in thirstily to the very bottom of my lungs. To my amazement, my weariness, my nervousness, my brain-fag slipped from me like a discarded garment.

"Say, Lee," I demanded, when I realized the delightful exhilaration that was stealing over me, "cook me up a couple of yen poks (pills). I'm going to smoke a few."

Willingly he toasted the brownish syrupy drug over his dim lamp, rolled the pill into shape, deftly attached it to the bowl and then handed me the pipe and guided it over the flame while I drew into my lungs my first pill of opium.

In sixty seconds I was another man. My barren brain, in which I had been conning over an introduction to the criticism I must write before I slept, leaped to its task. The ideas, the phrases, the right words, which, until then, had eluded my fagged mentality, came trooping forth faster than I could have written them had I been at my desk. My worries and responsibilities fell from me. I remember even to-day that as I smoked my third or fourth pill the solution of a problem that had been a bugbear for days came into my mind like an inspiration.

* * *

I smoked six pills before we left. As my friend and I separated he looked at me curiously.

"I've often wondered how you do the work you do and hold up," he said. "Now I know. I'm going to try that myself the next time I'm stuck for my Sunday page story. My brain is virile and as clear as crystal and I didn't take a pill—just breathed the air. I've surprised your secret, old man. Good night."

I didn't tell him he had seen me smoke my first pill.

A half hour later I wrote a column dramatic criticism that was quoted on the billboards and I reeled it off as fast as my fingers could hit the typewriter keys. I was never at a loss for a word. The story in its entirety seemed to lie ready in my brain. My task finished, I went to bed without my customary drink, and dropped asleep as peacefully as a child. For the first time in weeks I slept soundly and awoke refreshed and clear-minded with a zest for the day's labor.

That was the beginning. After that I visited Lee, first at intervals of several days, then, by degrees, more frequently, until finally I became a daily user of opium. I shall never forget one conversation with the old Chinese den-keeper on the occasion of my third or fourth smoke. He looked up with his bland smile of welcome as I came in. It was evident that the man *expected* me. This nettled me. Nothing could have convinced me then that the drug could ever become a necessity to me.

"Well, Lee," I said throwing myself on the bunk, "chef me up a few extra big ones to-night. I'll take more to-night, for this will be about my last smoke. I'm going to quit."

In silence he adjusted my favorite bowl to the pipe. In silence he deftly toasted the pill, completed the operation and twirled the ivory mouthpiece around to me. Greedily I drew the fragrant smoke into my lungs. He noticed my eagerness. Indeed, I could not even pretend to conceal it. He watched me inhale the smoke until my lungs puffed out like a pigeon's breast, then exhale it slowly, in little puffs, regretting each. At last he spoke.

"You no quit," he said softly. "Every man alleetime say he quit. Every man alleesame you. Smoke one time, smoke two time, smoke tlee time, then smoke alleetime. Chineman, white man, chokquay (negro) alleesame. No can quit. Bimeby you die you quit. Bimeby maybe you bloke,—no more money, no more fliend bollow money, no can stealem money, maybe you quit one, two days. Bimeby maybe you go jail, no got fliend bling you hop, no got money givem policeman catchem hop, you quit. You got money, no go jail, you no quit. I heap sabe. Bimeby you see."

I laughed at his warning. Had I but known it, the wisdom of ages, the experience of untold thousands of wrecked lives were summed up in the halting words I allowed to pass me unheeded.

When I became a regular smoker I bought a "layout"—pipe, bowls, lamp, tray, yen hocks, everything—and indulged my habit in the "joint" of a white smoker where I was a favored patron and could lie at ease, privately, without fear of discovery.

* * *

By this time the cost of opium had become a very appreciable and permanent expense. From a few pills at first I increased my allowance day by day until it took thirty or forty "fun" (a Chinese measure; there are seventy-six fun in an ounce) to give me the mental relief I craved. The physical craving—the body's demand for it—can be satisfied with approximately the same amount each day. The mental craving—the mind's demand—increases daily. What satisfies to-night is too little tomorrow, and so on. To feel even normal I now needed three or four times the half-dozen pills which at first had given me such exquisite pleasure. To get the exhilaration, the soothed nerves, the contentment I craved, I, like each of the millions before me, had to use more and more each day.

Thirty-six fun of opium at retail costs, at an average, three dollars. A fifty-cent tip to my "cook" and a quarter for the privilege of the room in which I smoked made my habit cost me about four dollars a day, which made a ghastly hole in even the good salary I earned. I began to buy my opium by the can, paying from $25 to $30 [approximately $300 by today's standards] for tins averaging 460 fun. The elimination of the retailer's profit helped temporarily, but the ever-increasing demands of my habit soon overcame the saving.

It wrested from me bit by bit everything that a man holds dear and sacred, giving nothing in return but the temporary power to forget. The paper on which I worked was absorbed by another and I passed out of the newspaper business forever. I was rather glad at the time. I had just that many more hours a day to lie musing by my layout.

* * *

What were my thoughts during these hours? I have never read anything, not even De Quincey's "Opium–Eater," [Thomas De Quincey's autobiographical *Confessions of an English Opium Eater*, 1822] that gives a truthful and lucid impression of what "opium dreams" really are. The ordinary conception of them is miles from the truth. There is no riot of wonderful and strange colors dancing before the eyes. There are no visions of Orientalized beauty, no loving women, sweetly-perfumed, no luxurious air castles filled with jewels, gold and sensuous luxury. Instead, the brain works automatically on the important projects of everyday life. It plans and plots, rejects and reconstructs—always trickily and by devious means—and, finally, evolves a clean-cut idea. The intervening difficulties are lessened, the ultimate rewards accentuated.

"Every castle of the air
Sleeps in the fine black grains, and there
Are seeds for every romance, or light
Whiff of a dream for a summer night."
—Amy Lowell, "Sword Blades and Poppy Seeds," 1914

> All this is absolutely without effort. You lie quiescent, your whole being apparently deep in lethargy, your eyes half-closed and unseeing. You are perfectly content, at peace with the world and yourself. Meanwhile the brain, working of its own volition, independently of you exactly as if it were a distinct personality raps out with Gatling-gun rapidity various solutions of the problems it has set itself. It works always, however, in devious channels. If there is a direct road between two points, it mistrusts and rejects it, taking the crooked path.
>
> Time ceases to exist. Night after night I have lain down after the theater to smoke. Finally, rousing myself to leave, believing it midnight or a little later, I would look at my watch. Five o'clock! Impossible! Not until I raised the curtain to a gray dawn could I believe. Night after night this happened. I smoked for five years and was surprised anew each time when the day seemed to come hours before its time.

As French poet Henri Michaux said of the drug's effect, "One no longer dreams, one is dreamed."

A Pirate's Adventures with Captain Morgan Sacking Panama

Blackbeard, Captain William Kidd, and Captain Henry Morgan are undoubtedly the most famous of all the pirates. Captain Morgan was also the most successful pirate, with the possible exception of Captain John Avery or Sir Francis Drake. In addition, Captain Morgan was one of the most audacious pirates for he decided to attempt a monumental feat—the taking of Panama. Panama (the city, as the country didn't exist at this time) was the repository for the gold from that area's gold mines while it was waiting to be loaded on a galleon for shipment to Spain. Although it is not known how much gold Spain took from the New World, records indicate that the Veraguas mine—which shipped its gold through Panama—produced more than two tons of this precious metal in one year. At this time, the area around Panama was the greatest producer of gold in the world. It made a very tempting target for the pirates, but it was very heavily guarded. No one had ever attempted to take the city before.

The thirty-five-year-old Morgan had already achieved a great reputation among the buccaneers.[90] He even tried to establish a refuge and sanctuary for pirates on an island off Nicaragua. Though his privateering[91] commission allowed him to plunder Spanish ships, he decided on his own to sack the towns of El Puerto del Principe (now Camagüey) in Cuba, Portobello[92] on the Caribbean coast of what is now the country of

---

[90] Buccaneer is the Spanish name for privateers and pirates. It generally refers to those operating in the West Indies during the seventeenth and eighteenth centuries.

[91] Privateering was a legal form of piracy, used by countries to supplement their armed forces. A privateer was a privately owned warship that operated under a commission making it legal for them to capture and plunder ships of a specific country or countries. The government granting the commission usually received a portion of the booty. In England, from the fifteenth through the seventeenth centuries, these commissions were issued by the king. (Captain Kidd's commission was signed by King William the Third.) After 1702, they were issued by the Lord High Admiral, and later by colonial governors, some of whom were corrupt and granted commissions to pirates to make them "legal." Privateering was last used by Chile against Spain in 1865.

[92] While celebrating on board his ship after capturing this town, the ship suddenly exploded killing more than three hundred men, but Captain Morgan survived.

Panama, and Maracaibo in what is now Venezuela. With all these successes, when he announced his raid on Panama, pirates and privateers from all over the West Indies and the Caribbean flocked to join him. This excursion was in direct violation of the 1670 peace treaty between England and Spain in which England agreed to end attacks on Spanish towns in the West Indies.

The primary source for Captain Morgan's exploits in Panama and for the buccaneers in general is *The Buccaneers of America* (1678) written by John Esquemeling[93] (a.k.a. Alexander Oliver Exquemelin or Oexmelin), who was a buccaneer surgeon with Morgan on this expedition. Almost everything we know about the Panama raid comes from this book. Some historians feel this account is inaccurate and therefore unreliable, but we are faced with this problem with any firsthand account. By their nature, firsthand accounts are written from a single point of view and are bound to be influenced by that person's biases. In this case, Esquemeling did not like Captain Morgan, saying that at the end of their journey back from Panama, Morgan cheated the pirates out of most of the loot and then abandoned many—including Esquemeling—on the Caribbean coast without a ship and in Spanish territory to fend for themselves, which is more than enough to leave anyone bitter.

But though there are some inaccuracies, overall his account appears to be surprisingly reliable. The chief proof of this comes from the libel suit that Captain Morgan—who was Sir Henry Morgan by then—filed when the book was published. The main things he objected to were that he was called a pirate (though there is no doubt that he was) and that he went to the West Indies as an indentured servant. The court found in his favor, but he received only a token award. In later editions of the book, the publishers included weak apologies saying that a man of Morgan's obvious stature wouldn't condone such things as torturing prisoners and that priests weren't killed unless they were found to be carrying arms. Although no one came forward to support Esquemeling's account, only one short account defending Morgan was published anonymously by "P.A. Esq.," but it didn't claim to be an eyewitness account.

Captain Morgan obviously wanted to protect his reputation since he was working for the government of England when the book came out. It wouldn't be surprising if the things described by Esquemeling did happen, since these things were common practice at that time, but whether any of these atrocities were done under Captain Morgan's orders or with his consent or even his knowledge will never be known.

With all this in mind, let's move on to Esquemeling's account. In December 1670, the pirates began by capturing the fort at Chagre, a town on the Caribbean side of the Isthmus of Darien.[94] He reports that in this attack, 400 pirates went up against 314 entrenched Spaniards.

Esquemeling writes that during the battle:

> One of the pirates was wounded with an arrow in his back, which pierced his body to the other

[93] This was probably a pen name for Hendrik Barentzoon Smeeks from the town of Zwolle in Holland.

[94] The Isthmus of Darien is now called the Isthmus of Panama and is now just the eastern portion of the country of Panama and a small portion of Colombia. At that time, it was part of the province of Tierra Firma, which in turn, was part of the Spanish colony of New Spain.

> side. This instantly he pulled out with great valor at the side of his breast. Then taking a little cotton that he had about him, he wound it about the said arrow, and putting it into his musket, he shot it back at into the castle. But the cotton, being kindled by the powder, occasioned two or three houses that were within the castle, as being thatched with palm-leaves, to take fire, which the Spaniards perceived not so soon as was necessary. For this fire, meeting with a parcel of powder, blew it up, and thereby caused great ruin.

More than one hundred pirates were killed and more than seventy were wounded, but the Spaniards suffered more. Only thirty remained alive, and only about ten of these escaped being wounded. Morgan left 500 pirates in the fort to guard their escape route and another 150 in their ships, and he headed off for Panama with 1,200 men.

It was January 1671 when Captain Morgan and his men traveled by canoe and foot about one hundred miles winding through the jungle to reach Panama on the Pacific side of the Isthmus of Darien. By the time they arrived, they were starving and exhausted. Since they brought very few supplies on their nine-day trip, hoping to capture them on the way, many of the men had resorted to eating leather.

Preparing to face these pirates was Don Juan Perez de Guzman, the President of Panama and Captain-General of Tierra Firma, with his force of 2,700 soldiers—600 of which were cavalry. Perez was an old man, but he had many years experience as a soldier. Having distinguished himself in campaigns in Netherlands, he was made the captain general and president of Panama before Morgan became a buccaneer.

Captain Morgan surprised the Spaniards by not attacking them head-on as armies normally did at this time. Instead of gallantly charging into the thick of it, he sent out small parties to provoke the Spaniards into breaking their ranks. As this failed and both sides hesitated to attack, he circled his men around through a thick forest to a hill on Perez's right where he gained the advantages of height, wind, and the sun. This took several hours, but they caught the Spaniards completely off guard. Perez suddenly found his cannons were facing the wrong direction.

Perez intended to stampede a herd of 2,000 cattle into Morgan's attacking forces in order to break them up and throw them into disarray. He didn't get the chance to do this. Instead, he tried to run the cattle at the pirates from behind, but the noise of the battle scared the cattle away.

As Captain Morgan later described it:

> Although they worked such a stratagem that hath been seldom or never heard, that is when the [infantry] engaged in the flank, he attempted to drive two droves of cattle of 1500 apiece into the right and left angles of the rear, but all come to one effect, and helped nothing for their [the Spaniards] flight to the city. . . .
>
> [There] they had 200 fresh men and two forts, one with six brass guns, the other with eight, and the streets barricaded, and great guns in every street, which in all amounted to thirty-two brass guns, but instead of fighting [Perez] commanded the city to be fired [set on fire], and his chief forts to be blown up, the which was in such haste that they blew up forty of his soldiers in it. We followed into the town, where in the market

place they made some resistance and fired some great guns, killed us four men and wounded five.

In this battle, which lasted two hours, Esquemeling estimates that six hundred Spaniards died, and many others were wounded or taken prisoner. Morgan puts the fatalities at four hundred with the loss of only five pirates and ten wounded.

In his report to the Queen of Spain describing the destruction of Panama, Don Juan Perez de Guzman mentioned Captain Morgan, saying the pirates "brought with them an Englishman whom they called 'The Prince,' with the intent to crown him 'King of the Tierra Firma.'"

Morgan says Perez set his city on fire, but Esquemeling says it was done at Captain Morgan's orders, while Perez, in a letter to the Queen-Regent, María Anna of Spain, blames it on the fleeing house owners and their slaves. Whatever really happened, it's doubtful Morgan was responsible. General pirate procedure was to plunder a town first and then demand a ransom, threatening to set the town on fire. The pirates lost a considerable amount of loot because of the fire, and they were put in the position of trying to stop the fire. Before the fire, Panama was the second largest city in the New World (next to Cartagena) with some 7,000 houses, but only a small fraction were saved.

Morgan said:

> There we were forced to put the fire out of the enemy's houses, but it was in vain, for by 12 at night it was all consumed that might be called the City; but of the suburbs was saved two churches and about 300 houses; thus was consumed that famous and ancient City of Panama, which is the greatest mart for silver and gold in the whole world, for it receives the goods into it that comes from Old Spain in the King's great Fleet, and likewise delivers to the Fleet all the silver and gold that comes from the mines of Peru and Potosi.

A month later the fire still had not gone out.

Since the residents of Panama had several days' warning that the pirates were coming, most of the city's wealth was hidden, and much of it was loaded aboard a galleon that set out to sea just before the battle.

Immediately after seizing the city, many of the pirates organized themselves outside the city, thinking the Spanish army might rally, but they didn't, so their minds turned to plunder. Esquemeling continues:

> In the afternoon of this fatal day Captain Morgan reentered again the city with his troops, to the intent every one might take up his lodgings, which now they could hardly find, very few houses having escaped the desolation of the fire. Soon after, they fell to seeking very carefully among the ruins and ashes for utensils of plate or gold which peradventure were not quite wasted by the flames. And of such things they found no small number in several places, especially in wells and cisterns, where the Spaniards had hid them from the covetous search of the pirates.
>
> The next day Captain Morgan dispatched away two troops of pirates, of 150 men each, being all very stout soldiers and well armed, with

orders to seek for the inhabitants of Panama who were escaped from the hands of their enemies. These men having made several excursions up and down the campaign fields, woods, and mountains adjoining to Panama, returned after two days' time, bringing with them above 200 prisoners, between men, women, and slaves. The same day returned also the boat [they had captured] . . . which Captain Morgan had sent into the South Sea, bringing with her three other boats which they had taken in a little while. But all these prizes they could willingly have given, yea, although they had employed greater labor into the bargain, for one certain galleon, which miraculously escaped their industry, being very richly laden with all the King's plate [bars of silver or gold] and great quantity of riches of gold, pearl, jewels, and other most precious goods, of all the best and richest merchants of Panama. On board of this galleon were also the religious women belonging to the nunnery of the said city, who had embarked with them all the ornaments of their church, consisting in great quantity of gold plate, and other things of great value.

The strength of this galleon was nothing considerable, as having only 7 guns, and 10 or 12 muskets for its whole defense being on the other side very ill provided of victuals and other necessaries, with great want of fresh water, and having no more sails than the uppermost sails of the main mast. This description of the said ship the pirates received from certain persons, who had spoken with seven mariners belonging to the galleon, at such time as they came ashore in the cock-boat to take in fresh water. Hence they concluded for certain they might easily have taken the said vessel, had they given her chase and pursued her, as they ought to have done, especially considering the said galleon could not long subsist abroad at sea. But they were impeded from following this vastly rich prize by the lascivious exercises wherein they were totally at that present involved with women, which unto this effect they had carried with them and forced on board their boat. Unto this vice was also joined that of gluttony and drunkenness, having plentifully debauched themselves with several sorts of rich wines they found there ready to their hands. So that they chose rather to satiate their lust and appetite with the things above-mentioned than to lay hold on the occasion of such an huge advantage, although this only prize would certainly have been of far greater value and consequence unto them than all they purchased at Panama and other places thereabouts. The next day, repenting of their negligence and being totally wearied of the vices and debaucheries aforesaid, they sent forth to sea another boat well armed, to pursue with all speed imaginable the said galleon. But their present care and diligence was in vain, the Spaniards who were on board the said ship having received intelligence of the danger they were in one or two days before, while the pirates were cruising so nigh unto them, whereupon they fled unto places more remote and unknown to their enemies. . . .

[Though they continued to search for the galleon, they couldn't find it, but they did capture several boats and a ship.]

The convoy which Captain Morgan had sent unto the castle [or fort] of Chagre returned much about the same time, bringing with them very good news. For while Captain Morgan was upon his journey to Panama, those he had left in the castle of Chagre had sent forth to sea two boats to exercise piracy. These happened to meet with a Spanish ship, which they began to chase within sight of the castle. This being perceived by the pirates that were in the castle, they put forth Spanish colors, thereby to allure and deceive the ship that fled before the boats. Thus the poor Spaniards, thinking to refuge themselves under the castle and the guns thereof, by flying into the port were caught in a snare and made prisoners, where they thought to find defense. The cargo which was found on board the said vessel consisted in victuals and provisions, that were all eatable things. Nothing could be more opportune than this prize for the castle, where they had begun already to experience great scarcity of things of this kind.

This good fortune of the garrison of Chagre gave occasion unto Captain Morgan to remain longer time than he had determined at Panama. And hereupon he ordered several new excursions to be made into the whole country round about the city. So that, while the pirates at Panama were employed in these expeditions, those at Chagre were busied in exercising piracy upon the North Sea. Captain Morgan used to send forth daily parties of 200 men, to make inroads into all the fields and country thereabouts; and, when one party came back, another consisting of 200 more was ready to go forth. By this means they gathered in a short time huge quantity of riches and no lesser number of prisoners. These, being brought into the city, were presently put unto the most exquisite tortures imaginable, to make them confess both other people's goods and their own.

For many years after Capain Morgan's exploits, sailors and pirates would sing the following words attributed to Morgan in a ballad:

If few there be amongst us,
Our hearts are very great;
And each will have more plunder,
And each will have more plate.

Here it happened that one poor and miserable wretch was found in the house of a gentleman of great quality, who had put on, amidst that confusion of things, a pair of taffety breeches belonging to his master with a little silver key hanging at the strings thereof. This being perceived by the pirates, they immediately asked him where was the cabinet of the said key. His answer was: He knew not what was become of it, but only that, finding those breeches in his master's house, he had made bold to wear them. Not being able to extort any other confession out of him, they first put him upon the rack, wherewith they inhumanly disjointed his arms. After this, they twisted a cord about his forehead, which they wrung so hard that his eyes appeared as big as eggs and were ready to fall out of his skull. But neither with these torments could they obtain any positive answer to their demands. Whereupon they soon after hung him up by the testicles, giving him infinite blows and stripes while he was under that intolerable pain and posture of body. Afterwards they cut off his nose and ears, and singed his face with burning straw, till he could speak nor lament his misery no longer. Then, losing all hopes of hearing any confession from his mouth, they commanded a Negro to run him through with a lance, which put an end to his life and a period to their cruel and inhuman tortures. After this execrable manner did many others of those miserable prisoners finish their days, the common sport and recreation of these pirates being these and other tragedies not inferior to these.

They spared, in these their cruelties, no sex nor condition whatsoever. For, as to religious persons and priests, they granted them less quarter than unto others, unless they could produce a considerable sum of money, capable of being a sufficient ransom. Women themselves were no better used, except when they would condescend unto the libidinous demands and concupiscency of the pirates. For such as would not consent unto their lust were treated with all the rigor and cruelty imaginable.

Captain Morgan, their leader and Commander, gave them no good example in this point. For, as soon as any beautiful woman was brought as a prisoner to his presence, he used all the means he could, both of rigor and mildness, to bend her to his lascivious will and pleasure: for a confirmation of which assertion, I shall here give my reader a short history of a lady whose virtue and constancy ought to be transmitted unto posterity, as a memorable example of her sex.

Among the prisoners that were brought by the pirates from the Islands of Tavoga and Tavogilla, there was found a gentle woman of good quality, as also no less virtue and chastity who was wife unto one of the richest merchants of all those countries. Her years were but few, and her beauty so great as peradventure I may doubt whether in all Europe any could be found to surpass her perfections either of comeliness or honesty. Her husband, at that present, was absent from home being gone as far as the kingdom of Peru, about great concerns of commerce and trade, wherein his employments did lie. This virtuous lady, likewise, hearing, that pirates were coming to assault the city of Panama, had absented herself thence in the company of other friends and relations, thereby to preserve her life amidst the dangers which the cruelties and tyrannies of those hard-hearted enemies did seem to menace unto every citizen. But no sooner had she appeared in the presence of Captain Morgan instantly she was designed for his voluptuous pleasures and concupiscence. Hereupon he commanded they should lodge her in a certain apartment by herself, giving her a Negress, or black woman, to wait upon her, and that she should be treated with all the respect and regalement due unto her quality. The poor afflicted lady did beg, with multitude of sobs and tears, she might be suffered to lodge among the other prisoners, her relations, fearing lest that unexpected kindness of the Commander might prove to be a design upon her chastity. But Captain Morgan would by no means hearken to her petition, and all he commanded, in answer thereunto was she should be treated with more particular care than before, and have her victuals carried from his own table.

This lady had formerly heard very strange reports concerning the pirates, before their arrival at Panama, intimating unto her as if they were not men, but, as they said, heretics, who did neither invoke the Blessed Trinity nor believe in Jesus Christ. But now she began to have better thoughts of them than ever before, having experienced the manifold civilities of Captain Morgan, especially hearing him many times to swear by the name of God and of Jesus

Christ, in whom, she was persuaded, they did not believe. Neither did she now think them to be so bad, or to have the shapes of beasts, as from the relations of several people she had oftentimes heard. For, as to the name of 'robbers' or 'thieves,' which was commonly given them by others, she wondered not much at it, seeing, as she said, that among all nations of the universe there were to be found some wicked men who naturally coveted to possess the goods of others. Conformable to the persuasion of this lady was the opinion of another woman, of weak understanding, at Panama, who used to say, before the pirates came thither, she desired very much and had a great curiosity to see one of those men called pirates, for as much as her husband had often told her that they were not men, like others, but rather irrational beasts. This silly woman, at last happening to see the first of them, cried out aloud, saying, "Jesus bless me! These thieves are like unto us Spaniards."

This false civility of Captain Morgan, wherewith he used this lady, as a thing very common unto such persons as pretend and cannot obtain, was soon after changed into barbarous cruelty. For, three or four days being past, he came to see her, and entertained her with dishonest and lascivious discourses, opening unto her his ardent desires of enjoying the accomplishment of his lust. The virtuous lady constantly repulsed him, with all the civility imaginable and many humble and modest expressions of her mind. But Captain Morgan still persisted in his disorderly request, presenting her withal with much pearl, gold, and all that he had got that was precious and valuable in that voyage. But the lady, being in no manner willing to consent thereunto, nor accept his presents, and showing herself in all respects like unto Susannah for constancy, he presently changed note, and began to speak unto her in another tone, threatening her with a thousand cruelties and hard usages at his hands. Unto all these things she gave this resolute and positive answer, than which no other could be extorted from her, "Sir, my life is in your hands, but, as to my body, in relation to that which you would persuade me unto, my soul shall sooner be separated from it through the violence of your arms than I shall condescend to your request."

No sooner had Captain Morgan understood this heroic resolution of her mind than he commanded her to be stripped of the best of her apparel, and imprisoned in a darksome and stinking cellar. Here, she was allowed an extremely small quantity of meat and drink, wherewith she had much ado to sustain her life for a few days.

Under this hardship the constant and virtuous lady ceased not to pray daily unto God Almighty for constancy and patience against the cruelties of Captain Morgan. But he, being now thoroughly convinced of her chaste resolutions, as also desirous to conceal the cause of her confinement and hard usage, since many of the pirates, his companions, did compassionate her condition, laid many false accusations to her charge, giving to understand she held intelligence with the Spaniards and corresponded with them by letters, abusing thereby his former lenity and kindness.

I myself was an eye-witness unto these things here related, and could never have judged such constancy of mind and virtuous chastity to be found in the world if my own eyes and ears had not informed me thereof. . . . [He later states that

Captain Morgan started to take her to Jamaica with him, but then decided to release her.]

Captain Morgan, having now been at Panama the full space of three weeks, commanded all things to be put in order for his departure. . . . After this, Captain Morgan sent forth many of the Spaniards into the adjoining fields and country, to seek for money wherewith to ransom not only themselves but also all the rest of the prisoners, as likewise the ecclesiastics, both secular and regular. Moreover, he commanded all the artillery of the town to be spoiled, that is to say, nailed and stopped up. . . .

On the 24th of February of the year 1671 Captain Morgan departed from the city of Panama, or rather from the place where the said city of Panama did stand; of the spoils whereof he carried with him 175 beasts of carriage, laden with silver, gold, and other precious things, besides 600 prisoners, more or less, between men, women, children, and slaves.

Once on the coast, they divided some of the spoils, though Esquemeling says Morgan took off with most of the loot, leaving many men stranded on the coast of Darien to fend for themselves. Some say that each of his men received only £50. Morgan assessed his gains at £30,000, though one of the other surgeons on this trip, Richard Browne, estimated it at £70,000. Whatever the amount was, it was only a fraction what it could have been if the city hadn't caught fire or if the galleon hadn't escaped.

Despite the treaty between England and Spain, the Council of Jamaica passed a vote of thanks to Morgan for his successful expedition. Captain Morgan became Sir Henry Morgan in 1674 when he was knighted by King Charles II and made the Lieutenant Governor of Jamaica and commander of the English armed forces there. Now he found himself in the position of having to bring pirates to justice. Because of his intense fondness for rum and his abrasive nature, he was removed from these offices in 1683. He died in Jamaica in 1688 at the age of fifty-three. In the end, it was his passion for rum that did him in. No doubt he would be very pleased to know that there is a brand of rum named after him.

The Supposed Location of Blackbeard's Treasure

The following quote about where Blackbeard's treasure is supposed to be buried was made by the captain of the pirate-hunting ship H.M.S. *Salisbury*. On returning from a cruise to the pirate-infested waters around Madagascar in about 1719, Downing relayed the following information in an official report to his superiors, saying he received it from a Portuguese captain who was a former pirate. Blackbeard had been killed and some of his crew captured the previous year.

> At Guzarat [near Bombay, India] I met with a Portuguese named Anthony de Sylvestre; he came with two other Portuguese and two Dutchmen to take on in the Moor's [the Great Mogul of Delhi] service, as many Europeans do. This Anthony told me he had been among the Pyrates, and that he belonged to one of the sloops in Virginia when Blackbeard was taken. He informed me that if it should be my lot ever to go to York River [Virginia] or Maryland, near an island called Mulberry Island, provided we

went on shore at the Watering Place, where the Shipping used most commonly to ride, that there the Pyrates had buried considerable sums of money in great chests well clamp'd with Iron Plates. As my part, I never was that way, nor much acquainted with any that ever used those Parts. But I have made Enquiry, and am inform'd that there is such a place as Mulberry Island. If any Person who uses those Parts should think it worth while to dig a little way at the upper End of a small Cove, where it is convenient to land, he would soon find whether the Information I had was well grounded. Fronting the landing-place are five trees, among which, he said, the Money was hid. I cannot warrant the Truth of this account; but if I was ever to go there, I should find some means or other to satisfy myself, as it could not be a great deal out of my way. If anybody should obtain the Benefit of this account, if it please God that they ever come to England, 'tis hoped they will remember whence they had this information.

Downing's report was still in the uncataloged British naval and Colonial archives as late as the 1930s. This quote was published in the early 1900s. A later version withholds the name of the island, but says it's in North Carolina. It's not known if a search was ever made.

I Started World War I

On June 28, 1914, the Archduke Franz Ferdinand, heir to the Hapsburg throne, was assassinated in Sarajevo by Serb nationalist Gavrilo Princip. Austria used the assassination as an excuse to declare war on Serbia. Within weeks, the major powers of Europe were mobilizing their forces. World War I had begun.

Borijove Jevtic was one of Princip's co-conspirators. He wrote the following account, revealing the reason the world was plunged into war was that Archduke Ferdinand just happened to choose the wrong day to visit Serbia.

> A tiny clipping from a newspaper mailed without comment from a secret band of terrorists in Zagreb, a capital of Croatia, to their comrades in Belgrade, was the torch which set the world afire with war in 1914. That bit of paper wrecked old proud empires. It gave birth to new, free nations.
>
> I was one of the members of the terrorist band in Belgrade which received it and, in those days, I and my companions were regarded as desperate criminals. A price was on our heads. Today my little band is seen in a different light, as pioneer patriots. It is recognized that our secret plans hatched in an obscure cafe in the capital of old Serbia, have led to the independence of the new Yugoslavia, the united nation set free from Austrian domination.
>
> The little clipping was from the *Srobobran*, a Croatian journal of limited circulation, and consisted of a short telegram from Vienna. This telegram declared that the Austrian Archduke Franz Ferdinand would visit Sarajevo, the capital of Bosnia, 28 June, to direct army maneuvers in the neighboring mountains.
>
> It reached our meeting place, the cafe called Zeatna Moruana, one night the latter part of April, 1914. . . . At a small table in a very humble cafe, beneath a flickering gas jet we sat and read it. There was no advice nor admonition sent with it. Only four letters and two numerals were

sufficient to make us unanimous, without discussion, as to what we should do about it. They were contained in the fateful date, 28 June.

How dared Franz Ferdinand, not only the representative of the oppressor but in his own person an arrogant tyrant, enter Sarajevo on that day? Such an entry was a studied insult.

Twenty-eight June is a date engraved deeply in the heart of every Serb, so that the day has a name of its own. It is called the *vidovnan*. It is the day on which the old Serbian kingdom was conquered by the Turks at the battle of Amselfelde in 1389. It is also the day on which in the second Balkan War the Serbian arms took glorious revenge on the Turk for his old victory and for the years of enslavement.

That was no day for Franz Ferdinand, the new oppressor, to venture to the very doors of Serbia for a display of the force of arms which kept us beneath his heel.

Our decision was taken almost immediately. Death to the tyrant!

Then came the matter of arranging it. To make his death certain twenty-two members of the organization were selected to carry out the sentence. At first we thought we would choose the men by lot. But here Gavrilo Princip intervened. Princip is destined to go down in Serbian history as one of her greatest heroes. From the moment Ferdinand's death was decided upon he took an active leadership in its planning. Upon his advice we left the deed to members of our band who were in and around Sarajevo under his direction and that of Gabrinovic, a Linotype operator on a Serbian newspaper. Both were regarded as capable of anything in the cause.

The fateful morning dawned. Two hours before Franz Ferdinand arrived in Sarajevo all the twenty-two conspirators were in their allotted positions, armed and ready. They were distributed 500 yards apart over the whole route along which the Archduke must travel from the railroad station to the town hall.

When Franz Ferdinand and his retinue drove from the station they were allowed to pass the first two conspirators. The motor cars were driving too fast to make an attempt feasible and in the crowd were Serbians: throwing a grenade would have killed many innocent people.

When the car passed Gabrinovic, the compositor, he threw his grenade. It hit the side of the car, but Franz Ferdinand with presence of mind threw himself back and was uninjured. Several officers riding in his attendance were injured.

The cars sped to the Town Hall and the rest of the conspirators did not interfere with them. After the reception in the Town Hall General Potiorek, the Austrian Commander, pleaded with Franz Ferdinand to leave the city, as it was seething with rebellion. The Archduke was persuaded to drive the shortest way out of the city and to go quickly.

The road to the maneuvers was shaped like the letter V, making a sharp turn at the bridge over the River Nilgacka. Franz Ferdinand's car could go fast enough until it reached this spot but here it was forced to slow down for the turn. Here Princip had taken his stand.

As the car came abreast he stepped forward from the curb, drew his automatic pistol from his coat and fired two shots. The first struck the wife of the Archduke, the Archduchess Sofia, in the abdomen. She was an expectant mother. She died instantly.

The second bullet struck the Archduke close to the heart.

He uttered only one word; "Sofia"—a call to his stricken wife. Then his head fell back and he collapsed. He died almost instantly.

The officers seized Princip. They beat him over the head with the flat of their swords. They knocked him down, they kicked him, scraped the skin from his neck with the edges of their swords, tortured him, all but killed him.

Then he was taken to the Sarajevo jail. The next day he was transferred to the military prison and the round-up of his fellow conspirators proceeded, although he denied that he had worked with anyone.

He was confronted with Gabrinovic, who had thrown the bomb. Princip denied he knew him. Others were brought in, but Princip denied the most obvious things.

The next day they put chains on Princip's feet, which he wore till his death.

His only sign of regret was the statement that he was sorry he had killed the wife of the Archduke. He had aimed only at her husband and would have preferred that any other bullet should have struck General Potiorek.

The Austrians arrested every known revolutionary in Sarajevo and among them, naturally, I was one. But they had no proof of my connection with the crime. I was placed in the cell next to Princip's, and when Princip was taken out to walk in the prison yard I was taken along as his companion.

On July 28, 1914, Austria-Hungary declared war on Serbia and the next day began to bombard Belgrade. Russia rushed to assist the Serbs causing Germany to declare war on Russia, thereby joining Austria-Hungary. Because of France's alliance with Russia, Germany declared war on that country as well. The next day Great Britain was forced to enter the fray. Countries continued to join in, with the United States entering the war in 1917. Eventually, it was the countries of Austria-Hungary, Germany, Bulgaria, and what remained of the Ottoman Empire all fighting against Serbia, Russia, France, Great Britain, Italy, Rumania, Belgium, Greece, Portugal, Montenegro, Liberia, San Marino, Siam, China, Japan, the United States, Cuba, Panama, Guatamala, Brazil, Nicaragua, Costa Rica, Honduras, and Haiti. World War I was the second most bloody and costly war in modern history. At least 10 million people were killed.

Though the war probably would have started without this assassination, history certainly would be very different today if the Archduke Franz Ferdinand had chosen any other day except June 28 to visit Sarajevo.

Emperor Nero's Mother Pleads for Her Life

In A.D. 59, Roman Emperor Nero ordered the execution of his mother, Agrippina Minor. Actually, if it wasn't for Agrippina's efforts, Nero never would have become emperor.

Agrippina was the daughter of Germanicus and Agrippina Major. During the reign of her brother, Caligula, she became involved in a conspiracy against him and was banished from Rome. After Caligula's assassination, she was able to return when her uncle Claudius became emperor. After Claudius's wife was executed for adultery and treason, Agrippina courted him until he married her. He did this even though most Romans considered it incestuous. She then talked Claudius into adopting Nero—her son from a previous marriage—and naming Nero as his heir-designate, even though Claudius's son by his first wife was the rightful heir. Then, in 54 A.D., Agrippina murdered Claudius, and Nero became emperor.

As emperor, Nero devoted himself to the pursuit of pleasure. Described as "potbellied," he thought of himself as an Apollo and liked to wander around in the nude. Nero also considered himself to be a great musician, actor, athlete, and poet. He devoted much of his time to writing a history of Rome, which was to eventually consist of four hundred books of verse. When much of Rome was destroyed by fire, many thought Nero had started it so that he could rebuild the city on a more magnificent scale.

Nero was responsible for the murders and suicides of many of his friends. When people bored him, he would send them a note saying their suicide would not be unwelcome to him and the state. The philosopher and statesman Seneca, who had also been the emperor's tutor, received one of these notes and promptly stabbed himself with a sword.

While Nero was emperor, Agrippina quarreled often with her son and interfered with the affairs of state. Eventually, Nero falsely accused his mother of treason and ordered her execution. This was engineered by Nero's mistress, Poppaea Sabina—the wife of Otho (who later became emperor). Although some scholars question the authenticity of the following letter, it is said to be from Agrippina to her son, pleading that he spare her life:

> I do not wonder that barren Silana has no sense of maternal affection. One who has never borne a son naturally would not know how to bear the loss of one. Nature renders either hateful or indifferent those objects that we do not ourselves experience. . . . I am amazed that even the most skillful sorcery of words could make you pay the least attention to such barbarous inhumanity. . . .
>
> Don't you know, my son, the affection all mothers naturally bear their children? Our love is unbounded, incessantly fed by that tenderness unknown to all but ourselves. Nothing should be more dear to us than what we have bought with the risk of our lives; nothing more precious than what we have endured such grief and pain to procure. These are so acute and unbearable that if it were not for the vision of a successful birth, which makes us forget our agonies, generation would soon cease.
>
> Do you forget that nine full months I carried you in my womb and nourished you with my blood? How likely is it, then, that I would destroy the dear child who cost me so much anguish to bring into the world? It may be that the just gods were angry at my excessive love of you, and used this way to punish me.
>
> Unhappy Agrippina! You are suspected of a crime of which nobody could really think you guilty. . . . What does the title of empress mean to me, if I am accused of a crime that even the basest of women would abhor? Unhappy are those who breathe the air of the court. The wisest of people are not secure from storms in that harbor. There even a calm is dangerous. But why blame the court? Can that be the cause of my being suspected of parricide? . . .
>
> Tell me, why should I plot against your life? To plunge myself into a worse fate? That's not likely. What hopes could induce me to build upon your downfall? I know that the lust for empire often corrupts the laws of nature; that justice has no sword to punish those who offend in this way; and that ambition disregards wrong so long as it succeeds in its aim. . . . Nay, to what deity could I

turn for absolution after I had committed so black a deed? . . .

What difficulties have I not surmounted to crown your brow with laurels? But I insult your gratitude by reminding you of my services. My innocence ought not to defend itself but to rely wholly on your justice.

Farewell

Agrippina was executed by strangulation. In a fit of anger, Nero later kicked his mistress, Poppaea. She was pregnant, and the blow resulted in her death. After a fourteen-year reign, Nero himself was condemned to death by the Roman Senate. He promptly committed suicide by stabbing himself with a sword. His last words reportedly were: "What a pity for such an artist to die!"

American PRESIDENTS

Extramarital Affairs of the Presidents (and a Few Other Indiscretions)

Accusations of infidelity have haunted presidents all the way back to the creation of the office. Such allegations are difficult to prove beyond all doubt, and they often lead historians into hot debates. Although some are more likely to be true than others, here are a few of them.

George Washington professed his love for Sally Fairfax—the wife of his best friend. Though he was suspected of having had an affair with her, this was never proved. During his engagement to Martha Custus, Washington did write two letters to Mrs. Fairfax professing his love for her. They cautiously wrote to each other throughout his marriage, and in the last year of his life, he asked the widowed Sally to return from England to live at Mount Vernon. Though he hadn't seen her since before the Revolution, he wrote, "None of the important events since I have last seen you nor all of them together have been able to eradicate from my mind the recollection of those happy moments, the happiest of my life, which I have enjoyed in your company."

British propaganda charged that Washington had fathered several children by one of his slaves, but this was a lie. There were rumors of other illegitimate children, but there's nothing to support these accusations.

As a young man, **Thomas Jefferson** attempted to seduce Betsey Walker—the wife of his friend and neighbor. Of this, he later wrote, "When young and single, I offered love to a handsome lady. I acknowledge its incorrectness." As her husband, Jack Walker, described it, Jefferson tried to convince his wife "of the innocence of promiscuous love" while he was away on business in 1768. He said Jefferson continued making advances several times over the next three years and even approached her "in an indecent manner" a few months after Jefferson was married. He added, "And all this time I believed him to be my best friend and so felt and acted toward him." His wife confessed all this to him years later when he was about to make Jefferson the executor of his estate.

Jefferson's wife died in 1782, ten years after they were married. As she was dying, he promised her he would never marry anyone else. In 1784, while he was ambassador to France, he fell in love with Maria Cosway. Maria was unhappily married at the time, and her husband was most understanding. He not only had no problem with the affair, he remained Jefferson's close friend. The affair lasted more than a year.

Jefferson was later accused of fathering seven children with his slave, Sally Hemings. The scandal became public during Jefferson's administration and raged for two years. Many rude ballads were written about it at the time. One rather offensive little ditty appeared in the *Boston Gazette* and then in the Philadelphia *Port Folio* in 1802. Sung to the tune of "Yankee Doodle," it went:

Of all the damsels on the green,
On mountain, or in valley,
A lass so luscious ne'er was seen,
As Monticellian Sally.

Chorus:
Yankee doodle, who's the noodle?
What wife were half so handy?
To breed a flock of slaves for stock,
A blackamoor's the dandy.

Search every town and city through,
Search market, street, and alley;
No dame at dusk shall meet your view,
So yielding as my Sally.

Chorus

When press'd by loads of state affairs,
I seek to sport and dally,
The sweetest solace of my cares
Is in the lap of Sally.

Chorus

Let Yankee parsons preach their worst—
Let tory wittling's rally!
You men of morals! and be curst,
You would snap like sharks for Sally.

Chorus
She's black, you tell me—grant she be—
Must colour always tally?
Black is love's proper hue for me—
And white's the hue for Sally.

Chorus

What though she by her glands secretes?
Must I stand, Shill-I-shall-I?
Tuck'd up between a pair of sheets
There's no perfume like Sally.

Chorus

You call her slave—and pray were slaves
Made only for the gallery?
Try for yourselves, ye witless knaves—
Take each to bed your Sally.

Chorus:
Yankee doodle, whose the noodle?
Wine's vapid, tope me[95] brandy—
For still I find to breed my kind,
A negro wench the dandy!

Sally Hemings was his dead wife's half-sister, and in many ways was very similar to her. Although Sally was a slave, she was only one-quarter African American. It's said the thirty-eight-year affair began when he was forty-four and she was fourteen. While Jefferson was minister to France, Sally escorted his daughter there. Madison, her son, claimed she was pregnant when they returned to America in 1789 and that this child died in infancy. She had four other children—Beverley (born 1798), Harriet (1801), Madison (1805), and Eston (1808). Madison wrote of Jefferson, "He was uniformly kind to all about him. He was not in the habit of showing partiality or fatherly affection to us children. We were the only children of his by a slave woman.

[95] I.e. "give me a full helping of brandy."

He was affectionate toward his white grandchildren, of whom he had fourteen, twelve of whom lived to manhood and womanhood."

It has never been conclusively proven that Jefferson was indeed the father of Sally's children and some have suggested the father was either Peter Carr or Samuel Carr. Both were Jefferson's nephews.

Although all this caused a great scandal, an even greater one was created a few years later by **Richard Johnson**, who openly admitted he had two daughters by a slave named Julia Chinn and even tried to introduce them into white society. Despite the tremendous furor, he ignored the vicious attacks and eventually became vice president in the Van Buren administration.

Jefferson quietly endured the derision heaped on him, but was pleased when it briefly shifted to his arch-enemy, **Alexander Hamilton.** Hamilton was the patriot primarily responsible for the ratification of the Constitution. A close friend and advisor to George Washington, he was also the leader of the Federalist party. Jefferson, as head of the Democratic-Republican party, had many clashes with him.

When in 1797, Congress began investigating accusations that Hamilton had used confidential government information for his personal gain in his association with James Reynolds, a notorious financial speculator, Hamilton denied the charges, but admitted Reynolds was blackmailing him. He made this embarrassing statement:

> This charge against me is a connection with one James Reynolds for purposes of improper pecuniary speculation. My real crime is an amorous connection with his wife, for a considerable time with his privy and connivance, if not originally brought on by a combination between husband and wife with the design to extort money from me.
>
> This confession is not made without a blush. I cannot be the apologist of any vice because the ardour of passion may have made it mine. I can never cease to condemn myself for the pang, which it may inflict in a bosom [i.e., that of Hamilton's wife] eminently intitled to all my gratitude, fidelity and love. But that bosom will approve, that even at so great an expence, I should effectually wipe away a more serious stain from a name, which it cherishes with no less elevation that tenderness. The public too will I trust excuse the confession. The necessity of it to my defense against a more heinous charge could alone have extorted from me so painful an indecorum.

The adulterous affair occurred in the summer of 1791. Hamilton admitted he'd since paid large sums of money from time to time to keep the couple silent. All this prompted Jefferson to write, "I understand that finding the strait between Scylla and Charybdis too narrow for his steerage, he preferred running plumb on one of them. In truth, it seems to work very hard for him; and his willingness to plead guilty seems rather to have strengthened than weakened the suspicion that he was guilty of speculations."

In 1791, **Andrew Jackson** unknowingly married his wife Rachel while she was still married to her first husband, Lewis Robards. Although Robards had filed for divorce on the grounds of desertion that year in Virginia, it was rejected. But he was later granted a divorce in Kentucky because of his wife's obvious adultery with Jackson. When the divorce finally went through, Andrew and Rachel were remarried in 1794.

People throughout the countryside didn't forget this and often referred to her as "the harlot" and "the immoral adulteress." Even John Quincy Adams referred to Jackson as "an adjudicated adulterer." Jackson continuously horsewhipped and fought duels with everyone who questioned her honor. In fact, it's said he fought more than a hundred duels. He was seriously wounded twice. One bullet remained in his arm for nineteen years before he allowed a surgeon to remove it. In a 1806 duel with Charles Dickinson, a fellow Nashville lawyer, Dickinson's bullet fractured Jackson's rib. If the coat Jackson was wearing hadn't slowed the bullet down, it probably would have pierced his heart. Dickinson wasn't as fortunate. Jackson's bullet sent him to his grave.

Some people have suggested several presidents had homosexual tendencies, but there is only weak circumstantial evidence to support these claims. The most often cited is **James Buchanan**. Buchanan remained a bachelor throughout his life, and Washington gossip at the time linked him with **William Rufus King**, who was vice president during Franklin Pierce's administration. King had been given the nickname "Miss Nancy." But there is no direct evidence Buchanan was gay. Or that **Abraham Lincoln** was, for that matter, though some claim he might have been.

"Marriage is neither heaven nor hell, it is simply purgatory."

—Abraham Lincoln

Anthony Summers, author of *Official and Confidential: The Secret Life of J. Edgar Hoover* (1993), has reported that FBI Director **J. Edgar Hoover** had an intimate relationship with Clyde Tolson from about 1927 until his death in 1972. Hoover had personally chosen Tolson for the FBI and had elevated him from rookie to Assistant Director in less than three years. In a 1943 letter to Tolson, Hoover wrote, "Words are mere man-given symbols for thoughts and feelings, and they are grossly insufficient to express the thoughts in my mind and feelings in my heart that I have for you." On Hoover's death, Tolson inherited the lion's share of Hoover's half-million-dollar fortune—more than $1.5 million if adjusted to today's value—plus there are hints that much more was stashed away in secret accounts. In accordance with their wishes, Tolson is buried less than ten yards from Hoover in Arlington National Cemetery.

Summers interviewed many of their friends and associates and was told some startling things. Several spoke of incriminating photographs that were in the possession of James Angleton of the CIA and Mafia boss Meyer Lansky. It's said this was the reason Hoover denied that the Mafia even existed until the 1960s and how they were able to flourish. According to Army Supply Sergeant Joe Bobeck, who was also gay, he once saw about half a dozen photographs of Hoover in drag lying on a bed with other people around. He also said he'd been to gay parties when Hoover was there. Susan Rosenstiel insisted she'd been to two orgies with her bisexual husband, Hoover, Roy Cohn, and two young men about eighteen years old. Both times Hoover was decked out in a wild dress, wig, makeup, false eyelashes and, underneath it all, a garter belt. Summers's book contains a lot more detail, but I've devoted enough space to the former FBI director already.

JFK hated J. Edgar Hoover and often called him "a queer son-of-a-bitch." LBJ considered getting rid of him, but decided it would probably be too difficult. "Well," he reasoned, "it's probably better to have him inside the tent pissing out, than outside pissing in."

So, getting back to presidents: Based largely on circumstantial evidence, several people have suggested **Abraham Lincoln** had an illegitimate daughter who was born in Hazelwood, Illinois, in either 1855 or 1856 and was raised by three sets of foster parents who all had connections with Lincoln. They interpret Lincoln's statement, "I regret the necessity of saying I have no daughter," to mean that he had a daughter, but necessity forced him to say that he didn't.

Lincoln's close friend, law partner and biographer, William Herndon[96] insisted Lincoln was "true as steel" to Mary Todd throughout their marriage, adding, "Lincoln had terrible strong passions for women, could scarcely keep his hands off them, and yet he had honor and a strong will, and these enabled him to put out the fires of his terrible passion." It may have been much more than will and honor that kept Lincoln in line. In his younger days, Herndon believed, Lincoln had caught syphilis. "About the year 1835–36," Herndon wrote, "Mr. Lincoln went to Beardstown and during a devilish passion had connection with a girl and caught the disease. Lincoln told me this. . . . "

In these pre-penicillin days, there was an epidemic of syphilis and the disease was usually incurable. After a long bout with it, Lincoln was apparently cured by Dr. Daniel Drake of Cincinnati, though Herndon suspected he might have first passed it on to Mary Todd, which would explain the premature deaths of three of their sons and the deterioration of her brain that was revealed in her autopsy. If Lincoln had inadvertently caused his son's deaths, this would also explain his fits of melancholy. Herndon wrote that Lincoln once said, "What caused the death of these children? I have an opinion which I shall never state to anyone."

Although **Grover Cleveland** doubted whether he was the father of the illegitimate son born in 1874 to Maria C. Halpin, an attractive thirty-five-year-old widow, he did provide her with child-support payments. After she began drinking heavily and neglecting the baby, he arranged to have the child placed in an orphanage, to which Cleveland donated five dollars a week. All this became public while he was running for president. Though party officials wanted him to deny it, Cleveland, who was extremely honest, refused and openly admitted what had happened. He won the election after his opponent was hit with a worse scandal. Some Democrats celebrated the election victory with: "Hurrah for Maria, hurrah for the kid. I voted for Cleveland. And I'm damn glad I did!" The forty-nine-year-old president soon stirred up controversy again when he married the twenty-one-year-old daughter of his late friend and law partner. On his friend's death, Cleveland had become her legal guardian when she was eleven.

When **Warren Harding** ran for president, the Republican National Committee paid hush money of $20,000 plus $2,000 per month during his presidency to Carrie Phillips to keep her from revealing his extramarital affair with her to the press. They also sent her and her husband on an

96 Although Herndon's secondhand material is sometimes shaky, his firsthand material on Lincoln is generally sound.

expense-paid vacation to Europe, where they remained until after Harding's death. The Phillipses were close friends of Harding and his wife. The affair began in 1905 and lasted more than fifteen years. It was kept secret until 1964 when the existence of 250 of Harding's love letters to her were revealed to the public. These letters are now in the Library of Congress, but are sealed until the year 2014. Francis Russell, the biographer who discovered the letters, wrote:

> Compared to what is available today at any drugstore book rack, Harding's eroticism as expressed in his letters is naïve, and even pathetic as the quality of his mind peeps through the boudoir phrases. . . . The letters if they can be considered shocking—and some of them can—more so because they were written by the President of the United States, than through the tumescence of their content. When I first read them, I felt a sense of pity for the lonely Harding, for Carrie Phillips was clearly the love of his life, and he was more loving than loved.

Nan Britton began her affair with Harding while he was senator. In 1919, she had his illegitimate daughter, and he began making payments of $500 or more every month for her support. Harding had found out about her infatuation with him when she was thirteen and they began writing secret letters to each other when she was sixteen or seventeen. She said in her book, *The President's Daughter*, that the affair didn't actually begin until 1916 when she was twenty and he was fifty-one. She said they often had sex in the Senate Office Building—which is where she became pregnant—and later in a small closet near the Oval Office. She said the closet was "evidently a place for hats and coats, but entirely empty most of the times we used it, for we repaired there many times in the course of my visits to the White House, and in the darkness of a space not more than five feet square the President of the United States and his adoring sweetheart made love."

Their affair continued until 1923.

Harding died suddenly and some people have suggested he was poisoned by his wife because of his affairs, but this has yet to be proved or disproved. Some historians believe that if Harding had lived, he would have been impeached because of the Teapot Dome and other financial scandals. The first lady died in a sanitarium fifteen months later.

Franklin Roosevelt's affair with his secretary, Lucy Page Mercer, began twenty years before he became president and continued while he was in the White House. Roosevelt's wife (who was also his cousin) had stopped sleeping with him in 1916—about the time his affair with Lucy Mercer began. Mercer had been hired as Eleanor's social secretary a couple years earlier. They were able to keep their activities secret until 1918, when Eleanor found some love letters from Lucy. According to the Roosevelt's son, Elliott, in his book *An Untold Story* (1973), FDR's mother stepped in, telling him his allowance would be cut off and he would be disinherited if the affair continued. He agreed, and she married a rich, elderly man named Rutherfurd. Their relationship stopped for a while, but eventually resumed in secret, as it had before. In 1921, FDR lost the use of his legs in his bout with polio. Twenty-four years later, when Roosevelt suffered the stroke that killed him, Lucy was at his side, not his wife. Lucy was rushed off as Eleanor was rushed in.

Although Lucy Mercer Rutherfurd and FDR had a special relationship, she may not have been the love of his life. He had another mistress whom he may have been even closer to. Marguerite (Missy) LeHand lived in the White House and was treated as the unofficial first lady. While Eleanor assisted FDR by assuming many of his duties as chief executive, Missy ran the household and controlled the finances, including Eleanor's spending money. They were relatively discreet, but they didn't hide their relationship. As Michael John Sullivan wrote in *Presidential Passions* (1991), "In the evening Missy was seen by everyone in her nightgown in Roosevelt's bedroom sitting on his lap. She would also sit on his lap at other private occasions where friends and family were present." She was diagnosed with a brain tumor in 1941 and was soon incapacitated by a stroke. She then began losing her sanity and tried to commit suicide by setting herself on fire. Roosevelt changed his will so that up to half of his estate would be used to pay her medical bills, and though she died before he did, he didn't change his will back.

There were rumors that FDR was also romantically involved with the young Crown Princess Martha of Norway, who was living with her children near the capital during the war while her husband remained in Europe. Their house was selected by Roosevelt and under the protection of U.S. agents.

Throughout this time, Eleanor Roosevelt is alleged to have carried on a lesbian relationship with Lorena Hickok. Hickok was no beauty. Wearing mannish suits and weighing two hundred pounds, she had a penchant for smoking cigars. She lived in the White House for many years, though for most of that time she had to stay out of FDR's sight. FDR didn't like having her around because he felt she might give the White House a bad name. Still, she and Eleanor were almost constant companions. Here are a few excerpts from the more than 2,300 letters the otherwise unemotional Eleanor wrote to her:

> Hick darling . . . Oh, I want to put my arms around you. I ache to hold you close. Your ring is a great comfort. I look at it and think she does love me, or I wouldn't be wearing it.

> I can't kiss you so I kiss your picture goodnight and good morning! Don't laugh! This is the first day I've had no letter and I miss it sadly but it is good discipline.

> Dear one, and so you think they gossip about us, well they must at least think we stand separations rather well! I am always so much more optimistic than you are—I suppose because I care so little what they say.

> Dear, I've been trying today to bring back your face—to remember just how you look. Funny how even the dearest face will fade away in time. Most clearly I remember your eyes, with a kind of reassuring smile in them, and the feeling of that soft spot just northeast of the corner of your mouth against my lips. I wonder what we'll do when we meet—what we'll say. Well, I'm rather proud of us, aren't you? I think we've done rather well.

Eleanor and Lorena remained together until Eleanor's death in 1962.

During World War II, there were rumors going around that **Dwight Eisenhower** was having an affair with his personal assistant, Kay

Summersby—an Irish divorcee who was almost young enough to be his daughter. She confirmed these rumors in her book, *Past Forgetting* (1976). It turns out that right after the war ended, Eisenhower wrote to General Marshall requesting he be relieved of duty so he could return home to divorce his wife, Mamie, and marry Kay. Kay was unaware of all this until it was revealed by President Harry Truman in Merle Miller's *Plain Speaking* (1973).

> It was a very, very shocking thing to have done, for a man who was a general in the Army of the United States [said Truman in 1961 or 1962].
>
> Well, Marshall wrote him back a letter the like of which I never did see. He said . . . if Eisenhower even came close to doing such a thing, he'd not only bust him out of the Army, he'd see to it that never for the rest of his life would he be able to draw a peaceful breath. He said it wouldn't matter if he was in the Army or wasn't. Or even what country he was in.
>
> Marshall said that if he ever again even mentioned a thing like that, he'd see to it that the rest of his life was a living hell. General Marshall didn't very often lose his temper, but when he did, it was a corker.
>
> I don't like Eisenhower; you know that. I never have, but one of the last things I did as President, I got those letters from his file in the Pentagon, and I destroyed them.

In an interview on the television news program "60 Minutes," First Lady Betty Ford revealed that she was in favor of premarital sex, as it might help reduce the divorce rate.

Then there was **John Kennedy**, who confided with friends that he could only be satisfied with three women a day. Apparently, this was no exaggeration. Kennedy's closest friend, Lem Billings said, "Jack could be shameless in his sexuality, simply pull girls' dresses up and so forth. He would corner them at White House dinner parties and ask them to step into the next room away from the noise, where they could hold a 'serious discussion.'"

Peter Lawford, Kennedy's brother-in-law, rounded up many women for him. Jean Martin, the ex-wife of Dean Martin, said:

> I saw Peter in the role of pimp for Jack Kennedy. It was a nasty business—they were just too gleeful about it, not discreet at all. Of course there was nothing discreet about either of the Kennedys, Bob or Jack. It was like high-school time, very sophomoric. The things that went on in that beach house were just mind-boggling. Ethel could be in one room and Bobby could be in the other with this or that woman. Yes, Bobby was a grabber, but not in the terms that Jack was. Jack was really instinctive, you know, straight for the jugular—"Come upstairs, come in the bathroom, anything." Bobby didn't have eyes for me, but I do know this. I have a friend who was in the library with him, and before she knew it the door was locked and he threw her on the couch—amazing! It was so blatant. Here were the President of the United States and the Attorney General.

JFK's supposed conquests are said to include Marilyn Monroe, Audrey Hepburn, Jayne Mansfield, Angie Dickenson, Brazilian actress Florinda Bolkan, and the famous burlesque stripper Blaze Starr. It's also said that both

Monroe and Dickenson were then passed to his brother Robert, as he did with many others.

"One is astonished in the study of history at the recurrence of the idea that evil must be forgotten, distorted, skimmed over. We must not remember that Daniel Webster got drunk but only remember that he was a splendid constitutional lawyer. We must forget that George Washington was a slave owner . . . and simply remember the things we regard as creditable and inspiring. The difficulty, of course, with this philosophy is that history loses its value as an incentive and example; it paints perfect men and nation, but it does not tell the truth."

—W. E. B. Du Bois

Judith Exner (née Campbell) in her book, *My Story* (1977), also claimed she had an affair with Kennedy and then with Mafia godfather Sam Giancana. She says she acted as a go-between for the president and the Chicago mob boss in 1961 and 1962, carrying sealed envelopes back and forth between them and arranging ten face-to-face meetings, some of which apparently concerned the rigging of the Democratic primary in Illinois and West Virginia[97] and the following presidential election and assassinating Fidel Castro.[98] The official White House telephone log shows there were more than seventy calls between Judith and the president from the end of 1960 to mid-1962, and many of these calls were from Sam Giancana's home. Peter Lawford later said of Judith, "She began to believe she meant something to Jack. She thought he cared for her. But Jack wasn't the type to confuse sex with love."

Kennedy was also involved with Maria Novotny, who headed the New York branch of an international prostitution ring. Jack once went to her apartment where they were joined by two other prostitutes to play doctor and nurse. The big problem with all this was that Novotny's husband was Harry Alan Towers, a Soviet spy whose mission was to compromise top-level American political figures. Fortunately, the FBI chased him from the country before he apparently did any damage. The FBI also investigated JFK's association with two prostitutes who had been involved in Britain's Profumo scandal.

97 Illinois and West Virginia were essential for Kennedy to win the primary. James Spada's biography, *Peter Lawford: The Man Who Kept the Secrets* (1991), notes the following:

> Ovid Demaris, a Mafia specialist, analyzed the 1960 Illinois results and found that although Nixon had won 93 of the state's 102 counties, he lost Illinois by 8,858 votes—because of a huge Kennedy majority in Cook County, which includes Chicago. A partial, unofficial Republican recount of the Cook County vote reportedly turned up an extra 4,539 votes for Nixon, but an official recount was blocked by Chicago's Democratic mayor, Richard Daley. Indeed, the Chicago Mafia boss, Sam Giancana, boasted that he had been responsible for Kennedy's victory.
>
> Eisenhower urged his vice-president to contest the election results, but Nixon declined. . . . A careful investigation would surely have uncovered local fraud that benefited the Republican ticket as well. And Nixon was aware that Bobby Kennedy knew but had decided not to leak the fact that Nixon had sought psychiatric counseling in the 1950s. . . .
>
> Not only did it make Nixon think twice about demanding a recount, but it kept him from releasing information . . . that Jack Kennedy was an adulterer.

98 JFK's father also had ties with the Mafia. In the 1920s, Joe Kennedy largely made his fortune by illegally smuggling liquor into the United States during Prohibition and turning it over to organized-crime boss Frank Costello for distribution and sales.

Michael John Sullivan writes, "On numerous occasions, Kennedy placed his personal pleasure ahead of the duties of his office, even to the extent of seriously endangering national security in the process." Adding that one time JFK even ditched his Secret Service escorts and ran off to some woman's apartment, making himself completely unavailable if an emergency had arisen. On another occasion, the president was seeing so many women that an Irish teenager who had asked to see Kennedy was quickly ushered into the Oval Office before it was discovered she had just been released from a Dublin mental hospital and was carrying a butcher knife in her bag.

In contrast to Kennedy's obsession with sex, (which *Newsweek* and others describe as "monomaniacal") his wife, Jackie, had very little interest in it. As her step-brother, Gore Vidal, once put it, "She finds it untidy."

Apparently, **Lyndon Johnson's** infidelities were also numerous. His White House press secretary, George Reedy, wrote that Johnson was continually on the lookout for women he could add to what his staff referred to as "the Harem."

The affair between Johnson and Alice Glass began in late 1938 or early 1939 according to Alice's sister, Mary Louise Glass, and her cousin and closest friend, Alice Hopkins. At the time, Alice was in a relationship with Charles Marsh, and although she had had two children by him, she refused to marry him for many years. The two couples spent a lot of time together and though Marsh was seemingly unaware of the affair, it's thought that Lady Bird knew about it, but said nothing. Mary Louise Glass reflected, "The thing I could never understand was how she stood it. Lyndon would leave her on weekends, weekend after weekend, just leave her home. I wouldn't have stood it for a minute." This relationship is said to have lasted for more than twenty-five years, until Alice became so upset over his failure to end the Vietnam war that she cut off all contact with him.

Madeleine Brown claims she was his mistress for twenty-one years and gave birth to his illegitimate son in 1950. In 1987, when she thought she was dying, she revealed all this to Steven, the son in question, and filed a lawsuit against Lady Bird to gain recognition of this and $10.5 million. Madeleine Brown says the affair began in 1948 when she was twenty-three and he was a forty-year-old congressman. She adds, "He was a little kinky and I loved every second of it. So did he." But she says she was very upset when she found out he was having other affairs. The affair with Brown ended when her face was seriously scarred in an automobile accident.

While I'm not aware of any intimations that **Ronald Reagan** had any extramarital affairs, he does hold the distinction of being America's first divorced president. Further, Nancy was pregnant with their first child before they got married. Reagan has a son and daughter from each of his marriages.

"Blondes have the hottest kisses. Red-heads are fair-to-middling torrid, and brunettes are the frigidest of all. It's something to do with hormones, no doubt."

—Ronald Reagan

A former U.S. ambassador said he had to make arrangements for **George Bush** and his longtime aide, Jennifer Fitzgerald, to occupy adjoining bedrooms in a separate cottage while they attended a conference in Geneva in 1984. The ambassador explained, '"It became clear to me that the [then] vice president" and the aide "were romantically involved and this was not a business visit. . . . It made me very uncomfortable." Bush denied this when asked about it, but he refused to say whether or not he had ever had an extramarital affair.

Gennifer Flowers said she had a fourteen-year undercover relationship with **Bill Clinton**, while two former members of his security detail alleged that they and other Arkansas state troopers had helped Clinton meet women, book hotel rooms for liaisons, and brought a woman into the Arkansas governor's mansion after he was elected president.

And, of course, presidents weren't the only ones to join in the fun. A proper discussion of congressional indiscretions would fill an entire book. But to give one outstanding example: it has been reported that shortly after World War II, two senators—Scoop Jackson and Warren Magnuson—staged a race to see who would be the first to have sex with women from all of the then forty-eight states.

So, what does all this mean? Well, it either means we need to be more careful selecting our chief executives, or it means that none of this has anything to do with their leadership abilities. Or depending on how you feel about these presidents, we might even want to make promiscuity a requirement for the office. I'm afraid I'll have to leave that to you and the political analysts to determine. I'm just a historian.

Presidential Nicknames

Most of these nicknames were given to presidents by their enemies during elections and most were undeserved.

John Adams—"King John the Second" (accusing him of being a snobbish aristocrat), "His Rotundity"

William Henry Harrison—"Granny Harrison," "Old Tip-ler" (because supporters called him "Tippecanoe" and "Old Tip")

John Tyler—"His Accidency" (because he assumed the presidency on Harrison's death), "The Accident of an Accident," "Executive Ass"

James K. Polk—"The Plodder"

Franklin Pierce—"Doughface" (meaning a Northern man with Southern principles)

Ulysses S. Grant—"Grant the Butcher" (by some in the North during the Civil War because of the high number of casualties among his men)

Rutherford B. Hayes—"The Usurper" (because some felt the election was rigged; actually, both parties had resorted to fraud), "Rutherfraud B. Hayes," "His Fraudulency"

Chester A. Arthur—"The Dude President" (because of his flashy attire)

Grover Cleveland—"His Obstinacy," "The Beast of Buffalo," "The Hangman of Buffalo" (from when he twice filled in as executioner while he was a sheriff in Buffalo, New York)

Benjamin Harrison—"Little Ben" (because he was 5'6" tall), "White House Iceberg" (because of his icy demeanor; he was also described as being "a cold fish" and "a wilted petunia")

Woodrow Wilson—"Peck's Bad Boy" (because of allegations Wilson had an extramarital affair with divorcée Mary Allen Peck)

Richard Nixon—"Tricky Dicky" (he was called this long before his illegal activities came to light)

Though not a nickname, Gerald Ford was not President Ford's original name. He was born Leslie King, Jr., but after his mother divorced and remarried, his name was changed to that of her new husband. The same sort of thing happened to Alexander Hamilton. He was born Alexander Levine. Several presidents changed their names on purpose. Grover Cleveland's real first name was Stephen, Calvin Coolidge's was John, and Woodrow Wilson's was Thomas. Hiram Ulysses Grant's name was changed to Ulysses Simpson Grant by the congressman who sponsored him for the West Point Military Academy so that his initials would be U.S.

Another Look at Some Presidents

We were all taught about the presidents, right? But wait! Here are a few things they forgot to mention:

President John Hanson

Some historians consider John Hanson to be the first president of the United States. He was the first to hold that title. Actually, his full title was "President of the United States in Congress Assembled." Shortly before the Revolution began, the Continental Congress was formed. The Continental Congress operated from 1774 to 1789 and had sixteen presidents. Although John Hanson was the ninth of these presidents, he was the first to serve under the Articles of Confederation, which united the thirteen states, and he was the first to be called president of the United States. Even General George Washington referred to him by this title. However, Congress still retained full executive power. Hanson presided over the Congress and so could be considered the head of the government, but not the head of state. The presidents after Hanson were Elias Boudinot, Thomas Mifflin, Richard Henry Lee, John Hancock, Nathaniel Gorham, Arthur St. Clair, and Cyrus Griffin. In 1789, the Constitution established the Congress as we know it, and George Washington became president. But back in 1783 when George Washington appeared in the Continental Congress to resign as commander in chief of the Continental Army, he handed his resignation to President Thomas Mifflin.

President George Washington

George Washington was one of the richest men in the country at that time. At his death, his estate was valued at about a half a million and included 33,000 acres of land. A tremendous amount at that time. His family motto was "Exitus acta probat," meaning "the end justifies the means."

Washington had a fiery temper that, as Thomas Jefferson put it, "was naturally irritable" and when "it broke its bonds, he was most tremendous in his wrath." On one occasion, Jefferson said Washington became "much inflamed, [and] got into one of those passions when he cannot command himself." After his temper flared up, it usually subsided quickly and he would regain control. On another occasion, Washington chewed out Alexander Hamilton for keeping him waiting for ten minutes. Hamilton, who said it was only two minutes, promptly resigned from Washington's staff.

Like Mark Twain, Benjamin Franklin, and even Abraham Lincoln, Washington enjoyed dirty jokes and often told obscene anecdotes. Although he and Martha destroyed most of his letters, a few did survive. In the late 1920s, multimillionaire J. P. Morgan bought some, but he burned them saying they were "smutty."

President John Adams

The latter half of John Adams's administration was known as the Federalist Reign of Terror. Because the Alien and Sedition Acts were used by the Federalists to jail anyone who criticized the government, Thomas Jefferson, who was then the vice president, stopped signing his letters out of fear that postal clerks were searching his mail for evidence to charge him with treason. His fears were justified in that more than twenty Republican editors were indicted for criticizing Adams and his administration. Most of them were convicted and sent to jail. Many agents and writers fled the country to avoid prosecution. Members of Congress were also under surveillance and Representative Matthew Lyon was sent to jail for four months and fined $1,000 for criticizing the president in a Vermont newspaper. His constituents took up a collection to pay his fine and reelected him to Congress while he was still in jail. The Alien and Sedition Acts expired when Jefferson became president. If they hadn't, he would have repealed them.

Ben Franklin said President Adams was "always an honest man, often a wise one, but sometimes, and in some things, absolutely out of his senses." While Adams did have his good qualities, he was also petty, vain, outspoken, abrasive, and crusty. He once described Alexander Hamilton as "the bastard brat of a Scottish peddler" and Thomas Paine's *Common Sense* as "a poor, ignorant, malicious, short-sighted, crapulous mass."

President Thomas Jefferson

During the election, Jefferson refused to discuss his religious beliefs, leading many people to believe he didn't have any. This prompted the Reverend Cotton Mather to accuse "the ungodly Jefferson" of being guilty of "gross immorality." The Reverend John M. Mason claimed anyone who voted for Jefferson "would do more to destroy the gospel of Jesus than a whole fraternity of infidels." When Jefferson was elected, some believers hid their Bibles so they wouldn't be seized by "the satanic Jefferson." Actually, Jefferson was religious and did attend church (Episcopal), though he didn't believe in the divinity of Christ. "To the genuine precepts of Jesus Himself," he wrote, "I am a Christian in the only sense in which He wished any one would be; sincerely attached to His doctrines in preference to all others; ascribing to Him every *human* excellence and believing He never claimed any other."

President John Quincy Adams

As president, John Quincy Adams liked to go skinny-dipping in the Potomac. On one occasion, someone stole his clothes and he had to ask a passing boy to run back to the White House to get him some more.

President Andrew Jackson

Andrew Jackson's wife, Rachel, was the only first lady who smoked a pipe.

President William Henry Harrison

William Henry Harrison was killed by his own inaugural address. The sixty-eight-year-old general delivered it on a cold winter's day and he droned on for two hours without a hat, coat, or gloves. He caught pneumonia and died a month later. In his address, he had promised not to run for a second term.

President John Tyler

Following Harrison's death, John Tyler was down on his knees playing marbles when he was found and told he had just become the president of the United States. He later joined the Confederacy during the Civil War and sat in its provisional Congress before becoming a member of the Confederate House of Representatives.

President David Rice Atchison

Atchison was president for only one day. The term of James K. Polk ended at noon on March 4, 1849, but because this was a Sunday, Zachary Taylor refused to be sworn in until the next day. Since Polk's vice president had resigned a few days earlier, by law the president pro tempore of the Senate automatically became president during this vacancy. That was Atchison. He later said, "I slept most of that Sunday." On his gravestone, it says, "President of U.S. one day."

"[President Warren] Harding was not a bad man. He was just a slob." So said Alice Roosevelt Langworth, Theodore Roosevelt's daughter. She also loved repeating someone's statement that Calvin Coolidge looked as though he'd been weaned on a pickle.

President Zachary Taylor

When it was first proposed that this old general run for president, his response was, "Stop your nonsense and drink your whiskey!" He loved chewing tobacco and was known as a "sure-shot spitter." As a military officer, he disliked wearing uniforms. "He looks more like an old farmer going to market with eggs to sell than anything I can . . . think of," one officer said, while another man described him as wearing "a dusty green coat, a frightful pair of trousers and on horseback he looks like a toad."

President Franklin Pierce

While Pierce was president, he accidently ran down an old woman with his horse and was arrested. The officer released the president when he discovered who he had in custody. A few chief executives later, President U. S. Grant was arrested for speeding in his horse carriage.

President James Buchanan

President James K. Polk wrote in his diary, "Mr. Buchanan is an able man, but in small matters without judgment and sometimes acts like an old maid." After Polk made Buchanan his secretary of state, Andrew Jackson strongly objected to the appointment. To which Polk replied, "But, General, you yourself appointed him minister to Russia in your first term." "Yes, I did," Jackson explained. "It was as far as I could send him out of my sight, and where he could do the least harm. I would have sent him to the North Pole if we had kept a minister there!" Buchanan was an alcoholic who consumed large amounts of alcohol with no outward signs of drunkenness. This prompted one journalist to write, "More than one ambitious tyro who sought to follow his . . . example gathered an early fall."

President Abraham Lincoln

Lincoln was America's first non-Christian president. Not only did he reject Christianity, he once wrote a booklet titled *Infidelity*, by which he meant a lack of faith in God. William Herndon, Lincoln's close friend and biographer, wrote that when Lincoln "read his manuscript to Samuel Hill, his employer said to Lincoln: 'Lincoln, let me see your manuscript.' Lincoln handed it to him. Hill ran it in a tin-plate stove, and so the book went up in flames. Lincoln in that production attempted to show that the Bible was false: first on the grounds of reason, and, second, because it was self-contradictory; that Jesus was not the son of God any more than any man." Later, as President, considerable pressure was placed on him to mention God in his speeches. This he increasingly did—but he never mentioned Jesus.

President Andrew Johnson

Andrew Johnson was a tailor and made all of his own clothes until he became a congressman. He was a Southerner and had held slaves, but he was against the South's seceding from the Union, prompting many Southerners (including those in his home state of Tennessee) to consider him a traitor. Returning home after Lincoln's inauguration, a mob in Lynchburg, Virginia, dragged him from the train, beating, kicking, and spitting on him. They were about to hang him when an old man shouted, "His neighbors at Greenville have made arrangements to hang their Senator on his arrival. Virginians have no right to deprive them of that privilege." When Tennessee seceded from the Union, Johnson was forced to flee his own state.

Three presidents had little or no schooling: Andrew Jackson, Zachary Taylor, and Andrew Johnson.

President Ulysses S. Grant

U. S. Grant was the first person to be promoted to the rank of full general after George Washington. Yet, despite having sent his men into some of the Civil War's bloodiest battles, he hated the sight of blood, disliked hunting, and was sickened at the sight of a Mexican bullfight. If he ate meat, it had to be cooked black because rare meat made him queasy.[99] A shy, mild-mannered man with little interest in the military and a dislike of wearing uniforms, his father had to force him to go to West Point. Grant once said, "I am more of a farmer than a soldier. I take little or no interest in military affairs." Though Grant fought in the Mexican War, he thought it was "one of the most unjust wars ever waged by a stronger against a weaker nation. It was an instance of a republic following the bad example of European monarchies, in not considering justice in their desire to acquire additional territory." He felt the Civil War was America's punishment for what the country did in Mexico, saying, "We got our punishment in the most sanguinary and expensive war of modern times."

President Grover Cleveland

That President Clinton avoided the draft during the Vietnam war by going to college in England is well known, but he's not the only

[99] Another of Grant's culinary peculiarities was that he usually ate a pickle soaked in vinegar for breakfast.

president who got out of being drafted. During the Civil War, Grover Cleveland was drafted but paid a substitute $150 to take his place. Like Clinton's maneuver, this was completely legal at the time and was actually quite common in both the Civil and Revolutionary wars. Two of Cleveland's brothers were off fighting for the Union, and he stayed behind to support his mother and sister.

He was definitely not a conscientious objector, though. Later, when he was Sheriff of Erie County, New York, one of his duties was to fill in as executioner when the usual executioner was unavailable. In this capacity, he killed two men by placing and tightening the nooses around their necks and then dropping the trapdoors. This earned him the nickname "the Hangman of Buffalo."

President Theodore Roosevelt

Teddy Roosevelt was exactly like the ninety-six-pound weakling in the old Charles Atlas advertisements. He once confessed that "owing to my asthma I was not able to go to school, and I was nervous and self-conscious." A weak, scrawny kid with poor eyesight, after a humiliating run-in with some bullies, he decided, "I'll make myself a body" and began working out. He developed a love of sports, adventure, and war.

For many years, he tried unsuccessfully to push the country into war. He wrote to a friend in 1897, "In strict confidence . . . I should welcome almost any war, for I think this country needs one." Dying to prove himself in battle, eventually the Spanish-American War came along, and he immediately rounded up some men to go and fight in defense of Cuba. Of his famous charge up Kettle Hill[100] near San Juan, he said, "I waved my hat and we went up the hill with a rush. . . . I killed a Spaniard with my own hand . . . like a jackrabbit." Following the charge, he proudly said, "Look at those damned Spanish dead." And later he added, "The charge itself was great fun. Oh, but we have had a bully fight!" Though he did have to admit, "The percentage of loss of our regiment was about seven times that of the other five volunteer regiments."

Though the Rough Riders had trained as a mounted cavalry regiment for two months prior to going to Cuba, most of them were on foot during the charge because there wasn't room on the ship for their horses to go with them. Further, Roosevelt wasn't actually the leader of the regiment. That was Colonel Leonard Wood.

In all, Roosevelt's campaign in Cuba lasted one week, with one day of heavy fighting. Still, he published a book on it and became a national hero. He summed it all up saying, "San Juan was the great day of my life."

While Theodore Roosevelt was running for governor of New York, he and seven of his Rough Riders toured the state by train. At one station, ex-Sergeant Buck Taylor told the crowd, "I want to talk to you about mah colonel. He kept ev'y promise he made to us and he will to you. When he took us to Cuba, he told us . . . we would have to lie out in the trenches with the rifle bullets climbing all over us, and we done it. . . . He told us we might meet wounds and death and we done it, but he was thar in the midst of us. And when it came to the great day, he led us up San Juan Hill like sheep to slaughter, and so he will lead you!"

---

100 Kettlehill is the actual name of what later became known as San Juan Hill.

When he was nominated as McKinley's vice president, the chairman of the Republican National Committee exclaimed, "Don't any of you realize that there's only one life between this madman and the White House?" After McKinley's assassination, one citizen pleaded with him not to start any wars and he replied, "What! A war, and I cooped up here in the White House? Never!" True to his word, there were no armed conflicts during his seven-and-a-half-year presidency.

Gradually, many—including the chairman of the Republican National Committee—grew to like him. But he did offend many others by inviting Booker T. Washington, the illustrious African-American educator, to dinner at the White House and by trying to remove "In God We Trust" from U.S. coins. He also launched an antitrust suit against J. P. Morgan's Northern Securities Company. In addition, he was responsible for the overthrow of the Panamanian government so the Panama Canal could be built, and because of his policies, he annexed the Dominican Republic, though he said he did so with as much desire "as a gorged boa constrictor might have, to swallow a porcupine wrong-end-to."

Roosevelt was shot by a madman while campaigning for a third term in office and insisted on delivering his campaign speech with the bleeding, undressed bullet hole in his chest before he allowed anyone to rush him to the hospital. When World War I came along, he volunteered to lead a unit into battle, but President Wilson refused to allow him. After one of his sons was killed in the war, Roosevelt's health rapidly declined and he died a year later.

Theodore Roosevelt was America's youngest president. Kennedy, at age forty-three, was just the youngest person to be *elected* president. Roosevelt wasn't elected to his first term and was forty-two years old when he assumed the office.

President Woodrow Wilson

Woodrow Wilson was a hard-core racist and white supremacist, and his wife was even worse. She often told "darky" stories, while he segregated the federal government and tried to pass legislation curtailing the civil rights of African-Americans. Through his efforts, the Democratic party was essentially closed to African-Americans for an additional two decades, and parts of federal government were segregated through the 1950s. The only time he met African-American leaders in the White House ended with him practically throwing them out of his office. With the wave of racism coming out of the White House, the Ku Klux Klan experienced a tremendous resurgence, antiblack race riots swept the country, and lynchings of African-Americans spread as far north as Duluth.

Wilson prejudices also extended to other ethnic groups, which he referred to as "hyphenated Americans." He insisted, "Any man who carries a hyphen about with him carries a dagger that he is ready to plunge into the vitals of this Republic whenever he gets ready."

Under Wilson's leadership, the United States made more military interventions in Latin America than at any other time in American history. U.S. troops landed in Haiti, the Dominican Republic, Cuba, Panama, and eleven times in Mexico. The U.S. military was used to select Nicaragua's president and to force that country to accept a treaty favorable to the United States.

In a largely forgotten war against the Soviets, the United States invaded the Soviet Union in an attempt to assist White Russian forces in overthrowing the Russian Revolution. In the summer of 1918, American forces, under a joint command with the Japanese, penetrated to Murmansk, Archangel, Vladivostok, and then west to Lake Baikal. After reaching the Volga, the White Russian forces disintegrated, and the U.S. troops were forced to flee from Vladivostok on April 1, 1920. This action convinced the Soviets that the United States and the Western powers were determined to destroy them if given a chance.

President Warren Harding

From the ages of twenty-two to thirty-five, Warren Harding had five nervous breakdowns that landed him in Dr. Kellogg's famous clinic in Battle Creek, Michigan. Harding's wife continuously went to fortune tellers and tailored her life around their advice.

President Calvin Coolidge

It's said Calvin Coolidge loved to eat breakfast in bed while having his head rubbed with Vaseline.

President Herbert Hoover

Herbert Hoover apparently ordered two men—naval intelligence officer Glenn Howell and his civilian aide Robert J. Peterkin—to burglarize a Democratic party office in New York in 1930. Jeffery M. Dorwart, a Rutgers University professor, discovered Howell's long-overlooked diary in naval archives in 1983. In it, Howell wrote that Hoover ordered the break-in after "he received a confidential report alleging that the Democrats had accumulated a file of data so damaging that if made public it would destroy both his reputation and his entire Administration." He said they searched the office but found nothing. He also said that other naval officers broke into the homes and offices of radicals and Japanese citizens looking for national security information and that these break-ins were approved by President Hoover and then by President Franklin Roosevelt. Nixon, on the other hand, was charged with covering up break-ins, but not ordering or approving them, though he did order at least one break-in that was not carried out.

President Franklin Roosevelt

Keeping the presidency all in the family, FDR was a relative of William Howard Taft, Theodore Roosevelt, Benjamin Harrison, Ulysses S. Grant, Zachary Taylor, William Henry Harrison, Martin Van Buren, John Quincy Adams, James Madison, John Adams, and George Washington. FDR and his relatives contolled the presidency for one-third of its existence.

President John F. Kennedy

Kennedy was considered a war hero because of his actions after his patrol boat PT-109 was rammed by a Japanese destroyer. Actually, the incident did not occur during a battle, and since it would be practically impossible for a destroyer to hit a fast, highly maneuverable patrol boat, some have suggested the crew was napping or possibly drunk. Many historians wonder how Kennedy escaped being court martialed.

Kennedy was awarded a Pulitzer Prize in 1957 for *Profiles in Courage*—a book that he didn't write. It's believed his ghostwriter was Theodore Sorensen, one of his speech writers.

President Lyndon Johnson

According to articles that appeared in *Newsweek* and *National Review* in 1977, Johnson was elected to the Senate in 1948 by fraud. In a statewide recount, Johnson gained 202 votes in Jim Wells County that officials said they had missed in the first count. These 202 votes were all in the same handwriting and in the same ink, plus they were all in alphabetical order . . . and they were all votes for Johnson. One of the votes was reportedly cast by William F. Buckley, Jr.'s grandfather, who had died forty-four years earlier. A brief investigation saw nothing irregular in any of this, and Johnson was declared the winner by eighty-seven votes. A former Johnson aide later said, "Of course they stole the election. That's the way they did it down there [in Texas]. In 1941, when Lyndon ran the first time for the Senate, he went to bed one night thinking he was 5,000 votes ahead . . . and when he woke up that next morning [he was] 10,000 votes behind. He learned a thing or two between 1941 and 1948."

President Richard Nixon

Richard Nixon's involvement in the Watergate coverup is common knowledge. One thing that is not quite as well known is that he was also accused of being involved in illegally raising the price of the McDonald's Quarter Pounder cheeseburgers. According to a book published by the *New York Times* titled *The Offences of Richard M. Nixon* (1973), among twenty-eight criminal violations by the president is one for receiving bribes from Ray Kroc, Chairman of the Board of McDonald's. After McDonald's raised the price of their cheeseburger from 59¢ to 65¢ without authorization or notification, the Price Commission ordered the price lowered. But after Kroc gave over $200,000 to Nixon's campaign, the Price Commission reversed its decision. This money was "solicited and obtained. . . . in violation of article II, section 4 of the Constitution and sections 201, 372, 872 and 1505 of the Criminal Code." The book also lists ten similar instances of bribery and fraud, plus one of embezzlement. Of course, Nixon didn't believe anything he did was wrong. In 1977, he said, "When the President does it, that means that it is not illegal."

"Really, we are all fake heroes."

—President Theodore Roosevelt, 1898

President Ronald Reagan

For the former actor and actress, Ronald and Nancy Reagan's images were extremely important, and both of them underwent plastic surgery to give themselves a more youthful appearance. According to one of their physicians, "Both of them have had numerous face lifts. From the scars behind his ears, I'd say the President has had two lifts, and she's probably had three or four." And this probably doesn't count when she had her eyes lifted just before Reagan announced he was running for governor of California.

Both Reagan and Nancy relied heavily on astrologers when making decisions, but they were not the first in the White House to do so. The wives of both Lincoln and Harding also relied on them. Reagan first became interested in astrology when he was a young actor, and he later got Nancy interested in it. From then on, their schedules were dictated by their astrologers—who included Jeane Dixon, Carroll Righter, Ed Helin, and Joan Quigley. British witch Sybil Leek claimed credit for Reagan changing his inauguration as governor from noon to just after midnight. Ed Helin, who began doing Reagan's charts in 1949, said, "As President, he was primarily concerned with the timing of events and how his popularity would be affected by his actions. He called me to determine the best timing for invading Granada, for bombing Libya, for launching the *Challenger*—things like that." Helin was paid by the Republican National Committee and was still doing work for them in 1990.

Although the Reagans professed to be very religious, they almost never went to church. But for their 1980 campaign, arrangements were made for them to attend an Episcopal service in Virginia. As they were about to take communion, Nancy asked Mike Deaver, "Are those people drinking out of the same cup?" He explained that they would be given wafers first and they would dip it into the cup. Reagan couldn't hear these instructions and was asking, "What? What?" To which Nancy responded, "Ron, just do exactly as I do." As the tray of wafers came by, she took one, dipped it in the chalice, accidentally dropped it in the wine, and turned to Deaver with a horrified expression. Reagan promptly took the host, dipped it, and dropped it into the wine as well. Deaver said, "I watched the minister move on, shaking his head, staring at these blobs of gunk floating in his wine."

The president's reliance on astrology was first revealed to the public by Reagan's former chief of staff, Donald Regan, but it was later confirmed by several other White House employees and the president's son, Ron. These revelations prompted Speaker of the House Jim Wright to comment, "I'm glad the President was consulting somebody. I was getting worried there for a while."

But then, maybe the reliance on astrology by the Reagans and the Republican party isn't all that unusual, considering the CIA spent $750,000 on psychic research between 1972 and 1977, and the Pentagon spent $20 million on just one of its psychic projects—code named Star Gate—from about 1985 to 1995. Pentagon psychic projects date back at least to 1952.

Great Turnarounds

Thomas Jefferson owned slaves, but continuously tried to pass antislavery legislation and even wrote an antislavery passage in the Declaration of Independence that was later removed. Zachary Taylor also owned slaves (he had 182 of them when he died), but he adamantly opposed extending slavery into the newly acquired territories. And though Andrew Johnson had slaves, he was responsible for the amendment to Tennessee's constitution that outlawed slavery in that state.

After he was president of the United States, John Tyler became one of the leaders in the Confederate government.

Grant and Harding were both very honest presidents who had very corrupt administrations.

Theodore Roosevelt, a hawk who desperately sought war before becoming president, had two peaceful terms in office and was awarded the Nobel Peace Prize.

Kennedy was considered a liberal president, but he got the country deeper into the Vietnam quagmire, he dragged his feet on civil rights, had Martin Luther King's phone tapped through his Attorney General Robert Kennedy, launched the

Bay of Pigs invasion of Cuba, and approved the CIA's attempts to assassinate Fidel Castro.

It's reported that during his final years as president, Lyndon Johnson admitted about the Vietnam war, "The kids were right. I blew it."

Nixon was considered conservative and rose to prominence with his anti-Communist witch-hunting, but he was the president who established relations with both the Soviet Union and Communist China. And despite the Domino Theory, he was the one who got the United States out of the war that was supposed to save Southeast Asia from Communism. He also established the Occupational Safety and Health Administration, the Environmental Protection Agency, the Legal Services Administration, and the Equal Opportunity Commission. He expanded the food-stamp program and more than doubled funding for the National Endowment of the Arts and the National Endowment of the Humanities. He promoted affirmative action and instituted government-mandated racial quotas. Nixon also supported the Equal Rights Amendment and produced the nation's last balanced budget. Some programs he was unable to get passed include a national health insurance plan requiring businesses to pay for 75 percent of their employees' insurance and the Family Assistance Plan, which would have given poor families a guaranteed annual income.

Reagan became president with promises of a smaller government and less taxes, but then he spent money like there was no tomorrow. From the end of World War II until the year Reagan was elected president, the national debt had slowly increased by $649 billion over thirty-five years, but during his administration it skyrocketed by $1.7 trillion in just eight years. When he left, the debt was $2.6 trillion—almost three times what it was before he became president. The amount owed for each U.S. citizen shot up to $10,534. As a result, much of today's national debt is the *interest* owed on the money spent during the Reagan years. This also resulted in the United States becoming a debtor nation in 1985, losing its status as the world's financial leader—a position it had maintained since 1914—to Japan.

Reagan often insisted he would never make concessions with terrorists. He continued saying this while he was selling arms to Iran.

The more peaceful presidents who led the country into war are Madison, Lincoln, McKinley, Wilson (who was elected on the slogan "he kept us out of war"), FDR (who was reelected with the 1940 campaign promise, "I have said this before, but I shall say it again and again and again; your boys are not going to be sent into any foreign wars"), and Bush (who was called a wimp and talked of a kinder, gentler nation). Besides the Persian Gulf War, the United States also overthrew the government of Panama while Bush was president. Even though less than half of America's presidents never served in the military, the country entered two thirds of its wars[101] under those nonmilitary presidents.

Unintelligible Quotations of U.S. Presidents

As Nixon used to say, let me make one thing perfectly clear. Sometimes certain presidents have had some difficulty making themselves perfectly clear. In fact, some-

101 Excluding the Revolution and the Indian Wars.

times these distinguished leaders of our great nation don't make any sense at all. It's as if they've suddenly started speaking in some weird foreign language that uses English words, only they mean something completely different. Perhaps they are speaking in tongues . . . or maybe extraterrestrials are trying to channel important messages to us . . . or maybe there's just something about being president that sometimes causes their brains to short circuit. Whatever it is, the results occasionally find their way into the media, though the general public usually ignores them or quickly forgets. It's probably just as well. Most people get a bit uneasy when the man in the nation's highest office starts blathering like an idiot.

In his time, President Warren G. Harding was well known for utilizing the English language in some rather unusual ways . . . and *he* was a former *newspaper editor*. Usually, his pronouncements were just a bit unconventional, such as, "we must prosper America first" or "Despite all the deprecation I cannot bring myself to accept the notion that the inter-relation among our men and women has departed." But occasionally he would come up with statements like, "Progression is not proclamation nor palaver. It is not pretense nor play on prejudice. It is not the perturbation of a people passion-wrought, nor a promise proposed." In one of his more lucid moments, he once commented, "Oftentimes . . . I don't seem to grasp that I am President."

Sometimes when newspapers printed interviews with President Ronald Reagan or excerpts from his press conferences, they could not report exactly what he said. If they did, few people would understand him; therefore his quotes had to be altered in order to get across what he was trying to say. However in 1981, a few newspapers did decide to quote him directly. Here are some of those quotations.

When asked whether a U.S./Soviet nuclear confrontation could be limited, Reagan replied (remember, this quote is verbatim now), "I don't honestly know. I think, again, until someplace—all over the world this is being, research going on, to try and find the defensive weapon. There never has been a weapon that someone hasn't come up with a defense. But it could—and the only defense is, well you shoot yours and we'll shoot ours." (These are completely free of typos. I promise.)

When asked about the Soviet's SS-20s, he asserted, "Well, the SS-20s will have, with what they're adding, 750 war heads, one of them capable of pretty much leveling a city, and they can sit right there and that's got all of Europe, and including England, on target."

When asked if there could be a tactical exchange of nuclear weapons without a strategic exchange, Reagan explained, "Well, I would—if they realized that we—again, if—if we led them back to that stalemate only because that our retaliatory power, our seconds, or strike at them after our first strike, would be so destructive that they couldn't afford it, that would hold them off."

On another occasion he was asked about gross national product. "Well," he explained, "you can't have the gross national product . . . here's a thing for the return of the people and so forth on that without reflecting those who are paying the taxes."

Following in the footsteps of his mentor, George Bush also had his moments of eloquence, but he tended to add an extra dimension. Bush would suddenly change the subject midsentence and take off in an entirely new direction. Sometimes he would change the subject so many times, so quickly, that it's hard to identify what he was talking about at all. And sometimes one has to wonder if even he knew what he was talking about.

Take the following shining example where Bush attempted to sympathize with some disgruntled New Hampshire workers:

> And the other thing, and I guess—is that I expect it's difficult for somebody working in a plant here in New Hampshire to wonder, to know if the president really cares about what's happening in the economy. And I think I know this state. I went to school a thousand years ago across the border and—would go up every summer of my life, except 1944, to Maine, spending a fair amount of time. Almost—you could see it, practically, coming in on the plane. So when you get clobbered on the seacoast by a storm, I get clobbered on the seacoast by a storm. It goes further than that. When you get hurting because you worry whether you're going to have a job or you get thrown out, I do care about it and I just wanted to say that.

Or how about when he somehow came up with this lead-in to a speech on family values:

> Somebody—somebody asked me, what's it take to win? I said to them, I can't remember, what does it take to win the Super Bowl? Or maybe Steinbrenner, my friend George, will tell us what it takes for the Yanks to win—one run. But I went over to the Strawberry Festival this morning, and ate a piece of shortcake over there—able to enjoy it right away, and once I completed it, it didn't have to be approved by Congress—I just went ahead and ate it—and that leads me into what I want to talk to you about today. . . ."

Now try deciphering these comments he made about pollution in Clinton's home state during the 1992 presidential campaign: "You talk about the environment—take a look at the Arkansas River. And I'll have more to say about that in a minute. We've even seen some chickens along the way. Here's one back here. But I can't figure that out or maybe he's talking about the Arkansas River again where they're dumping that—I've got to be careful here—that fecal—some kind of bacteria into the river. Too much from the chicken."

And then one time the former president said, "High tech is potent, precise, and in the end, unbeatable. The truth is, it reminds a lot of people of the way I pitch horseshoes. Would you believe some of the people? Would you believe our dog? Look, I want to give the high-five symbol to high tech."

Though it must be mentioned that he did admit, "Fluency in English is something that I'm often not accused of." And on another occasion, "I've been talking the same way for years, so it can't be that serious."

Here are a few more Bushisms:

"I have opinions of my own—strong opinions—but I don't always agree with them."

"If a frog had wings, he wouldn't hit his tail on the ground."

"Well, I'm going to kick that one right into the end zone of the secretary of education."

Then there were times when one had to wonder if President Bush really had all of his marbles. Such as when he visited some children in a Head Start program and said, "And let me say in conclusion, thanks for the kids. I learned an awful lot about bathtub toys—about how to work the telephone. One guy knows—several of them know their own phone numbers—preparation to go to the dentist. A lot of things I'd forgotten. So it's been a good day."

Or even during his first presidential conference when he talked to reporters about a present Reagan left him:

> Let me see whether I dare read you this. "Dear George:"—this is from Reagan—"You'll have moments when you want to use this particular stationery. Well, go to it. George, I treasure the memories we share, and wish you all the very best. You'll be in my prayers. God bless you and Barbara. I'll miss our Thursday lunches. Ron." And the heading on the paper is, "Don't let the turkeys get you down." So, nobody here should take personal this at all. I mean this is a broad, ecumenical statement. "Do not let the turkeys get you down." And it shows a bunch of turkeys trying to get an elephant down. Then it says "Boynton" on the bottom.

Or the time during his 1992 presidential campaign when he said, "Don't just ask me about what's wrong with our legal system. Check with the opinion of that famous enforcer of American justice. I'm not talking about Oliver Wendell Holmes or John Marshall. I mean someone even more famous than that—Hulk Hogan."

Or how about when he greeted some international tourists with (note, "nihaoma" is Mandarin for "how are you?"), "Hey, hey, nihaoma. Hey, yeah, yeah. Heil, heil—a kind of Hitler salute." This unusual greeting, no doubt, left them completely bewildered.

And then once while he was still vice president he exclaimed, "There's no difference between me and the president on taxes. No more nit-picking. Zip-ah-dee-doo-dah. Now, it's off to the races!"

Demonstrating that he's made of the same stuff as his predecessors, President Bill Clinton showed off his elocution skills in a Cleveland shopping mall in 1993 with the following: "I've been criticized for doing more than one thing at once. . . . Would it be nice if you could pay your bills and not earn any money to pay them? I don't understand this whole—you can't do one thing at once. But anyway, that's what they say."

Richard Nixon began showing that he had presidential abilities long before he entered the White House when in 1952 he said, "Now, what was wrong? And let me say that it was wrong—I'm saying, incidentally that it was wrong and not just illegal. Because it isn't a question of whether it was legal or illegal. That isn't enough. The question is was it morally wrong." He continued to prove he had a talent for advanced semantics in 1971 by explaining, "Then you have two Secretaries of State. You cannot have that, there being only one."

At least President Gerald Ford was not incoherent when he said during a 1976 debate with Jimmy Carter, "There is no Soviet domination of Eastern Europe and there never will be under the Ford administration." When he was asked to clarify this, he answered, "I don't believe . . . the Rumanians consider themselves dominated by the Soviet Union. Each of these countries is independent, autonomous. It has its own territorial integrity and the United States does not concede that those countries are under the domination of the Soviet Union."

All this was news to everyone else in the country (and probably to everyone in Eastern

Europe, too). A few days later his advisors insisted he clarify his statements further, so he told the press that "we are going to make certain to the best of our ability that any allegation of domination is not a fact." Eventually, he was forced to admit that Eastern Europe was under Soviet control. "I did not express myself clearly—I admit," he said.

All in all, at least President Ford could be understood when he made such memorable comments as, "Things are more like they are now than they have ever been" and "If Lincoln were alive today, he'd probably roll over in his grave."

Yes, the author of such unforgettable lines as "Fourscore and seven years ago, our fathers" etc., etc. probably would.

Actually, it's kind of scary when you remember that all these men (Lincoln and Harding excluded) had their fingers on the button.

U.S. Presidents Are Not Elected by the People

The president and vice president are the only elected officials who are not elected by the people. They are actually elected the Electoral College—or, if none of the candidates get enough electoral votes, by the House of Representatives—which leads to some situations where the candidate receiving the most votes from the people might still lose the election. In fact, this has happened several times.

This is a bit complicated at first, but I hope you can bear with me. It's important for what comes later.

When people vote in a presidential election, they are not actually voting for the candidates, they are voting for the electors of the candidate's political party. Whichever party receives the most votes in a particular state gets to send all its electors to the Electoral College to represent the entire state. As a result, all the people who voted for the electors of the other political parties lose all of their influence in choosing the president. It's the same as if they didn't vote at all. For example, looking at figures from the 1984 Reagan/Mondale election, Mondale's party lost in California so Reagan's party grabbed up all the electoral votes, even though Mondale received 3,815,947 popular votes. These voters had absolutely no influence on the Electoral College, where the president is actually elected. In Wyoming, Reagan's party won a majority with 133,241 votes, giving him three electoral votes. So in the end, just over 100,000 voters got Reagan 3 electoral votes, whereas almost 4 million voters got Mondale zilch.

Since usually only about half of the eligible voters actually vote in presidential elections and these votes are divided between several candidates (or rather their parties), it's usually only a small fraction of the country's population that actually determines the winner.

Now let's look at the Electoral College itself. Since the Electoral College has 538 members, it actually only takes 270 votes to win the presidency. Although these members are elected by the people, they can legally vote for anyone they want. The only requirement is that each elector must vote for at least one candidate, president or vice president, that is not from that elector's home state. This is to prevent the president and vice president from being from the same state. Because electors can vote for anyone, there have been instances where some did vote for different candidates than the one to which they were pledged. So far this hasn't altered the outcome of an election, but that doesn't mean someday it won't.

The electoral votes are taken to Congress and counted on January 6. If none of the presidential candidates receives a majority, then the House of Representatives chooses the winner from the three top candidates. Each state is allowed to cast only one vote, and the majority of the state's representatives decide how that state will vote. Then the Senate chooses the vice president with each senator casting one vote.

In the election of 1800, Thomas Jefferson and Aaron Burr both received seventy-three electoral votes, so the decision went to the House of Representatives, and they chose Jefferson as president. Unfortunately, the popular vote for this election isn't known.

In 1824, Andrew Jackson received 50,551 more popular votes and 15 more electoral votes than his opponent, John Quincy Adams, but Adams won the election. Though Jackson got more electoral votes, it was not enough to constitute a majority because the votes were divided among several candidates, so the decision again went to the House, and they made Adams president.

In the 1876 election, Samuel J. Tilden got 250,807 more popular votes than Rutherford B. Hayes, and he got only one less electoral vote. He lost as well. In this election, fraud was suspected and the returns from Florida, Louisiana, South Carolina, and Oregon were contested, so Congress met in a joint session and chose Hayes as the winner.

Then in 1888, Benjamin Harrison won in the Electoral College with 233 votes, as opposed to Grover Cleveland's 168 votes, so Harrison won the presidency by 65 electoral votes, even though Cleveland got 95,703 more popular votes.

Recent discussions by Ross Perot and others about forming a third party greatly increase the likelihood the election will have to be decided by the House of Representatives, as those of 1800 and 1824 were, and as almost happened when Lincoln was first elected president. This makes some people very nervous. If an independent or a third-party candidate gets just enough electoral votes to prevent either of the other two candidates from getting the required majority of 270 votes out of the 538 and it goes to the House, then almost anything can happen. That wildcard candidate might even prevent the House from reaching an absolute majority, which means they'll have to keep voting until they can agree on someone.

Then there are other ways of becoming president that don't involve voting of any kind. Gerald Ford had never run in a presidential election before he became president, and he wasn't elected by either the Electoral College or the House of Representatives. He became the first nonelected vice president because of the resignation of Spiro Agnew and then became the first nonelected president—with Nelson Rockefeller as the second nonelected vice president—when Nixon resigned.

Fortunately, most of the time the Electoral College elects the person who receives the most popular votes. But this still doesn't change the fact that the president is not actually elected by the presidential election; nor does it change the fact that about 10 percent of our presidents attained that office without receiving a majority of the popular vote. There have been several attempts by Congress to alter or abolish the Electoral College, but so far all have failed. Basically, this is because smaller states have more power in choosing the president under the current system, and they don't want to give that up.

So the next time you get mad at the president, you can console yourself by remembering: He wasn't really elected by the people.

Nixon on Watergate

"I don't think you're going to see a great, great uproar in this country about the Republican committee trying to bug the Democratic headquarters."

—President Nixon, four days after the Watergate break-in

"No one in the White House staff, no one in this administration, presently employed, was involved in this very bizarre incident. . . . What really hurts in matters of this sort is not the fact that they occur, because overzealous people in campaigns do things that are wrong. What really hurts is if you try to cover it up."

—President Nixon

"I was not lying. I said things that later on seemed to be untrue."

—President Nixon in 1978

"I'd like to see people, instead of spending so much time on the ethical problem, get after the problems that really affect the people of this country."

—President Nixon

"What was Watergate? A little bugging!"

—President Nixon

"I was under medication when I made the decision not to burn the tapes."

—President Nixon

"Break into the place, rifle the files and bring them out."

—President Nixon, ordering aides to steal files from the Brookings Institution in 1971, one year before Watergate

"The President is guilty of misdemeanors. It is inherent in the office."

—Special White House consultant Leonard Garment on President Nixon's involvement in Watergate

Strange RELIGION

The X-Rated Bible

Originally, the Church didn't want the Bible to be translated into a language that everyone could read. As long as the Bible was available only in Latin translations, then only those who were taught Latin (and had been properly indoctrinated) could read it. Not only did the Church burn the first English translations of the Bible, it even burned one of the translators—William Tyndale. But all the Church's Bible burnings didn't help. English translations were soon readily available. Since then, some have believed that reading the Bible without first receiving the Holy Ghost (read "proper indoctrination") could cause insanity. As a result, the Bible has been one of the world's most banned and censored books. Part of the reason for all this fuss is that the Bible contains an awful lot of stuff that goes against what the Church teaches. And then there are some parts of it that completely contradict other parts. And not only that, there are also some parts that are downright pornographic. Understandably, the naughty bits are usually skipped over in church. So in the interest of providing you with a complete, well-rounded religious education, I have gathered some of the more unsavory portions. But remember, this is for educational purposes only. Don't try some of this stuff at home. It could land you in prison.

These quotations are all from the King James translation (1611) since it is the most widely used.[102]

Adultery

"Passing through the street near her corner; and he went the way to her house, In the twilight, in the evening, in the black and dark night: And, behold, there met him a woman with the attire of an harlot, and subtle of heart. (She is loud and stubborn; her feet abide not in her house: Now is she without, now in the streets, and lieth in wait at every corner.) So she caught him, and kissed him, and with an impudent face said unto him, I have peace offerings with me; this day have I payed my vows. Therefore came I forth to meet thee, diligently to seek thy face, and I have found thee. I have decked my bed with coverings of tapestry, with carved works, with fine linen of Egypt. I have perfumed my bed with myrrh, aloes, and cinnamon. Come, let us take our fill of love until the morning: let us solace ourselves with loves. For the goodman is not at home, he is gone a long journey: He hath taken a bag of money with him, and will come home at the day appointed. With her much fair speech she caused him to yield, with

[102] My thanks to Poppy Dixon and the PostFundamentalist Press for providing some of these quotations. She can be contacted at her Internet Web Site: www.postfun.com/pfp.

the flattering of her lips she forced him. He goeth after her straightway . . . " (Proverbs 7:8–22)

"And [King] David sent and inquired after the woman. And one said, Is not this Bathsheba, the daughter of Eliam, the wife of Uriah the Hittite? And David sent messengers, and took her; and she came in unto him, and he lay with her; for she was purified from her uncleanness [i.e. menstruation]: and she returned unto her house. And the woman conceived, and sent and told David, and said, I am with child." (2 Samuel 11:3–5)

"And it came to pass, when Israel dwelt in that land, Reuben [Jacob's son] went and lay with Bilhah his father's concubine and Israel [Reuben's grandfather] heard it." (Genesis 35:22)

Adultery and Possible Exhibitionism

"Thus saith the Lord, Behold, . . . I will take they wives before thine eyes, and give them unto thy neighbour, and he shall lie with they wives in the sight of this sun." (2 Samuel 12:11)

Adultery and Prostitution

" . . . they then committed adultery, and assembled themselves by troops in the harlots' houses. They were as fed horses in the morning: every one neighed after his neighbour's wife." (Jeremiah 5:7–8)

Anti-Family Values

"Think not that I [Jesus] am come to send peace on earth: I came not to send peace, but a sword. For I am come to set a man at variance against his father, and the daughter against her mother, and the daughter in law against her mother in law. And a man's foes shall be they of his own household." (Matthew 10:34–36)

"And call no man your father upon the earth: for one is your Father, which is in heaven." (Matthew 23:9)

"If any man come to me [Jesus], and hate not his father, and mother, and wife, and children, and brethren, and sisters, yea, and his own life also, he cannot be my disciple." (Luke 14:26)

Bigamy, Polygamy and Harems

[For Lamech's bigamy, see Genesis 4:19. For Abraham's concubines, see Genesis 16:3 and 25:6. For Nahor's wives and concubines, see Genesis 22:20–24. For Esau's three wives, see Genesis 36:2–3. For Gideon's wives and concubines, see Judges 8:30–31. For King David's wives and concubines, see 1 Samuel 25:39–44; 2 Samuel 3:2–5, 5:13, 12:24, 15:16; 1 Chronicles 3:1–9, 14:3 and others. For Belshazzar's wives and concubines, see Daniel 5:2–3. For Abijah's fourteen wives, see 2 Chronicles 13:21. For Rehoboam's eighteen wives and sixty concubines, see 2 Chronicles 11:21. Note that a concubine can either be a man's secondary wife—which is polygamy—or they would not be married and she would be more akin to a mistress—in which case it's adultery. If she's his slave, then it would be sexual slavery.]

"But king Solomon loved many strange women, together with the daughter of Pharaoh, women of the Moabites, Ammonites, Edomites, Zidonians, and Hittites; . . . And he had seven hundred wives, princesses, and three hundred concubines . . . " [He was quite the libidinous profligate, wasn't he?] (1 Kings 11:1, 3)

"If a man have two wives, one beloved, and another hated, and they have born him children . . . he shall acknowledge the son of the hated for the firstborn . . . " (Deuteronomy 21:15, 17)

Bigamy or Polygamy and Surrogate Mothers

[Jacob married Leah and her sister Rachel, but at first only Leah became pregnant.] "And when Rachel saw that she bare Jacob no children, Rachel envied her sister . . . And she said, Behold my maid Bilhah, go in unto her . . . And Bilhah conceived, and bare Jacob a son . . . And Bilhah conceived Rachel's maid again, and bare Jacob a second son. . . . When Leah saw that she had left bearing, she took Zilpah her maid, and gave her Jacob to wife. And Zilpah Leah's maid bare Jacob a son. . . . And Zilpah Leah's maid bare Jacob a second son." [And the pregnancy wars continued.] (Genesis 30:1, 3-5, 7, 9-10, 12)

[Abraham had a similar problem. See Genesis 16:1–4.]

Breasts

" . . . he shall lie all night betwixt my breasts." (The Song of Solomon 1:13)

"Let thy fountain be blessed: and rejoice with the wife of thy youth. Let her be as the loving hind and pleasant roe; let her breasts satisfy thee at all times; and be thou ravished always with her love." (Proverbs 5:18–19)

Breasts (Metaphorical)

"That ye may suck, and be satisfied with the breasts of her consolations; that ye may milk out, and be delighted with the abundance of her glory." (Isaiah 66:11)

Castration

"For there are some eunuchs, which were so born from their mother's womb: and there are some eunuchs, which were made eunuchs of men: and there be eunuchs, which have made themselves eunuchs for the kingdom of heaven's sake. He that is able to receive it, let him receive it." (Matthew 19:12)

"For thus saith the Lord unto the eunuchs . . . I will give them an everlasting name, that shall not be cut off." (Isaiah 56:4–5)

Child Murder

"And they came to the place which God had told him of; and Abraham built an altar there, and laid the wood in order, and bound Isaac his son, and laid him on the altar upon the wood. And Abraham stretched forth his hand, and took the knife to slay his son." [But he was stopped at the last minute.] (Genesis 22:9–10)

"And the king said, Bring me a sword. And they brought a sword before the king. And the king said, Divide the living child in two, and give half to the one [woman], and half to the other." (1 Kings 3:24–25)

[Here is the end of the psalm that begins, "By the rivers of Babylon. . . ."] "O daughter of Babylon, who art to be destroyed; happy shall he be that rewardeth thee as thou hast served us. Happy shall he be, that taketh and dasheth thy little ones against the stones." (Psalm 137:8–9)

"For every one that curseth his father or his mother shall be surely put to death . . . " (Leviticus 20:9)

Child Murder, Rape and Possible Pedophilia

[Following a battle with the Midianites, in which the Israelites had killed all the men and taken the women and children captive, Moses said,] "Now therefore kill every male among the little ones, and kill every women that hath known man by lying with him [i.e. kill all the prisoners except the female virgins]. But all the women children, that have not known a man by lying with him, keep alive for yourselves." (Numbers 31:17–18)

[After the tribe of Benjamin was wiped out except for six hundred men, the problem arose, what were these men to do for wives? It was decided the other tribes would attack the people of Jabesh-gilead and steal some women.] "And this is the thing that ye shall do, Ye shall utterly destroy every male, and every woman that hath lain by man. And they found among the inhabitants of Jabesh-gilead four hundred young virgins, that had known no man by lying with any male . . . " [But this was still not enough women.] "Therefore they commanded the children of Benjamin, saying Go and lie in wait in the vineyards; And see, and, behold, if the daughters of Shiloh come out to dance in dances, then come ye out of the vineyards, and catch you every man his wife of the daughters of Shiloh, and go to the land of Benjamin." [This was done, and so the Benjaminites took wives by force.] (Judges 21:11–12, 21)

One interesting law from Colonial Connecticut read, "If any Childe or Children above fifteen years old, *and of sufficient understanding, shall Curse or Smite their natural Father or Mother, he or they shall be put to death, unless it can be sufficiently testified, that the Parents have been unchristianly negligent in the education of such Children." Another Connecticut law read, "If any man have a stubborn or rebellious Son, of sufficient understanding and years,* viz. fifteen years of age, *which will not obey the voice of his Father, or the voice of his Mother, and that when they have chastened him, he will not hearken unto them; then may his Father and Mother, being his natural Parents, lay hold on him, and bring him to the magistrates assembled in Court, and testifie unto them, that their Son is Stubborn and Rebellious, and will not obey their voice and chastisement, but lives in sundry notorious Crimes, such a Son shall be put to death,* Deut. *21. 20.21."*

Child Prostitution?

"And they have cast lots for my people; and have given a boy for an harlot, and sold a girl for wine, that they might drink." (Joel 3:3)

Coitus Interruptus

"And Judah said unto Onan, Go in unto thy brother's wife, and marry her, and raise up seed to thy brother. And Onan knew that the seed should not be his; and it came to pass, when he went in unto his brother's wife, that he spilled it on the ground, lest that he should give seed to his brother." (Genesis 38:8–9) [The term *onanism* originated with this story. Its primary meaning is "coitus interruptus"—or pulling out just prior to ejaculation. But the term also means "masturbation," as we saw in Mark Twain's speech on this topic.]

Exhibitionism

"At the same time spake the Lord by Isaiah the son of Amoz, saying, Go and loose the sackcloth from off thy loins, and put off thy shoe from thy foot. And he did so, walking naked and barefoot. And the Lord said, Like as my servant Isaiah hath walked naked and barefoot three years for a sign and wonder upon Egypt and Ethiopia; So shall the king of Assyria lead away the Egyptians prisoners, and the Ethiopians captives, young and old, naked and barefoot, even with their buttocks uncovered, to the shame of Egypt." (Isaiah 20:2–4)

"And he [Saul] stripped off his clothes also, and prophesied before Samuel in like manner, and lay down naked all that day and all that night . . . " (1 Samuel 19:24)

" . . . I will go stripped and naked . . . " (Micah 1:8)

Exhibitionism (Metaphorical)

[And the Lord said,] "Behold, therefore I will gather all they lovers, with whom thou hast taken pleasure, and all them that thou hast loved, with all them that thou hast hated; I will even gather them round about against thee, and will discover thy nakedness unto them, that they may see all they nakedness." (Ezekiel 16:37)

Gang Rape, Homosexuality, Possible Polygamy and Murder

[A man and his concubine were traveling through an unfamiliar city and were going to sleep in the streets when they were taken into an old man's house as guests. Since the text refers to the man as "her husband," the concubine was his secondary wife.] "Now as they were making their hearts merry, behold, the men of the city, certain sons of Belial, beset the house round about, and beat at the door and spake to the master of the house, the old man, saying, Bring forth the man that came into thine house, that we may know him. And the man, the master of the house, went out unto them, and said unto them, Nay, my brethren, nay, I pray you, do not so wickedly; seeing that this man is come into mine house, do not this folly. Behold, here is my daughter a maiden, and his concubine; them I will bring out now, and humble ye them, and do with them what seemeth good unto you: but unto this man do not so vile a thing. But the men would not hearken to him: so the man took his concubine, and brought her forth unto them; and they knew her, and abused her all the night until the morning: and when the day began to spring, they let her go. Then came the woman in the dawning of the day, and fell down at the door of the man's house where her lord was, till it was light. And her lord rose up in the morning, and opened the doors of the house, and went out to go his way: and behold, the woman his concubine was fallen down at the door of the house, and her hands were upon the threshold. And he said unto her, Up, and let us be going. But none answered. Then the man took her up upon an ass, and the man rose up, and gat him unto his place. And when he was come into his house, he took a knife, and laid hold on his concubine, and divided her, together with her bones, into twelve pieces, and sent her into all the coasts of Israel." (Judges 19:22–29)

[Similarly, Lot offered his two daughters to a sex-crazed crowd in an attempt to spare two men from being gang raped in Genesis 19:8.]

Genitals

"When men strive together [fight] one with another, and the wife of the one draweth near for to deliver her husband out of the hand of him that smiteth him, and putteth forth her hand, and taketh him by the secrets [his genitals]: Then thou shalt cut off her hand, thine eye shall not pity her." [Note that the New International Version translates "taketh him by the secrets" as "seizes him by his private parts."] (Deuteronomy 25:11–12)

Genital Mutilation

"And Saul said, Thus shall ye say to David, The king desireth not any dowry, but an hundred foreskins of the Philistines, to be avenged of the king's enemies. . . . Wherefore David arose and went, he and his men, and slew of the Philistines two hundred men; and David brought their foreskins, and they gave them in full tale to the king, that he might be the king's son in law." (1 Samuel 18:25, 27)

"And Dinah the daughter of Leah, which she bare unto Jacob, went out to see the daughters of the land. And when Shechem the son of Hamor the Hivite, prince of the country, saw her, he took her, and lay with her, and defiled her. And his soul clave unto Dinah the daughter of Jacob, and he loved the damsel, and spake kindly unto the damsel. And Shechem spake unto his father Hamor, saying, Get me this damsel to wife. . . . [So they pleaded with the Israelites to allow the marriage.] And the sons of Jacob answered Shechem and Hamor his father deceitfully, and said, because he had defiled Dinah their sister: And they said unto them, we cannot do this thing, to give our sister to one that is uncircumcised; for that were a reproach unto us: But in this will we consent unto you: If ye will be as we be, that every male of you be circumcised; Then will we give our daughters unto you, and we will take your daughters to us . . . And their words pleased Hamor, and Shechem Hamor's son. And the young man deferred not to do the thing, because he had delight in Jacob's daughter: and he was more honourable than all the house of his father. . . . [So they went back and talked all of their men into doing this to themselves] and every male was circumcised, all that went out of the gate of his city. And it came to pass on the third day, when they were sore, that two of the sons of Jacob, Simeon and Levi, Dinah's brethren, took each man his sword, and came upon the city boldly, and slew all the males." [And they retrieved Dinah and took all the women and children prisoner. Note that there is nothing to indicate that Dinah was forced to have sex against her will. She may have fallen in love with the prince and wanted to marry him. So much for trying to do the "honorable thing," aye?] (Genesis 34:1–4, 13–16, 18–19, 24–25)

Harems and Pedophilia

[First a word about the following two texts. Although God is not mentioned in either Esther or the Song of Solomon, they do contain some sex. In fact, the Song of Solomon is the most erotic book in the Bible. Rabbinic writings indicate that when they were deciding which books were actually holy and which were not, there was quite a dispute over these two books and Ecclesiastes. There were also lesser disputes over Ezekiel, Proverbs, Ruth and Ecclesiasticus. In the end, only Ecclesiasticus didn't make it into the Old Testament—though the Roman Catholic Church, the Eastern Orthodox Church, and the Anglican Communion did include this and the other thirteen books of the Apocrypha in their Bible.[103] The primary objection to Esther and the Song of Solomon was that they lacked religious value, not mentioning God at all. And then there

[103] There was a similar disagreement over which New Testament books were actually holy. This time, 2 Peter, 2 and 3 John, James, and Jude were suspect. In the end, it was primarily their suitability for public reading in church that determined which ones made it. And there were many others that didn't.

was the heavily erotic tone—somewhat obscured in King James's version—of the Song of Solomon. In the end, it was argued that this book was not really a love poem between a King Solomon and his fiancée, but an allegory of God's love for Israel, and it was decided the book was holy after all. The Christians also had difficulty with the book's erotic nature and interpreted it as an allegory of Christ's love for the church. Reading through this book, one has to wonder how they ever came up with the allegory idea—especially when reading references to the harem (Song of Solomon 6:8) and such thinly shrouded sexual metaphors as "My beloved put in his hand by the hole of the door, and my bowels were moved for him. I rose up to open to my beloved; and my hands dropped with myrrh, and my fingers with sweet smelling myrrh, upon the handles of the lock. I opened to my beloved; but my beloved had withdrawn himself. . ." (Song of Solomon 5:4–6). But then, religions are full of such imponderables.

[The dialogue in the Song of Solomon actually shifts back and forth between the royal lover (Solomon), his fiancée/wife (the girl), and her friends and relatives. That this girl is prepubescent—as many marriages were at that time and still are in some parts of the world—is indicated in the verse where her relatives say of her, "We have a little sister, and she hath no breasts: what shall we do for our sister in the day when she shall be spoken for?" (The Song of Solomon 8:8) This is after the marriage has taken place in the royal palace and they are ratifying their love covenant in her family's home. Solomon would have been much older than her. And it should be remembered, as quoted earlier, that she was just one of his seven hundred wives and three hundred concubines.

"Reason is the greatest enemy that faith has: it never comes to the aid of spiritual things, but—more frequently than not—struggles against the divine Word, treating with contempt all that emanates from God."

—Reverend Dr. Martin Luther, Table Talk *(1569).*

[The book of Esther tells of how the King of Persia (which is now Iran) decided to get rid of his queen. He needed a replacement, so he had all the "fair young virgins" gathered from all over the land so he could choose one as his new queen. A young Jewish girl named Esther quickly caught his fancy, but he wanted to try out all the virgins before he made his decision.] "Then thus came every maiden unto the king; whatsoever she desired was given her to go with her out of the house of the women [the harem] unto the king's house. In the evening she went, and on the morrow she returned into the second house of the women [a different harem so she wouldn't be brought to the king again by accident], to the custody of Shaashgaz, the king's chamberlain [eunuch], which kept the concubines: she came in unto the king no more, except the king delighted in her, and that she were called by name. . . . So Esther was taken unto king Ahasuerus into his house royal . . . And the king loved Esther above all the women . . . " [She became the new queen and later saved the Jews from an attempted genocide.] (Esther 2:13–14, 16, 17)

Homosexuality

"And it came to pass, when he [David] had made an end of speaking unto Saul, that the soul of Jonathan was knit with the soul of David, and Jonathan loved him as his own soul. . . . And Jonathan and David made a covenant, because he loved him as his own soul." (1 Samuel 18:1, 3)

"Then Saul's anger was kindled against Jonathan, and he said unto him, Thou son of the perverse rebellious woman, do not I know that thou hast chosen the son of Jesse [i.e. David] to thine own confusion, and unto the confusion of thy mother's nakedness?" (1 Samuel 20:30)

" . . . they [David and Jonathan] kissed one another, and wept one with another . . . " (1 Samuel 20:41)

[Following Jonathan's death, David said,] "I am distressed for thee, my brother Jonathan: very pleasant hast thou been unto me: thy love to me was wonderful, passing the love of women." (2 Samuel 1:26)

King James I (1566-1625), who was responsible for the most widely used translation of the Bible—the King James Version—was gay and fell in love with several young men. In 1607, the forty-one-year-old king began a relationship with the penniless seventeen-year-old Robert Carr, which lasted for about seven years. In that time, Carr became a wealthy earl and was married. After his relationship with the king hit the rocks, both he and his wife were imprisoned in the Tower of London. They were sentenced to death, but the king commuted their sentence, and they remained in the Tower for six years.

Impotence

"Now king David was old and stricken in years; and they covered him with clothes, but he gat no heat. Wherefore his servants said unto him, Let there be sought for my lord the king a young virgin: and let her stand before the king, and let her cherish him, and let her lie in thy bosom, that my lord the king may get heat. So they sought for a fair damsel throughout all the coasts of Israel, and found Abishag a Shunammite, and brought her to the king. And the damsel was very fair, and cherished the king, and ministered to him: but the king knew her not." (1 Kings 1:1–4)

Incest

"And Lot went up out of Zoar, and dwelt in the mountain, and his two daughters with him; for he feared to dwell in Zoar: and he dwelt in a cave, he and his two daughters. And the firstborn said unto the younger, Our father is old, and there is not a man in the earth to come in unto us after the manner of all the earth: Come, let us make our father drink wine, and we will lie with him, that we may preserve seed of our father. And they made their father drink wine that night; and the firstborn went in, and lay with her father; and he perceived not when she lay down, nor when she arose. And it came to pass on the morrow, that the firstborn said unto the younger, Behold, I lay yesternight with my father: let us make him drink wine this night also; and go thou in, and lie with him, that we may preserve seed of our father. And they made their father drink wine that night also: and the younger arose, and lay with him; and he perceived not when she lay down, nor when she arose. Thus were both the daughters of Lot with child by their father." (Genesis 19:30–36)

[Incest is implied in Adam and Eve's family since their sons had no one else to marry but their own sisters. Such intermarriage is also implied in Noah's family.]

Incest and Rape

"And it came to pass . . . that Absalom the son of David had a fair sister, whose name was Tamar; and Amnon the son of David loved her. And Amnon was so vexed, that he fell sick for his sister Tamar; for she was a virgin; and Amnon thought it hard for him to do any thing to her. . . . So Amnon lay down, and made himself sick: and when the king was come to see him, Amnon said unto the king, I pray thee, let Tamar my sister come, and make me a couple of cakes in my sight, that I may eat at her hand. . . . And when she had brought them unto him to eat, he took hold of her, and said unto her, Come lie with me, my sister. And she answered him, Nay, my brother, do not force me; for no such thing ought to be done in Israel: do not thou this folly. And I, whither shall I cause my shame to go? and as for thee, thou shalt be as one of the fools in Israel. Now therefore, I pray thee, speak unto the king; for he will not withhold me from thee. Howbeit he would not harken unto her voice: but being stronger than she, forced her, and lay with her. Then Amnon hated her exceedingly; so that the hatred wherewith he hated her was greater than his love wherewith he had loved her. And Amnon said unto her, Arise, be gone. And she said unto him, There is no cause: this evil in sending me away is greater than the other that thou didst unto me. But he would not harken unto her. Then he called his servant that ministered unto him, and said, Put now this woman out from me, and bolt the door after her." (2 Samuel 13:1–2, 6, 11–17)

Live Sex Show and Either Adultery or Incest

[After King David left his palace in the care of ten of his concubines, his rebellious son, Absalom, decided to try to take over the kingdom.] "Then said Absalom to Ahithophel, Give counsel among you what we shall. And Ahithophel said unto Absalom, Go in unto thy father's concubines, which he hath left to keep the house; and all Israel shall hear that thou art abhorred of they father: then shall the hands of all that are with thee be strong. So they spread Absalom a tent upon the top of the house; and Absalom went in unto his father's concubines in the sight of all Israel." [If David was not married to these concubines, then Absalom was also committing adultery. But if they were some of David's secondary wives, then Absalom was having sex with his some of his step-mothers. Absalom later died in battle and David imprisoned these women for the rest of their lives. The text says their life sentences were spent "living in widowhood," suggesting they were indeed secondary wives.] (2 Samuel 16:20–22, 20:3)

"But as an adolescent I had prayed a pitiful prayer for a clean life, saying, 'Give me chastity and give me control over myself, but not yet.' I was afraid you [God] might answer me too quickly and straighten me out before I was ready; for what I really wanted was not to be cured but to be fulfilled."

—*St. Augustine,* Confessions *A.D. 398–400).*

Mud and Watersports

"But Rab-shakeh said unto them, Hath my master sent me to thy master, and to thee, to speak these words? hath he not sent me to the men which sit on the wall, that they may eat their own dung, and drink their own piss with you?" (II Kings 18:27, Isaiah 36:12)

Prostitution

"Then went Samson to Gaza, and saw there an harlot, and went in unto her. . . . And Samson lay till midnight, and arose at midnight . . . " (Judges 16:1, 3)

"And Joshua the son of Nun sent out of Shittim two men to spy secretly, saying, Go view the land, even Jericho. And they went, and came into an harlot's house, named Rahab, and lodged there." (Joshua 2:1)

"When Judah saw her [Tamar, Judah's daughter-in-law in disguise], he thought her to be a harlot; because she had covered her face. And he turned unto her by the way, and said, Go to, I prey thee, let me come in unto thee; (for he knew not that she was his daughter in law.) And she said, What wilt thou give me, that thou mayest come in unto me? And he said, I will send thee a kid from the flock. And she said, Wilt thou give me a pledge, till thou send it? And he said, What pledge shall I give thee? And she said, Thy signet, and they bracelets, and they staff that is in thine hand. And he gave it her, and came in unto her, and she conceived by him. . . . And it came to pass about three months after, that it was told Judah, saying, Tamar thy daughter in law hath played the harlot; and also, behold, she is with child by whoredom. And Judah said, Bring her forth, and let her be burnt." [Of course, he changed his mind when he found out he was the father.] (Genesis 38:15–18, 24)

[And the Lord said,] "I will not punish your daughters when they commit whoredom, nor your spouses when they commit adultery: for themselves are separated with harlots: therefore the people that doth not understand shall fall." (Hosea 4:14)

Rape

[The laws in Deuteronomy 23:25–29 state that if a man rapes a young woman who is engaged to be married, he shall be executed. But if she doesn't have a fiancée, then he shall marry her—in other words, she will be forced to marry her rapist. The idea behind this is that since such importance was placed on a woman's virginity as a prerequisite for marriage, no one else would want her after she was raped. Although a woman needed to keep proof she was a virgin when she married—usually a bloody cloth from her nuptial bed—the man's virginity was not considered important.]

Ritual Child Genital Mutilation

"And he that is eight days old shall be circumcised among you . . . " (Genesis 17:12)

Sexual Metaphors

"The word of the Lord came again unto me saying, Son of man, there were two women, the daughters of one mother: And they committed whoredoms in Egypt; they committed whoredoms in their youth: there were their breasts pressed, and there they bruised the teats of their virginity. . . . And Aholah played the harlot when she was mine; and she doted on her lovers, on the Assyrians her neighbours . . . Neither left she her whoredoms brought from Egypt: for in her youth they lay with her, and they bruised the breasts of her virginity, and poured their whoredom upon her. . . . And when her sister Aholibah saw this, she was more corrupt in her inordinate love than she, and in her whoredoms more than her sister in her whoredoms. . . . And the Babylonians came to her into the bed of love, and they defiled her with their whoredom, and she was polluted with them, and her mind was alienated from them. So she discovered her whoredoms, and discovered her nakedness: . . . Yet she multiplied her whoredoms, in calling to remembrance the days of her youth, wherein she had played the harlot in the land of Egypt. . . . Thus thou calledst to remembrance the lewdness of thy youth, in bruising thy teats by the Egyptians for the paps of thy youth. . . . Thus will I make thy lewdness to cease from thee and thy whoredom brought from the land of Egypt . . . and shall leave thee naked and bare and the nakedness of thy whoredoms shall be discovered both thy lewdness and thy whoredoms. . . . Thou shalt even drink it [i.e. the cup of astonishment and desolation] and suck it out, and thou shalt break the sherds thereof, and pluck off thine own breasts: for I have spoken it, saith the Lord God. . . . Then said I unto her that was old in adulteries, Will they now commit whoredoms with her and she with them? Yet they went in unto her, as they go in unto a woman that playeth the harlot: so went they in unto Aholah and unto Aholibah, the lewd women." (Ezekiel 23:1–3, 5, 8, 11, 17–19, 21, 27, 29, 34, 43–44)

Sexual Slavery

"When thou goest forth to war against thine enemies, and the Lord thy God hath delivered them into thine hands, and thou hast taken them captive, And seest among the captives a beautiful woman, and hast a desire unto her, that thou wouldst have her to thy wife; Then thou shalt bring her home to thine house . . . and after that, thou shalt go in unto her, and be her husband, and she shall be thy wife. And it shall be, if thou have no delight in her, then thou shalt let her go whither she will; but thou shalt not sell her at all for money, thou shalt not make merchandise of her, because thou hast humbled her." [Obviously, she has no choice in the matter.] (Deuteronomy 21: 10–14)

"And whosoever lieth carnally with a woman, that is a bondmaid, betrothed to an husband, and not at all redeemed, nor freedom given her; she shall be scourged; they shall not be put to death, because she was not free." (Leviticus 19:20)

Unwed Teen Pregnancy

[As one wise guy put it, "The virgin Mary should have just said no and waited until she finished school and gotten married."]

Voyeurism

"And it came to pass in an eveningtide, that David arose from off his bed, and walked upon the roof of the king's house: and from the roof he saw a woman washing herself; and the woman was very beautiful to look upon." (2 Samuel 11:2)

"Woe unto him that giveth his neighbour drink, that puttest thy bottle to him, and makest him drunken also, that thou mayest look on their nakedness! Thou art filled with shame for glory: drink thou also, and let thy foreskin be uncovered . . . " (Habakkuk 2:15–16)

Who's the Antichrist?

During the late-1970s, some born-again Christians became convinced Henry Kissinger was the Antichrist prophesied in the Book of

Revelation. As proof, they pointed out that if you assign a number to each letter of the alphabet—A=1, B=2, C=3, and so on—and you convert "Kissinger" into numbers and add them together, then you come up with 111. And if you multiply this by 6, then you get the 666 mentioned in Revelation 13:18 as the number of the beast (the Antichrist).

Around the mid-1980s, they had decided President Reagan was actually the Antichrist. Since his names, Ronald Wilson Reagan, each have six letters, so once again you have 666. It was also about this time that Universal Product Code (UPC) seals were appearing on products and merchandise throughout the country, and some saw these as the Mark of the Beast, noting they use three sixes to separate other numbers in the bar code (though this only applies to one of the two popular types of UPCs and it's not actually 6-6-6, but 06-60-66). And then some people assigned numbers to letters—as they did with Kissinger—and found that when they add up the word *computer* and multiply it by 6, it also adds up to the dreaded 666.

By the mid-1990s, some Christian fundamentalists, including former presidential candidate Pat Robertson, were saying that Mario Cuomo was the Antichrist, pointing out that "Mario Cuomo" and "Antichrist" both have ten letters. Others suggested it was actually Bill Gates, because if you take the ASCII-values of "Bill Gates III" and add them, you get 66+73+76+76+71+65+84+69+83+1+1+1=666 (though "the third" should be III, not 111). Plus, if you do the same with "MS-DOS 6.21" or with "Windows 95" (if you add a 1 to it), you also come up with 666. Then some people hinted that President Clinton might be the Antichrist. According to evangelist Tex Marrs, "He wants to turn America's public schools into occult, black magic laboratories."

Other supposed Antichrists include Nero, Attila the Hun, Genghis Khan, Merlin, all of the popes (especially Pope Boniface VIII and Pope John XXII), Frederick II, Napoleon, Kaiser Wilhelm II, Adolf Hitler, and Mikhael Gorbachev (because of the "mark" on his forehead). There were also times when two religious groups would each claim that the other was the Antichrist.

Some people have even said that *they* were the Antichrist. Probably the most famous of these was the occult figure Aleister Crowley, who earned himself the nickname "the Beast." And then Johnny Rotten (née John Lydon), the lead vocalist of the Sex Pistols, sang "I am an antichrist. I am an anarchist."

Mormon Polygamy

Mormonism is a relatively new religion having been founded in 1830 by twenty-four-year-old Joseph Smith, Jr. (1805–1844). He claimed that between 1823 and 1827, God the Father and Jesus Christ appeared to him, along with an angel named Moroni who led him to some ancient gold plates that were buried under a rock in a New York forest. Using special translating spectacles called Urim and Thummim that were buried with the plates, he was able to decipher their strange characters, dictating them to several of his followers from behind a sheet, so as to keep the plates hidden. The results were published as the *Book of Mormon* in 1830. Moroni took back the plates, though eleven of Smith's friends and relatives later testified that they saw them.

There is another version of the origin of the *Book of Mormon*. In 1812 Reverend Solomon Spaulding, a Presbyterian minister and Dartmouth graduate, was inspired by an archaeological excavation in Ohio to write a historical novel about the discovery of some ancient plates that told of how the lost tribes of Israel had ended up in ancient America. Before he died, Reverend Spaulding left copies of the manuscript with his wife and a Pittsburgh bookseller. Then in 1825, while Joseph Smith was working as a well-digger for the next-door neighbor of Spaulding's wife, her copy of the manuscript disappeared. After reading the *Book of Mormon*, she accused Joseph Smith of plagiarism and at least eight of Spaulding's relatives and neighbors gave affidavits and statements to this affect. Mormons say they were influenced by an ex-Mormon with a grudge.

The Book of Mormon is a history of the lost tribes of Israel from 600 B.C. to A.D. 421. It describes how the tribes migrated from Babylon and Jerusalem to ancient America and how they fought each other through continual wars. It also tells how Jesus Christ, after his resurrection, descended from heaven in ancient America in order to present his teachings to the rest of the chosen people though most of them eventually rejected it. The Native Americans are supposed to be the descendants of the Israelite tribe called Lamanites—whose skins were darkened by apostasy. According to Mormon prophecy, they will eventually be converted and once again become "a white and delightsome people" (II Nephi 30:6). The Mormons also believe that the church Jesus established in the New Testament did not survive in its original form, which is why it had to be reestablished in 1830. This is also why it's called the Church of Jesus Christ of Latter-Day Saints.

Characters on one of the golden plates from which the Book of Mormon *was transcribed from. (above)*

One of six additional plates Joseph Smith said were revealed to him at Kinderhook, Illinois, in 1843. These were bell shaped and made of brass. Smith said they were a history of a descendent of Ham. (below)

Oddly, but not surprisingly, the *Book of Mormon* is written in something of a pseudo-sixteenth-century King James English, with lots of *thee*s and *thou*s, and tons of and *it came to passe*s. "The book is a curiosity to me," wrote Mark Twain, "it is such a pretentious affair, and yet so 'slow,' so sleepy, such an insipid mess of inspiration. It is chloroform in print. If Joseph Smith composed this book, the act was a miracle—keeping awake while he did it was, at any rate. . . . The book seems to be merely a prosy detail of imaginary history, with the Old Testament for a model; followed by a tedious plagiarism of the New Testament." Twain also points out that if Smith had left out all the and it *came to passes*, "his Bible would have been only a pamphlet."

Here is a sample from the very aptly named *Book of Ether:*

> And it came to pass that in the first year of Lib, Coriantumr came up unto the land of Moron, and gave battle unto Lib. And it came to pass that he fought with Lib, in which Lib did smite upon his arm that he was wounded; nevertheless, the army of Coriantumr did press forward upon Lib, that he fled to the borders upon the seashore. And it came to pass that Coriantumr pursued him; and Lib gave battle unto him upon the seashore. And it came to pass that Lib did smite the army of Coriantumr, that they fled again to the wilderness of Akish. And it came to pass that Lib did pursue him until he came to the plains of Agosh. And Coriantumr had taken all the people with him as he fled before Lib in that quarter of the land whither he fled. And when he had come to the plains of Agosh he gave battle unto Lib, and he smote upon him until he died; nevertheless, the brother of Lib did come against Coriantumr in the stead thereof, and the battle became exceeding sore, in the which Coriantumr fled again before the army of the brother of Lib. Now the name of the brother of Lib was called Shiz. And it came to pass . . . (Ether 14:11–17)

Mormon scriptures include two other books. *Doctrine and Covenants* is a collection of revelations made by God to Joseph Smith, and the *Pearl of Great Price* contains Smith's writings and some more translations of ancient records. The Bible is also considered sacred, though Joseph Smith revised it and published his version as *The Inspired Version.*

Here is a brief outline of a few other Mormon beliefs: God the Father is a flesh-and-bone person with a glorified body. He created Jesus and then the rest of the human race as His spirit-children, though Jesus was the only one to be born by the father in the flesh. Jesus is also God, and he's the one who created the world, under the Father's direction. The Holy Ghost is a spirit being without a flesh-and-bone body. All non-Mormons (including Jews) are Gentiles. People existed as spiritual infants before being born, waiting for a body. On a person's death, that person moves back into a spirit existence until the body is physically resurrected. Those who aren't called to the church during their lifetime, will have their chance while in this state. Through the church, the saints are progressing toward a godlike existence and will ultimately have a heaven of their own to rule. This is summarized in their phrase, "As man is, God once was; as God is, man may become." This evolution includes God, who was at one time himself a man and who is just one among many gods with many heavens.

The temples are essential for many Mormon ceremonies, such as the baptism of the dead by proxy, marriages of the dead and the sealing of eternal marriages. Some of their ceremonies contain elements lifted from Masonry.[104]

After founding the church, Smith attempted to build the new Kingdom of Zion four times in various places. Financial difficulties and dissension lead to the first failure. The other three times, they were chased out by their neighbors. At the last of these places, a newspaper published a sensational story about how women were being brought over

104 Joseph Smith had once been a Mason, though the *Book of Mormon* condemns such secret fraternities.

from other countries and ordered by Smith to have sex with him "or be damned to hell." After Smith—who was then running for president—and his men destroyed the press, non-Mormons rose up in fury. Smith was arrested for inciting a riot, but the charge was later changed to treason.

While he was in jail, a lynch mob broke into his cell. Smith wounded three of them with a gun one of his supporters had smuggled in to him. He then quickly crawled out a window onto the second-story ledge where he was hit by gunfire from both inside the jail and from the crowd below. Some said he was dead before he hit the ground. Others said he was still alive, so they propped him up and had a firing squad of four men execute him. His brother was also killed at this time.

After many more of his followers were executed, Brigham Young finally led the rest of them into Native American territory and settled at the Great Salt Lake to get out of the United States. This was in 1847. The following year, the United States won the Mexican War and obtained what would become Texas, New Mexico, Arizona, California, Nevada, Utah, and part of Colorado from Mexico. The Mormons then tried to establish their own state called Deseret, but Congress made it the Territory of Utah instead, and President Fillmore appointed Brigham Young as governor.

"I do not think that he believes in his own religion."

—Ann-Eliza Young referring to her husband, Brigham Young

Shortly after arriving at the desolate Salt Lake, a group of the struggling Mormons attacked a wagon train of settlers and murdered 120 men, women, and children. This became known as the Mountain Meadow Massacre. Only one of the culprits was executed as a scapegoat. Then in 1857, after appointing a non-Mormon as territorial governor, President Buchanan had to invade Utah with 1,500 troops in order to restore U.S. authority.

But probably the most sensational circumstance surrounding the Mormons involved their doctrine of polygamy. This set them completely at odds with intensely monogamous mainstream Christianity.

Polygamy—or as they prefer to call it, plural marriage or celestial marriage—was publicly announced by Brigham Young in 1852, though he insisted it actually began in secret nine years earlier when Joseph Smith received a revelation from the Lord (i.e., Jesus) commanding him to take more wives.

Establishing polygamy as Church doctrine was a bit tricky since the *Book of Mormon* contains only admonishments against it. For example, Jacob 2:24 and 27 says, "Behold, David and Solomon truly had many wives and concubines, which thing was abominable before me, saith the Lord. . . . Wherefore, my brethren, hear me, and hearken to the word of the Lord: For there shall not any man among you have save it be one wife; and concubines he shall have none."[105]

But Mormon leaders cited the examples of polygamy in the Old Testament, adding that in a previous existence, Adam had many wives and that Eve was one of them. Ann-Eliza Young, one of Brigham's many wives, says that in one sermon, Brigham Young declared that even Jesus Christ was a polygamist, that Mary Magdalen was one of

---

105 For other examples, see Jacob 1:15, 3:5; Mosiah 11:–4, 14 and Ether 10:5–7.

his wives, as were the sisters of Lazarus, Mary and Martha, and that the bridal feast where Jesus turned the water into wine was actually one of his own marriages.

Convincing the church of his new doctrine was tough, but Joseph Smith also had his wife to contend with. She was very much against the idea and it's said when Smith showed her the original revelation, she destroyed it by throwing it on the fire.[106] It survived only because another church leader had made a copy. Smith's marriage wasn't going too well, and at one point he said God told him to offer his wife a divorce, but later he backpeddled, saying God was just testing them.

Smith had anticipated her reaction to the revelation, for the revelation contained a couple of sections directed specifically at her. One part reads, "And I command mine handmaid Emma Smith to abide and cleave unto my servant Joseph, and to none else. But if she will not abide this commandment, she shall be destroyed, saith the Lord; for I am the Lord thy God, and will destroy her if she abide not in my law."

Convincing the other wives was a bit easier. As Ann-Eliza Young wrote in her exposé on plural marriages titled *Wife No. 19* (1875):

> They appealed to women through their maternal as well as through their religious natures. Not only did they teach them that they could never be saved except by the intervention of some man, who should take upon himself the duty of resurrecting them at the last day, but they were also told that floating through space were thousands of infant spirits, who were waiting for bodies; that into every child that was born one of these spirits entered, and was thereby saved; but if they had no bodies given them, their wails of despair would ring through all eternity; and that it was, in order to insure their future happiness, necessary that as many of them as possible should be given bodies by Mormon parents. If a woman refused to marry into polygamy, or, being married, to allow her husband to take other wives, these spirits would rise up in judgment against her, because she had, by her act, kept them in darkness.

The revelation also said, " . . . behold, I reveal unto you a new and everlasting covenant, and if ye abide not that covenant, then are ye damned . . . he that receiveth a fulness thereof must and shall abide the law, or he shall be damned, saith the Lord God."

Ann-Eliza Young's father, Chauncey G. Webb, said to his doctor on his deathbed in 1903, "No matter what the Church authorities tell you to do—do it. If it's right, it's right. If it's wrong, they'll be accountable, not you."

Ultimately, the women had very little choice in the matter. They'd been taught Smith's revelations came directly from God and disobeying them was unthinkable. For those who did think about it and might have decided this idea wasn't

106 After her husband's death, Emma Smith split off from Brigham Young's brand of Mormonism and with her son formed the Reorganized Church of Jesus Christ of Latter-Day Saints, which today has a U.S. membership of about 200,000. The courts have recognized this as the actual successor to the church founded by Joseph Smith, making Brigham Young's church a splinter group from the original Mormon church. There are several other small splinter groups.

divinely inspired after all, even if they were willing to risk eternal damnation and possible physical destruction, it meant being booted out of the Church. It must be remembered, these women were stuck in a religious community out in the middle of nowhere where they would be heavily slandered and ostracized. Most of them had no place else to go to and no means of getting anywhere. If they thought of it, they might possibly get assistance from other churches or the military, but then what? It also meant leaving their family, friends, and everyone they knew.

No one knows how many wives Joseph Smith ended up with, but Mormons place the number between twenty-eight and forty-nine. As for Brigham Young, when Ann-Eliza Young designated herself wife number nineteen, she wasn't counting any of his wives who had died or who didn't live in one of his several houses. Some say she was actually his twenty-seventh wife, while the Church's Genealogical Society roster lists her as wife number fifty out of a total of fifty-two.[107] It's unlikely Brigham Young even knew how many wives he had.

Ann-Eliza tells how once "Brigham met a lady in the streets of Salt Lake City . . . who recognized him, and addressed him as Brother Young, greeting him quite cordially. He scrutinized her closely, with a puzzled expression. 'I know I have seen you somewhere,' he said; 'your face is very familiar, but I cannot recall you.' 'You are right,' replied she; 'you have most certainly seen me before; I was married to you ten years ago. I have never seen you since,' she continued, 'but my memory is more retentive than yours, for I knew you the moment I saw you.'"

107 He married thirty-one of his wives in 1846 and seven of them on the same day.

"There is one advantage in a plurality of wives; they fight each other instead of their husbands."

—Humorist Josh Billings, who also said, "All girls marry Young—in Utah."

Part of the problem in determining the number of wives comes from the fact that the Mormons had several different types of marriages. First of all, all marriages not performed by the Church were not recognized. In addition, all contracts—including marital contracts—made prior to Smith's "Celestial Marriage" revelation were declared null and void by the revelation unless they were ratified by him. This even applied to Smith's first marriage though his wife chose to remarry him rather than face destruction by Jesus.

A Mormon woman's first sanctified marriage was considered to be eternal, meaning that her husband would still be her husband in the afterworld. A second type of marriage was for their time on earth only. This occurred when a woman's eternal husband died and she remarried. Thirteen of Brigham Young's wives were for life only because they had previous husbands, and eight of these were official widows of Joseph Smith.

A third type of marriage was in name only. The husband wanted these spiritual marriages to build up his heavenly kingdom, and as mentioned earlier, women needed a spiritually powerful man to resurrect them in their glorified bodies and to protect them in the afterworld. No sex was involved here, and these "wives" didn't live with their "husbands." This is why some people say Brigham Young only had twenty-seven "real wives" out of the fifty-two—the rest being these spiritual wives.

Then there are marriages of the dead. Here, someone can stand in for the dead person and be baptized or married for them. In this way, a woman who had ended her earthly existence could be sealed to a powerful husband for eternity. These marriages probably aren't included in most of the listings of wives.

Of course, the polygamy doctrine applied only to men. Polyandry—a woman having more than one husband—was definitely out of the question. A man could have a harem, but a woman had to be monogamous.

The Mormon practice of polygamy offended so many non-Mormons that Congress decided to put a stop to it by passing the Antibigamy Act in 1862. With the Constitution in mind, Congress had to first decide whether or not it had the authority to interfere with people's private lives. Because of their uncertainty, this act was rather weak.

"Is it not true . . . that marriage is the basis of society? . . . And is it not therefore within the legitimate scope of the power of every civil government to determine whether marriage shall be polygamous or monogamous under its dominion?"

—Colonel O. J. Hollister, the Federal Revenue Collector for Utah, 1879

By the 1880s, Congress was a little more sure of its authority to limit people's personal freedoms and the Antibigamy Act was supplemented by additional, much stricter, laws in 1882 and 1887. As a result, more than 900 Mormon men and women were imprisoned, church property was confiscated and many Church leaders—including Prophet John Taylor, Brigham Young's successor—went into hiding. Finally, in 1890, the government placed enough pressure on the Church to force their fourth Prophet, Wilford Woodruff, to renounce polygamy as a church doctrine. Though the church was now officially against plural marriages, the practice continued in secret, and apparently, while in hiding, Prophet John Taylor received a revelation from God to continue plural marriages.

Irving Wallace, in *The Twenty-seventh Wife* (1961), wrote, "In 1959 a high official of the Mormon Church admitted to this writer that there were 2,000 polygamists in Salt Lake City; an attorney connected with the city administration placed the figure at closer to 5,000 polygamists [scattered throughout the country]." It's estimated that today there are between 25,000 and 35,000 polygamous marriages in the United States (not all of them Mormon), while a survey of 437 financially successful men revealed that some maintained two separate families that were completely ignorant of one another.

"Brigham Young has pleaded that he is living in a condition of mystical concubinage. A United States court confirms that view, so far as the concubinage is concerned."

— New York Times, *May 2, 1877*

Obviously, polygamy didn't agree with Ann-Eliza Young. At one lecture she said, "I was neglected, insulted and humiliated in every way imaginable, and I saw that it was impossible for me to ever interest my husband." Not surprisingly, she finally decided to file for a divorce.

This prompted the *San Francisco Chronicle* to aptly describe her as the "unfortunate victim of too much matrimony."

Today, there are more than 4 million Mormons in the United States.

Rev. Dr. Martin Luther and the Fairy Changeling

Belief in the actual existence of fairies still exists today. I happen to know a couple of people who believe in them, and I know of many more believers. The two I know personally both live in England and are serious

Brigham Young (top) and a few of his wives. Ann-Eliza is pictured immediately to the right.

and intelligent individuals. But believers aren't restricted to the United Kingdom by a long shot. There are also many in the United States, Canada, Australia, and throughout the rest of the world. Because most of society associates fairies with childhood fantasy, these believers—with a few brave exceptions—tend to keep their beliefs to themselves to avoid ridicule. (Oddly, the similar belief in angels is widely accepted. Go figure.)

Reverend Dr. Martin Luther never nailed his ninety-five theses to a church door according to scholar Erwin Iserloh. What he really did was make a few copies and pass them around for his friends to read. Later on, after he left the Church, he helped kidnap a dozen nuns from the Nibschen convent and smuggled them off in a herring wagon (some say in herring barrels). He did this to free them so they could get married . . . and he married one of them himself—Katherine von Bora—in 1525.

Some of the more illustrious believers include Sir Arthur Conan Doyle (1859–1930, the creator and author of the Sherlock Holmes mysteries) and Nobel Prize winner William Butler Yeats (1865–1939, the Irish poet, author and playwright, who was also a member of the Irish Senate). William Blake (1757–1827, the famous English writer, poet, and painter) once turned to a woman who happened to be sitting next to him and asked, "Did you ever see a fairy's funeral, Madam?" to which she quickly replied, "Never, Sir!" "I have," he said, "but not before last night. I was walking alone in my garden [in London], there was a great stillness among the branches and flowers and more than common sweetness in the air; I heard a low pleasant sound, and I knew not whence it came. At last I saw the broad leaf of a flower move, and underneath I saw a procession of creatures of the size and colour of green and grey grasshoppers, bearing a body laid out on a rose leaf, which they buried with songs, and then disappeared. It was a fairy funeral." Blake also said his book, *Europe: A Prophecy*, was dictated to him by a fairy he found sitting on a tulip.

In the past, the fairy faith was much more common than it is today. The beliefs have evolved somewhat over the years. Although today's view of fairies as elemental nature spirits has existed for centuries, the fairy faith of old also included a broad spectrum of many other types of fairies—most of them extremely dangerous. Not only did they maim, torture, and kill people, some would torment people to insanity. Dogs that chased them were said to return with all of their fur ripped off their bodies. Few dogs suffering this punishment survived more than a couple days in agony. Another punishment was being pinched by fairies. This is often looked upon today with mild amusement, but it was actually described as a very painful ordeal resulting in huge welts and bruises. It was said to be similar to being stung by a hoard of wasps.

Christians were once commonly anti-Semitic, blaming Jews for killing Christ. This included the Reverend Dr. Martin Luther, who some consider to be the father of German anti-Semitism. He wrote in "On the Jews and Their Lies" (1543), "First, their synagogues should be set on fire, and whatever does not burn up should be covered or spread over with dirt so that no one may ever be able to see a cinder or stone of it." He went on to say that their homes should also be destroyed and they should "be put under one roof, or in a stable, like Gypsies, in order that they may realize that they are not masters in our land." But if they were still considered to be too dangerous after this, then these "poisonous bitter worms" should be stripped of their belongings "which they have extorted usuriously from us" and be driven out of the country "for all time."

Sentiments that would make Hitler proud, coming from the man who probably had a greater influence than anyone on modern Chistianity. Unfortunately, all these Jew-hating so-called Christians conveniently forgot that Christ and all of his apostles were Jewish.

It was also commonly believed that the fairies would kidnap people as servants or human lovers or to increase their numbers. Because of their fascination with youth and beauty, when it came to increasing their numbers they almost exclusively chose infants and children. Those chosen would wither and die with their spirit going to the fairies, or they would be replaced by a changeling. There were basically two types of changelings. One was a fairy child, which either the fairy mother hoped would be raised by humans or was too ugly to remain with the fairies. The other type were ancient fairy imps disguised as infants who often behaved atrociously, ate fantastic amounts of food, and had knowledge of things that would be far beyond that of any children. Usually, the changeling appeared exactly like the baby it replaced, then its appearance would gradually change, becoming shriveled and ugly.

The founder of the Protestant religion, Reverend Dr. Martin Luther (1483–1546) wrote in 1543 about how he was tempted to murder a changeling he had met. This excerpt is from his book *Table Talk*:

> Eight years ago there was a changeling in Dessau [Germany], which I, Dr. Martin Luther, have both seen and touched: it was twelve years old, and had all its senses, so that people thought it was a proper child; but that mattered little, for it only ate, and that as much as any four ploughmen or thrashers, and when any one touched it, it screamed: when things in the house went wrong, so that any damage took place, it laughed and was merry; but if things went well, it cried. Thereupon I said to the Prince of Anhalt, "If I were prince or ruler here, I would have this child thrown into the water, into the Moldau, that flows by Dessau, and would run the risk of being a homicide." But the Elector of Saxony, who was then at Dessau, and the Prince of Anhalt, would not follow my advice. I then said they ought to cause a pater-noster to be said in the church, that God would take the devil away from them. This was done daily at Dessau, and the said changeling died two years after.

"The Mass is the greatest blasphemy of God, and the highest idolatry upon earth, an abomination the like of which has never been in Christendom since the time of the Apostles."

—Reverend Dr. Martin Luther, Table Talk *(1569)*

Murder was once accepted by the Church as a proper way to deal with changelings. Manuscripts dating back to the ninth or tenth centuries detail the childhood of St. Stephen—one of Christ's apostles—saying that when he was a baby, Satan took the form of a man and stole him from his cradle, leaving a changeling in his place. After Stephen grew up, he returned to his parent's house and revealed the changeling for what it was. In the series of fifteenth-century paintings titled *The Life of Saint Stephen*, the Saint is then shown presiding over the burning of the changeling. Two other saints who were substituted with changelings according to fourteenth- and fifteenth-century manuscripts were St. Lawrence and Christ's apostle St. Bartholomew.

Weird Saints

Here a few of the more unusual saints, along with their feast days in parentheses and some of their more notable achievements.

St. Adam (December 24): There are several St. Adams with this feast day. One of them is the Adam from the Garden of Eden, who was later released from Hell sometime after his death by Christ himself. Another was a British bishop in the thirteenth century who raised tithes all the way up to one handful of butter for every ten cows. This amount was considered so outrageously high that his parishioners burned his house down with him in it.

St. Adrian (September 8): The patron saint of prison guards, arms dealers, and butchers. According to Sean Kelly and Rosemary Rogers' book *Saints Preserve Us* (1993), "A Roman officer in fourth-century Nicodemia, Adrian was so impressed by the bravery of his Christian captives that he asked to be jailed with them. His wife, Natalia, was delighted, and shaved her head in order to disguise her sex and be able to visit him in prison, where she kissed his chains and urged him to endure martyrdom. When his legs were cut off, she prayed that his hands might be removed as well, as befitted a true Saint." When they burned his remains, she tried to jump into the fire with them but was restrained. Still, she was able to make off with one of his hands as a relic. She also became a saint. St. Adrian's sword is now in Walbech, Germany.

"The hatred of women in the Old Testament is pathological. St. Paul is no improvement. Worse, Christianity is based on murder and torture . . . that one result of all this emphasis on blood and pain should be S and M is hardly surprising. Which other major religion is based on the Godhead incarnate being whipped, tacked to a cross, stabbed? Only the Marquis de Sade could have made up a sicker religion. It's no wonder that those brought up in such a culture hate life and enjoy inflicting pain. All societies are sick but some are sicker than others. Christian societies are certainly the sickest."

—Gore Vidal, 1977

St. Agatha (February 5): The symbol of this third-century virgin from Sicily is two breasts on a plate. After she rejected the advances of the governor, he subjected her to various tortures, such as ripping her skin with iron hooks and throwing her on hot coals. He also had her breasts sliced off. She is invoked against breast diseases.

St. Anthony the Great (January 17): The patron saint of butchers and gravediggers, St.

Anthony lived in Egypt until his death in 355 at the age of 105. He lived in a tomb for twenty years where the Devil sometimes appeared to him as a naked woman. His disciple, Athanasius wrote of him, "he always fasted, his outer garment was a sackcloth and his inner garment a hair shirt. He never washed his body or his feet." Which may be the reason one of his emblems is the pig. His followers were the first monks. They hung out in the desert and caves trying not to eat, sleep, or think impure thoughts.

St. Barbara (December 4): The patron saint of detonations, ammunition manufacturers, and artillery. She lived at Nicomedia in Bithynia in about 236 A.D. Because of her great beauty, her father, Dioscurus of Heliopolis, locked her up in a tower, but a man disguised as a doctor was able to gain access to her and convert her. When Dioscurus tried to chop her in two with his sword, she jumped out the window and flew off to a cave in the mountains. He eventually found her and dragged her by her hair to the magistrates. They stripped her, flogged her, "burn[ed] her sides with burning lamps . . . and hurted her head with a mallet . . . and cut off her paps." They finally allowed her father to decapitate her. God was not pleased and caused him to explode. The California city, Santa Barbara, was named after her.

St. Bartholomew (August 24): One of the twelve apostles, he reportedly came to the assistance of the English fleet and their magician, Stephen Crabbe, when they went into a battle with the French fleet. They needed his help because the French fleet had been made invisible by their magician, Eustace the Monk, who also happened to be an English traitor.

St. Catherine of Alexandria (November 25): On her conversion, "she underwent a 'mystical marriage' with the infant Jesus." Later she was sentenced to death and miraculously survived being run over by a giant wheel studded with spikes (called a Catherine Wheel in her honor). They finally cut off her head and limbs, but a miracle occurred and milk issued forth instead of blood. Angels arrived and carried her parts off to Mt. Sinai. Her voice was one of the voices heard by St. Joan of Arc.

St. Catherine of Sweden (March 24): She is invoked against abortions. Married at the age of fourteen, she convinced her husband to allow her to remain a virgin. On a later pilgrimage to Rome, though many men tried to seduce or rape her, they were prevented by a shining white doe.

St. Colman or Coloman (October 13): There are more than three hundred official saints with this name. One of them is the patron saint of hanged men. In 1012, he tried to go to the Holy Land through Austria, but was arrested as a spy. Since he couldn't speak German, they hanged him. But when his body refused to decompose, they decided he must be a saint. They also decided he must have been descended from Scottish royalty.

St. Dominic Savio (March 9): This patron saint of juvenile delinquents was the youngest nonmartyred person to achieve sainthood. He died at the age of fifteen in Turin in 1857 after organizing the Company of the Immaculate Conception. He was noted for stealing and tearing up porn magazines belonging to his fellow students.

St. John Chrysostom (January 27) was "revered for his saintliness, incomparable eloquence and passion for social justice." Sometime between A.D. 390 and 407, this venerable saint wrote, "What else is woman but a foe to friendship, an unescapable punishment, a necessary evil, a natural temptation, a desirable calamity, a domestic danger, a delectable detriment, an evil of nature, painted in fair colors!"

St. Elmo or Erasmus (June 2): This fourth-century Syrian Bishop had his intestines pulled out on a ship's capstan and is invoked to heal bowel and stomach problems.

St. Gregory the Great (March 12): Born into a wealthy Roman family in about 540, after his mother became a nun, he became a monk, spending his inheritance on building monasteries. He didn't want to become pope, calling it "the height of embarrassment," but he did anyway in 590. He believed all sex—even for procreation—was evil. In fact, he believed everything fun was evil, saying, "pleasure can never be without sin." To prove his point, he would tell a story about a woman who went to church right after having sex with her husband and then went insane. He also believed all babies were born damned because they were the product of their parent's lust. Prague, Lisbon, Sens, Constance, and other cities all claim to have his skull as a sacred relic.

St. Joseph (March 19 and May 1): Jesus' stepfather is invoked for a happy death. Although he's also invoked against Communism, he is the patron saint of Vietnam. Highlighting his blue-collar image, Pope Pius XII turned May Day into the Feast of St. Joseph the Worker. According to St. Epiphanius (315–403), Joseph was eight-nine years old when he married the Virgin Mary. Sometimes referred to as "the Divine Cuckold," it's said he remained celibate all his life and is also called "the Virgin Father." Since the Church also teaches that Mary was a virgin her entire life, her other four sons (Mark 6:3) must have been conceived by the Holy Ghost, just as Jesus was. And the same must be true for her daughters (Matthew 13:56).

The doctrine of immaculate conception has nothing to do with Jesus' birth. It really means that Mary was conceived completely free of sin. The idea dates back to the 1100s, but it didn't become official until Pope Pius IX made it so in 1854.

St. Joseph of Copertino (September 18): After becoming a monk, St. Joseph decided he didn't need his underwear, so he sent them home to his mother. For the next two years, he didn't take off his robe. He was dubbed the "flying monk" after he began levitating. This freaked out his superiors and they brought him before the Inquisition, but they eventually came around. He performed this feat more than a hundred times, once carrying a large cross thirty-six feet in the air. He would also give the other monks rides on his back. He died in 1663 and later became the patron saint of astronauts.

St. Julian the Hospitaller (February 12): Fulfilling a prophecy spoken by a deer, St. Julian accidentally sliced his parents in half thinking they were his wife and her lover. He founded a hospital and did many other good deeds as penance.

St. Kea (November 5): Became the patron saint of toothache sufferers after he had a tooth knocked out in a fight with a Welsh prince. He is invoked with the words, "Holy Kea, holy kai. Well again, by and by."

St. Kenelm (July 17): In about 811, at the age of seven St. Kenelm became King of Mercia. His sister Ascebert (or Quendreda or Quoenthryth) was not pleased with this, so she whacked him on the head. A dove immediately emerged from his split skull and flew off to inform the pope. After his body was found, his sister tried to mess up the funeral by reading the Cursing Psalm (either Psalm 107 or 108) backwards, but her eyes burst.

St. Lawrence (August 10): Made the patron saint of cooks and bakers after he was roasted alive in Rome in A.D. 258, it's reported his final words were, "You've cooked me on one side, now turn me over so I can be eaten well done."

St. Lucia (December 13): In order to avert the affections of an unwanted suitor, St. Lucia plucked her eyes out. No doubt that did the trick.

St. Marcel of Paris (November 1): When a non-Christian woman was buried in a Christian cemetery, a big black serpent erupted out of her grave, exposing her corpse. St. Marcel, who became the Bishop of Paris in 400, rushed to the site to find the serpent munching on the cadaver. He promptly bonked the offending creature on the head with his staff and hauled it off in his robe to the accolades of his admirers. He is invoked to ward off vampires.

St. Mark (April 25): The author of one of the gospels is invoked against fly bites. It's said that he was once aroused by a beautiful woman kissing his hand, so he promptly cut his hand off. Fortunately, it was later restored by the Virgin Mary.

St. Nicholas and the three pickled children.

St. Martin of Tours (November 11): The patron saint of drinking and revelry. He was the replacement of the god Bacchus. According to one legend, this fourth-century Bishop of Tours died while he was in the form of a cow, which was why cows were often slaughtered on this day in Europe.

St. Nicholas (December 6): The patron saint of beer drinkers and pawnbrokers. Better known to us as Santa Claus (from his Dutch name Sinte Klaas), he was a bishop in Turkey and was martyred in 305. Old St. Nick got an early start on sainthood. As a baby, he refused to suckle his mother's breast on fast days and Fridays. Later he saved three girls from prostitution by giving them money. As bishop, he once went to a butcher's shop where he was given some meat. Suspecting something was up, he descended into the cellar where he found the bodies of three murdered boys in a barrel of brine. He promptly resurrected the pickled children. The image of Santa Claus has changed radically over the years. Until the early 1800s, pictures depicted him as being tall, thin, and clean shaven. The Catholic Church unsainted him in 1969.

St. Odhran or Otteran (October 27): When St. Columba wanted to dedicate his new church on the island of Iona in 563, he decided the best way to guarantee the church's success was to have a human sacrifice. St. Odran quickly volunteered, and they buried him alive. They later uncovered him and found he was amazingly still alive. Odran promptly announced that the doctrines of Heaven, Hell, salvation, and damnation were not quite as straightforward as everyone thought, saying, "The saved are not forever happy, the damned are not forever lost." St. Columba was so offended that he immediately ordered Odran to be buried again before he could say any more.

St. Patrick (March 17): Probably one of the most famous saints, St. Patrick is closely associated with Ireland. He wasn't Irish though. He was English. Although he was responsible for converting the Irish to Christianity, he described the Irish as "savage barbarians" and according to one of his biographers, E. J. Dillon, "Even at the end of his life he expected daily a violent death, to be robbed or reduced to slavery." Probably not surprising considering his first trip to Ireland was when he was taken there unwillingly after being captured by Irish pirates. He spent six years in slavery before he escaped. It was on his second trip that he brought Catholicism to the Emerald Isle.

St. Sebastian (January 20): Pictures of this third-century saint almost always show him shot full of arrows, but according to his story, he was actually clubbed to death. After the Emperor Diocletian had his archers use him for target practice, a woman named Irene nursed him back to health, so Diocletian then had him clubbed. Oddly, St. Sebastian is the patron saint of archers.

St. Sithney (August 4): When God offered to make him the patron saint of girls, St. Sithney was outraged, so God offered him mad dogs instead and he accepted.

St. Teilo (February 9): The bones of this sixth-century Welsh saint were kept as relics by three different churches, but there was some rivalry between them because each church claimed to have his skull. Over time, all the bones—including his three skulls—were lost. Fortunately, his "genuine" skull was found in Hong Kong in 1994, and it now resides in Llandaff Cathedral in Cardiff.

St. Thecla or Tegla (September 23): St. Thecla was one of the durable martyrs. During the first century, after being converted, she broke off her marriage engagement and dedicated her virginity to Christ. Because of this, people tried to burn her at the stake, but a gust of wind blew out the fire. When she was thrown to the ferocious beasts, they suddenly lost their appetites. At the age of ninety, they came for her a third time, but she was sucked into the ground and hasn't been seen since.

St. Theresa of Avila (October 15): St. Theresa Sánchez de Capeda y Ahumada (1515–1582), who was partly Jewish, is well known for her reform of the Carmelite nunneries. After becoming a nun when she was about twenty, she was "frequently rapt in ecstasy" with spiritual experiences that included the "mystical piercing of her heart by a spear of divine love." Discerning the danger in this, she eventually learned to love God "in and through all things." Following her death, her body was dismembered for relics. While her right foot and part of her jaw were hauled off to Rome and her left hand taken to Lisbon, one cleric bit off her toe and smuggled it away in his mouth.

In 1977, María Rubio of Lake Arthur, New Mexico, put a tortilla in her oven. When she pulled it out, it had a picture of Jesus Christ on it. The three-inch image soon attracted pilgrims from all over the world—often as many as two dozen a day. María says the tortilla caused her husband to stop drinking and helped her through a difficult pregnancy. Because of the steady stream of visitors, the Rubios built a shrine for what is probably the world's only holy tortilla. Not to be outdone, in 1996 the Bongo Java Coffee Shop in Nashville, TN built a shrine for a cinnamon roll they said looked like Mother Teresa. For a while they sold NunBun T-shirts, pictures, bookmarks, prayercards and coffee mugs. Personally, I think the roll looks more like a troll.

St. Ursula (October 21): Her legend is a bit garbled because the Latin abbreviation for "11 martyrs" apparently was misinterpreted as "11,000." During the fourth century, this daughter of a British king was leading 10 virgins (or 10,999 virgins), plus their spouses and children (yes, virgins with children again) on a pilgrimage to Rome when they were attacked by the Huns. Unfortunately, the angels who came to their defense arrived too late to save them and all 11 (or 11,000) were slaughtered.

St. Vincent of Saragossa (January 22): The patron saint of drunks. Another durable martyr, Vincent was subjected to fierce tortures, his flesh was ripped with iron hooks, he was roasted on a red-hot gridiron, and he was thrown into a dungeon with broken pottery on the floor. He survived all this, until his friends put him in a nice, soft bed they had made for him. That was too much for him, and he kicked the bucket. I'll bet they were bummed. Anyway, St. Vincent is the groundhog of vintners. If his feast day is bright and sunny, then that year's wine crop will be a good one. If it's not, then you should probably drink beer instead.

St. Walstan (May 30): This saint from Norwich, England, was celibate until he died in 1016. It's said that men who have "lost their genitals" and wish to have them restored should go to St. Walstan's Well in Bawburgh, Norfolk, England.

In 1946, **St. Frances Xavier Cabrini** (1850-1917) became the first American citizen to be made a saint, though she was born in Italy. She is credited with four miracles. The first saint born in America was **St. Elizabeth Ann Bayley Seton** (1774-1821), who was canonized in 1975. There are more than 2,000 "registered" saints. About two-thirds of them are French or Italian. Between 1978 and 1995, Pope John Paul II canonized 273 new saints, and more than 500 more were beatified (or nominated for sainthood).

So What Are Saints Good For?

The following are some things saints can be called on to cure or ward off:

- Bruises—St. Amalburga (Jul. 10)
- Frenzy—St. Walburga (Feb. 25)
- Gravel in the urine—St. Drogo or Druon (Apr. 16)
- Worms—St. Benignus or Benen (Nov. 9)
- Hangovers—St. Bibiana or Viviana (Dec. 2)
- Scruples or too sensitive a conscience—St. Igantius of Loyola (July 31)
- Evil eye—St. Januarius or Gennaro (Sept. 19)
- Plagues of storks—St. Agricola of Avignon (Sept. 2)
- Freethinking—St. Titus (Feb. 6)
- To find lost keys—St. Zita (Apr. 27)

And here are some of the interesting professions and entities that saints are the patrons of:

- Pallbearers and undertakers—St. Joseph of Arimathaea (Mar. 17)
- Fallen women—St. Margaret of Cortona (Feb. 3) and St. Afra (Aug. 5)
- Fortune-tellers—St. Agabus (Feb. 13)
- Geese—St. Ambrose (Dec. 7)
- Blood banks—St. Januarius or Gennaro (Sept. 19)

Television—St. Clare of Assisi (Aug. 12)
Draft dodgers—St. Besse (Aug. 10)

January 1 is designated as the day to celebrate Christ's circumcision, while July 1 is the day to celebrate his blood, and August 22 is for Mary's immaculate heart. Then on August 29, it's the feast day for the beheading of John the Baptist.

Truss makers—St. Lambert of Maestricht (Sept. 17)
Spelunkers—St. Benedict (July 11)
Outer Mongolia—St. Francis Xavier (Dec. 3)
Bastards—St. John Francis Regis (June 16)
Popes—St. Gregory the Great (Mar. 12)

Sorry, I couldn't find out who the patron saint of Elvis impersonators is. I also didn't see one for politicians.

Phallic Worship in Japan

"The union of male and female, of man and woman, symbolizes the union of the gods themselves at the moment when the world was created. The gods smile upon your lovemaking, enjoying your pleasure! For this reason both husband and wife must strive to please each other and themselves when they embrace. If you are both satisfied, the gods will be satisfied . . . good sex brings more honor to Daikoku [a god of wealth] than a well-tended altar."

This quotation from *The Pillow Book*, which was written between 1192 and 1333, clearly illustrates a fundamental difference between Eastern and Western religious views of sex. In Western religions, sex tends to be viewed as being evil and animalistic—sometimes even within the confines of marriage. Virginity and celibacy are still often regarded as being a step closer to godliness. In the East, however, sex is usually seen as being completely natural and good. In fact, sexual imagery sometimes even plays an important role in worship.

Originally a holdover from prehistoric fertility religions, phallic and vulvar worship have survived the introduction of Buddhism and Confucianism and became a part of Shintoism. They continued to remain an important feature of Japanese religion even during periods of suppression. Christian missionaries and contact with Western cultures finally began to change this in the nineteenth century. Though the phallic cults and many of the festivals were outlawed by the Meiji government in 1868 in the name of modernization, they continued in many parts of the countryside.

On a trip from Tokyo north toward Nikko in 1871, British scholar W. G. Aston wrote:

> I found the road lined at intervals with groups of phalli, connected no doubt with the worship of the sacred mountain Nan-tai . . . I once witnessed a phallic procession in a town some miles north of Tokio. A phallus several feet high, and painted a bright vermilion colour, was being carried on a sort of bier by a crowd of shouting, laughing coolies with flushed faces, who zig-zagged along with sudden rushes from one side of the street to another. It was a veritable Bacchic rout. The Dionysia, it will be remembered, had their phalli. A procession of this kind invaded the quiet thoroughfares of the Kobe foreign settlement in 1868, much to the amazement of the European residents.

At one time massive phalluses carved from a tree trunk were the centerpieces of Shinto temples and shrines. Today, only about forty Shinto shrines devoted to sexual deities remain in Japan. Like the ancient shrines, the alters of those still remaining are usually graced with very large representations of phalluses or vulvas. The vulvas are thought to be good at repelling numerous demons, but the phalluses are considered to be much more powerful, which is why phallic temples greatly outnumber vulvar ones. One temple in the city of Kawasaki contains hundreds of phalluses and vulvas made of almost every material imaginable—some of which are hundreds of years old.

Those who pray to the phallic deities include sufferers of venereal diseases or sexual dysfunctions, infertile women, newlyweds, anyone seeking a mate, or anyone seeking divine intervention. Caressing and stroking the massive wooden phalluses is an important part of the prayers. Two temples—one in Tatebayashi and one in Atami—boast ancient statues of the goddess Kannon squatting with her legs parted. The genitals of both statues are well worn from centuries of caressing. Sometimes babies are presented at temple altars covered with phalluses and both parents and grandparents put their toddlers astride huge phalluses that rest on wooden frames like cannons.

While genital-shaped statues still appear along roadsides to ensure fertility and ward off evil, they are quickly disappearing, and stones with relief pictures of gods copulating are pretty much gone, though some retain hidden sexual imagery. These groups of statues usually appear near or between rice fields. Some have shelters or fences around them which used to provide a degree of privacy for romantic trysts. It was believed that making love in or near the fields on certain auspicious days encouraged the gods to increase the fertility of the crops.

Some of the phallic statues have been disguised as statues of gods, though their true nature is often revealed when viewed from behind. Then these bald-headed old men clearly resemble penises. But while many of the genital statuary have gone undercover, the idea of the sacredness of sex lingers on. Interestingly, the image of the goddess Benten is still a common decoration on the dildos used in Japanese strip clubs.

The fertility festivals were also once very common, but they're rapidly vanishing as well. Some of the surviving festivals are held by specific temples, whereas others are a bit more widespread. For instance, the annual *bonten* festival is held in scattered rural areas throughout Japan on the lunar new year's day. At Inuyama in the Aichi prefecture, the phallic Tagata shrine holds a festival on March 15 of every year, while a short distance away the vulvic Ogata shrine holds its festival on the same day. Once every five years, the two festivals combine for one very auspicious celebration. Also in mid-March, the Kanamara-sama jinja ("the Metal Phallus Deity Shrine") holds its festival. This shrine, located in Daishi, near Kawasaki, is the last urban shrine devoted primarily to a phallic god. The farming town of Yokote, in the Akita prefecture, attracts about 100,000 visitors for its day-long drunken celebration of sexuality.

During these fertility festivals, the gigantic penises are removed from the temples, loaded onto palanquins, and paraded through the streets from one temple to the next, sometimes with the bearers chanting "*Yo-i-cho!*" which means "Heave ho!" Some of these giant organs measure thirteen feet long and three feet wide, though there are no doubt larger ones. Until recently, one huge stone phallus weighing two tons was carried through the streets of Nagano by hundreds of bearers during the summer solstice festival of Kamiyamada Natsu Matsuri. Some penises made of straw were set on fire and thrown into the sea, while at the climax of one festival, the giant wooden penis was thrust into a giant straw vagina as worshippers splattered the organs with milk-white raw sake.

At some of these festivals, huge banners resembling Shunga prints of genital close-ups are hung in the streets. There are women who dress in their best kimonos and carry two-foot-long wooden penises as if they were holding a baby, while some of the men wear large papier-mâché phalluses in the appropriate spot as part of their costume. Children suck on phallic lollipops or bananas with a crown of pink chocolate on the end. There are phallic cakes, phallic signs, phallic pictures, phallic sculptures, and even phallic toys.

The early Roman Catholic Church actually made eating sausage a sin because it was associated with the fertility festival Lupercalia, and Roman Emperor Constantine the Great (A.D. c. 280–337) banned it after he converted to Christianity, but the Romans bootlegged so much sausage that the officials finally had to lift the prohibition.

As surprising as all this may sound, many of the more blatant customs have already disappeared—some only recently. The men used to dance through the streets prodding women with their wooden phalluses and pinching their bottoms, and the women welcomed it on this occasion because it meant the following year would be a happy one for them. Going farther back in time, the men used to knock on doors and enter houses prodding every female of child-bearing age. And even farther back, some of the prodding that took place was the real thing. But all these traditions have pretty much faded away.

In ancient times, the festivals ended with the young men and women getting together for huge orgies. This was especially common during the Heian period (794–1185) and one document presented to Emperor Saga in 810 even said, "The union between youths and girls on auspicious days is of primordial importance in human law."

At various times the government tried to put a stop to the orgies, but they persisted right up into the twentieth century. Donald Richie and Kenkichi Ito in *The Erotic Gods* describe what used to happen at the Rokusho shrine after the municipal electricity supply was shut off for the night, plunging the town into darkness: "Eventually the streets were filled with screaming boys and girls more possessed than drunk, all making for the temple grounds. These, although already large enough, soon became packed as the youth of the entire city forced its way in and milled about singing, dancing and pleasing the gods in other ways until dawn." The government finally succeeded in putting an end to this particular celebration in 1953. At another night festival in Uji, near Kyoto, the celebrants wandered around naked and made love in the fields.

Related to this is the practice of *yobai*, or "night creeping," which may have started when the sacred orgies were banned. *Yobai* usually took place after Shinto rice-planting ceremonies and on other auspicious occasions. It generally began with the village bachelors gathering for a party at the house of the village's headman. At the conclusion of the party, the youths would creep in small groups through the village until they found themselves outside the house of a local girl. After playing *janken-pon* (scissors-paper-stone) to determine who would get to have sex with her, the winner would sneak into her room through the door that she left open for this purpose, and the others would continue on to the house of the next available girl.

The farmhouses usually only had one floor, with the bedroom doors opening to the outside. Sometimes the house was raised up on stilts, in which case the rooms opened onto a veranda. This made entering the girl's bedroom relatively easy.

Some villages had a variation of *yobai* in which all the young people got together for a party, and after pairing off, they would head to the privacy of an inn for young people called a *Wakamono-yado*, where the real fun would begin.

Of course, the parents were well aware of what was going on and would have taken part themselves when they were younger. Many of the parents probably met their spouses in this manner. It was completely accepted, but not usually talked about. Discretion had to be maintained, which accounts for all the creeping.

"A scandalous custom, which could only proceed from the blindness of idolatry, prevails amongst the people of these parts [in Tibet], who are disinclined to marry young women so long as they are in their virgin state, but require, on the contrary, that they should have had previous commerce with many of the other sex; and this, they assert, is pleasing to their deities, and that a woman who has not had the company of men is worthless."

—*Marco Polo,* The Book of Marco Polo, *c. 1298*

As Nicholas Bornoff writes in *Pink Samurai* (1991):

> Parents knew exactly when it was scheduled to occur, but they feigned ignorance. Rooms were separated by thin wooden partitions, so it seems very unlikely that anyone could sleep very well through all that humping on a creaking wooden floor. Nevertheless, in some places, before entering the maiden's room, the young Lothario urinated against the base of the sliding door to prevent any noise when it was drawn open against the saturated groove. Rather as with the spraying of a tom cat, the reek informed any other *yobai* aspirants that the house had already been visited.
>
> Not that all the young women necessarily ended their evening with a single postulant. Many a bawdy *yobai* tale tells of ladies of a generous disposition, and these no doubt hold a kernel of truth. In many instances, the process was spiced with voyeurism. As some erotic prints show and the modern striptease parlour implies, voyeurism is seen not as a perversion but as a perfectly normal sexual stimulus in Japan. Gluing their ears to the wall of the love nest or even holding aloft a candle to watch the ecstatic undulations of their winning comrade, many night-creepers must have been worked up into a frenzy considerably curtailing their staying power when their turn came.

Although arranged marriages were usual in more populous areas, they were not the general rule in the more remote spots in which *yobai* was common. Until the Meiji period, many peasants, like the urban poor, never bothered with marriage anyway. Nor was *yobai* necessarily a determinant in the selection of a mate; if the affair had not gone to the satisfaction of the parties concerned, there was always next time. Fulfilling their purpose, such nocturnal adventures often resulted in offspring and, if they didn't, the young lady made herself available for more *yobai*. . . .

But what about the women? Although chances are the boy was not a stranger, could a girl really enjoy a one-night stand with an unchosen partner? To one woman journalist often covering feminist issues in the *Asahi Shimbun*, the answer, surprisingly, was yes. "Unlike their city counterparts, country women were not especially demure," she says, "and the scope of their enjoyments was extremely limited." . . .

On July 8, 1996, the Scottish newspaper Daily Record *reported that two men in Botosani, Romania, were not allowed to become Orthodox priests because their penises "don't reach the minimum length set down in the rules." Exactly how this would have affected their priestly duties is uncertain.*

For some, *yobai* and the old sacred orgies no longer made any sense; for others they had been fun. And it is precisely because they were fun that they were on the way out: in the eyes of the "modern" authorities, fertility observances no longer had an excuse.

Bornoff also points out that *yobai* "is a custom which died out so very recently that whether or not it actually survives in very remote villages is still being discussed."

In industrialized Japan, fertility is not as important as it once was, but another reason these festivals and deities are largely disappearing is the fashion-conscious young aren't interested in such relics from the past. Interestingly, it is the Japanese conservative movement that is trying to maintain such traditions.

Fertility religions and festivals were once common all over the world. Quoting from the Roman scholar Marcus Terentius Varro (116–27 B.C.), St. Augustine presents a picture of a Roman fertility festival that's almost a mirror image of those in Japan. This quote is from *St. Augustine's De Civitate Dei* (*The City of God*; A.D. 413–426).

> Varro says among other things that the rites of Liber were celebrated at the crossroads in Italy so immodestly and licentiously that the male genitals were worshipped in honor of the god—and this not with any modest secrecy but with open and exulting depravity. That shameful part of the body was, during the festival of Liber, placed with great pomp on wagons and carried about to the crossroads in the country and at last into the city.
>
> In the town of Lanuvium, a whole month was dedicated to Liber. During it, all the citizens used the most disgraceful words until the Phallus had been carried across the marketplace and put to rest again. It was necessary that the most honorable of the matrons should publicly place a wreath on that disgraceful effigy. The god Liber had to be propitiated to ensure the future of the

crops and the evil eye had to be repelled from the fields by compelling a married woman to do in public that which not even a harlot might do under the eyes of married women in the theater.

The ancient Greeks had Priapus, the son of Aphrodite and the god of the perpetual erection. It's said that in the thirteenth century, one Greek priest who was unable to prevent his flock of sheep from dying finally threw away his rosary and carved a large phallus from the branch of a fig tree. Once he did this, his flock began their recovery. Some remnants of phallic worship survive in Greece today, just as obscure bits of ancient fertility religions persist in the West in the form of Easter bunnies and Easter eggs. Elsewhere, phallic worship still exists among the Lapps, Hindus, Thai, the Arandas of Australia, some African tribes, and some South Pacific islanders, though none of them do it up quite like the Japanese. Though the Hindus come close. In 1996 about 112,000 Hindus made the annual pilgrimage to Amarnath cave, which is in the Kashmir mountains at an altitude of 12,725 feet, to pay homage to an ice stalagtite they regard as the god Siva's lingam (or phallus).

To most Westerners, all this doesn't sound much like religion at all, being so used to religions emphasizing the negative aspects of sex. These fundamentally different religious views are made much more apparent by the fact that the oldest Shunga sketches—those graphic pictures of sexual intercourse with the massive, dripping genitals that most of the Western religions would consider pornography—were preserved in Buddhist temples and were drawn by Buddhist artists in the seventh and eighth centuries. Even the famous, highly respected print artists Utamaro (1753–1806) and Hokusai (1760–1849) created Shunga prints.

Japanese creation myths are also seeped in sexual imagery. According to one, "In the beginning Izanagi (the first male) and Izanami (the first female) stood on the rainbow bridge of heaven and watched the lightning lance thrust down into the waters of chaos. The foam around the jeweled lance solidified to become the first island of Japan. Soon Izanagi and Izanami learned how to imitate the act of creation with their own bodies, and from them came the whole world."

Sex also appears in the legends of some gods and goddesses. For example, "The dance of the goddess Ame-no-Uzume grew wilder as she recalled a thousand orgasms she had enjoyed: her nipples stiffened and she felt her sex open when she remembered the phalluses of the countless lovers who had penetrated her. When at last she brought herself to the crisis, she opened her clothes to reveal herself to the kami [god]: wet to the knees, her sex throbbing with joy."

You'd certainly be hard pressed to find religious imagery like that in the West.

"Some will march on a road of bones,
and others will be nailed up on telephone poles.
That is the way it works."

—Dr. Hunter S. Thompson

INDEX

H

I

J

K

L

M

N

O

P

T

U

V

W

X

Y

Z

About the Author

John Richard Stephens has had many different occupations ranging from driving an armored truck and working as a professional photographer to being a psychiatric counselor at a couple of hospitals and a security officer for the U.S. Navy. He was an intelligence officer and squadron commander in the U.S. Air Force before he moved on to writing full time in 1990. Since then, he's written over three dozen articles, poems, and short stories for newspapers and magazines that range widely from a short story for the literary journal *Nexus* to an article about anti-American propaganda on postage stamps for *Penthouse*. He's also the author/editor of seven other books—*The Enchanted Cat*; *The Dog Lover's Literary Companion*; *Mysterious Cat Stories* (co-edited with Kim Smith); *The King of the Cats and Other Feline Fairy Tales*; *Vampires, Wine and Roses*; *Wyatt Earp Speaks!*; and *Captured by Pirates: 22 Firsthand Accounts of Murder and Mayhem on the High Seas*. His books have been selections of the Preferred Choice Book Club, the Quality Paperback Book Club, and the Book of the Month Club. He's also on the board of directors of the Wyatt Earp Society and is the editor of their journal, *The Wyatt Earp Review*. The material in *Weird History 101* was gathered over a 20-year period and what's presented here is just the tip of the iceberg. There's definitely no shortage of weird history. More information on John's work can be found at www.thegrid.net/fern.canyon